MANDELSTAM

Clarence Brown

PROFESSOR OF COMPARATIVE LITERATURE
PRINCETON UNIVERSITY

CAMBRIDGE
AT THE UNIVERSITY PRESS
1973

Published by the Syndics of the Cambridge University Press
Bentley House, 200 Euston Road, London NW1 2DB
American Branch: 32 East 57th Street, New York, N.Y.10022

© Cambridge University Press 1973

Library of Congress Catalogue Card Number: 72–90491

ISBN: 0 521 20142 X

Composed in Great Britain
at the University Printing House, Cambridge
(Brooke Crutchley, University Printer)
and printed in the United States of America

CONTENTS

List of illustrations v   *Note on transliteration* vii
Abbreviations viii

1	Preliminary	1
2	The most abstract and intentional city	9
3	Studies abroad and at home	32
4	Beginnings	53
5	Snapshots from the Revolution and Civil War	69
6	From the insane ship to hunchbacked Tiflis	85
7	The wing of approaching night	99
8	1925–1938: Silence, prose, arrest, exile, sickness, death	121
9	The romance of the precise	135
10	*Stone*	159
	I. Mandelstam's books of poems	159
	II. Seashell	161
	III. Silence	164
	IV. Patterns, visual and kinetic	168
	V. Theater of interrupted words	173
	VI. Down from the tower	176
	VII. Animated temples	183
	VIII. That has such people in't	194
11	*Phaedra*	207
12	Three poems of *Tristia*	219
13	Transparent sadness: the classical in *Tristia*	253
14	Here writes Terror: Poems, 1921–1925	276
	Notes to the text	297
	Bibliography	311
	Index of names	315

FOR NADEZHDA YAKOVLEVNA MANDELSTAM

By mourning tongues
The death of the poet was kept from his poems

ILLUSTRATIONS

between pages 48 *and* 49

1 *a* Osip Mandelstam at the age of 16 or 17 before the painted backdrop of a photographer's studio in Paris, 1905–6

1 *b* Osip Mandelstam, *c.* 1915–16. Note the Pushkinian side-whiskers

2 *a* Osip Mandelstam, Moscow 1922

2 *b* Osip Mandelstam, Voronezh 1936

3 *a* Osip Mandelstam, Leningrad 1927. Photograph by Nappelbaum

3 *b* Nadezhda Yakovlevna Mandelstam, *née* Khazina, the wife of Osip Mandelstam, Moscow 1922

4 As a pensioner Mandelstam was entitled to this streetcar pass, issued on 7 March 1933

5 *a* Osip Mandelstam in the winter of 1933–4, but without the beard to be seen in other pictures of this time

5 *b* Flora Osipovna Mandelstam, *née* Verblovskaya, the mother of Osip Mandelstam. The photograph comes from a postcard mailed from Halle and dated 30 August 1910

6 An autograph of poem No. 63. The poet's signature appears in the lower right corner

7 A page from the manuscript of Mandelstam's novella *Egipetskaia marka* (The Egyptian Stamp), Chap. VI. In my translation (*Prose*, 1967 edn), this passage begins on p. 177 at the words 'In Jewish apartments...' The figure in the left margin, who begins as a triangle and acquires greater and greater reality as he proceeds, might be Mandelstam's rendering of old Pergament

8*a* Koktebel, *c.* 1935. Nadezhda and Osip Mandelstam are seated in the middle row at the right; Andrey Bely (wearing the skullcap) second from the left in the same row

8*b* In the apartment on Nashchokinsky Pereulok, now Furmanov Street, Moscow, in the winter of 1934. From *l.* to *r.*, Alexandr Emilevich Mandelstam, the poet's brother; Mariya Sergeevna Petrovykh; Emil Veniaminovich Mandelstam, the poet's father; Nadezhda Mandelstam; Osip Mandelstam; Anna Andreevna Akhmatova

A NOTE ON THE TRANSLITERATION

The system of transliteration is that of the Library of Congress, modified in accordance with recommendations in J. Thomas Shaw, *The Transliteration of Modern Russian for English-Language Publications* (Madison: The University of Wisconsin Press, 1967). Except where noted, other systems of transliteration in quoted material have been changed to conform with the system of this book. The spelling 'Mandelstam' is that preferred by the poet himself.

ABBREVIATIONS

References to volume and page alone are to Mandelstam's three-volume *Sobranie sochinenii* (Collected Works). See Bibliography.

Akhmatova	Anna Akhmatova, *Sochineniia* (Works), in two volumes
Hope	Nadezhda Mandelstam, *Hope Against Hope: A memoir.* New York, 1970
NZh	*Novyi zhurnal* (New Review). New York
Prose	Clarence Brown (ed. and trans.), *The Prose of Osip Mandelstam*, 2nd, revised edition. Princeton, 1967
SEEJ	*Slavic and East European Journal*
Vestnik	*Vestnik russkogo studencheskogo khristianskogo dvizheniia* (Messenger of the Russian Christian Student Movement). Paris–New York
VL	*Voprosy literatury* (Problems of Literature). Moscow
VP	*Vozdushnye puti* (Aerial Ways). New York

1

Preliminary

There had been an earlier evacuation of Voronezh – that is to say, the citizens had left with the assistance of the government – but on that occasion the Germans had not come. Later on, though everyone could sense that the fall of the city to the invaders was merely a matter of time, all talk of evacuation was treated as 'counterrevolutionary.' Luckily, however, for Natalya Yevgenevna Shtempel,[1] the director of the technical school where she taught managed to save his staff and students by the sort of ruse that comes naturally to the Soviet managerial class: he applied for permission to leave, saying that he was taking them all to the village of Arkhangelskoe to help out in the fields. Though it was only the end of June, a time when such mobilization in the cause of agriculture was unusual, he was able to get the necessary papers. They got away on 4 July 1942. The first leg of the trip was easy, for there was a train that ran all the way to Anna, a small station at the end of a railway *cul de sac*. From there it was a difficult trek to Arkhangelskoe, some 75 kilometers away. Once they'd arrived the Voronezh teachers and their pupils did in fact engage in some sort of farm work for a time, then moved on to Borisoglebsk, and were finally evacuated to the city of Kuybyshev.

During all this time and until she was able to return to Voronezh in October of 1944 Natasha Shtempel carried with her most of the unpublished poems and letters of Osip Mandelstam. Among them were three notebooks of the kind used by school children for their exercises. These were the so-called 'Voronezh Notebooks,' containing the poems written between 1934 and 1937. They were in the hand of Nadezhda Yakovlevna, his wife, and each poem bore the inscription 'V' (for Voronezh), its date, and the poet's initials as a sign that he looked upon it as final. Owing to this ceremoniousness, the Mandelstams had another name for the collection: the 'Vatican Codex.'

The medieval flavor of the name is not inappropriate, for the means by which the later poems of Mandelstam 'came down' to us recall the age anterior to Gutenberg, not to mention that of the typewriter and the photostatic copier. Many readers will find it difficult to realize that we live in a time when poetry has had to survive in the most ancient of its repositories, the human memory. The lady to whom this book is dedicated carried not only the poems but also the prose of Mandelstam in her head – 'entire in the interior dark' – until about the year 1956, when she sensed that age was weakening her grasp. Not that she had ever depended entirely upon the daily routine of systematic practice: it was she who had seen to it that Natasha Shtempel salvaged the letters and notebooks from the destruction of Voronezh by the Wehrmacht, it was she who distributed many other copies to trusted friends (some of whom betrayed her trust), it was she who presided for years over the intricacies of this scattered and clandestine archive, ensuring that autographs, when such existed, and copies were secure in separate places, and it was in fact she who had insisted to Mandelstam himself that the poems be written down. In the most literal sense, he was no 'writer.' He was contemptuous of paper and ink, kept his poems in his head, and believed so strongly in their objective existence that once he had finished them he had no fear of losing them. 'Entire in the interior dark' translates a line from the cycle of eight-line poems containing his thesis on this point. In the autobiographical *Chetvertaia proza* (Fourth Prose) he furiously megaphones:

> I have no manuscripts, no notebooks, no archives. I have no handwriting because I never write. I alone in Russia work from the voice while all around the bitch-pack writes. What the hell kind of writer am I!? Get out you fools![2]

One might reduce the underlying statement of many of the early poems to the ancient formulaic truth *ars longa, vita brevis*, which is not less true for being, as it often was there, little more than a convenient subject. As the 1930s wore on, however, not proverbial wisdom but immediate experience must have taught that although poems may endure, men do not, and hence had better not be exclusively relied upon.

Whence all this sedulous memorization, concealment and copying? Perhaps the answer to that had better be spelt out in the beginning, since it will overshadow everything to come in this book.

The possibility that the poems might have perished along with the ninety-five per cent of Voronezh destroyed by the Germans was only one of the dangers. The eternal tragedy of the lost manuscript, the history of the French Revolution burnt by a careless chambermaid – these were also merely minor dangers. What really threatened the survival of his work was that it might at any moment be confiscated or destroyed by the governmental authorities of his own country. Mandelstam was living in Voronezh not by choice but as punishment for a political crime. He had written a derogatory poem on Stalin (No. 286) and been informed upon. That he was alive at all was something of a miracle. The miracle had been brought about in part by highly placed protectors, but so singular was it that its true origins will probably always be lost in conjecture. What is known about it can be found in Nadezhda Yakovlevna's invaluable memoir, *Hope Against Hope*, a book to which my indebtedness will become apparent as we proceed.[3] For the moment, let the bare fact of his being a suspect political exile in Voronezh at the beginning of the Terror account for the extreme vulnerability of anything that he might write. After all, it was a poem that had landed him there in the first place.

The story of Mandelstam's life in exile, of his being set free and then taken once again in the wave of 'second arrests,' of his last months of agony, and of his eventual death in one of the camps in 1938 can be read in detail in his widow's book (and in outline in Chapter 8 below). The question may arise – why, then, I have begun at this dismal end of the story. Perhaps we have been sufficiently informed as to the martyrdom of Russian writers? Perhaps the dreary tale of persecution, systematic provocation, torture, slow death from disease and inanition, or sudden death from drowning, shooting, etc., etc. – this has been so often rehearsed that we can take it all for granted without being reminded of it, and would rather prefer to do so? Would it not expedite matters simply to apply Hannah Arendt's phrase 'banality of evil,' invented for her account of the Eichmann trial in Jerusalem, to the conditions that have attended the making of poems and novels for the last half century in Russia and go on at once to the study of that writing itself? Evil may be interesting, but banality? Is it not, in fact, a shade too automatically 'interesting' to begin with the martyrology? To talk of spectacular persecutions and tragedies in the life before having shown, in the writing itself, why that life might possibly concern anyone?

The answer to these questions points to a thesis underlying this book, namely, that the 'writing itself' can hardly be treated in isolation from the life that formed it. It was his life in large part that occasioned the policy of the Soviet state towards his work; that policy in turn affected the nature of his life no less than of his work; and to a greater extent than will be easily believed it has affected and still affects our access both to the one and to the other. Such *apologia* as I can now make for the plan and scope of this book depends in large measure from this nexus of conditions, a point upon which I shall now enlarge.

For some two decades after his death, Mandelstam was a 'non-person' – which is to say not only that his work was suppressed, and confiscated when it could be found, but that all mention of his ever having existed was systematically deleted. Or if he was mentioned in passing, he was mentioned in some list of disreputable survivals from a past that had been irreversibly superseded. The first official turn in this policy came in August 1956, when a flimsy slip of mimeographed paper with the blanks filled in was issued by an office of the Supreme Court of the USSR.

It carried the information that Mandelstam was 'rehabilitated' (though the word itself, reserved for persons deemed to be of exceptional importance, did not appear). This meant that the occasional editor of some outlying journal, remote from the glacial censorship of the capitals, might print a poem of Mandelstam's if he wished. In February 1957, the usual 'commission' to oversee a writer's literary remains was appointed by the Writers' Union. Mandelstam's commission included Nadezhda Yakovlevna, Anna Akhmatova, Ilya Ehrenburg, Yevgeny Yakovlevich Khazin (his brother-in-law), Z.S. Paperny, A.A. Surkov, and N.I. Khardzhiev. Plans to publish a selection of his poetry went forward – and, just as often, backwards. At this writing the book has been in physical existence literally for years, but it has never been released. In 1966 a responsible editor on the staff of the 'Poet's Library,' the series in which Mandelstam's book has for so long been scheduled to appear, told me that a decision had been taken to bring it out the following year. But the decision was revoked, the grounds being that Mandelstam was an unsuitable poet to appear in the jubilee year of the 1917 Revolution (the mental leap that would connect the two parts of this thought ought not to be attempted), and the book was to come out in 1968. But it did not come out in 1968, or thereafter.

I will not conceal one further rumor: that the book is being withheld pending the expiration of copyright, which at the moment of this writing is imminent, whereupon no royalites will have to be paid the poet's widow – a motivation of which the most voracious bourgeois publisher might feel ashamed. It may in fact never appear, or it may appear in such a form as to make it worse than nothing at all, or bits of it may come out during one of those brief paroles that sometimes occur in Russian cultural affairs, or...but who can tell?

At any rate, there seems little further point in waiting for it. This is all the more true since there does exist a three-volume edition of practically all the known works of Mandelstam, published in Russian in New York. This collection, which has been expanding and improving in various editions since 1955, is the work principally of two men, Professor Gleb Struve and Mr Boris Filippov, who have also collaborated to edit and publish, in the United States but in their native language, many other suppressed or partially suppressed Russian writers. It is owing to their extraordinary effort that most of what the general public now knows of Mandelstam's work is known. He might otherwise be, for us, an admired figure of the early part of the century whose later life and work belonged to rumor.[4]

But the works of Mandelstam, especially those that did not appear while he was alive, have made their way into what I shall hereafter call the New York edition under circumstances that should be clear from what I have said above. They derive from copies, and from copies of

4

copies, and even from things put down by memory. That they have reached the West at all is a *de facto* if not a *de jure* violation of Soviet law. The editors themselves – no less than the present writer, who contributed an English introduction – realize the inevitable lacunae and inaccuracies that must result from their conditions of work. What is remarkable is not that the edition has drawbacks, but that it exists at all and that it is under the circumstances remarkably full and exact.

If you were to diagram our present knowledge of Mandelstam's life in relationship to our knowledge of his poetry, the figure resulting would be an X, an elegant chiasm, for the one is inversely proportionate to the other. Of his early poetry we have pretty precise texts, which he himself saw through the press, but we know maddeningly little of his early life; of his later poetry we have texts the authenticity of which it is difficult to judge in minute particular, but there exists an account of his later life, his widow's memoir, filled with unimpeachable and intricate detail. The temptation in the former case is to allow the poems to supply the deficiency in our knowledge of the life, and in the latter, to amend the texts by presuming that since we know what he was doing we know also what he must have written. Even though Mandelstam's work was censored with increasing severity, we are still able to rely fairly confidently upon what appeared in book form while he was alive. This means that critics may deal with these poems while enjoying the primary sense of security required by all critics, namely, that they are dealing with what the poet actually wrote. On the other hand, it is exceedingly difficult to come by reliable information on the author's life before the early 1920s, by which time he had produced his first two books. As for the poems of the 1930s, never seen through the press by the author and evidently unpublishable in his own country even today, one relies upon the best available texts – and the notion of 'best available' has changed considerably as the New York edition went through its successive versions.

Lest it be assumed that even the early texts are all in a satisfactory state, I have dwelt at some length on one of them (No. 101; p. 259 below), which chances to be in a spectacularly unsatisfactory state. It is somewhat daunting to realize that the text of this poem – one of the most famous, most often discussed and frequently translated – was published three times in Mandelstam's own collections, and that in spite of this, no two versions are identical. That in the New York edition is, alas, different from them all. The variations are minor indeed, but the result of them has been a persistent misreading of the poem even by the best of Mandelstam's increasing number of students and commentators. How difficult such questions are in the poems of the 1930s I leave to the imagination of readers, who will perhaps understand better the limited scope of this book.

In general, I ignore the demands that specialist readers would have a right to make concerning the texts. The analysis of No. 101 will have to stand as a lonely example, applicable to many other cases, of how difficult it sometimes is to know what Mandelstam even wrote, let alone what he meant. In this work we are at a much more preliminary stage than is commonly believed.

Given the conditions sketched above, what can the reader expect from the present book?

The limitations of it have been imposed no less by the circumstances which I have outlined than by my own abilities and interests. It deals with Mandelstam's life and poetry through the 1920s – with that part of the life that has heretofore remained obscure and unwritten, and with that part of the poetry, the collections culminating in 1928, upon which his fame chiefly rests and about the authenticity of which we can be most confident. Chapters 2 through 8 deal with Mandelstam's life, and 9 through 14 with his poetry; but the boundary between these two parts is deliberately permeable, with the result that poems are also treated in the first part, and the life in the second.

It is an introduction to Mandelstam, and it is not for specialists in Russian literature. I include the Cyrillic texts of every poem discussed, but I also include a full translation. If it is possible at this long remove from its beginnings to recall the audience that I first had in mind, I suppose it would consist of the university students and colleagues to whom I have attempted on various occasions to convey, in spite of their lack of Russian, a sense of Mandelstam as a poet. Whether that is a feasible ambition is not for me to decide, but it was and remains my ambition.

The book seeks also to be a kind of anthology. For the most part, therefore, it eschews a technique that is – especially, it seems, in the traditional way of writing about Russian poetry – best described in Vladimir Nabokov's novel *The Gift*. When Valentin Linyov, a hack reviewer, wrote about poetry,

> he artlessly employed the device of so-called 'inter-quotational footbridges.' His discussion of Koncheyev's book boiled down to his answering for the author a kind of implied album questionnaire (Your favorite flower? Favorite hero? Which virtue do you prize most?): 'The poet,' Linyov wrote of Koncheyev, 'likes [there followed a string of quotations, forcibly distorted by their combination and the demands of the accusative case]. He dreads [more bleeding stumps of verse]. He finds solace in – [*même jeu*]; but on the other hand [three-quarters of a line turned by means of quotes into a flat statement]; at times it seems to him that' – and here Linyov inadvertently extricated something more or less whole.[5]

In this book I have tried not only to discuss but also to display Mandelstam's poems, and not 'more or less whole,' but whole.

As for the English translations, my hope was to make them as attractive as possible. Most of them aim modestly enough at no more than accuracy; some aim a little higher. Experts will enjoy distinguishing the one from the other. I hope that my primary audience will enjoy the translations themselves.

I should like to conclude these preliminaries, which supply the place of a preface, and have become more and more personal, with a thoroughly personal note.

The real beginning of this book, I suppose, was in the mid-to-late 1950s, when I was a graduate student at Harvard and when Mandelstam's works first appeared (in New York, in Russian) after a lapse of time during which he had scarcely existed, save in the memory of those who had known him and, in a sort of covenant with his memory, preserved his works. Casting about for a dissertation topic, I lit upon Mandelstam. After so long an association with him it is not easy to say what first drew me to him. An equally long association with the processes of graduate education, and a wish to be honest, compel me to admit that his then obscurity, in every sense, had a seductive appeal: few knew Russian (I supposed that I knew Russian) and even fewer had ever heard of him, let alone written about him. His fate was utterly mysterious, even the little that was known of his life was a web of surmise, for the most part, and his poetry, in the context of what I then knew of Russian poetry, seemed even more miraculously *sui generis* than it later proved in fact to be. The dissertation was duly written, and that part of it relating to his autobiographical and imaginative prose, together with translations of the prose, appeared as a book in 1965.[6]

The present book, like the dissertation which it thoroughly supersedes and the study of the prose, began in the spirit of an introduction, and remains there, but it reaches the light of day at a time when Mandelstam's name, at least, is familiar to what is, retrospectively, an astonishingly large readership. I write these words in the year 1972. The life to which they refer ended in 1938 and the poetry a decade earlier. Yeats died in 1939, Joyce in 1941, Stevens in 1955, Eliot in 1965, and Pound is still alive (to mention some modern writers in whose company Mandelstam belongs) and about each of them there already exist small libraries of biography, commentary, explication, concordances, letters, and even variorum editions.

Set beside this the state of our knowledge of Mandelstam in the late 1950s. It was not definitely known, at least in the West, whether or not he was dead. To this day the exact time and manner of his death cannot be publicly verified. There is no grave. He vanished into space and time with less trace than Hart Crane, more anonymously than the victims of Dachau. At the time when I began to write what became this book, there were rumors that he was obscurely alive, though terminally insane, in some vague Russian hinterland. The notion could be remotely entertained of sitting down to coax from even the demented relic of a great poet whether, say, he had read Dickens in English, or ever travelled in Italy. Not even the editors of the New York edition, who knew more than anyone else in the West, had ever heard of the existence of Mandelstam's wife. Today not only her name but also her genius, courage, and awesome literary power are familiar around the world. In the 1950s and early 1960s we ignorantly supposed ourselves to be more or less in possession of the canon itself, allowing for the obvious oversights that plague all rooting in archives, especially those to which entry could be gained only haphazardly, or clandestinely, but in any case incompletely. Today the little brick-red book of 1955 has a frail and faded charm beside the three large volumes that have superseded it.

It is surely not necessary to dwell upon the quantum leap that our knowledge has made between that day and this for the reader to understand that a book written over that period was several times near completion when it had to be discarded and begun anew. It is no part of the reader's concern to overlook the resulting deficiencies, but the facts might shape his expectation of what is to come.

It is, finally, one of the endless ironies of Mandelstam's fate that this book should have been written where, when, and by whom it was written. The years when this Russian Jew was enduring exile and death for having been a poet of genius were years when all I had to cope with was a Christian childhood in the American South. My acknowledgments, were they even to approach fullness, ought to begin with Thomas Winner, who first guided my steps in the great and beautiful language of Russia and continue with all my benign Russian drillmasters in the Army Language School, as it was then called. The limitations that such a background must impose upon the ambitions and the possible achievements of this book will not require further emphasis. I have tried to repay a forever unrepayable debt to Nadezhda Mandelstam, to such great Soviet scholars as Viktor Zhirmunsky and Nikolay Khardzhiev, to my professors Roman Jakobson, Vsevolod Setchkarev, and Renato Poggioli, and to the editors of Mandelstam's works in this country, Gleb Struve and Boris Filippov. It was my purpose to make the greatest modern poet of their language available to speakers of mine. Responsible for what might be good in the book, they are blameless for its shortcomings. The endurance and devotion of my wife have made the disappointments seem small, and the joys much greater.

2

The most abstract and intentional city

I

Osip Emilevich Mandelstam was born in Warsaw. The fact seems slightly discordant, something like Robert Frost's having been born in San Francisco, though of course the differences, spiritual and geographical, between Warsaw and St Petersburg are not so great as those between the Coast and the country north of Boston. In everything but literal fact St Petersburg was Mandelstam's native city. That is where he grew up after having moved there with his family at an early age (unknown to me). It is where he received his first impressions of the world outside the apartment, went to school, began to write, and earned his first fame. It is the place with which, in everyone's mind, Mandelstam is associated, and when he wrote in 1930 a famous poem beginning 'I've returned to my city, familiar to the point of tears,' no one who knew him could possibly have mistaken the place or disputed the possessive even if the poem had not borne as its title the new name: Leningrad.

He was much drawn to the West, especially the classical Mediterranean world, and within Russia itself he felt an enormous attraction to the south, especially to the Crimea and Armenia, with their ancient classical and Christian associations. And the truth is that he spent about as much of his creative lifetime in Moscow as in St Petersburg. About all of these other places he left memoirs and poems. He is nevertheless a St Petersburg poet.

Probably he is so not only because of the literary world's notable tendency to retain its first impressions of a man but also because there really is some special quality that distinguishes those who were formed as artists in the salons and in the streets of the imperial Russian capital. The subject is risky. It has a long history of having been taken to lyrical and sentimental extremes, and most readers interested in the topic of this book will no doubt be familiar with it. Still, nothing so eccentric as St Petersburg can go without mention, especially in view of Mandelstam's identification with it.

It was and is an anomaly among Russian places. There can be little doubt that its external aspect contributed to Mandelstam's enthusiasm for the Mediterranean world, for this northern city with its loathsome climate and seemingly endless winter, its ice-blocked river and soot-blackened snow, remains in the mind as a pattern of immense avenues, canals, and broad perspectives of water lined with serenely classical, columned buildings – many of them, in fact, built by Italian architects. While it is Russian and Western at once, the foreign element dominates. The little Church of the Resurrection on the Catherine Canal, with its nine domes and its enamels, mosaics and gilding in the exhuberant Russian seventeenth-century style, strikes one as a curiosity imported from abroad, which is practically the case, since it is largely a copy of the familiar St Basil's on Red Square in Moscow.

To be sure, it is also the city of Dostoevsky, that detester of the West. For the kind of unnerving atmosphere that fills, for instance, the opening of *The Eternal Husband* he preferred the brief, dusty, unnatural summer of Petersburg, especially the period known as the 'white nights,' when the sun makes a merely perfunctory dip of a few hours beneath the horizon, leaving the city bathed in what is neither night nor day. It has been said that for T. S. Eliot any city, not only London, would have been 'unreal.' One wonders what he would have made of the scene on Nevsky Prospekt, up and down which knots of compulsive strollers plod in the low sun of eleven o'clock at night. Such dislocations of the biological clock, clinging as it does to the diurnal rhythm, wreak havoc with one's sense of well-being. Even if the history of St Petersburg had furnished no other cause for anxiety, this alone is enough to engender the sense that it is a kind of mirage, or as Mandelstam wrote in the *Noise of Time*, quoting Tyutchev, 'a covering thrown over the abyss.'[1]

II

Like much else besides, though with less excuse, the year of Mandelstam's birth has been often misreported. He was born on 15 January 1891. In the Old Style, that is, in the style of the Julian calendar used in Russia before the Revolution, the date would be 3 January 1891. For some reason the date has been repeatedly given as 1892, but Mandelstam himself is the conclusive guide: 'My first conscious, sharp perceptions were of gloomy crowds of people in the streets. I was exactly three years old. It was 1894 and I had been brought from Pavlovsk to Petersburg for the purpose of seeing the funeral of Alexandr III.' Years later, in 1931, he wrote in a notebook, 'In January I turned forty.'[2] Reliable Russian works of reference give 1891 as the year of his birth.

In 1937, near the end of his life, he wrote some lines that give the time of his birth with a precision that even astrologers might savor:

> —Я рожден в ночь с второго на третье
> Января в девяносто одном
> Ненадежном году...
>   (No. 362)

The most abstract and intentional city

I was born on the night between the second and the third
of January in the untrustworthy year
of eighteen-ninety something or other...

though the casual blur of the digit seems prophetic of later confusion.

Mandelstam loved the sharpest possible historical juxtapositions, and
in his notes on Darwin's style he even prescribed them as the best rule
for prose. So he would probably think it appropriate to mention that
the year 1891 was the year when construction was begun on the Trans-
Siberian railroad, across the tracks of which, to its eastern terminus,
Vladivostok, the poet would be shipped forty-seven years later to die in
one of Stalin's camps.

III

Practically the only source we have for a knowledge of Mandelstam's
childhood happens, luckily, to be a good one – Mandelstam himself.
In a book of recollections and character portraits published in 1925
under the title *Shum vremeni* (The Noise of Time),[3] he summons up, as
the title indicates, some of the buzzing confusion of the two decades on
either side of the turn of the century. Since the chief intent is a recreation
of the noise and smell and feel of the times, one has to glean the actual
facts of his own personal life where one can find them.

He wrote very little about his immediate family – nothing at all, for
example about the two brothers with whom he grew up, Alexandr and
Yevgeny – and the fact is that he never appears to have spoken about
his family with much willingness. Most memoirists who can be relied
upon agree that the young Mandelstam was reticent to the point of
secretiveness about his close relations.

The name Mandelstam is not an uncommon one among Russian
Jews. The directory *Ves' Peterburg na 1909 g.* (All Petersburg for the
Year 1909)[4] lists 14 Mandelstams. But at the time when the poet was
growing up the best known man by that name appears to have been
a certain physician, an eye specialist, in Kiev. Yury Trubetskoy asserts –
on, as the saying goes, no less an authority than his own – that this
Dr Mandelstam was a cousin of the poet.[5] But Dr Aaron Steinberg of
London, who knew Mandelstam during the winter of 1909–10 in Heidelberg and had kept some very valuable notes dating from that time, told
me that he had once asked him whether the famous ophthalmologist was
a relative and got the answer: 'I am not interested in my kinfolk.' That
does not of course answer the question – which is not in itself of much
importance – but neither is this fit of hauteur a transient one, for it
conveys what seems to have been Mandelstam's normal public attitude
on the matter. Georgy Adamovich, one of the few émigré writers whose
reminiscences of Mandelstam have proven to be free of fiction, recalls

11

that he never invited anyone to his family's apartment and never discussed his life at home.

The poet's father, Emil Veniaminovich Mandelstam, was a leather merchant. He stemmed from Kurland, a former Polish duchy and in the nineteenth century one of the Russian gubernias, lying on the shore of the Baltic Sea and the Gulf of Riga. It was he, destined in his youth for the rabbinate, who had made the break with religious orthodoxy. Mandelstam's picture of his father is, typically, rather more like the history of an idea than the history of a man, and in his published memoirs the tone of it is more amused and kindly than it is affectionate.

> In essence, my father transferred me to a totally alien century and distant, although completely un-Jewish atmosphere. These were, if you will, the purest eighteenth or even seventeenth century of an enlightened ghetto somewhere in Hamburg. Religious interests had been eliminated completely. The philosophy of the Enlightenment was transformed into intricate Talmudist pantheism. Somewhere in the vicinity Spinoza is breeding his spiders in a jar. One has a presentiment of Rousseau and his natural man. Everything fantastically abstract, intricate and schematic. A fourteen-year-old boy, whom they had been training as a rabbi and had forbidden to read worldly books, runs off to Berlin and ends up in a higher Talmudic school, where there had gathered a number of such stubborn, rational youths, who had aspired in godforsaken backwaters to be geniuses. Instead of the Talmud, he reads Schiller – and mark you, he reads it as a new book. Having held out there for a while, he falls out of this strange university back into the seething world of the seventies in order to remember the conspiratorial dairy shop on Karavannaya whence a bomb was tossed under Alexandr, and in a glove-making shop and in a leather factory he expounds to the paunchy and astonished customers the philosophic ideals of the eighteenth century.[6]

Mandelstam describes the results of such training in the only other passage in his writing devoted directly to his father:

> My father had absolutely no language; his speech was tongue-tie and languagelessness. The Russian speech of a Polish Jew? No. The speech of a German Jew? No again. Perhaps a special Kurland accent? I never heard such. A completely abstract, counterfeit language, the ornate and twisted speech of an autodidact, where normal words are intertwined with the ancient philosophical terms of Herder, Leibnitz, and Spinoza, the capricious syntax of a Talmudist, the artificial, not always finished sentence: it was anything in the world, but not a language, neither Russian nor German.[7]

This is clearly hyperbole, a beloved device of Mandelstam. It might be simply dismissed as such had it not become the subject of a small dispute that throws some further light upon the character of Emil Mandelstam and a great deal of light on the obstacles in the way of his son's biographer.

Attempting to compose the first biographical sketch of Mandelstam in the 1955 edition of his works, Gleb Struve, one of the editors, relied upon the above passage to observe that the poet's father 'apparently wrote and spoke poor Russian and poor German,' which, on the evidence, would seem to say the least of it.[8] The émigré poet Georgy Ivanov, a former acquaintance of Mandelstam, seized upon this remark when he reviewed the 1955 edition in an exasperatingly truculent article. Though he could not testify as to the German, he said, Mandelstam's father spoke excellent literary Russian without the least trace of accent. Ivanov continues: 'I think that he wrote in the same way. At least, during the time of the Provisional Government, he did give several talks at the Manufacturers' Society. Occasionally we would be drinking tea in the parlor and the "barin" [master], as Mandelstam's father was called in his family, would take his glass into the study to write a talk.'[9]

IV

What was Emil Mandelstam like as a person? How did he talk? Was he an irrascible domestic tyrant, a Jewish merchant aspiring to the title 'barin' in his own house, at least? Was he, as Ivanov writes in another memoir devoted to Mandelstam, 'eternally out of sorts...a perfect Leiden jar: touch him and you're dead'? Did he, to take the present by no means minor point, speak perfect literary Russian or was his language the jumbled linguistic litter described by his son?

There would seem on the surface to be no problem at all. For all its clear autobiographical slant, *The Noise of Time* belongs after all to the realm of *belles lettres*, and is thus dangerous ground for those seeking hard facts about the real world. Besides, Mandelstam's account bears all the marks of exaggeration for the sake of effect. And the effect is one that Mandelstam adored and even explicitly recommended as the rule of prose: the sharpest possible juxtaposition. Juxtaposed to this passage on his father's language is one on his mother's: 'The speech of my mother was clear and sonorous without the least foreign admixture.' And there is a perfectly plausible reason why these two vividly contrasting portraits are side by side in the same paragraph. They answer the question posed at the beginning of it: 'The speech of the father and the speech of the mother – does not our language feed through all its long life on the confluence of these two, do they not compose its character?'

It is clear, then. Typically, Mandelstam is speaking of himself, of his own language, his own 'Russian Latin,' as it has been called, by the oblique method of deriving it from the chaotic linguistic environment of his earliest childhood. Having realised this, we need not take what he says about his father's language as anything more than a vague gesture in the general direction of the truth.

Ivanov, on the other hand, who knew Mandelstam from 1910 until 1922 and was, by his own account, one of the poet's most intimate acquaintances, appears simply to have been setting the record straight for the sake of history. Except for the painfully evident personal animus against the editors of the 1955 edition, it would be difficult to adduce any reason for his disputing Struve's innocuous remark and offering his own version of the elder Mandelstam. In his own memoir of Mandelstam, written years earlier and collected in his book *Peterburgskie zimy* (Petersburg Winters),[10] there is not the slightest apparent reason why Ivanov should have distorted the facts of his friend's biography.

But perhaps there are less apparent reasons. Let us leave aside, charitably, the itch of the publicist to be 'interesting' – an itch, after all, for which we readers have reason to be grateful. And anyway, Ivanov was a poet first of all and a publicist *faute de mieux*. The point is that he was a poet in exile, and among people for whom the rule *rossica non leguntur* was as sovereign then as it generally is today. It must have seemed to him at certain moments of loneliness that he had 'imagined Russia,' to quote a phrase from one of Vladimir Markov's poems. Could there really have been Akhmatova and Mandelstam and the others, who were now so incommunicado as to be practically dead? Might one not conjure back into existence those lost years, the desperate gaiety that reigned even at the height of the Revolution, a time when one's every poem had an audience waiting round the corner?

There is the problem and the tragedy. Ivanov's testimony to the period that he lived through, one of the most interesting and inaccessible periods of Russian literary history, simply cannot be believed. He made no distinction between what was and what merely might or even ought to have been the truth. But the literary artist's perfectly commendable desire not to bore his reader led to the vicious practice of attaching real names of living people to his fictitious personages. Ivanov's character, mysterious and imponderable always, deteriorated in sordid ways under the bitterness of exile, which appears to have warped his nature at the same time that, by general agreement, it improved his poetry. A mere 'school' poet as a junior Acmeist in Petersburg, he became in Paris one of the masters of modern Russian poetry. His strange disregard for those who had been among the warmest friends of his youth appears to have extended later to the world in general, but out of this final moral vacuum emerged poems of indubitable power.

Here is a rather innocuous example of Ivanov's technique. In Chapter XIII of *Petersburg Winters* he tells the story of a drunken midnight ride from Petersburg to Tsarskoe Selo, a nearby town of intensely literary associations. The time was 1914. The participants were Gumilyov, Akhmatova, Gorodetsky, Mandelstam (the high command of Acmeism) and of course Georgy Ivanov. The object of their lighthearted ride through night and snow was a pilgrimage to the park bench where Innokenty Annensky, a poet revered by the Acmeists, used to sit. He had died five years earlier. When they arrived at the spot they were startled to see a man 'like a hunch-backed shadow' sitting on the bench and reciting poetry. This turned out to be the mysterious figure of Count Vasily Komarovsky, a little-known poet, who, in his rare moments of lucidity, wrote delicately wrought poems on themes from the classical world. He spoke to them of some recent suicides that had taken place on the Annensky bench, then took them all to his house, which Ivanov pictures chiefly in terms of the blinding amount of light that the count required his servants to furnish:

> 'Light the girandoles!'
> 'At once, your excellency!'

Ivanov describes in some detail, from Count Komarovsky's own unembarrassed conversation, the mental illness that kept him institutionalized much of the time. We learn that the count, whose heart was as frail as his mind, later fainted and died on reading the news of the declaration of war.

This decayed romance, with its midnight and madness, its Smyrna carpets and its Sèvres, owes about as much to Huysmans as to reality. No such drunken ride ever took place. Ivanov's description of Komarovsky's house is pure invention, and the likelihood is that Ivanov was obliged to invent it since he had never been there (Count Komarovsky lived modestly with a maiden aunt in the house of a man named Palkin). Nor was that the time or the manner of his death.

The refutation of Ivanov comes from a memoir of Komarovsky written by Ivanov's fellow émigré in Paris, Sergey Makovsky, the former editor of the journal *Apollon*. 'I don't know why Ivanov needed this romantic fabrication,' Makovsky writes. 'I remember that about twenty years ago, in Paris, I asked him, "What was that for?" Ivanov laughed in reply and admitted that he had "indulged his fancy."'[11] Since Makovsky himself was not averse to 'indulging his fancy' on occasion, it is comforting to be able to add that Anna Akhmatova herself, one of the supposed trippers to Tsarskoe Selo that night, told me that it was all pure invention.

In seeking some justification for Ivanov, one might point to the paragraph that opens the chapter on Komarovsky: 'There are memories like dreams. There are dreams like memories. And when you think about what happened "so recently and so endlessly long ago" you sometimes don't know what is memory and what is dream.' There follows a page of lyrical impressionism on the general topic of transitoriness and irreality, but nowhere is it said that the account of Komarovsky and the others is a dream. Or, to be more exact, we are not told which parts are dream, for it seems to me that we are bound to suppose

15

that some parts of it are genuine memory. Some truth must have crept in – if only in moments of flagging imagination. Perhaps Count Komarovsky *did* wear 'American shoes.'

It might perhaps also be argued that Ivanov, in this instance at least, was not actually up to any mischief. The story is innocuous enough, or must seem so to those reading it now. Considering the vertiginous scope afforded to malice in the community of Russian literary exiles, it is an innocent and amusing anecdote.

But we may perhaps be excused for finding the jokes of Ivanov and other such memoirists unfunny. Something more important is involved than the damned nuisance to researchers. What might seem at another time to be an innocent frivolity is not so now. In order to understand why Anna Akhmatova, a woman of rare equanimity who could herself be grimly humorous even about such phenomena as Andrey Zhdanov, could be set in a rage by Ivanov and other such inventive memoirists, one must understand the value assigned to absolute veracity by those whose lives are smothered in an atmosphere of lying. They have for so long read gross distortions of their lives in print – for reasons that have nothing to do with merely amusing a readership – that no possible goal could justify departures from the truth. It seems to them the depth of iniquity for those in the West who *could* write the truth to indulge a taste for fancy lying.

Another Paris émigré and, like Ivanov, one of the very best of modern Russian poets, Vladislav Khodasevich, once went to a lecture in Paris on the Russian Symbolists, most of whom he had himself known well. Returning home, he wrote a melancholy essay prompted by the occasion.[12] The lecturer had read the poets sensitively. He had read what there was to read about the period. In short, he had done an honest, conscientious job. But how far from the mark! How distorted and basically misconceived it all was. For the point is that the poems of the Symbolists cannot be more than superficially understood without knowing, often in intimate detail, the lives of the poets. Khodasevich argues with great cogency a thesis that, while it was critical anathema throughout my own education, has increasingly come to underlie my studies of Mandelstam. It applies of course not only to the Symbolists but to most of the Russian poets of the modern period. Perhaps it is true that the more smothered the life, the greater will be its relevance to a reading of the poems through which it breathed.

There will be occasion enough to lament Ivanov's distortions later on, but before returning to the narrative of Mandelstam's early life, I should like to consider one other memoirist from the Paris émigré world. This is Irina Odoevtseva. She knew Mandelstam for a period of a few months after his return in 1920 to St Petersburg from the south, and she has left a rather extensive memoir of that time in her book *Na beregakh Nevy*

The most abstract and intentional city

(On the Banks of the Neva).[13] Russians as a people strike me as indubitably the greatest memoirists in the world, and Odoevtseva has the national talent for recreating people and moods from the past. Her book is comfortably and attractively furnished with the appointments of reality – with all the precise addresses, street corners, names of servants, and the hard factualness that one would expect from a dedicated Acmeist (she was one of several gifted young poetesses who briefly formed part of Gumilyov's retinue). Her portrait of Mandelstam seems natural and true to life. She is even at some pains to correct the widespread exaggerations of other memoirists.

What is most striking of all is the abundance of the dialogue. There are no memoirs of Mandelstam in which he is given so many lines of his own to speak. Alas – that is precisely what his 'conversations' with Odoevtseva come down to: lines of his own. For the memoirist has merely adapted passages from Mandelstam's own prose. The *New Yorker* would no doubt put the following into the 'Department of Funny Coincidence':

'You know, as a child I conceived a love for Tchaikovsky, a life-long love, to the point of painful frenzy. We lived at our dacha in the summer and I heard the music from behind a barbed-wire fence. I often tore my sailor's jacket and covered my hands with scratches by making my way to the orchestra shell without paying. It was there in Dubbeln on the Riga coast that an orchestra first strained at Tchaikovsky's *Symphonie Pathétique* for me, and I drowned in it as in the Baltic Gulf.'
Odoevtseva, *Novyi zhurnal* (New Review) 72, June 1963, 79.

In Jewish Dubbeln the orchestra strained at Tchaikovsky's *Symphonie Pathétique*, and one could hear the two nests of strings calling back and forth to each other.
At this time I conceived for Tchaikovsky a painfully nervous and tense love that recalled the desire of Dostoevsky's Netochka Nezvanova to hear the violin concerto behind the red flame of the silk curtains. The broad, flowing, purely violin passages in Tchaikovsky I heard from behind a barbed-wire fence and more than once tore my clothes and covered my hands with scratches as I made my way gratis to the orchestra shell.
Mandelstam, *Shum vremeni* (The Noise of Time), Chap. VI.

'And then there appeared for me, as the center of the world, the Pavlovsk railroad station. I rushed into it as into some Elysium...it was an Elysium of sounds and spirits in which Tchaikovsky and Rubinstein reigned.'
Odoevtseva, loc. cit.

What, in a word, were the nineties? Ladies' bouffant sleeves and music in Pavlosk: the balloons of the ladies' sleeves and all the rest revolve around the glass railroad station in Pavlovsk, and Galkin, the conductor, stands at the center of the world.
In the middle of the nineties all Petersburg streamed into Pavlovsk as

'Suddenly, I'd be terrified – another second and it would all end in a frightful scandal, I'd be thrown out in shame. They'd take me by the arms and out of the concert hall, out of the salon of some wealthy patroness, out on my neck I'd go and head over heels down the stairs. They'd disgrace me. Ruin me.'
Odoevtseva, loc. cit.

into some Elysium. Locomotive whistles and railroad bells mingled with the patriotic cacophony of the *1812 Overture*, and a peculiar smell filled the huge station where Tchaikovsky and Rubinstein reigned.
Mandelstam, op. cit., Chap. I.

They will throw you out one of these days, Parnok, throw you out with frightful scandal and shame...they'll take you by the arms and pf-f-t!... out of the Symphony Hall, out of the Society of Friends and Amateurs of the Last Word, out of the Circle for Grasshopper Music, out of the salon of Mme Bookbinder...who knows where else?...but out you will go, disgraced, vilified...
Mandelstam, *Egipetskaia marka* (The Egyptian Stamp), Chap. II.

'The Petersburg cabby was always a myth...he should be put in the meridian or the zodiac.'
Odoevtseva, loc. cit.

The Petersburg cabby is a myth, a Capricorn. He should be put in the zodiac.
Mandelstam, op. cit., Chap. V.

Even if we suppose that writers might offer oral redactions of some of their happier sentences, and of course that conversation is flabbier and more ill-considered than published writing, still it strains our credence to read that Mandelstam, notable self-quoter though he was, should have united in one conversation with Mme Odoevtseva so many literal citations from such widely scattered places in his own writing. The fact is that she has simply cribbed from the pages of Mandelstam conversations that she never had.

There can be no question of malice; the author is merely promoting her claim to intimate association with the great. But her memoirs falsify the record on every hand, not only in the dialogue, and, as in the case of Ivanov's, one cannot depend on any part of them unless there is some collateral evidence for what she says (in which case, of course, we do not require hers). The only danger is that they will be believed by those seeking to know the truth or utilized by those promoting some particular version of the truth. Did Mandelstam conceive a 'life-long' love of Tchaikovsky? That is the memoirist's embellishment on the text from which she was fabricating her 'conversation' with the poet. I do not believe it, for he never wrote it.

The most abstract and intentional city

V

Whatever Emil Mandelstam's pronunciation may have sounded like when he spoke Russian, as of course he certainly did, his written language was German. He carried on his commercial correspondence in German, and years later, in the 1930s, he even wrote his memoirs in German. Nadezhda Yakovlevna, the poet's widow, who told me of this, does not know what became of them. If they should ever prove to have survived the war and other calamities, they will no doubt be an invaluable source of information about Osip Mandelstam's earlier life. In the little bookcase that Mandelstam makes into a sort of ikon of the family's intellectual history, his father's books were the Germans – Schiller, Goethe, Kerner, and Shakespeare in German translation.[14] Mandelstam's paternal grandparents, who lived in Riga, knew no Russian at all and presumably spoke German as their normal language at home, for he writes that he never heard Yiddish as a boy.

Mandelstam's mother, Flora Osipovna Verblovskaya, came from Vilno. Her language, to continue with the same linguistic portrait of the poet's parents, is described thus:

> The speech of my mother was clear and sonorous without the least foreign admixture, with rather wide and too open vowels – the literary Great Russian language. Her vocabulary was poor and restricted, the locutions were trite, but it was a language, it had roots and confidence. Mother loved to speak and took joy in the roots and sounds of her Great Russian speech, impoverished by intellectual clichés. Was she not the first of her whole family to achieve pure and clear Russian sounds?[15]

This last question is a reminder of the fact that in the little Mandelstam has to say about his parents one theme emerges: each of them broke significantly with a family heritage to which only the most occasional allusions are made. Emil Mandelstam rejected the religion and Flora Verblovskaya the linguistic stigma of a minority culture.

As he grew older Mandelstam evidently changed his mind about his Jewishness, but it is important to record how he felt about it as a child. This may in a certain sense tell us more about his real relationship to his family than many more direct references.

His parents were not religious. 'Once or twice in my life I was taken to a synagogue as if to a concert,' he writes in *The Noise of Time*. It was an alien spectacle, nothing like those other concerts of which Mandelstam left affectionate memorials, and it formed no part of the boy's idea of himself. The title of the chapter from which this sentence comes is 'The Judaic Chaos,' a phrase pregnant with meaning. It points in fact to one of the central motifs of the book of recollections and of much else in Mandelstam's life besides: the contrast between order and chaos. Being

19   2-2

a Jew was a disorderly thing. St Petersburg and the ritualized life that took place with a certain grand ceremoniousness in its embassies, cathedrals and imposing avenues – that was order, Russian order. Mandelstam felt vaguely misplaced as a Jew, the victim of a slightly comic but also unpleasant and even shameful miscalculation by Fate. 'All this,' he writes, referring to the grand spectacle of the capital, 'may very well have been proper to some son of a corps commander with the appropriate family traditions, but it was completely out of keeping with the kitchen fumes of a middle-class apartment, to Father's study, heavy with the odor of leathers, kidskin and calfskin, or to Jewish conversations about business.'[16] The penetrating smell of leather was always to remain for him, as he says elsewhere, 'the smell of the yoke of labor.' It is striking how often he refers to the 'smell' of his heritage and one cannot escape the impression that it had a smothering effect

> As a little bit of musk fills an entire house, so the least influence of Judaism overflows all of one's life. O, what a strong smell that is! Could I possibly not have noticed that in real Jewish houses there was a different smell from that in Aryan houses? And it was not only the kitchen that smelled so, but the people, things and clothing. To this day I remember how that sweetish Jewish smell swaddled me in the wooden house of my grandfather and grandmother on Klyuchevaya Street in German Riga.[17]

Those were the parents of his father. The boy visited them very unwillingly – 'It seemed to me that I was being taken to the native country of my father's incomprehensible philosophy' – and resisted their efforts at religious education, which only terrified him.

> My grandfather, a blue-eyed old man in a skull cap which covered half his forehead and with the serious and rather signified features to be seen in very respected Jews, would smile, rejoice, and try to be affectionate – but did not know how. Then his dense eyebrows would draw together. When he wanted to take me in his arms I almost burst into tears... Suddenly my grandfather drew from a drawer of a chest a black and yellow silk cloth, put it around my shoulders, and made me repeat after him words composed of unknown sounds; but, dissatisfied with my babble, he grew angry and shook his head in disapproval. I felt stifled and afraid.[18]

But the ceremonies of his inherited religion inspired him with other emotions than terror. Chief among them was disgust, the sort of disgust felt by children for their familiar circumstances at certain periods of life, and felt no doubt by all children who are not only growing up but also growing out of one culture into another. 'But how offensive was the crude speech of the rabbi – though it was not ungrammatical; how vulgar when he uttered the words "His Imperial Highness," how utterly vulgar all that he said!'[19]

In the emblematic bookshelf that I have mentioned the books relating to Jews occupied a despised position.

I always remember the lower shelf as chaotic: the books were not standing upright side by side but lay like ruins: reddish five-volume works with ragged covers, a Russian history of the Jews written in the clumsy, shy language of a Russian-speaking Talmudist. This was the Judaic chaos thrown into the dust. This was the level to which my Hebrew primer, which I never mastered, quickly fell. In a fit of national contrition they went as far as hiring a real Jewish teacher for me. He came from his Torgovaya Street and taught without taking off his cap, which made me feel awkward. His correct Russian sounded false. The Hebrew primer was illustrated with pictures which showed one and the same little boy, wearing a visored cap and with a melancholy adult face, in all sorts of situations – with a cat, a book, a pail, a watering can. I saw nothing of myself in that boy and with all my being revolted against the book and the subject. There was one striking thing in that teacher, although it sounded unnatural: the feeling of national Jewish pride. He talked about Jews as the French governesses talked about Hugo and Napoleon. But I knew that he hid his pride when he went out into the street, and therefore did not believe him.[20]

Worst of all perhaps was simply the intolerable sense of otherness, of isolation from the world that he saw around him and loved with all his heart. As a child Mandelstam evidently felt that to submit to his Jewish heritage would have meant to renounce the festive splendor that the real world held and was always to hold for him.

The strong, ruddy, Russian year rolled through the calendar with decorated eggs, Christmas trees, steel skates from Finland, December, gaily bedecked Finnish cabdrivers, and the villa. But mixed up with all this there was a phantom – the New Year in September – and the strange, cheerless holidays, grating upon the ear with their harsh names: Rosh Hashana and Yom Kippur.[21]

Mandelstam's rejection of his Jewish inheritance was not permanent. In a remarkable work known as *Chetvertaia proza* (Fourth Prose)[22] he would fling 'the honorable name of Jew, of which I am proud' into the teeth of his tormentors. Nor did it amount to a rejection of religion altogether. On the contrary, it probably intensified a striving after religious conviction that he would otherwise not have felt. In an important letter written to his teacher V. V. Gippius in 1908, when he was 17, Mandelstam said of himself that as a result of the unreligious surroundings in which he had grown up, his family and school, he had 'long since striven toward religion.'[23]

It would be a great mistake to conclude from the foregoing remarks that Mandelstam's childhood was generally solemn or sad. That is emphatically not the impression conveyed by *The Noise of Time*, which is a book brimming with life and delighted surprise at the variousness and oddity of life. He pictures himself as a busy and ubiquitous little boy, clambering over parade stands, overwhelming policemen with questions, blundering into the female balcony at the synagogue, and eternally on the *qui vive* to catch all the color and flavor of the city. His childhood comes to life with great vividness. The sense impressions give pleasure: snow-cold, blindingly white bed linen; the odor of resin, leather, and bread; swift sleighs, punch, cards, a Swedish toy fortress of cardboard; the 'everyday spiritual beauty, the almost physical charm' of his mother's edition of Pushkin; and oozy, pure yellow sand on the Riga seacoast.

Later on, Mandelstam's life was to be a paradigm of modern tragedy, but he had at all times an indomitable love of life and a buoyancy that seems to have been strangely invulnerable. At the bleakest moments he could sustain himself with frank and humorous gladness in simple things: a goldfinch, a child on a sled, fresh bread. Perhaps that artistic euphoria itself, the strength of character and will, the utter self-reliance of the man are the best arguments we have for the boy's having felt generally secure and happy in his father's house.

VI

The buildings on Mokhovaya Street in Leningrad that once housed the famed Tenishev School still contain a school, and there is a theater (for young people) in the auditorium. In other respects little appears to have survived from the institution to which Mandelstam, probably in 1899 at the age of eight,[24] was admitted for the secondary education needed to supplement the efforts of his tutors and French governesses at home.

One recent summer day I sought permission to photograph the building that contained the classrooms. It is located in a courtyard that one reaches from Mokhovaya Street through the rather imposing façade of the building containing the auditorium. An uncivil janitor whom I finally located at the end of one squalid hallway (what could he have been doing there?) would neither grant nor deny permission, for which it is hard to blame him. A policeman whom I found on a nearby streetcorner leapt with similar grace at the chance to be responsible and suggested that I apply to the head of the school, which was, in that particularly vacant period of the summer, not much help. There is little point in dwelling upon the shabbiness, the crumbling masonry and the rickety palisade, for the assumption that the school was once in better shape is, after all, based only upon the general prejudice that everything in Russia has declined – a rule to which there are numerous exceptions.

But whatever the buildings themselves looked like, the life inside them must then have had a different and slightly more zestful quality. The Tenishev School was a progressive institution. It combined the usual classical education with a practical scientific and commercial curriculum. The eight-year course was, in American terms, equivalent to the last six years of school and the first two of college. Intellectually, it was on a very high level and was evidently the elite school of the foremost city in Russia, though its determined modernism included a policy of ignoring the racial and social distinctions that elsewhere made all the difference. This democratic spirit made it eminently suitable in the eyes of the egalitarian Vladimir Dmitrievich Nabokov (1870–1922) as a place to send his son Vladimir (b. 1899), the future great novelist, who entered the school in 1911, four years after Mandelstam had left. Nabokov's memoirs (*Speak, Memory*)[25] provide us with a good bit of the exterior detail for which Mandelstam's memoirs supply the inner essence. Thanks, too, to their widely different angles of vision, the school emerges spectroscopically, with an illusory third dimension. Nabokov earned for himself the cordial dislike of the generality of students (a throng-emotion for which his relish was later to become a permanent public stance) by arriving in a limousine driven by a liveried chauffeur and by holding himself utterly aloof from all the clubs, circles, and debating societies that flourished among what he called the 'good little democrats.'

Mandelstam is characteristically silent on the point of his own reception among the students. Unsurprisingly, he was not so impressed as Nabokov was by the liberal air of the school. 'There was in the school a military, privileged, almost aristocratic undercurrent that was forever threatening to break through: this was composed of the children of certain ruling families who had landed here by some strange parental caprice and now lorded it over the flabby intellectuals.'[26] The boy who rode the streetcar from the Jewish quarter must have had to join in the compulsory ceremony when 'a certain Voevodsky, the son of a court official and a strikingly handsome boy with a classical profile in the style of Nicholas I, proclaimed himself "commander" and compelled everyone to take an oath of fealty to him, kissing the cross and the Bible.'[27]

More or less predictably, there was a certain hiatus between the genial intentions of the school's constitution and the reality that obtained among the students. Anti-Semitism was not lacking. The student press loyally deplored it but reported it, citing a scrawled election slogan (NO YIDS! VOTE FOR RUSSIANS!) and a note found in a classroom ('Yids and Sicilians are strictly forbidden to sit on this bench!!!'). In other schools it would conceivably have been worse.

The orientation of this young and still self-conscious academy was wholly modern and Western – English, to be precise. The students were even dressed in what Mandelstam imagined to be 'the Cambridge fashion' – short trousers, English shirts, and wool stockings. Where else would the intensely Anglophile Nabokovs have sent their son, who was himself soon to go to the real Cambridge?

But one is left with more conjecture about Mandelstam's feelings in these matters, for his own description of the place has that same tough-minded luminosity that we find elsewhere in his memoirs. Something of

23

his human surroundings can be seen in what he called a 'portrait gallery' of his classmates. 'Portraits' they certainly are not, in any ordinary sense of graphic word-painting. They are rather more like socio-economic dossiers, compressed to a sentence or two; for Mandelstam, while scarcely noting their physical presences, sees them all as concentrates of their cultural heritages. This is a good example of that peculiar historical 'intuition' of Mandelstam's that so impressed Prince Mirsky.

> Vanyusha Korsakov. Nicknamed 'Porkchop.' Flaccid boy from a family with ties to the *zemstvo* tradition (Petrunkevich, Rodichev). Wore his hair in a bowl cut. A Russian shirt with a silk belt.
>
> Barats. His family intimate with Stasyulevich *Vestnik Yevropy* (Messenger of Europe). A passionate mineralogist, mute as a fish, talks only of quartz and mica.
>
> Leonid Zarubin. Large coal-mining industry in the Don Basin. To begin with, dynamos and batteries; later on, nothing but Wagner.
>
> Przesiecki. Poor Polish gentry. Specialist at spitting.
>
> Słobodzinski. Top student. A person from the second part of *Dead Souls*, burnt by Gogol. Positive type of the Russian *intelligent*. Moderate mystic. Truth lover. Good mathematician. Well read in Dostoevsky. Later on he ran a radio station.
>
> Nadezhdin. A classless intellectual. Sour odor from the apartment of a minor clerk. Gaiety and insouciance, since there was nothing to lose.
>
> The Krupenskys. Twins. Landed gentry from Bessarabia. Connoisseurs of wine and Jews.
>
> And finally, Boris Sinani. Belonged to the generation that is now active, having ripened for great events and historical work. He had hardly graduated before he died. How he would have shone during the years of the Revolution![28]

And with his usual penchant for seeing his surroundings through the eyes of a passionate museum-goer, he compares his classmates to the children in the portraits of Serov and to those in the sculptures of Fyodor Tolstoy. One of the distinguishing marks of Mandelstam as a writer both of poetry and prose is a sacred horror of telling the reader what he already knows. There must be few writers in any age who have had such utter confidence in and respect for their audience. It was therefore not necessary to dwell upon the outward aspects of those schoolboys: they were the portraits of Serov and the sculptures of Fyodor Tolstoy, and everyone knows what is meant.

The curriculum was varied and resolutely up-to-date. Hygiene was taught by a Dr Virenius, described by Mandelstam with his unerring sense of the incongruous as a 'ruddy-cheeked old man like the child on the can of Nestlé's,' who gave a talk every fall, when the water was frozen solid for miles in every direction, on the beneficial effects of swimming. There was also biology, chemistry, German, and, at the end of the day, training in the skills of manual labor:

...heavy with lessons and sated with conversations and demonstrations, we would gasp with fatigue among the wood shavings and sawdust, unable to saw a board in half. The saw would get bent, the plane would go crooked, the chisel would strike against fingers: nothing came out right. The instructor would busy himself with two or three of the skillful boys, and the others would damn all handicrafts.[29]

The Tenishev School was a hotbed of political discussion.

What a hodge-podge, what true historical dissonance lived in our school, where geography, puffing away at a pipeful of 'Capstan' tobacco, was transformed into anecdotes about American trusts...No, Russian boys are not English. You won't catch them with sport or with the boiled water of political amateurism. Life, with all its unexpected interests and its passionate intellectual diversions, life will burst in upon the most hothouse-like, the most completely sterilized Russian school, as it once burst into Pushkin's lycée.

Mandelstam's particular enthusiasm was for the 'Erfurt Program' of Karl Kautsky, which he read and responded to as if it were a book of poetry. He describes himself, indeed in a conventionally 'poetic' landscape with Kautsky's brochure in his hand: strolling by the banks of the river Aa in his father's native Kurland one clear autumn day, when the spider webs glistened in the fields of barley, he was able, he says,

to populate, to socialize the visible world, with its barley, dirt roads, castles, and sunlit spider webs, breaking it down into diagrams and setting up under the pale blue firmament ladders, far from biblical, upon which not the angels of Jacob but small and large property holders ascended and descended, passing through the stages of capitalist economy.[30]

Many of the student 'circles' had distinct political colorings. There was one whose members announced their allegiance to the SR Party (Socialist Revolutionary). Kozmin asserts that Mandelstam himself was at the age of sixteen a member of the SR group and even engaged in propaganda work at mass meetings.[31] The age is by no means too precocious; Ehrenburg and Mayakovsky, to name only two, were similarly engaged in re-fashioning the world at a similar age. As for the 'propaganda work,' there is no other evidence known to me, though he does declare himself to have been, at this period, 'an altogether finished and perfect Marxist.' But he was not the sort of Marxist who regarded *Das Kapital* as a sacred text. In fact, he found it a bore. 'Marx's *Kapital* is the same as Kraevich's *Physics*. Surely no one can think that Kraevich leads to any new ideas.'[32] The 'finished and perfect Marxist' (this is the Mandelstam of 1925 looking back upon his childhood) could not have been all that perfect, since there was in his 'Marxism' a strong admixture of religion. In the letter to Gippius from which I have already quoted he writes, 'My religious experiences date from the period of my childish attraction to Marxist dogma and cannot be separated from that attraction.'

His Marxism, like that of many another youthful revolutionary was a generalized desire for social justice and, to give it an English name that Mandelstam would doubtless have approved, fair play. It must also have been satisfying to a hunger that Mandelstam intensely felt: a desire to bring the confusion of history under some general rule – to channel, chastise, subdue and control the messy waywardness of life. Viewed in this way, the step from Marxism to Classicism is a brief one, and Andrey Sinyavsky, in his essay on 'Socialist realism,' the deposit of Marxism upon literature, wittily corrected 'realism' to 'classicism.'

VII

His chief opponent in political arguments was the last figure in the short portrait gallery, Boris Sinani, a friend who deserves special mention in any account of Mandelstam.

Among the hyperbolic and sometimes even grotesque figures who populate his autobiographical prose as well as his fiction, Boris Sinani emerges as a real, sympathetic personality in three dimensions, and one cannot but feel the genuine affection and attachment with which Mandelstam speaks of him.

> When he had listened intently to my self-assured speeches, there came up to me a boy wearing a thin belt around his waist, his hair almost red, and somehow narrow all over – narrow in the shoulders, with a narrow face, gentle and manly, narrow hands, and little feet. Above his lip he had a red splotch, like a fiery mark. There was little in his dress to recall the Anglo-Saxon style of the Tenishev School. It was as if they had taken an old, old pair of trousers and a shirt, scrubbed them very hard with soap in a cold stream, dried them in the sun, and given them to him, unironed, to put on. Anyone looking at him would have said, 'What frail bones!' But anyone glancing at his high, modest forehead would have been astonished at his almost slanted eyes, which had a greenish cast to their smile, and would have been stopped by the expression of his small mouth, bitterly proud. His movements, when necessary, could be large and bold, like the gesture of the boy playing jacks in Fyodor Tolstoy's sculpture, but he generally avoided sharp movements, saving his precision and lightness for play. His walk was astonishingly light – a barefoot walk. It would have suited him to have a sheep dog at his legs and a long staff in his hands. His cheeks and chin were covered with a golden, animal down. He was something between a Russian boy playing a Russian game and an Italian John the Baptist with a barely noticeable hook in his sharp nose.[33]

Of Mandelstam's capacity for emotional attachment to others we know from the memoirs of his friends. But there are few paragraphs like this one in his own writings. That makes all the more precious this declaration of his youthful love for Boris Sinani, whose longing for glory, cut short by his early death, touched Mandelstam's heart. He causes it to touch ours: 'Boris, lying in a Finnish meadow, loved to gaze into the blank sky with the cold astonished eyes of Prince Andrew.'

Mandelstam devotes some of the vividest pages of his memoirs to the family of Boris Sinani. Boris Naumovich Sinani, the father, was a psychiatrist and an affectionate, unpredictable, stimulating domestic tyrant. He 'was a widower, and about his widowerhood there was something stubborn and wolfish. He lived with his son and two daughters, Zhenya, the elder, slant-eyed as a Japanese and very miniature and elegant, and the little hunchback Lena.' The mother of Mandelstam's friend had been Russian, but his father was a Karaite Jew from the Crimea.

'The central feature of the Sinani household,' Mandelstam writes, 'was what I should call an aesthetic of the intellect. Positivism is usually hostile to aesthetic contemplation, the disinterested pride and joy of the movements of the mind. But for these people the intellect was joy, health, sport, and almost religion, all at once.'[34] It seems clear that Mandelstam's real education took place at least as much within the walls of the Sinani house on Pushkin Street as it did in the Tenishev School. There, too, his education was intensely involved with the burning questions of the day. The Sinanis ran something like a political salon. Their house was the headquarters, the Senate, of Populism, and Mandelstam's entry into the earliest years of manhood was accomplished to the tune of passionate, even beautiful, if, to him, slightly silly debates on the role of the horseless peasant.

Mandelstam's essential contempt for ideology, and his poet's appreciation of the human personality at the core of even the most wrongheaded *enragé*, can be seen more distinctly, perhaps, than anywhere else in his loving description of the Sinanis.

VIII

Around the time of Mandelstam's fourteenth birthday, on 9 January 1905, the priest Georgy Apollonovich Gapon (1870–1906) led a procession of workers through the streets of the capital to present a demand for the redress of certain grievances. The marchers were fired upon by the police, and the revolution of 1905, a sort of dress rehearsal for what was to happen a dozen years later with greater success, was on. That day is now known to history as 'Bloody Sunday,' and it was followed by revolutionary events around the country.[35] There were peasant uprisings, burnings of the estates of landowners, and even mutinies, the most famous of them being that on the battleship *Potemkin*. A general strike occurred in October, and order had not really been restored until the summer of 1907, the end of Mandelstam's school career. The unrest was general in Russia, but it naturally centered in the capital.

Alexander Pushkin had also been a schoolboy in Tsarskoe Selo (a short distance to the south of St Petersburg) when an even greater convulsion, the Napoleonic invasion of 1812, took place. It more or less passed them by, but their tranquility, with the rest of the country in flames, only exacerbated their dreams of heroic patriotism. That is what Mandelstam was thinking of when he wrote,

> Life, with all its unexpected interests and its passionate intellectual diversions, life will burst in upon the most hothouse-like, the most completely sterilized Russian school, as it once burst into Pushkin's lycée.[36]

But if the life of the 1905 uprising burst from the street outside into the Tenishev School, Mandelstam's account of the event is singularly indirect, for he reduces all the strife and the ultimate disappointment of the first revolution to the one emblematic figure of Sergey Ivanych. Perhaps because his significance was thereby made more general, or perhaps simply because the original was still alive in 1925, Mandelstam gives him no last name. He was clearly another of those extracurricular masters, like the Sinanis, whose instruction filled out the more formal if hardly less political education that Mandelstam was receiving within the walls of the Tenishev School.

> For me the year 1905 is in Sergey Ivanych. There were many of them – the tutors of the revolution! One of my friends, a rather haughty person, used to say, not without some justice, 'Some men are books, others – newspapers.' Poor Sergey Ivanych would not have found a place in such an analysis; for him it would have been necessary to establish a third category: some men are interlinear translations. Interlinear translations of the revolution poured from him, in his cold-stuffed head their cigarette-paper pages rustled, he shook from the cuffs of his sea-green cavalry jacket an ethereally light contraband literature, his Russian cigarette burned with a forbidden smoke, as if it had been rolled out of illegal paper.[37]

With this profound nihilist and subversive Mandelstam collaborated on a 'grandly futile' project – a long paper on the reasons for the fall of Rome. His apartment was repellently filthy and contained, instead of air, some other substance entirely. And yet (there is always the 'and yet' in any character portrait by Mandelstam) Sergey Ivanych was capable of preparing 'the most magnificent, thick, and aromatic hot chocolate.'

And yet, again: when the fateful hour approached, the grim promise of his violence seemed to dissipate harmlessly. In fact, he promised to come, in the event of a pogrom of the intelligentsia, to protect one and all with his Browning.

And the further fate of Sergey Ivanych was what happened essentially to the revolution of that year.

> I chanced to meet him many years after 1905. He was totally faded. He had absolutely no face, so erased and bleached were his features. A faint shadow of his former disgust and authority. It turned out that he had found a place and served as an assistant in the astronomical observatory at Pulkovo.[38]

IX

It is a testimony to the intellectual ferment in the Tenishev School that the students there managed to publish at least two independent journals during Mandelstam's time. The more viable of these was called *Tenishevets* (The Tenishev Student) during 1906–7; in 1908–9 it appeared as *Tovarishch* (The Comrade) but in 1910 expired under its original title. Its less durable rival, *Probuzhdennaia mysl'* (Awakened Thought), lasted for only two issues in 1906.

For all its brevity, however, *Awakened Thought* contains in its stormy pages much that illuminates the life of the school and is therefore of interest to the student of Mandelstam. It was imbued with a bracing spirit of bold, free-thinking student revolt (rather clouded, to be sure, in its second and last number by an apology for some of its more independent sallies). The usual student pranks are soberly reported (a stolen doorknob held the pupils of the XIIIb Semester prisoner in their classroom), there is a report on the demonstration of a marvelous new apparatus, the vacuum cleaner (called 'pylesobiratel'' (dust collector) in *Awakened Thought* but 'pyleunichtozhatel'' (dust destroyer) in the *Tenishev Student* account of the same event: the machine finally became known in Russian as 'pylesos' (dust sucker)). And there is the customary institutional humor ('Dear Mr Editor, I have lost a second pair of boots.' 'Inquire in the school kitchen.')

The most absorbing feature of its short life is undoubtedly an open letter from the students to Vladimir Vasilevich Gippius, a teacher of Russian literature at the school who evidently played a large part in Mandelstam's conception of that subject. He is the subject of the chapter entitled 'In a Fur Coat Above One's Station in Life' in *The Noise of Time*.[39]

Dear Vladimir Vasilevich!
At one lesson you announced to us that when you arrive in our classroom you have already determined in advance to have such-and-such students recite and that even if they should not be present (regardless of whether or not they have serious reasons for being absent) you will nevertheless give them the grade which they would have received for an unsatisfactory answer. When we naturally asked why, you said that you would tell us after the lesson, but...you didn't tell us. Now we hope that you will, in the next issue of *Awakened Thought*, satisfy our just request.

Little wonder that practically all the contributors to the journal were anonymous. One can only speculate whether Mandelstam published any of his 'prehistoric' poetry there, nor do I find any evidence of his having written for the rival *Tenishev Student*. The principal mainstay of that paper, which was much more sober in tone and probably indebted for a relatively long life to its general solidarity with the Establishment, was

29

the youthful Viktor Zhirmunsky, a friend of Mandelstam's who was one class behind him at the school. He subsequently became one of the most outstanding scholars of the Soviet Union.[40] The first issue (1 October 1906) opens with his 'étude' in lyrical prose entitled 'Svoboda' (Freedom), later to be flatteringly compared in a letter from some parent with Gorky's 'Burevestnik' (Stormy Petrel).

The *Tenishev Student* provides a far more three-dimensional view of the life in the school. The opening assembly at the beginning of the academic year, which always contained the annual performance of the hygienist Dr Virenius, described by Mandelstam, was duly reported. At the ceremony on 8 September 1906, Virenius expressed his dissatisfaction with the physical condition of the students and placed the blame on deficiencies in the home. The boys over fifteen, seemed to him surprisingly strong, since their maturing muscles were forever breaking his dynamometer. He then showed a graphic table of the lung capacities of the students, but the correspondent of *Tenishev Student* explains that those in the back rows could not make it out.

I find only one mention of Mandelstam in the pages of *Tenishev Student*. It is there owing to the editors' strong support of the *vecherinki*, a series of informal evening gatherings at the school for the purpose of reciting poetry, performing plays, and discussing literary topics. The same names turn up over and over again. V. V. Gippius was the most frequent participant from among the teachers, and Viktor Zhirmunsky is practically always reported to have recited some verse, such as Balmont's translation of Poe's 'Raven,' and the poetry of Nadson and Sergey Gorodetsky.

On the evening of 14 September 1907 about sixty of the students gathered for their first evening of the new academic year. It began at 9:00. Goder and Kantakuzin played musical selections on the piano.

> Then Mandelstam called forth a storm of applause with his poem 'Kolesnitsa' (Chariot), which greatly exceeds in artistic quality the majority of our school *belles lettres* and perhaps of modern *belles lettres* generally. The somewhat unclear diction of the author, however, rather detracted from the impression made by his poetry.

The article is unsigned, but it belongs to that part of the magazine edited by Zhirmunsky, so it is possibly the first of many assessments of Mandelstam's poetry made by his schoolmate. It is certainly the earliest of many accounts of many observers of the poet's platform style.

The title is all that we have, but this must be the earliest reference to a particular poem by Mandelstam. The earliest known poem containing the word *kolesnitsa* is 'Zverinets' (Menagerie), dated January 1916.

Mandelstam had finished the Tenishev School the previous spring, but it was common for a number of the old boys to return to the auditorium on Mokhovaya Street for the schoolboy soirées as well as for the more mature literary evenings that often took place on the premises of the Tenishev School. In the same issue, Słobodzinski, the 'top student' in Mandelstam's portrait gallery of his own classmates, is reported to have participated in the opening ceremonies for that year. Mandelstam himself was often to be invited back to the school to read his poetry after he had earned the fame that was already foreseen by his well-disposed young critic.

3

Studies abroad and at home

Mandelstam spent the greater part of the next few years (1907–10) in Western Europe. Our knowledge of his life there consists of one or two unexpected pinpoints of clarity that occasionally pierce a general murk of ignorance and surmise (he lived in Paris at No. 12, rue de la Sorbonne, and on the evening of 24 December 1907 met Mikhail Karpovich at a café on the Boulevard St Michel).

Under what circumstances and when, between that September evening of poetry in the Tenishev auditorium and Christmas Eve in Paris, Mandelstam left home we don't know. But it is hardly necessary to speculate about the reason. The immemorial attraction of Paris for young men with talent had been magnified beyond all telling when the Russian cultural renascence, roughly coincident with the year of Mandelstam's birth, had brought about one of the periodic rediscoveries of France and Germany. For an aspiring poet whose sense of current literature had been fashioned by the reigning Symbolist school – and by his own teacher, Vladimir Gippius, himself a minor figure of the school – there was nowhere else to go.

The first and fullest witness of Mandelstam in Paris was the late Mikhail Karpovich, who left a precious memoir of the occasion when they met.[1] Those familiar with other memoirs of Mandelstam will appreciate Karpovich's modesty and his fastidious refusal to invent conversations that he honestly can't recall.

This happened in the distant past – nearly a half century ago. I was living in Paris at the time and attending lectures at the Sorbonne. I can give the exact day when I first met Mandelstam: 24 December 1907. As everyone knows, the French celebrate Christmas Eve in the same way that we greet the New Year. On that evening I was also 'making merry' in one of the cafés on the Boul' Miche along with a small group of Russian young people. Sitting at a separate table nearby was a certain youth who had attracted our attention by his not altogether usual appearance. More than anything else, he looked like a young chicken, and that resemblance gave him a rather comic aspect. But along with that there was in his face and in his beautiful, sad eyes something very attractive. As soon as he heard that we were speaking Russian he became interested in us. It was clear that in the midst of the loud celebration going on about him he felt lost and lonely. We invited him to join us and he agreed with obvious pleasure. We learned that his name was Osip Emilevich Mandelstam.

He and I fell to talking that evening and quickly established the fact of our common literary interests. I gave him my address, and I'm not sure that it wasn't the very next day when he came to see me. Between that time and my departure for Russia in the spring of 1908 we met very often – at least several times a week. I can't remember where he lived, which makes me think that he must have normally come to my room, or rather to fetch me, since our talks generally took place while we were sitting at a café or wandering about the streets of Paris. We would sometimes go to concerts, exhibitions, and lectures together. Mandelstam was then seventeen, I was nineteen. Of course, I wasn't able to foresee that he would become one of the greatest Russian poets of our time. And besides, when one is a very young man personal relationships are more immediate and disinterested. I did not, therefore, try to 'study' Mandelstam or 'appraise' him, and I didn't write down my conversations with him. And my memory, alas, has not preserved much.

I was struck most of all by his extraordinary impressionability. It seemed that for him 'all the impressions of existence' were still really new, and to each of them he responded with his entire being. At that time he was filled with a youthful effusiveness and romantic enthusiasm which are difficult to reconcile with the later image that we have of him as a poet. In the future author of *Kamen'* [Stone] there was as yet nothing stony. Nor can I remember anything specifically 'Mandelstamian' in the aesthetic tastes and literary enthusiasms that he showed then. I recall them as being rather eclectic. I remember his ecstatic declamation of Bryusov's poem 'The Coming Huns.' But he also recited Verlaine's lyrical poetry with the same enthusiasm and even wrote his own version of Gaspard Häuser [*sic*]. Once, he and I were at a concert of Richard Strauss's works, conducted by the composer himself. We were both, I am sorry to say, profoundly moved by 'Salomé's Dance,' and Mandelstam immediately wrote a poem about Salomé. To my shame, I didn't memorize a single one of the early poems of Mandelstam. Nor do I recall whether they included any of those with the date '1908' at the beginning of *Stone*. In April 1908 I went for two weeks to Italy. Mandelstam took that first Italian pilgrimage of mine very much to heart and responded to it by writing a poem. But for some reason all that my memory retains – even of that poem, dedicated to me – is one line

поднять скрипучий верх соломенных корзин
to raise the creaking lid of the straw baskets

(among my luggage there really was such a basket, brought from Russia).

Whether we ever spoke about social or political themes I don't remember. In *The Noise of Time* Mandelstam, writing about his school years, also tells about the Erfurt Program which had for a while turned him into a 'perfect Marxist' and about his contact with the SRs through the Sinani family. I doubt that these early impressions left any lasting *political* traces in his mind. Gershuni died in Paris in the spring of 1908 and the SRs arranged a gathering in memory of him. Mandelstam expressed the strongest desire to go there with me, but I don't think politics had anything to do with it. It was of course the personality and the fate of Gershuni that attracted him. The principal speaker was B. V. Savinkov. The moment he began to speak, Mandelstam sat bolt upright, got up from his seat, and listened to the whole speech standing in the aisle. He listened to it in a kind of trance, his mouth half open and his eyes half closed and his whole body leaning over so far backwards that I was even afraid he might fall. I must confess that he made a rather comic sight. I remember that A. O. Fondaminskaya and L. S. Gavronskaya, who were sitting across the aisle, could not, for all the seriousness of the moment, refrain from laughing when they looked at Mandelstam.

What Karpovich has to say about Mandelstam's family is illuminated by his usual common sense and serves to balance what is often found on the subject in the memoirs of other acquaintances.

About his family Mandelstam told me practically nothing, and I did not inquire (the biographical interest in people also makes its appearance later in life). Only on one occasion – I don't recall in what connection – he gave me to understand that his relationship with his parents was not altogether satisfactory. He even exclaimed, 'It's terrible! terrible!' But since he was in general prone to abuse that expression, I immediately suspected him of overdoing it. And I still think that if Mandelstam's parents permitted him to live in Paris and occupy himself with whatever he wished they must not have been so indifferent to his desires, and the family bonds did not lie so heavily upon him. In any case, he did not give one the feeling that he was constrained and bound. He was helpless in practical affairs, but spiritually he was independent and, I think, sufficiently confident in himself.

The next year, in Russia, Karpovich saw him again on a couple of occasions, which he described (see below), but that is the extent of his memoir of Mandelstam in Paris, the most circumstantial that we have for the years between school and university. It raises tantalizing questions. Will we ever see those poems to which Karpovich listened without ever realizing the retrospective value that they were some day to have? Where is Mandelstam's version of Verlaine's poem ('Je suis venu, calme orphelin') on the foundling Kaspar Hauser? The mention of a poem on Strauss's (and Oscar Wilde's and the Bible's) Salomé teases the mind to speculate on some connection with a later famous poem, 'Solominka.' But they are questions that will for the present remain unanswered.

Until a short while ago, this memoir was the only writing that shed the least light on Mandelstam's life in Paris. Very recently, however, another document of the greatest value came to light. In the month when Mandelstam saw his friend off on the exciting 'pilgrimage' to

Studies abroad and at home

Italy – April 1908 – he wrote the following letter to Vladimir Gippius. It seems to me important enough to give a full translation of it.[2]

Paris 27/IV/1908

Dear Vladimir Vasilevich!

If you recall, I promised to write you 'when I got settled.' But I am still not settled, that is, up to the present moment I don't have the feeling that I am doing 'what I should' and therefore I haven't broken my promise.

I always felt the *need* to have a talk with you, though not once did I manage to tell you what I regarded as important. The history of our relationship, or perhaps of my relationship to you, strikes me in general as rather remarkable.

For a long time now I've felt a special attraction to you and at the same time felt a special distance separating me from you.

No closeness was possible, but certain wicked tricks gave [me] a special pleasure, the feeling of triumph: 'better than nothing...'

And you will forgive my being so bold as to say that you were for me what some people call 'friend-enemy.' It cost me a lot of time and trouble to realize what that feeling was.

But I always saw in you a representative of some principle that was precious and inimical at the same time, its duality even constituting the charm of the principle.

It's now clear to me that that principle is nothing other than religious culture, whether Christian or not I don't know, but in any case religious.

Having been brought up in a milieu where there was no religion (family and school), I have long striven toward religion hopelessly and platonically – but more and more consciously.

My first religious experiences date from the period of my childish infatuation with Marxist dogma and can't be separated from that infatuation.

But for me the connection between religion and society was already severed when I was a child.

At the age of fifteen I passed through the cleansing fire of Ibsen, and though I couldn't hold to the 'religion of the will' I finally took a stand on the ground of religious individualism and against society.

Tolstoy and Hauptmann, the two greatest apostles of love for people, I grasped fervently but abstractly, and the same is true of the 'philosophy of the norm.'

My religious consciousness never rose above Knut Hamsun and worship of his *Pan*, that is, an unacknowledged God, and that is, to this day, my 'religion.'

(Oh, don't be alarmed, that isn't 'Maeonism' and, in general, I have nothing in common with Minsky.)

In Paris I've read Rozanov and taken a great liking to *him* but not to the concrete cultural content to which he is devoted with his pure, biblical devotion.

I have no specific feelings towards society, God, and man – but my love is all the stronger for life, faith, and love. From this you will understand my enthusiasm for the music of life, which I have found in certain French poets and, among the Russians, in those of Bryusov's school. In the latter I was captivated by their ingenious boldness of negation, pure negation.

I live very alone here and am occupied with practically nothing aside from poetry and music. In addition to Verlaine, I've written something about Rodenbach and Sologub and am planning to write about Hamsun.[3]

After that, a little prose and poetry. I'm planning to spend the summer in Italy, and when I get back to enter the university and make a systematic study of literature and philosophy. Please forgive me, but there is really absolutely nothing for me to write about except myself. Otherwise the letter would become a 'report from Paris.'

If you answer me, perhaps you will tell me some things that might be of interest to me.

Your pupil,

Osip Mandelstam

My address: rue Sorbonne, 12.

II

By the spring of 1909 Mandelstam was back home in Russia, though he was already preparing to leave again, this time for Heidelberg. He continued his 'trials of character and talent,' to use one of his own phrases from the *Puteshestvie v Armeniiu* (Journey to Armenia), and some of these very early poems from the 'prehistoric' Mandelstam have only very recently come to light. Of the 22 poems all but seven come from recently unearthed letters written in 1909 and 1911 to Vyacheslav Ivanov, the arbiter of poetic elegance and doyen of the Symbolists.[4] They are deeply respectful, not to say worshipful letters from a young man who would soon be hurling defiance from the ramparts of a different 'school' at, among others, Vyacheslav Ivanov.

But, as Anna Akhmatova notes in her memoir of Mandelstam, these are letters from Mandelstam the Symbolist, the participant in Vyacheslav Ivanov's 'Wednesdays' in 'The Tower,' as his apartment in Petersburg was known.[5] As the second letter in particular demonstrates, however, Mandelstam was sufficiently independent of Ivanov, despite his admiration for him, to point rather bluntly to what struck him as faults in a collection of the master's poems. 'They were written by a boy of eighteen,' Akhmatova writes, 'but one could swear that the author of these letters was forty.' She adds, 'By 1911 Mandelstam felt no piety whatsoever for Vyacheslav Ivanov.'

20 June 1909[6]

Very respected and dear Vyacheslav Ivanovich!

No matter where my letter catches you, I beg one thing of you: send me your address, and also whether you will be in Switzerland and when. For the time being before I go abroad I am living with my family in Tsarskoe and never go anywhere. Your seeds have lodged deep in my soul and it frightens me when I look at the enormous shoots coming out.

I take great pleasure in the hope of meeting you somewhere this summer.

From the almost ruined by you, but corrected,

Osip Mandelstam

Petersburg, Kolomenskaya 5

In August of the same year Mandelstam wrote Ivanov another much
longer letter. He was now in Switzerland, staying in a sanatorium near
Montreux, an asylum to which he had been driven, one supposes, by the
'frail health' to which he darkly alludes, no doubt in an excess of appealingly
youthful romanticism.

13–26 August 1909

Kurhaus de Territet et Sanatorium l'Abri

Montreux-Territet

Dear Vyacheslav Ivanovich!

First of all permit me a few reflections on your book.[7] It seems to me that
one can't argue with it, it is captivating and destined to conquer hearts.

Is it true that a man reflects on the truth of Catholicism when he steps
under the vaults of Notre Dame and doesn't become a Catholic simply by
virtue of being under those vaults?

Your book is splendid with the beauty of great architectural creations
and astronomical systems. Every genuine poet, if he could write his books on
the basis of the exact and immutable laws of his art, would write as you do.

You are the most incomprehensible and, in the everyday sense of the
word, the obscurest poet of our time, precisely because you surpass everyone
in your fidelity to your own nature, to which you have consciously entrusted
yourself.

Only it seemed to me that the book is too round, as it were, without
angles.

There's no direction from which one can get at it to smash it, or smash
oneself against it.

Not even the tragedy in it constitutes an angle, because you consent to it.

Not even the ecstasy is dangerous, because you foresee the outcome
of it. And only the breathing of the Cosmos wafts about your book, giving
it a charm which it shares with the *Zarathustra* and compensating for the
astronomical roundness of your system, which you yourself flaunt in the
best parts of your book, and even flaunt unceasingly. Your book also has
in common with the Zarathustra the fact that every word in it carries out
its assignment with flaming hatred and sincerely hates its place and its
neighbors.

You will forgive me this effusion...

I spent two weeks at Beatenberg but then decided to spend several weeks
at the sanatorium and moved to Montreux.

Now I observe a strange contrast: the holy hush of the sanatorium,
interrupted by the dinner gong, and the shout in the evening from the
roulette game in the casino: 'Faites vos jeux messieurs! – remarquez
messieurs! – rien ne va plus!' – exclamations full of a symbolic horror.

I have strange taste: I love the patches of reflected electric light on the
surface of Lake Leman, respectful lackeys, the silent flight of the elevator,
the marble vestibule of the hotel and the Englishwomen who play Mozart
with two or three official listeners in the half-darkened salon.

I love bourgeois, European comfort and am devoted to it not only
physically but also emotionally.

Perhaps my frail health is to blame for this? But I never ask myself whether it's good or bad.

I also want to tell you the following.

In your book there is one place from which two immense perspectives open up, as from the postulate about the two parallel geometries, Euclid's and Lobachevsky's. That is the image of astonishing emotion where the one who doesn't agree to the choral dance leaves the circle, his face hidden in his hands.

Have our friends already gathered at Petersburg? What are *Apollon* and *Ostrov* [The Island][8] doing?

How I long to see someone that I know from among our poets – or even someone that I don't know! Do you know what, Vyacheslav Ivanovich? Write me (I'm so sure you'll write – but now what if you don't?) write me when someone goes abroad. Perhaps somehow I'll see somebody, and in order to see you I'm ready to travel a great distance if necessary. One more request. If you have an extra, an absolutely extra copy of *Kormchie zvezdy* [Pilot Stars],[9] could it not by some means find its way into my careful hands?

Also, Vyacheslav Ivanovich, write me who are the lyric poets in Germany at the moment. Aside from Dehmel I don't know a single one. The Germans don't know either, but still, there must be some lyric poets.

I embrace you warmly, Vyacheslav Ivanovich, and I thank you for – I myself don't know for what – which is the best sort of thankfulness there is.

P.S.
Osip Mandelstam

I am sending you some poems. Do with them what you want – what I want – what can be done with them.

The poems included No. 147, which appeared the next year in *Apollon*, No. 9, but which Mandelstam never subsequently reprinted in any of his collections, consigning it instead to the oblivion reserved for practically all of the poems sent to Ivanov at this period.[10] It must have been known to Ivanov even before he received the letter, for Vladimir Pyast recalls that Mandelstam had recited it on his first visit to the Tower, where it was duly praised by the master – 'his invariable custom,' according to Pyast. Writing in a student journal the following year,[11] Pyast praised the absolute metrical novelty of these lines, which, following a prosodic terminology popularized by Andrey Bely, he then saw as a combination of two feet called 'third paeon' and 'fourth paeon,' that is to say: $\smile \smile \perp \smile$ and $\smile \smile \smile \perp$. Years later, in his excellent memoirs *Vstrechi* (Meetings, 1929) Pyast returned to this poem with a somewhat different metrical analysis, to which he was helped by the great literary scholar Boris Tomashevsky, but with an undiminished enthusiasm for the epochal nature of the prosodic innovation, which he now looked upon as the birthday of the 'five-syllable foot.' He recalls that in 1926 the poet Iosif Utkin had published a poem exactly copying the meter of Mandelstam's poem and that no less a connoisseur of metrical novelty than Vladimir Mayakovsky had praised Utkin's great originality, unaware that it was in fact Mandelstam's invention. I find Pyast's championship of Mandelstam somewhat tempered, however, by his remark that in 1909 Mandelstam was 'of course oblivious' of having made such a discovery.[12] But other things besides the meter are interesting in this slight poem. It is very typical of the poetic concerns of the early Mandelstam, to be examined in greater detail when we come to his first book, and it provides a revealing counterpoint to the vaguely Proustian view of himself found in the letter:

Истончается тонкий тлен.
Фиолетовый гобелен.

К нам на воды и на леса
Опускаются небеса.

Нерешительная рука
Эти вывела облака,

И печальный встречает взор
Отуманенный их узор.

Недоволен стою и тих,
Я—создатель миров моих,

Где искуственны небеса
И хрустальная спит роса.   (No. 147, 1909)

The thin decay grows thinner.
The violet Gobelin.

The skies come down to us
onto the waters, the woods.

An uncertain hand
drew these clouds.

And a sad look
meets their hazy pattern.

I stand unsatisfied and silent,
I, the creator of my worlds,

where the skies are artificial
and a crystal dew is sleeping.

The letter gives us precious glimpses not only into Mandelstam's assured literary judgments at that time – an assurance already conveyed by Karpovich's memoir – but also into his own self-image. Or is it perhaps only the image that a young poet wished his mentor to see? In any case, it will provide welcome ammunition for all the ill-wishers who seek to portray Mandelstam as a blend of bourgeois and decadent and who will not be deterred by the pathetic irony that results when we juxtapose this youthfully defiant self-indulgence with what we now know of a life marked by other things than physical comfort. In the green April of an utterly changed world, in 1931, when the poet was at the height of his powers, he returned with what was under the circumstances much greater defiance to certain themes of this letter in a poem of buoyant, bitter gaeity – No. 233:

Я пью за военные астры, за все, чем корили меня:
За барскую шубу, за астму, за желчь петербургского дня,

За музыку сосен савойских, Полей Елисейских бензин,
За розы в кабине ролс-ройса, за масло парижских картин.

Я пью за бискайские волны, за сливок альпийских кувшин,
За рыжую спесь англичанок и дальних колоний хинин,

Я пью, но еще не придумал, из двух выбираю одно:
Веселое асти-спуманте иль папского замка вино...

I drink to the military asters, to all that I've been reproached for:
to the nobleman's fur coat, to asthma, to the bilious Petersburg day,

to the pines of Savoie, their music, to the Champs-Elysées gasoline,
to the roses inside the Rolls-Royce, to the oil of the paintings in Paris.

I drink to the waves in the Bay of Biscay, to the pitcher of alpine cream,
to the ruddy hauteur of English governesses and quinine from distant colonies.

I drink, but I've not yet decided which of the two I'll choose:
the jolly Asti-Spumante, or the Châteauneuf-du-Pape...

Mandelstam wrote five more letters to Ivanov in the fall and winter of 1909. They are all extremely brief and evidently had no other function than to convey poems for the older poet's judgment, for the correspondence seems to have gone in one direction only. At any rate, no reply of Ivanov's has yet come to light. On 26 October 1909 Mandelstam wrote from Heidelberg:

If you feel like writing me and you don't answer me for some sort of external reason, still, write to me anyway. I want to tell you a great deal, but I can't, I'm not able to.

That is the whole of the letter. Writing on 4 November from the same place and enclosing six poems,[13] Mandelstam ends with another faintly petulant hint at what must have been Ivanov's silence:

Dear, as before, Vyacheslav Ivanovich!
I can't refrain from sending you my lyrical explorations and achievements. As I am obliged to you for the former, so the latter belong to you by right – a right about which, perhaps, you never think.

Yours,
Osip Mandelstam

On 26 December 1909 Mandelstam evidently sent Ivanov two letters
from Heidelberg at the same time. Both contained versions of the poem
beginning 'Na temnom nebe, kak uzor' (In the dark sky, like a pattern),[14]
and the longer of the two letters is interesting for Mandelstam's commentary on his own poem. This must be the earliest extant example of
such self-criticism, and, since Mandelstam was very little given to observations on his own work, it is one of the few comments of this kind that
he ever put in writing. The poem precedes the first letter:

> На темном небе, как узор,
> Деревья траурные вышиты;
> Но выше, выше и все выше ты
> Возводишь изумленный взор;
>
> Божница неба заперта—
> Ты скажешь—время опрокинула
> И словно ночь, на день нахлынула
> Холмов холодная черта.
>
> Высоких, неживых дерев
> Темнеющее рвется кружево:
> О месяц, только ты не суживай
> Серпа, внезапно почернев!

On the dark sky, like a pattern,
the mourning trees are embroidered.
But you lift your astonished gaze
higher, higher and still higher.

The chapel of the sky is locked –
you would say the cold line of the hills
had overturned time and,
like night itself, swept over the daylight.

The darkening lace
of the tall dead trees is torn.
O crescent moon, only don't narrow
your sickle, suddenly grown black!

Dear Vyacheslav Ivanovich!
This poem would like to be 'romance sans paroles' (Dans l'interminable
ennui...). 'Paroles' – i.e. intimately lyrical, personal – I tried to use restraint,
to keep it in check with the reins of rhythm.
What concerns me is whether the poem is strongly enough bridled?
I can't help recalling your remark about the anti-lyrical nature of the iambic.
The anti-intimate nature, perhaps? The iambic is a rein on 'mood.'

> With profound respect,
> Osip Mandelstam

The second of these two letters contained No. 457b and No. 457v and
concluded with a postscript: 'Forgive me for all the bad stuff you have
received from me.'

The only other extant letters to Vyacheslav Ivanov belong to the year 1911. They contain no poems and little of any other interest, except for the signature of the letter dated 21 August 1911 (from Vyborg): Mandelstam signed himself – for the only time, to my knowledge – with the less emphatically Jewish form of his name: *Iosif* Mandelstam.

III

'End of the year 1909. Petersburg. *Apollon*...'[15] Thus begins a reminiscence by the late Sergey Makovsky – art critic, voluminous memoirist, and editor of the journal whose name, *Apollon*, accurately reflected the tranquilly classical harmony of its contents. There is still today a certain excitement (quite apart from one's interest in Mandelstam) about turning the elegantly dated pages of this journal. Its first issue had come out in October of 1909. From that time until its demise in 1917 it brought to its readership the work of the best writers, poets, scholars and artists of Russia and served as the center for news about the literary and artistic life in the principal European capitals. Beautifully printed in a luxurious format and with a typographical taste rare in that or any age, its program was Classicism. It began with essays by Innokenty Annensky, Professor of Greek at the famous lycée of Tsarskoe Selo, translator of Euripides into Russian, and a poet whose influence was decisive on the 'neoclassical' school of Acmeism, for which *Apollon* was eventually to serve as the central organ. The numerous expensively reproduced paintings and drawings tended heavily toward Grecian columns, fauns, nymphs, satyrs and classical nudity. Architectural photographs displayed the vaunted Petersburg style, such as that in the façade of the Azov–Don Bank, and the entire tone was resolutely that of Petersburg (the anonymous Moscow correspondent signed himself, in English, 'Outsider') and the classical world (a critic, thinking that the stylized Cyrillic letters of the title-page were actual Greek, complained that the two 'omicrons' were incorrect – a blunder noted with derisive glee by the editors in a department called 'Bees and Wasps of *Apollon*' and dedicated to stinging the aesthetic enemy). Its early contributors were the leading Symbolist poets – Blok, Bryusov, Vyacheslav Ivanov – foremost literary scholars such as Boris Eykhenbaum and Boris Tomashevsky – and Nikolay Gumilyov, leader of the Acmeists, wrote regularly in its pages from the time of its founding. Gumilyov's multiple reviews of current poetry appeared under the title 'Pis'ma o russkoi poezii' (Letters on Russian Poetry) and served as a platform for ideas that were to dominate a brief era in the art of Russian poetry.

Makovsky's memoir is set in the editorial rooms of the journal, then located on the Moika Canal at number 24, a building also occupied by the fashionable restaurant Donon. The Foreign Office, the Imperial Archives, and the School for Court Singers were close neighbors. This elegant scene provided the background for what Makovsky wishes us to believe was Mandelstam's formal entry into literature, or at least into publication. Alas, it is another of those émigré memoirs that reduce the historian to a kind of impotent frenzy, for it appears to be a concoction of truth and 'interesting' distortion. Anna Akhmatova several times recited to me a list of émigré authors whose testimony about her and her milieu was under no circumstance to be credited, and when I saw her in London in 1965 she had even put the list in writing, so as to omit none of those whom she called by a lusty Russian equivalent of 'scoundrels.' Georgy Ivanov headed the list, and Sergey Makovsky was next.[16]

Akhmatova's rage is more than understandable. What other emotion could a Soviet writer feel on contemplating the disgraceful use to which certain Russians who had it put their freedom to publish? And yet rage is no more reliable a guide to the truth than uncritical acceptance. There is no doubt some measure of historicity in the following account – the setting, the characters, the time of the event, and the general nature of the event itself – but we shall never know how much. Nadezhda Yakov-levna, in her memoir *Hope Against Hope*, is no more inclined to spare Makovsky than was her friend Akhmatova, but her complaint is more balanced and specific: what is chiefly objectionable is the cheap vulgarity attributed to Mandelstam's mother, who was, in her son's own memoir and in every other that I know, described as a women of cultured intellect. 'Evidently,' the poet's widow writes,

> Makovsky was trying to produce a cheap journalistic effect by contrasting the young genius with his vulgar family background. In fact, however, Mandelstam's mother was a woman of considerable culture, a music teacher who gave her children a good education and brought Mandelstam up to love classical music. She could never have said the preposterous things that Makovsky attributes to her. This is a good example of the kind of aristocratic superciliousness that prompted Mandelstam to declare himself a member of the 'fourth estate' of intellectuals from the lower classes.[17]

She adds that Mandelstam himself managed to see this memoir and was very upset by it. With these precautions, I shall put the reader in my own dilemma. Makovsky's secretary comes in to announce that an importunate lady named Mandelstam is in the outer office demanding to see the editor:

> In a moment there appeared a woman of middle age, rather plump, with a pale, excited face. She was accompanied by an ill-favored youth of some seventeen years – obviously embarrassed. He clung to her like a little boy, practically held her hand. His head was oversized, thrown back, on a very thin neck. His downy reddish hair had little tiny curls. In his sharp face, in all his figure, and in his little bouncy gait there was something birdlike.

The woman presented the youth to me:

'My son. Reason I've come to you. We've just got to know what to do with him. We're in business – leather goods. But he – poetry, and that's it. At his age it's time to help his parents. We brought him up, saw he got an education – and what his studying cost us! But so what – if he's got talent he's got talent; then it'll be the university and all the rest of it. But if it turns out to be just crazy ideas neither I nor his father are going to stand for it. Work, like everybody else, and don't go wasting paper on nothing. So there, Mr Editor...we're simple, poor people...do us a favor, give it to us straight: has he got talent or not?! What ever you say, that's the way it'll be...'

She took out of her purse several sheets of lined paper covered all over with writing and handed them to me.

'There!'

'Fine. Leave them here...for a few days. I'll read them.'

But the energetic mama would not hear of any delay and demanded that I read them then and there and pass the sentence.

I began to protest: 'No, I can't possibly...poetry requires attention... you've got to read it closely.'

Against neophyte poets in those days I had enough reason to be prejudiced: what a mass of amateurish verse was emptied into the editorial waste basket every day! But the last thing in the world that I wanted to do was distress the easily embarrassed boy. His eyes were most extremely expectant and sad. In his confusion he rolled them back in his head one moment, covered them with his enflamed lids the next, then again looked at me with imploring resignation.

Mama insisted: 'Read them and give us your decision...right now!'

Reluctantly, I unfolded the sheets and began to decipher the minute little lines. It was hard to make out the letters with their spidery little loops. I don't think I made any sense of a single poem that I read at that time. I do recall that those youthful poems of Osip Emilevich (to which he himself attached no importance later on) did not captivate me in any way, and I was ready to rid myself of the mama and her little boy by some vaguely encouraging formula of editorial politeness when, taking another look at the boy, I read in his gaze such tense and suffering entreaty, that I somehow gave in all at once and went over to his side: for poetry, against the leather business.

With an air of conviction, even rather solemnly, I said, 'Yes, madame, your son *has* talent.'

The boy beamed, exploded, leapt from his seat, began to mutter something, then suddenly burst out in a loud, choking laugh – and sat down again. Mama was silent with amazement: she had evidently not expected such a 'sentence' from me. But she quickly came to herself:

'Splendid. That suits me. Then print them!'

Things had not turned out in my favor: now there would be no rest from this tyro...But there was nothing to be done. As I said goodbye to him I asked him to 'bring some more.'

That Mandelstam 'brought some more' is evidenced by succeeding issues of *Apollon*, in the editorial offices of which he rapidly became a familiar figure, and remained so for the next eight years. His first poems (Nos. 8, 9, 13, 14, and 147) appeared in the ninth issue of the magazine for 1910, pages 5 to 7.

IV

That winter Mandelstam made his second and, so far as is known, his last trip outside of Russia. His journey took him to Switzerland (a poem, No. 152, is dated 'Lugano'), to Italy on two brief occasions, but principally to Heidelberg, where he spent two semesters as a student.

Switzerland left little trace in Mandelstam's life or poetry. Italy, on the other hand, provided him with such a rich fund of reference that it became one of the permanent realms of his imagination. This has prompted some speculation about his actual experience of that country, but the results have been as thin and unsatisfactory as Mandelstam's own brief trips apparently were. Nadezhda Yakovlevna writes that he once said, 'It's as though I'd never been there,' for his solitary excursions were so 'short and superficial' as to leave only a sense of frustration.[18] Anna Akhmatova, whose interest in Italy was fully as intense as Mandelstam's, even told me emphatically that he had never been there. 'Italy was a country of the mind for him,' she told me, 'an ethereal country.'[19]

Mandelstam's life and contacts at the university in Heidelberg are for the most part obscure, but there are a few patches of brilliant clarity, thanks largely to the memory of Aaron Zakharevich Steinberg, with whom I had a conversation in London in 1965 and who is no doubt the only available witness of the poet's brief sojourn in Germany.

Aaron Steinberg – born in 1891 and thus Mandelstam's exact contemporary – was also a member of the small colony of Russian students who gathered around the Pirogovskaya chitalnia (The Pirogov Reading Room), stocked with the Russian books and newspapers that once used to attract Turgenev there from his Baden-Baden. Others there at the same time were Boris Davidovich Kamkov (real name: Katz) and Alexandr Ivanovich Khainsky, whose names I record for the possible benefit of some future researcher.

At the end of the winter semester, on 10 February 1910, Steinberg read a paper in the Russian circle entitled 'Art and Criticism.' There was a discussion afterwards and Steinberg showed me the faded notes for his talk together with a memo of the discussion, in which Mandelstam participated. The thesis of his talk was that a work of art must be considered as an autonomous whole, a system of its own, to be treated by the critic as such, uncontaminated by subjective or biographical considerations. Let us note in passing that Steinberg's thesis, in 1910, was by no means yet a cliché. In his memo of the discussion the place following Mandelstam's name was left blank, though the other discussants' views were meticulously noted down. Steinberg smiled as he told me that Mandelstam was so hypnotic a speaker on that occasion that he absorbed everyone's complete attention, leaving none free for note-taking. Then he closed his eyes and reconstituted from memory what Mandelstam had said. He had been more concerned with the 'criticism' of Steinberg's title than with the 'art,' and he observed that criticism, whether subjective or not, could also be 'an organic whole,' valuable in its own right – in fact, a work of art. These paraphrased remarks seem little enough to have remained from that evening, but it is revealing to note that as early as 1910 Mandelstam expressed the ideas that gave shape to the great essay on Dante of 1933 and indeed to all of his criticism, early and late.

Steinberg told me that his conversations with Mandelstam generally turned on two themes: philosophy and the 'Jewish question.' On the latter, Mandelstam's attitude struck Steinberg as 'not altogether normal.' The poet seemed vaguely ashamed and distressed by his Jewishness. Asked by Steinberg whether the famous eye-specialist who bore his name was a relative, Mandelstam replied with some coldness: 'I am not interested in my kinfolk.'

Mandelstam attended the lectures of Fritz Neumann on Old French and, with a good deal less regularity, the lectures on Kant by the famous historian of philosophy, Wilhelm Windelband, whom he found dull. Years later, however, still trying to pass his university exams in 1916 in Petersburg, he would ask his mother to send him Windelband's history of ancient philosophy.[20] Steinberg is convinced that the ideas of a young professor of philosophy named Emil Lask, whose lectures Mandelstam found lively and even 'poetic,' will be shown by further research to have had a deep influence on the poet's world view.[21]

V

Back home in 1911, Mandelstam continued his studies in the Faculty of History and Philology at the University of St Petersburg. How he managed to gain admission to the University has always been something of a mystery. As a Jew he could only be admitted with a brilliant scholarly record (average grade: 5 – i.e. our A+), and Viktor Zhirmunsky, Mandelstam's classmate at the Tenishev School, told me that his marks were generally poor. In a short biographical outline of his life, Nadezhda Yakovlevna includes a note that somewhat clarifies matters: around this time Mandelstam was baptized a Christian at some Lutheran church in Finland, a step that removed him from the Jewish quota but one to which he later attached no significance at all. This should finally put to rest the many other reports of Mandelstam's conversion.[22] He almost certainly never received his degree, although the Soviet *Literary Encyclopedia* (alone) indicates that he did, but the date is not given. In July of 1916

Mandelstam was still promising his mother to pass the examinations in the autumn of that year. According to the late Konstantin Mochulsky, who tutored him in Greek, Mandelstam did manage to cope with that exam. But his success astonished Mochulsky himself, and the brief memoir that he has left of their sessions together in 1912 fully justifies the astonishment.

> He would be monstrously late for our lessons and completely shaken by the secrets of Greek grammar that had been revealed to him. He would wave his hands, run about the room and declaim the declensions and conjugations in a sing-song voice. The reading of Homer was transformed into a fabulous event; adverbs, enclitics, and pronouns hounded him in his sleep, and he entered into enigmatic personal relationships with them. When I informed him that the past participle of the verb παιδέω 'to educate' was πεπαίδευκος he gasped with pleasure and was unable to study any more that day. He arrived at the next lesson with a guilty smile and said, 'I haven't prepared anything, but I've written a poem.' And without taking off his overcoat, he began to recite. I remember two stanzas:

> > И глагольных окончаний колокол
> > Мне вдали указывает путь,
> > Чтобы в келье скромного филолога
> > От моих печалей отдохнуть.
> >
> > Забываешь тягости и горести,
> > И меня преследует вопрос:
> > Приращенье нужно ли в аористе
> > И какой залог «пепайдевкос»?   (No. 419, 1912)

> And the bell of the verbal desinences
> shows me the way in the distance
> so that in the modest philologist's cell
> I might have respite from my griefs.
>
> Burdens and misfortunes are forgotten
> and the question that haunts me is:
> does the aorist take the augment,
> and which voice is πεπαίδευκος?

To the end of our tutorial sessions, Osip Emilevich did not decide that question. He transformed grammar into poetry and declared that the more incomprehensible Homer was, the more beautiful. I was very afraid that he would flunk the exam, but fate saved him again, and by some miracle he withstood the test. Mandelstam did not learn Greek, he intuited it.[23]

Mikhail Karpovich saw him for the last time in 1912. His picture of the change that had taken place in Mandelstam during the critical period since their last meeting (between the ages of 19 and 22) is valuable not only for the insight it provides into the development of his character but also for the indication of his literary interests at the time.

47

I did not go to Petersburg so often and was always there for a short stay. On one of these trips...I happened to meet Mandelstam at a lecture given by Burlyuk (in the Tenishev School, I think). It seemed to me that Mandelstam had greatly changed: his aspect was far more imposing, he had grown some side-whiskers à la Pushkin, and he already behaved himself like a *maître*. He met me without especial warmth and, in any case, without the least trace of his former effusiveness. We differed, moreover, in our attitude toward Futurism. I was strongly repelled by it, but Mandelstam defended it, to a certain extent, and in any case was seriously interested in it. To my remark that I 'preferred the ship of eternity to the ship of modernity'[24] (I should not now express myself in so flowery a manner) he replied, not without a certain annoyance, 'You don't understand that the ship of modernity *is* the ship of eternity.'[25]

The growing self-confidence of the young man in this picture, and his not altogether modest behavior, must have come all too easily to one whose poetry, about which he was so defensive and doubtful in the letters to Ivanov, had now begun to earn genuine prestige for their author among the exclusive literary circles of the capital. Georgy Adamovich, a fellow student, was only three years Mandelstam's junior, but he remembers himself to have been positively shy in the presence of the *maître* pictured by Karpovich, though he denies that Mandelstam showed any haughtiness at all. The literary parallel which he draws is modest in the extreme ('I could not bring myself to be "on a friendly footing" with him, like Khlestakov with Pushkin'),[26] but since Adamovich's recollections of Mandelstam are otherwise conspicuously restrained and balanced, this testimony is the more valuable.

Another fellow student recalls an episode which reveals that Mandelstam was not invariably treated with the deference shown him by Adamovich. Yury Ofrosimov describes a collection of comic verse put together by the student philologists under the title *Antologiia antichnoi gluposti* (Anthology of Classical Nonsense):

And here is the 'dedication' to Mandelstam, who had practically no front teeth, except for one in a gold cap which protruded. Mandelstam was very taciturn, smoked a lot, and had the habit of using his shoulder as an ashtray and throwing ashes all over his suit:

> Пепли плечо и молчи—
> Вот твой удел, Златозуб[27]

> Litter your shoulder with ash and be silent –
> There is your destiny, Goldtooth.

The *Anthology* must have enjoyed a considerable local fame, for it is recalled by Anna Akhmatova, Irina Odoevtseva, and Grigory Semyonovich Rabinovich. The work was apparently Mandelstam's own inspiration, or chiefly his. Rabinovich recalls an event of December 1911:

1*b* Mandelstam, c.1915–16

1*a* Mandelstam at 16 or 17 (Paris 1905–6)

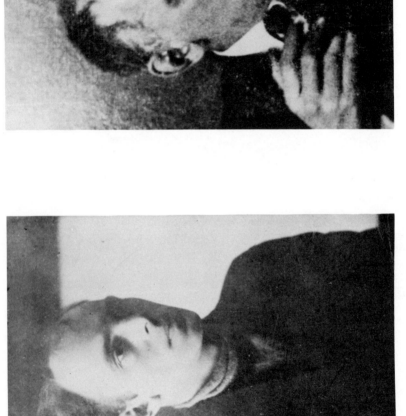

2a Mandelstam, Moscow 1922

2b Mandelstam, Veronezh 1936

3 b Nadezhda Mandelstam, Moscow 1922

3 a Mandelstam, Leningrad 1927

4 Mandelstam's streetcar pass, Moscow 1933. *detail on right*

5 *b* Mandelstam's mother, 1910

5 *a* Mandelstam, Moscow 1933–4

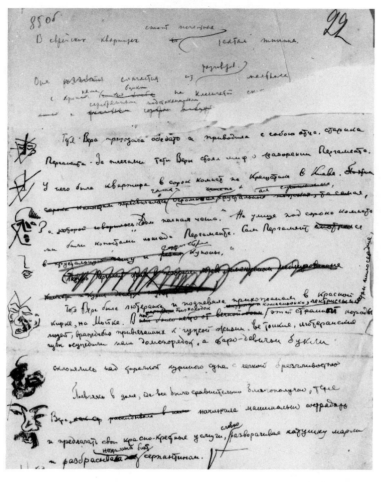

7 Manuscript page of Mandelstam's novella *Egipetskaia marka*

8*a* At Koktebel, *c.* 1933

8*b* Mandelstam with friends and relations, Moscow 1934

Mandelstam turned up in the Wandering Dog to recite some impromptu comic verses. 'Gentlemen!' he said, 'abroad, in Italy, I found some parchments of the unknown poet Caius Stultitius and translated them. They are distinguished by the most consummate classical nonsense. . .

Делия, где ты была?—Я лежала в объятиях Морфея.
Женщина! ты солгала!—в них я покоился сам!

Delia, where have you been? – Asleep in the arms of Morpheus.
Woman! You're lying! For *I've* been asleep there myself.[28]

The 'nonsense' of this particular gem is improved by knowing that Delia's interrogator is revealed by the form of the Russian past tense to have been a man.

VI AN ASIDE ON HOW HE LOOKED

When I first became interested in Mandelstam (on the basis of the 1955 edition of the Chekhov Publishing House), he existed for me solely as a creature of words – his own, of course, and those of others: the picture of him in life that could be assembled from the recollections of his friends. One was only frustrated by the little silhouette that appeared in Leonid Strakhovsky's book on the Acmeists,[29] and there were no other graphic images that I knew about at the time. I recall the joy of coming across a smudgy little photograph in the Soviet magazine *Ogonyok* (11 November 1923), but the poor quality and the usual crude retouching made the subject look rather exhumed.

Today, of course, all has changed, and no one need rely – not exclusively, at least – on the verbal portraits of his acquaintances. There remains, however, a curious mystery, for the photographs of Mandelstam at various stages of his life seem flatly to contradict what was said of his physical presence. I realize that photographs can also lie, and perhaps even more insidiously, but I should like to lay before the reader a sort of composite of the memoirists' Mandelstam and invite him to make his own comparison with the evidence of the pictures.

His acquaintances are almost unanimous in their testimony concerning the exceedingly poor figure that Mandelstam cut in a milieu that included the dashing, though far from conventionally handsome, Gumilyov and the poignantly beautiful Akhmatova. Like some of his own poetry, his appearance seemed to combine features of the grotesque, bordering on the comic, with a certain movingly pathetic element. Most witnesses agree as to the initial impression created by the young Mandelstam: it was unprepossessing, to say the least of it. His head was large, far too large for the scrawny neck on which it seemed to be imperfectly balanced, for it was always thrown back. The peculiarity of his head was utilized by an anonymous literary parodist of the poet's style to assure recognition of the victim.[30] Thin and emaciated, the face was sharply featured. His large forehead had begun to expand very early with the recession of his hairline, which left only a forelock in the middle, and was framed by a mass of reddish, curly hair, the quality of which is everywhere described as 'downy.' His ears protruded noticeably. Perhaps it was in an effort to reduce the effect of this that he wore the Pushkinian side-whiskers in young manhood.

His eyes were brilliant and arresting. He closed them when he read his poetry aloud, a fact which attracted much attention to his eyelids: various witnesses describe them as transparent, enflamed, and resembling those of a camel.

He was puny and delicate of body and moved about (he was seldom at rest) in a bouncy little gait on the tips of his toes, as if he were on a string.

His whole physical appearance – and even some of the impression produced by his personality – can be summed up in a word, some version of which occurs in practically every memoir that mentions his person as well as his behavior: *birdlike*. Mandelstam is repeatedly called a *bezdomnaia ptitsa*, 'homeless bird.' In the chapter entitled 'Starukhina ptitsa' (The Old Woman's Bird) of *The Noise of Time* he even calls himself a bird, and it is, incidentally, curious to note the words for bird and other fowl are among the most conspicuous in his lexicon, both in poetry and prose. The poet Velimir Khlebnikov, recalling no doubt Leskov's image of exquisite daintiness, the steel flea, reduced the scale without altering the essential sense of airy fragility: he called Mandelstam 'the marble fly.'[31]

The effect of Mandelstam's character, even on those who knew him well, seems to have been general bewilderment. The astonishing contradictions and contrasts, again recalling features of his own literary style, were summed up by Vladislav Khodasevich, who lived next door to Mandelstam in the Dom Iskusstv (House of the Arts) in Petersburg in the years following the Revolution. This can serve as a sample of what is customarily said about him:

> The neighboring...abode of Osip Mandelstam was something just as fantastic and whimsical as he himself – that strange and charming creature, in whom complaisance managed to exist alongside stubbornness, intelligence with frivolity, remarkable abilities with the inability to pass even a single university examination, laziness with diligence of the sort that compelled him to struggle literally for months over one intractible line of verse, the cowardice of a rabbit with courage that was practically heroic...[32]

The last sentiment was echoed in the name invented for Mandelstam by his other next-door neighbor in the House of the Arts, the gifted translator Mikhail Leonidovich Lozinsky: *kroliko-bars*, which suggests a hybrid creature, half rabbit, half snow-leopard.[33]

I hope that the reader will be struck, as I am, by the odd discrepancies between what Mandelstam's friends and acquaintances say about him and what the evidence of our senses presents as we look at the pictures. It would of course be arrant presumption on the part of one who never saw Mandelstam in life to assert that the eye-witness accounts of his physical presence are in error. They are perhaps not altogether in error. Perhaps it is a question of emphasis and selection. But emphasis and selection are the foundations of caricature. There can be little doubt, at any rate, that there are certain itinerant motifs in the word-picture of him that wander from one set of memoirs to the other. It is this fact which makes one almost certain that Mandelstam is the unnamed poet described in the memoirs of Vsevolod Rozhdestvensky: '*nizen'kii* (undersized), *shchuplyi* (puny), *nevzrachnyi* (ill-favored), *bol'shaia golova* (large head), *s pochti rebiach'ei naivnost'iu* (with an almost childish naivete), *ostrym, umnym glazom ptitsy* (with the keen, intelligent eye of a bird).'[34] Practically every one of these words can be found in several other notes on his appearance. The recently published memoirs of Em. Mindlin make Mandelstam look more like a caricature than perhaps any other.[35] It might be too extreme to speak here of a kind of mutual group hypnosis – if such a thing exists – but it cannot be denied that a considerable amount of cross consultation has taken place. Yuly Margolin, who never laid eyes on Mandelstam, furnishes the same description of him on the basis of the fact that his brother-in-law (who was ten at the time) had once heard the poet read when he stopped in Kharkov on his way to the south. The gifted poet Arseny Tarkovsky included a poem to Mandelstam in his collection *Zemle – zemnoe* (Earth to Earth, Moscow, 1966, pp. 15–17) and, while not naming the addressee of the poem, assured his recognition by using *ptichii* (birdlike) and several other such codewords.

Whatever may motivate this, I do not believe that it is malice. All those whom I have mentioned seem devoted to Mandelstam, and Mindlin, the most caricatural of all, writes in a tone that is worshipful, not to say fulsome. Princess Andronikova (see below, p. 244) was a close acquaintance of Mandelstam's and very fond of him, yet she wrote me (20 March 1961) that she had found him 'extremely ugly, with a hint of the absurd, which makes a man more than merely ugly.' Laying my hand upon my heart, as the Russians say, I cannot apply those words to the appealing young person whose image we now have before us in some quantity. The student just graduated from the Tenishev School is not, let us admit, strikingly handsome (those ears...), but neither is he ugly. There is also something distinctly appealing about the young poet with the arresting resemblance to Pushkin, and the portraits of Lev Bruni and P. Miturich must, if they conceal any ugliness of the subject, conceal it well. About the last photograph, that tragic rabbi out of Chagall, it can only be said that it has all the beauty which suffering and wisdom can confer upon human features.

Fortunately, one need not rely upon the pictures alone for a refutation of the 'little clown' image. Others who knew Mandelstam well recall an entirely different human being. The first of these, needless to say, is Nadezhda Yakovlevna herself. In Moscow in 1966 she was at some pains to disabuse me of the notion which she knew that I had acquired of her husband. Ehrenburg, one of the oldest and closest friends both of the poet and his wife, had written that Mandelstam was short. Taking me to Ehrenburg's apartment, she exacted from him the admission that Mandelstam was taller than he himself, an admission that he smilingly and readily gave. I am six feet, two inches tall. As Ehrenburg stood beside me, the top of his head was some seven or eight inches below the top of my own. It therefore strikes me that by Russian standards Mandelstam was anything but tiny. Nadezhda Yakovlevna has now conveyed this information in her memoirs,[36] where she adds: 'Neither was Mandelstam as frail as Ehrenburg makes him out to be. He was in fact quite broad-shouldered. Ehrenburg remembered him as he was in the Crimea when he was starving, and he was also aiming at a journalistic effect by describing him as a puny, delicate Jewish type like Ashkinazi – so weak and helpless, and look what they did to him! But Mandelstam was not like Ashkenazi at all – he was much more robust.' In 1962, Akhmatova had laughed: 'Of course he was an eccentric, but Osia was no absurd jack-in-the-box, no puppet on a string!'

When I later visited Korney Ivanovich Chukovsky in the writers' colony Peredelkino near Moscow, he was no less eager to correct Mandelstam's image. If I may say so without disrespect for the memory of that kindliest and most humane of men, Korney Ivanovich was something of a connoisseur of the human physique. His first memory was of a day in August 1914 when he and Mandelstam had gone for a swim at a place in Finland. The weather had already turned cold. Mandelstam swam vigorously, with practised movements (a triumph, no doubt, for Dr Virenius of the Tenishev School!) and was, in a state of nature, hardly the weak and scrawny little man of the caricature. Chukovsky remembered him as being well-built, with a strong, harmonious body, a sense of which he conveyed to me with graphic gesture and particular detail. 'But what a marvelous press you have,' he suddenly exclaimed, taking a current copy of the *New York Review of Books* from his table, 'just imagine a journal where Hemingway's penis can be discussed!'

Later that same August day, he and Mandelstam had their picture taken with Benedikt Livshits and Yury Annenkov.[37] Mandelstam, in his Pushkin guise, is already dressed against the cold in a long, heavy coat. Chukovsky sits beside him in the correct attire of a British diplomat. A tall, large-boned man, Chukovsky stood beside me at the age of 84 and was at least as tall as I, if not taller. The person seated to his right is not, to my taste, repellent or strange; as for his physical stature, taste has nothing to do with it.

4

Beginnings

When does a poet's career begin? With the first poems he writes, with the first publication, or is it with the time when he actually comes to the attention of a public beyond the circle of his close friends? If the latter, then one is justified in placing the start of Mandelstam's career in 1913. This is the first year when one might claim for him something like a readership, when the avocation of writer, as evidenced by an occasional printed poem, began to acquire the look and feel of a vocation. His poems continue to appear in *Apollon* (Nos. 38 and 39 were in the third number for 1913), but now they are also published in other monthly journals such as *Zavety* (Precepts; No. 171 was in the fifth number), *Severnye zapiski* (Northern Notes; Nos. 15 and 27 in the ninth number), and in Lozinsky's small and short-lived journal *Giperborei* (Hyperboreus) which carried Nos. 42, 45, and 37 in the February issue and Nos. 34, 49, and 173 in the May issue of 1913.

His first critical prose appeared, again in *Apollon*. The second issue carried the essay 'O sobesednike' (On the interlocutor),[1] a brilliant and meditative study by a beginning poet of what struck him as a central problem of poetry – that of the audience. It is extremely interesting to observe the urgency which the question of his listener seemed to have for him. Who is the addressee? The answer to the question whether poetry was more than an idle amusement involved the problem of who else, besides the poet, was vitally related to the poem. Mandelstam's prose writings about himself are relatively light and good humored, but when he wrote of poetry he was always serious. It seems, in fact, his art, to have been the one subject in life on which he was consistently and unfailingly serious. 'It was important to him,' wrote V. Kaverin of a conversation with Mandelstam in 1920, 'that I cease writing poetry, and what he was saying was a defense of poetry against me and those tens and hundreds of youths and maidens who were occupying themselves with word games. . .'[2] Mandelstam's answer to the question raised in his essay is that the poet must address himself to a presumptive reader in posterity, to an ideal rather than an actual reader. Like the seriousness

53

of the tone, the concern for permanence is a characteristic of his critical thought. As a judge of literature, his interest was always in what makes a work of art survive the particular circumstance surrounding its creation, and his conclusion was: the fullest and truest reflection of that particular circumstance. His rejoinder to Karpovich that 'the ship of modernity *is* the ship of eternity' was not so pat and unpremeditated as the occasion might have led one to believe. The essay also provides an insight into Mandelstam's vivid and intimate grasp of the essence of certain poets of the past: for Dante, Petrarch, Racine, Batyushkov he felt himself to be that reader in posterity, that ideal addressee become real, and this almost personal relationship gave him not only a feeling of gratitude but one of responsibility for their art. The third issue of *Apollon* carried Mandelstam's review of Huysman's *Parisian Arabesques*[3] and the fourth his essay on François Villon, written in 1910.[4]

Mandelstam's entry into literature with his publication in *Apollon* coincided with certain developments in the literary life of Russia that were to change its complexion entirely. The question of his personal relationship to Acmeism, one of the poetic schools in contention at the time, will be dealt with later (see Chap. 9) but it will be useful here to note some of the external manifestations of what was going on. The year of his first appearance in print, 1910, was a crucial one in the development of Russian poetry. It was for one thing the year of what is commonly called the 'crisis' of Symbolism, which had been for some two decades the reigning poetic school. Around Mandelstam's first poems in *Apollon* there raged a polemic concerning the plight in which Symbolism now found itself. In the preceding issue (no. 8 for May and June) two articles that had earlier been lectures delivered that spring in a literary society opened the debate. These were Vyacheslav Ivanov's 'Zavety simvolizma' (Precepts of Symbolism) and Alexandr Blok's 'O sovremennom sostoianii russkogo simvolizma' (On the present condition of Russian Symbolism). They called forth attack and defense in subsequent issues of the journal. Valery Bryusov, Andrey Bely and Dmitry Merezhkovsky were heard from in *Apollon*, and the debate, often acrimonious and personal, continued in the private meetings and correspondence of these writers.[5] To put the matter very briefly, the argument was over whether Symbolism, by which term one must understand practically everything of value being written at the time, was to be 'merely' an art or a species of philosophy, or rather theosophy. Vyacheslav Ivanov and Blok proposed the latter. At the end of the last century the Symbolists had emerged in opposition to the sort of utilitarian poetry for which the most fitting slogan was Nekrasov's versified apothegm: 'You may choose not to be a poet, but you are obliged to be a citizen.' Now Blok, too, would put the calling of poet in second place and called upon the writer to be first of all a *theurgist*, 'that is, possessor of secret knowledge, behind which there stands secret action.'[6] In the issue of Mandelstam's debut, Bryusov came to the defense of poetry *per se*, and upon this controversy – chiefly but not exclusively – Symbolism foundered as a unified, productive movement. Significantly enough, in that same number of *Apollon* Mikhail Kuzmin and Nikolay Gumilyov contributed retrospective reviews of the prose and poetry that had appeared in the recently defunct Symbolist journal *Vesy* (The Scales), and in the section chronicling artistic events outside Russia, Kuzmin began a note with the following words: 'A group of Italian poets and artists has united under the name of "Futurists."'

It was thus a moment of *ave atque vale* when Mandelstam's first poems made their appearance in print. Whether the revolution that it effected in technique and taste has ever ceased to be felt in Russian poetry, Symbolism itself was on the way out as a coherent 'school' in 1910. And Russian Futurism,[7] which derived its name if not its substance from the Italian group led by Marinetti and first mentioned in *Apollon* in Kuzmin's news note, had been officially launched that April with the publication by a group of avant-garde poets and artists, led by Vasily Kamensky of the work called *Sadok sudei* (A Fishtrap for Judges).

The third Russian modernist movement that had really lasting and widespread significance was Acmeism. As I mentioned, this will be characterized at length later on; here a brief note will suffice. Though much of its spirit and program had been adumbrated in the Symbolist Mikhail Kuzmin's article 'O prekrasnoi iasnosti' (On Beautiful Clarity) in *Apollon*, 4 (1910), and in Mandelstam's essay on Villon, written that same year, it was not officially to begin until the time, three years later, when Nikolay Gumilyov and Sergey Gorodetsky issued their manifestos in *Apollon*, 1 (1913). Gumilyov had established a closely related, but not identical, group called the *Tsekh poetov* (Guild of Poets) in the autumn of 1911. This rather informal but powerfully influential group at first included the Symbolists, but between 1913 and Gumilyov's departure for the war it became practically synonymous with Acmeism. The title can be variously translated, since the first word means either 'workshop' or 'guild.' I choose the latter because it conveys not only the interest of the Tsekh poets in the craft or technique of poetry, but also the exclusive-ness and even some of the medievalism that at times seemed essential features of the Acmeist physiognomy. This irregular group was something like a floating and continuous colloquy on the nature and technique of poetry, and its chairman and guiding spirit remained Gumilyov. In her brief memoir of Mandelstam, Anna Akhmatova devotes a few telegraphic sentences to the Guild. Between November 1911 and April 1912 (when she and Gumilyov left for a trip to Italy), the group met about three times a month. Later, from October 1912 to April 1913, it met twice a month. As secretary, Ahkmatova had the duty of mailing out the agendas, the cover of which bore the classical lyre that may also be

seen on the title-page of her collection *Vecher* (Evening). Her mailing list
included the following officers: Nikolay Gumilyov and Sergey Gorodetsky
('syndics') and Dmitry Kuzmin-Karavaev ('scribe'). And the members
were: Osip Mandelstam, Vladimir Narbut, Mikhail Zenkevich, Nikolay
Bruni, Georgy Ivanov, Georgy Adamovich, Vladimir Vasilevich Gippius,
M. Moravskaya, Yelena Kuzmina-Karavaeva, a certain Chernyavsky, and
Mikhail Lozinsky.[8]

Like the other modernist movements contemporary with it, Acmeism
is best understood as originally a reaction to Symbolism. The Symbolists'
Weltanschauung, one variant of which Blok expressed in his article, was
more important than their technique as a criterion for distinguishing
the school. And it was to the *Weltanschauung*, not the technique, that
the Acmeists chiefly reacted. They called for abandonment of the Symbolists'
metaphysical dualism and for a return to the things of this world, for
a classical and Mediterranean clarity as opposed to the gothic and
northern haze of the Symbolists, and for a firm and virile approach to
life. This latter trait caused the movement to go by the secondary name
of 'Adamism' for a while, but it was never a serious competitor. In its
early stages, at least, Acmeism deserved the apt phrase invented for it
by Kuzmin: 'veseloe remeslo' (merry craft). The Acmeist determination
to introduce some Mozartian – and Pushkinian – lightness into poetry
was again a revolt against the gathering and now often lugubrious gloom
of Symbolism.

The central event of Mandelstam's life in 1913 must have been the
appearance that spring of his first book of poems *Kamen'* (Stone). A small,
appropriately green brochure of some 33 pages (23 poems), it was
published at the author's expense.[9] On the title-page – under a rather
helpless drawing of a lion with an improbably serpentine tail and be-
stridden by a winged cupid with a lyre – appeared the imprint 'Akme.'
It sold for 50 copecks. A faint line on the last page tells us that it was
printed in the shop of one Yu. Mansfeld at 9 Gogol Street, information
with which I should not plague the reader were it not for the fact that
this printer later appeared in his client's autobiographical *Noise of Time*.
Akhmatova recalls that Mandelstam loved to repeat what Mansfeld had
said to him on bringing out *Stone*: 'Young man, you are going to write
better and better.'[10] In *Noise*, this remark is made by a certain Goldberg
who lives on Pushkin Street.

Stone itself became better and better. A second, much enlarged edition,
with a cover the color of dusty brick, appeared in 1916; and a third
edition, somewhat amplified and subtitled *Pervaia kniga stikhov* (First
Book of Poems), came out in 1923.

Mandelstam's first collection was well received by the critics. Specialist
readers of this book will find many of the reactions in the commentary

to·the New York edition, where they are quoted at considerable length. I shall cite here a few that are representative of its reception in three different ways, and are, incidentally, not so well known. Yelena Tager conveys the emotions felt privately by an ardent reader of poetry; Gumilyov supplies the more or less official estimate in the pages of *Apollon*; and Pasternak, in a letter to Mandelstam written some ten years later, confesses to a belated acquaintance with the book.

Yelena Mikhailovna Tager (1895–1964), an intelligent, well-educated woman four years Mandelstam's junior, was, as she says, not only of his generation but also of his milieu. She was Jewish on her father's side, Russian on her mother's. Under the name Anna Regatt she published her own poetry at the time when Mandelstam was also just beginning. Later on, after the usual dreary episodes of long imprisonment and exile, she published a book of short stories, *Zimnii bereg* (Winter Shore, 1929; reissued 1957), reminiscences of Blok, and was working at the time of her death on a novel about the life of Zhukovsky.[11] She was something more than the 'common reader.' Recalling in 1962 her reactions to the appearance of *Stone*, she wrote that it was not, after all, shocking that a student from that prodigiously fertile school should write verse:

> And now this keen-eyed Mandelstam – also from the Tenishev School and also writes poetry. Some surprise!
> And yet he really did surprise us – very soon and very greatly. There appeared a little book, thin as a revolutionary pamphlet. The cover was grey-green and bore the straight black letters: STONE. Common stone – not some semi-precious daisy-pearl, not 'a bit of quartz carefully saved' as in Balmont or Bryusov – but just stone, plain stone – uncut, unfaceted and, it must be, heavy. Strange name for a young poet's first collection...
> I read page after page and was more and more astonished. I had already come across some of these poems in the journals. But, collected in one place, they struck the heart with a mysterious force.

The utterly unadorned precision, so sharply contrasting with the Symbolist air of pregnant hinting, was what chiefly struck this contemporary. But she was also astonished by the metrical inventiveness and, like many another first reader of *Stone*, she cites No. 23 with its mesmerically rhythmical line, ending in two percussive beats side by side: 'Segodnia durnoi den',' the exact translation of which preserves, as it chances, the exact rhythm: Today is a bad day. _ ́_ _ _ ́ ́.

'No,' she writes, 'not since Pushkin have we encountered such intent, such powerful vision. Or such perfection in definition, in naming the object.'

Gumilyov included *Stone* along with books by Bryusov, Severyanin, Khlebnikov, Komarovsky, Annensky, and Sologub in one of his collective reviews for *Apollon* (no. 1/2 for 1914), but Mandelstam's debut was accorded equal space with the work of these better-known poets.

Gumilyov's chief concern was evidently to distinguish Mandelstam's Symbolist from his Acmeist work, and this he does with characteristic precision, pointing to the six lines on page 14 (see below, p. 178) as the first of the new manner.

> With this, he opened up the doors of his poetry to all of life's phenomena that exist in time, not merely in eternity or the instant: to the casino on the dunes, the parade in Tsarskoe Selo, the crowd in a restaurant, a Lutheran's funeral. With a purely southern passion, he has conceived a love for northern decorum or even simply for the harshness of ordinary life...I do not recall anyone else who has so completely destroyed the romantic in himself without at the same time touching the poet.[12]

Pasternak's comments come from a letter written in all probability (my copy is undated) in 1924. The copy that he mentions having just received is therefore no doubt the third edition, published in 1923.

> You know that I was only superficially acquainted with *Stone*? Yes, yes, of course; when we met you must have guessed that more than once from your knowledge of me and of those rough places in me that, with your knowledge of me, must inevitably have become blunders and gaps in our relationship, requiring an explanation. And you found it, didn't you – and guessed the truth? Once a long time ago, when I was visiting someone, I'm not sure it wasn't the Amaris, I did physically touch the book, but since that took place in an atmosphere saturated with the hosts' flighty touching all the things which at the time they had abundantly at hand, the event naturally belongs more to their domestic chronicle than it does to my recollections. Afterwards, I looked for the book whenever I had the chance, but since I always look for things in an unforgivably sleepy, half-way manner...I also asked you for it. Recently, this week, I had the good luck to get a copy. My dear fellow, I'm completely at a loss! What did you find that was good in me? Who inspired you with the notion of writing articles like those in *Rossiia* (Russia) or the one in *Russkoe iskusstvo* (Russian Art)?[13] What was that flattery for? For you know I shall never in my life write a book like *Stone*! And how long ago all that was done, and how many Americas were quietly discovered there in the silence...!

Mandelstam was 23 when the war started. He was not conscripted and did not, of course, emulate Gumilyov's prompt and voluntary donning of the uniform. How he received the 'white ticket' of exemption is not known, but his frail health or perhaps even his status as a creative artist might have been sufficient. Nadezhda Yakovlevna told me that he had worked in the Soiuz Gorodov (Union of Cities), which was the urban counterpart of the better-known Union of Zemstvos. This home-front auxiliary, known also by the acronym Zemgor, was initially organized to provide needed services, such as aiding refugees from Slavic areas of battle, but later on it became a political instrument of liberal forces and sided with progressive forces in the Duma against such reactionary ministers as Goremykin. As we shall see, Mandelstam did have some extraordinary associates in the Union of Cities, but whether he ever engaged in any political activity is not clear. At first he was probably more concerned, as the letter below indicates, with such matters as literary readings organized in aid of military hospitals.

The letter raises questions of an altogether different kind, though it can scarcely be said to answer them. It is nevertheless an irresistibly tantalizing document. The date of it is 27 April 1915, and the addressee Fyodor Sologub, a leading Symbolist poet and novelist, whose real name was Teternikov.

Dear Fyodor Kuzmich!
I have read your letter in utmost astonishment. In it you speak of your intention to keep a somewhat greater distance away from the Futurists, the Acmeists, and their associates. Not presuming to judge as to your relationship with the Futurists and their 'associates,' as an Acmeist I consider it my duty to remind you of the following: the initiative for your estrangement from the Acmeists derives wholly from the latter. Whatever your own wishes may have been, you were not invited to participate in the Guild of Poets, just as your collaboration was not sought for the magazine *Hyperboreus* nor your books for publication under the imprint of Guild of Poets, Hyperboreus, or Akme. The same applies to the public appearances of the Acmeists as such. As for my invitation to you to take part in the evening organized by the Tenishev School for the benefit of one of the military hospitals, I was acting then as a former student of that school and not as the representative of any particular literary group. It is true that certain of the Acmeists, and I among them, did visit your house at the invitation of yourself and A. N. Chebotarevskaya, but after your letter I have every ground to conclude that that was, on their part, a mistake.

With sincere respect,
Osip Mandelstam[14]

The circumstances that prompted so dismissive a letter are not known. In reviewing the 1955 edition, Georgy Ivanov took the editors to task for publishing it without explaining what events had produced it – and then failed to give any explanation himself. At one time, at least, Mandelstam felt seriously enough interested in the work of Sologub to study it critically. In his letter to his teacher Gippius from Paris he says that he has written something about Sologub, and that might have been a note later incorporated in the essay 'On the Interlocutor,' where he writes in warm admiration of the older poet. But what is most striking of all about the letter is the assured proprietary tone with which Mandelstam now speaks of Acmeism, a movement in which, a short a while before, he had been so junior a member that his manifesto, 'The Morning of Acmeism,' was not even published. Written in 1913, it was not printed until six years later.[15] But with Gumilyov absent at the front, Mandelstam evidently felt himself obliged to assume the role of spokesman.

In the year 1916 Mandelstam was much involved with a poet as remarkable in some ways as himself. This was Marina Tsvetaeva (1892–1941), who emigrated in 1922 but returned to Soviet Russia in 1939 and there hanged herself two years later.[16] It is thanks to another of Georgy Ivanov's inventions about his erstwhile friend that Tsvetaeva left a vivid memoir of her and Mandelstam's life during a short period of 1916. Entitled 'Istoriia odnogo posviashcheniia' (The Story of One Dedication), it is dated April–May 1931, a time when Tsvetaeva was living in Meudon, France. She had been helping a friend of hers who was leaving for Japan go through old papers, and on returning home continued the sorting process among her own archives and memorabilia. She comes upon someone's reminiscence of Osip Mandelstam, cut from an émigré newspaper, and is so angered by its falsehoods and inventions that she determines to put down her own recollections of the poet. She does not identify the article in question, but Professor Marc Slonim, who published the memoir in 1964,[17] notes that it is Georgy Ivanov's 'Kitaiskie teni' (Chinese Shadows) from the Paris Russian daily *Poslednie novosti* (Latest News) for 22 February 1930. The specific starting point of her memoir is the interpretation put by Ivanov upon Mandelstam's poem 'Ne veria voskresen'ia chudu' (Not believing the miracle of resurrection), and one must grant the authority from which she writes, since she is possessed of first-hand knowledge of every detail of the poem, it having been written, in fact, to her.

The second part of the memoir is devoted to Mandelstam, and bears the title 'Gorod Aleksandrov Vladimirskoi gubernii' (The City of Aleksandrov in the Vladimir Guberniya). It was here that Tsvetaeva was staying at her sister's in the summer of 1916 when Mandelstam, evidently in love with her, came for a visit. Her sister was away in Moscow, her brother-in-law away at his work during the day, and the little group left behind consisted of Tsvetaeva, Mandelstam, her daughter Alya, her nephew Andryusha (both aged three) and the old nursemaid Nadya.

Their pastime was strolling in the countryside, almost always in the direction of a nearby cemetery, untended and, to Tsvetaeva, charming in its neglect and disrepair. Mandelstam was horrified by the graves and delapidated crypts and offended by her absorption in them rather than in him. He was too much the Petersburger to find the cows and hikes and other country pleasures to his taste, but the prospect of loitering in a burial ground, especially one in which the crumbling vaults did not even conceal their contents, roused in him a fear of death that was, anyway, sufficiently acute. Tsvetaeva took no pity on him:

> 'It is good to lie there!'
> 'It isn't good in the least: you will lie there and be walked over!'
> 'And in life – you've not been walked over?'
> 'Metaphor! I'm speaking of feet, even boots.'

'But it won't be you. You will be...a soul.'

'That's just what I'm afraid of. Which of the two is more terrifying I don't know: a naked soul or a decomposing body.'

'What do you want to do – live forever? Without even a hope for the end?'

'Oh, I don't know! I only know that I'm afraid and I want to go home.'

Once as they returned from a stroll, they found that a nun had arrived bringing freshly laundered shirts. Tsvetaeva's recording of their dialogue tends, as always, toward stichomythia:

Mandelstam, in a whisper: 'Why is she so black?'

'Because *they* [the shirts] are so white!'

But a nun was too much to bear after the horrors of the graveyard. Mandelstam, whose eyes were as usual veiled by their heavy lids as his head tilted back in the manner so often described, stared roundly at the discomfiting figure in the black habit.

'Will she leave soon? Really, it isn't so cosy, you know. I am absolutely positive that I smell incense.'

'Mandelstam, you are imagining things!'

'And that ruined crypt with the bones – it was also imagined? Well, I'd simply like some tea, finally!'

While the nun bent over a shirt as though it were a corpse, Mandelstam said in a sibilant whisper:

'Won't you be afraid to wear these?'

'Just wait, my dear, when I'm dead that's the very one I'll put on – seeing that it is a nightgown – to appear before you!'

When he had had his tea Mandelstam relaxed somewhat.

'Perhaps it really isn't so frightening after all. Perhaps if one went every day one would become used to it? Still, we'd better not go there tomorrow...'

But, Tsvetaeva writes, the next day they inevitably went again.

There is a persistent theme, in most accounts of Mandelstam's encounters with the servant class, of mutual misunderstanding. A certain liberality of culture appears to have been needed to make allowances for his many eccentricities. The old family retainer of the Tsvetaevs, the nursemaid Nadya, had her difficulties with him, as he did with her. In separate conversations they complain to Tsvetaeva:

'Miss, what a queer one that Osip Emelich is! I'm feeding Andryusha his kasha just now and he says to me, "How lucky your Andryusha is, Nadya. He always has kasha enough ready for him, and his socks have all been mended. But as for me," he says, "no one feeds me kasha, and there's no one to mend my socks." And it was so-o sad, the way he sighed, the poor orphan...And I says to him, "But Osip Emelich, you ought to get married. Why, any girl would be glad to marry you. You want me to arrange it? There's a priest's daughter..."'

'But Nadya, seriously, do you really think that any girl would...?'

'Oh, get along, Miss...I just told him that to make him feel better. He made me feel so sorry for him. There's not a one that would marry him, let alone *any*, unless it was maybe some girl with only one arm. He's so peculiar!'

[Mandelstam:] 'Who is this Nadya you have? A nursemaid...and with eyes like a wolf. I wouldn't trust her with anything, not even a kitten, let alone a baby to look after. She does the washing and laughs all to herself, alone in an empty kitchen. I asked her for some tea. You'd gone out with Alya. She said, "We're all out."
    "Buy some," I say.
    "Can't leave Andryusha."
    "Leave him with me."
    "With *you*!!!"
And then that insulting laugh. Eyes like slits and huge teeth! A wolf!'

[Nadya:] 'Then I poured him a glass of boiling water and brought it to him. And he says to me in a little whining voice, "Na-a-dya, isn't there a little piece of chocolate?"
    "No," says I, "there's some jam."
    And he begins to groan: "Jam, jam, the whole day I eat jam. I don't want any of your jam! What a house – no chocolate!"
    "Osip Emelich, there is only one bar, only it's Andryusha's."
    "Andryusha's! Andryusha's! The jam's Andryusha's, the chocolate's Andryusha's, yesterday I wanted to sit in an armchair and that was also Andryusha's!...Now, just break off a piece..."
    "No, I won't break off a piece. I'll bring you some nice jam."
So he drank it – boiling water with jam.'

His departure took place unexpectedly – if not for me with my four-month experience (February to June) of these Mandelstamian arrivals and departures (raids and routs), then for him, with his childlike longing for home, whence he would always flee again. [...]
One morning – one fine morning, precisely – he came for his tea all ready to go.
    Breaking open his roll, he asked in a lordly way: 'What time does your train come through?'
    'Train? Ours? Where to?'
    'To the Crimea. I have to go today.'
    'Why?'
    'I...I...I can't stand it here any longer. Anyway, it's time to put an end to all this.'
    Knowing the departing guest, I did not try to dissuade him. I helped him pack: a razor and an empty notebook, I think it was.
    'Osip Emelich, how can you leave? Some of your things are still wet from the wash!'
    He, with the departing traveller's magnificent nonchalance: 'It will dry in the Crimean sun!' And to me: 'You'll see me off at the station, of course?'
    The station. On my left, just above my ear, the agitated Adam's apple

of his camel's neck, choking on Aleksandrovo as if it were a piece of fruit. Andryusha runs away from Nadya straight for the locomotive – to the 'little wheels.' The lyrical Alya, seeing that people are leaving, patiently sheds tears: 'He's coming back? He's not going away for a long, long time? Just a little time?' Nadya, with glistening tears and teeth, laments: 'You ought to have told me yesterday, Osip Emelich. I could have mended your socks for the trip... I could have baked a pie.'

The warning bell. First. Second. Third. One foot on the train steps, and he turns around.

'Marina Ivanovna, maybe I'm being stupid to leave?'

'Of course...' But I suddenly think better of it: 'Of course not! Just think: Max, Karadag, Pra'[18]... And you can always come back.'

'Marina Ivanovna!' (The train is already moving.) 'I'm sure I'm being stupid to leave! Here I've been... (I am walking alongside the rolling wheels.) 'With you I've been so... so...' (The car picks up speed and so do I.) 'Never with anyone have I felt...' I run, leaving behind Mandelstam, the train, and the sentence. End of the platform. A post. I also turn to a post. The cars go past: not his, not his, not his... his. I wave, as only the day before he and I had waved at the soldiers. He waves. Not one hand – both. As if waving something away! A shout is carried back along the steam-engine's mane: 'I don't want to go to the Crimea!'

[...]

The third and last part of Tsvetaeva's memoir is entitled 'Zashchita byvshego' (A defense of what was). It is a line by line rebuttal of Ivanov's elaborately dishonest commentary on Mandelstam's poem No. 90, 'Ne veria voskresen'ia chudu' (Not believing in the miracle of resurrection). Her technique is that of the marginal comment. She quotes a portion of Ivanov's article and immediately corrects it with withering scorn for the ignorance and invention which he offers as intimate knowledge. Perhaps the most effective stroke of all was to leave until the end her comment on the opening paragraph of Ivanov's article. In this, he introduces his subject with an outright protestation of his good faith, which, following Tsvetaeva's meticulous demonstration of his real method, has a very sorry ring to it.

Ivanov begins:

At a meeting in Paris of young people interested in literature I was re-proached in these words: 'Why do you distort Mandelstam, our favourite poet? Why do you present him in your memoirs as some sort of comical eccentric? Could he have been like that?' That is precisely what he was like. I have not invented a single word about Mandelstam.

His thesis is that we can find both lofty and ridiculous elements so intertwined in one human being, specifically in one writer, that it is impossible to know where one leaves off and the other begins. The entire article on Mandelstam, based on an explication of the poem, is offered as a substantiation of this view.

According to Ivanov, Mandelstam wrote the poem in the Crimea at a time when he was madly in love with a certain woman doctor. He had other difficulties, too. Since he would neither pay for his room and board nor leave, his landlords – i.e. Voloshin and his mother – attempted to drive him away by withholding water from him, an effective measure in that dry region. He suffered also from the persecutions of a certain evil-tempered servant woman. His food consisted of scraps and leavings. Whenever guests arrived he was evicted from his room and forced to sleep in an unheated storeroom, where he caught cold and an infection that caused his cheek to swell up. With his head bandaged, painted with iodine, he was followed about by a troop of taunting urchins. To top it all, 'she,' the woman doctor, laughed at Mandelstam's ridiculous condition. She was, Ivanov explains, a very pretty, rather vulgar brunette who could hardly be expected to accept such a gift as the handful of sand offered by Mandelstam in the poem, since she was already being kept in comfortable style by a fat Armenian merchant. He had brought her to the Crimea where he knew he would have no cause for jealousy except for the insignificant competition offered by Mandelstam. In Koktebel the only person who befriended Mandelstam was an old Jewish woman, the proprietress of a small stand where Mandelstam obtained cigarettes, matches, buns, etc., on credit. The final picture is of Mandelstam – 'unhappy, hungry, proud, absurd, hopelessly in love with the doctor' – walking dejectedly along the sunburnt coast while she, dressed in pink finery, sips coffee and eats hot buns on her balcony.

This further installment in the 'Jewish clown' legend was undoubtedly of use in the service of Ivanov's thesis, but it appears to have been invented. Tsvetaeva's refutation is in two parts. She first shows that virtually every assertion regarding Mandelstam's life in Koktebel (and life in Koktebel *tout court*) is flatly wrong or distorted for some effect. She then provides a true explication of the poem, dedicated to her and deriving from the very scenes and events contained in her earlier memoir of the poet's visit to Aleksandrovo.

Tsvetaeva and her husband, S. Ya. Efron, had met Mandelstam in Koktebel in the summer of 1915, a year before the episode in Aleksandrovo. Their encounter was brief: Mandelstam was just leaving the Crimea and they were just arriving. Both he and they were the guests of Voloshin and his mother, whose hospitality to many transient intellectuals has become legendary. Tsvetaeva is incensed by Ivanov's portrayal of them as malicious landlords, grasping at the pennies of their helpless client, feeding him on the leavings of more favored guests, and so on. Ivanov had obviously heard from Mandelstam or someone else some account of this period in Koktobel, since his narrative has, in its grosser aspect, some of the contours of reality. There was, for example, a servant in the house – not an evil old woman, however, but a kindly and even too generous old man called Socrates after the name of his boat. Mandelstam did sometimes move from his room to make way for other guests, but he was always shifted to Voloshin's wonderful study, not to a lumber room. There was a coffee shop, not a stand, operated by a Greek man in the prime of life, not an old Jewess, and so on. The entire episode of the woman doctor and her paramour, the fat Armenian merchant, comes from Ivanov's imagination. Tsvetaeva observes that it was hardly necessary to the thesis of the article to assert that Mandelstam combined his lofty gifts with such *poshlost*, an untranslatable Russian word signifying the most abysmal vulgarity.

Here is the poem, which I give in its published version. Tsevtaeva herself quotes its original form, where there are minor verbal differences:

Не веря воскресенья чуду,
На кладбище гуляли мы.
—Ты знаешь, мне земля повсюду
Напоминает те холмы

   .   .   .
   .   .   .

Где обрывается Россия
Над морем черным и глухим.

От монастырских косогоров
Широкий убегает луг.
Мне от владимирских просторов
Так не хотелося на юг,
Но в этой темной, деревянной
И юродивой слободе
С такой монашкою туманной
Остаться—значит быть беде.

Целую локоть загорелый
И лба кусочек восковой.
Я знаю—он остался белый
Под смуглой прядью золотой.
Целую кисть, где от браслета
Еще белеет полоса.
Тавриды пламенное лето
Творит такие чудеса.

Как скоро ты смуглянкой стала
И к Спасу бедному пришла,
Не отрываясь целовала
А гордою в Москве была.
Нам остается только имя—
Чудесный звук, на долгий срок.
Прими ж ладонями моими
Пересыпаемый песок.

Not believing in the miracle of resurrection,
We strolled in the cemetery
– You know, the earth everywhere
reminds me of those hills

. . .
. . .

where Russia suddenly comes to an end
above the black and desolate sea.

A wide meadow runs away
from the monastery slopes.
I was so reluctant to go south
from the wide expanses of Vladimir,
but to remain in that dark, wooden,
holy-fool settlement
with such a hazy nun
would lead to sure catastrophe.

I kiss your sunburnt elbow
and a waxen bit of forehead.
I know it has stayed white
beneath the strand of dark gold.
I kiss your hand where there is still
a white band from your bracelet.
The flaming summer of Taurida
performs such miracles.

How soon you became a brown-skinned girl
and came to the poor Saviour
and kissed without stopping
but you were proud in Moscow.
Only the name remains for us,
a miraculous sound, to last for long.
Take, then, this sand that I pour
from one palm to the other.

Much of the external reference will be clear from what has already
been given of the adventures in Aleksandrovo, but Tsvetaeva's comments
are also enlightening. The cemetery is that to which their daily strolls
took them. She suggests that the hills of line 4 are double: both the hills
of the countryside and the mounds in the cemetery. Lines 9 to 12 are
transparently clear in the context of Tsvetaeva's narrative, but the nun
of the following quatrain seems to her complex: the image comes from
the real nun, from Nadya with her 'holy-fool' laugh, and from Tsvetaeva
herself with her predilection for the graveyard. Hence also the haziness
of this triple personage. Why is there 'still' a white band from the
bracelet? Because, Tsvetaeva explains, it is left from the previous summer
of 1915, it being one of the miracles of the Crimean sun that its burn
lasts so long. In lines 25 to 28, upon which Ivanov had put an erotic

interpretation, Tsvetaeva sees the reflection of an episode in Moscow, when she had kissed an icon of the crucifixion.

As Marc Slonim observed on publishing this memoir, it is remarkable not only for the hitherto unknown picture of one moment in the lives of two great poets, but also as a specimen of what he aptly calls Tsvetaeva's 'dynamic and muscular prose.' It also shows Tsvetaeva in a role very seldom played by poets of genius – that of the exegete. She fully realizes what she is about, that she has touched upon a central problem in the study of literature, how 'reality' gets into a poem, and she does not fail to caution her reader against the assumption that the poem is 'really' – or worse, 'merely' – the mechanical product of its varied origins in life:

> I do not know whether in general we need real-life interlinear translations for poetry: who lived, when, where, with whom, under what circumstances, etc., as in the high-school game familiar to everyone. The poetry has ground life up and cast it out, and out of the siftings that remain the biographer, who creeps after them practically on his knees, endeavors to recreate what actually happened. To what end? In order to bring us closer to the living poet. But surely he must know that the poet lives *in the poem*, while *in essence* he is far away.

But, relenting somewhat in her picture of the humble biographer, she writes that 'one way or the other, the biographer *has* an official right to the factual past (the *document*),' and her own final paragraph presents the ultimate justification, and the poet's *apologia* for pursuing even the meanest truth behind the Truth of the poem as art:

> One thing more: had I limited myself to refuting a lie, i.e. to writing a mere exposé, I should have played the role that I hate most of all – the prosecutor's. But when I confront a lie with living life – and isn't my Mandelstam charming, for all his fear of dead people and passion for chocolate, or maybe because of that? – when I affirm life, itself an affirmation, I remain within the role that is native to a poet – that of the defender.

There are results other than this memoir from Mandelstam's short infatuation with Tsvetaeva. In addition to the poem quoted above, he wrote at least two others to her (see below, pp. 221ff.) and she wrote a number of poems to him, among them those numbered 23, 24, and 25 in the 1965 Moscow edition of her works: 'Nikto nichego ne otnial' (No one has taken anything away), 'Ty zaprokidivaesh' golovu' (You throw your head back), and 'Otkuda takaia nezhnost'' (Whence such tenderness). By the time their poems to each other appeared in print, however, Mandelstam was already married and no addressee was indicated. Writing privately to her friend Alexandr Bakhrakh in 1923, Tsvetaeva explained that the dedications had been removed on account of Mandelstam's wife – 'recent and jealous.'[19]

Tsvetaeva's admiration for Mandelstam and his poetry apparently endured long beyond the end of their affair, but Mandelstam, if indeed he ever thought highly of Tsvetaeva's work, ceased to do so. In one version of Akhmatova's memoir of Mandelstam, he is reported as saying to her: 'I am an anti-Tsvetaevan.'[20] (She puts this in the context of her own observation that Mandelstam was capable of being 'monstrously unfair,' as she herself once painfully learned.) And Mandelstam was nowhere so 'anti-Tsvetaevan' as in the 1922 essay entitled 'Literary Moscow',[21] where he simply lumped her together with some other women poets as an example of shrill femininity, tastelessness, and historical falsity. It is a dismaying passage and quite indefensible. One can only remark that such lapses were rare in his critical writing.

By July 1916 Mandelstam was in the Crimea, whence he wrote to his mother from Koktebel:

Dear Mama!
Everything has been arranged favorably. Shura has got well and got into the rut of a peaceful life. He no longer feels dull and looks altogether different. The day before yesterday we were driven to Feodosia with great pomp – automobiles, dinner with the governor. I read, gleaming white in my tennis things, from the stage of the summer theater. We returned in the morning and spent yesterday resting. I will definitely pass my exams this autumn. Find out the dates, please, and send Windelband's or Vvedensky's ancient philosophy...

5

Snapshots from the Revolution and Civil War

I

Whether Mandelstam kept his promise to his mother is not recorded. But he returned to Petersburg, and we see him next on the very eve of 1917: he was greeting the New Year in the 'Prival Komediantov' (The Mummers' Halt), a cabaret in the cellar of a house near the Field of Mars, which had now succeeded the 'Wandering Dog' as the gathering place for poets and artists. The proprietor was the same Boris Pronin, an actor and producer, who had run the Dog. He moved about among the tables of his new establishment with a flea-bitten mongrel in tow as a sort of souvenir of the old place. The Halt was decorated in the everlastingly 'new' fashion of the avant-garde: the vaulted walls and ceilings covered, not yet with abstract, but with daring 'left' paintings. Bright country fabrics replaced tablecloths, and the electric light came through the eye-holes of black half-masks. Negro boys in colorful Arabian costume waited on the crowded little tables. The clientele was mostly but not exclusively the *jeunesse dorée* left behind by the war, for Adamovich recalls having seen very important persons there as well: Boris Savinkov, terrorist and later Minister of War under Kerensky, and Lunacharsky, Lenin's famous Commissar of Education. Mandelstam was sitting that evening between two poetesses, Maria Levberg and Margarita Tumpov-skaya, when Pronin succeeded in pursuading him to read some of his recent poetry.

At that time [Tager writes], all poets more or less observed the meter in reading their poems aloud, but Mandelstam's reading was more than rhythmical. He didn't just scan or pronounce his lines – he sang them like a shaman seized by visions.

That New Year's Eve he sang us poems about the war, the European war that had lasted since the early autumn of 1914 and was now preparing to sweep over 1917. There was no trace of the patriotic lexicon often heard at the time in war poems. His iambics contained no perfidious Teutons, none of our invincible bayonets and shells, not even the super-modern dirigibles and zeppelins to which people had not yet become altogether accustomed. The poet sang of how the lion, the cock, and the eagle went into battle. Not the zoo lion nor the rooster from the barnyard, but creatures of mystical power – the salient principles of European history in the make-up of heraldic beasts. The poem was fantastic, frightening, irresistible. I don't think it was ever published. There was something similar in *Tristia* – 'Zverinets' (The Menagerie [No. 83]) – but that is not it.

When he had finished his reading, Mandelstam sat down next to Tager. She asked him whether the poem was to be published.

'Not now at least,' he answered. 'Perhaps after the war.'

Then he added, 'I'm afraid none of us is going to appear in print for a long time. A time of silence is coming.'[1]

II

3 July 1917. Mandelstam is standing on the balcony of the building housing the Union of Cities organization with two of his associates (and fellow Jews), Lev Borisovich Kamenev and Grigory Yevseevich Zinovev. Rozenfeld and Radomylsky, to give them their respective real names, were associates of Mandelstam's only, to be sure, in the home-front auxiliary to which they belonged. Mandelstam was at this time closest politically to the SRs, the Socialist Revolutionary Party, to which his great friends the Sinani family belonged. According to one reference work as we have seen Mandelstam had been an SR at the age of 16, and had even engaged in propaganda work at mass meetings.[2] Kamenev and Zinovev, of course, were Bolsheviks of long standing and would, on the death of Lenin, form a short-lived triumvirate with Stalin, who executed them both in 1936 as one of the first steps in the Great Purge. By the summer of 1917 Mandelstam had conceived an intense dislike for the Bolsheviks. 'It was very like him,' said Nadezhda Yakovlevna, as she told me of this episode, 'to choose two powerful opponents like Kamenev and Zinovev to listen to his objections. He told them that Bolshevism could not escape becoming a kind of "upside-down church."'

III

Artur Sergeevich Lourié (1892–1966), the composer and essayist, was a close friend of Mandelstam and Akhmatova in the years preceding and including the Revolution. Before emigrating to Paris – and, ultimately, to Princeton – he was briefly Lenin's first Commissar of Music, having headed the Muzo (Music Section) in Lunacharsky's Narkompros (People's Commissariat of Education). He had been close to the Futurists and in 1914 even issued one of their manifestoes together with Benedikt Livshits and Georgy Yakulov. One of his best-known musical works is 'Notre marche,' using Mayakovsky's famous poem as the text. Endowed with a rich memory and a vast acquaintance among the most eminent writers, artists and musicians of this century, Lourié was adamantly reticent about writing his memoirs. Akhmatova once sent him (through me) an outright order to do so – 'Skazhite emu, chto ia *velela*!' (Tell him that I command it), she said in her most regal manner – but the disease that finally ended his life had by that time advanced too far for compliance. Nevertheless, it is to Lourié that we owe an odd picture of Mandelstam in the autumn or winter of 1917:

> At the height of the Revolution Mandelstam, having by some miracle got a room in the Astoria [the most elegant hotel in St Petersburg], took a tub bath several times each day, drank the milk that had been left at his door by mistake, and lunched at the Donon, where the proprietor, out of his mind, extended credit to everyone.[3]

IV

Another of Mandelstam's associates in these years was a character who might have been ordered from Central Casting to play Russian Revolutionary Wild Man. This was Yakov Grigorevich Blyumkin, a Left SR (i.e. a member of that wing of the Socialist Revolutionary Party that entered a coalition with the Bolsheviks just after the Revolution) and, on 6 July 1918, the assassin of the German ambassador, Count Mirbach. The best source of information about Blyumkin is now Nadezhda Mandelstam's memoir *Hope Against Hope*. In fact, she had known him in Kiev before either of them had ever met Mandelstam. He was the very type of the terrorist and seems to have had a revolver where most other men have a right hand. He would brandish the revolver on the slightest provocation – even at home among his family, according to Nadezhda Yakovlevna. Roman Jakobson, who also knew Blyumkin, remembers him as a cultivated, even learned man, who struck Jakobson as more likely to be reading the Avesta or some Old Hebrew text than shooting diplomats. Nevertheless, Jakobson told me of an incident that does not differ in tone from all the others told of this naturally violent man. He (Jakobson) was sitting with Mayakovsky and Shershenevich in a café during the NEP period. The place was full. Blyumkin, denied entrance at the door, immediately flourished his weapon and shouted that he would deal with the hapless doorman as he had dealt with the German ambassador. 'Blyumkin seemed to look for ways to risk his life,' Jakobson said.

Nadezhda Yakovlevna also admits that Blyumkin was a rare example of natural murderer and lover of poetry combined in one man. He was, in particular, an admirer of Gumilyov's robust and strenuous poetry, which does not seem so surprising. Gumilyov repaid this admiration by actually including Blyumkin in a poem entitled 'Moi chitateli' (My Readers):

Человек, среди толпы народа
Застреливший императорского посла,
Подошел пожать мне руку,
Поблагодарить за мои стихи.

A man who amid a crowd of people
shot the Emperor's ambassador
came up to me to shake my hand
and thank me for my poetry.[4]

It seems more surprising that he should also have been an admirer of the somewhat more demanding poetry of Mandelstam. If he was, he must have understood poetry better than men, to judge by a suggestion he made to Mandelstam in November 1917. There was, he told Mandelstam, a new organization in process of formation which looked like developing into something quite powerful. It was called, unrevealingly enough, the Extraordinary Commission. Would Mandelstam not like to be in on the ground floor? Mandelstam declined. But no such proposition, declined or not, can be made without leaving in the imagination a ghostly image of Osip Mandelstam as a member of the organ that came to be known by the Russian initials for 'Extraordinary Commission,' the Cheka.

V

March 1918. Mandelstam, employed in Lunacharsky's education ministry, moved to Moscow along with the government. What precisely he did in the organization is not clear. His widow told me, 'They gave him the art education section.' Sheila Fitzpatrick's thoroughgoing history of Narkompros for the years 1917–21 does not, however, mention him.[5] Mandelstam himself seems to have been rather vague about his duties. 'He was completely at a loss as to what he was supposed to do,' said Nadezhda Yakovlevna, 'and he was terrified of his secretary. The only thing he did was organize something called the Institute of Rhythmics and rescue a church choir.' This was the famous choir led by Alexandr Kastalsky (1856–1926), which was to have been disbanded, but Mandelstam convinced the authorities that it must be preserved as part of the cultural heritage, nationalized and supported.

He had made the move to Moscow with N. P. Gorbunov, a leading official of the ministry, and stayed one or two nights at his apartment in the Kremlin. Gorbunov proposed that he stay longer, but at breakfast one morning Mandelstam heard that Trotsky was about to enter the dining hall and fled, as he repeatedly fled the presence of the mighty. Invited by the Foreign Minister, Chicherin, to put his knowledge of languages at the service of the new government, Mandelstam also ran from what would have been (for a while at least) a secure post, his principal reason being that far too powerful an individual had made the offer.[6]

One of his acquaintances in Narkompros later proved to be a godsend. Mandelstam invited Boris Lvovich Lopatinsky, an artist associated with Diaghilev's *Mir Iskusstva* (World of Art), to join his section and organize the art education of children. Later on, during the Civil War, in the spring of 1921, Lopatinsky had become head of an immense organization that had charge of the evacuation of the Caucasus. He was able to shelter Mandelstam and his wife and aid their escape, on one of his trains, to the relative calm of Georgia.[7]

VI

The same pistol-brandishing Blyumkin who had proposed that Mandelstam join him in the Cheka furnished the occasion for an extraordinary adventure in July 1918. Georgy Ivanov, impatient as always with the truth, sought in his memoirs to make the episode more extraordinary still, but Mandelstam's widow and others have now restored a measure of reality to the account of what happened.

Ivanov's fictionalized account places Mandelstam at a drunken party attended for the most part by Bolsheviks and their coalitionists, the Left SRs. Blyumkin, drunk, was haphazardly making out some death warrants already bearing the signature of Felix Dzerzhinsky, head of the secret police, and boasting of his power to dispose of human life. Outraged, Mandelstam rushes up to the armed terrorist, snatches the papers from his hand, tears them up, and flees from the room before anyone can recover from his astonishment. When he has calmed down, he goes into the Kremlin to the apartment of Kameneva, the wife of Lev Borisovich Kamenev and sister of Trotsky, and together they report on Blyumkin to Dzerzhinsky himself.

Beneath this colorful embroidery, as usual, there is an actual fabric of truth. Mandelstam told the story to Nadezhda Yakovlevna, who devotes a page of her memoir to it.[8] And the other witness was an actual participant in part of the story, Felix Dzerzhinsky, whose account can be found in a collection of documents relating to the history of the Cheka.[9]

What happened can be put together from these two sources. Blyumkin did in fact boast in Mandelstam's presence one night in late June or early July 1918 that his position in the Cheka gave him the power of life and death. He referred in particular to his power over a certain Hungarian or Polish Count whose name Mandelstam later forgot, though he thought he was an art historian. In his deposition concerning the murder of the German ambassador, Count Mirbach, Dzerzhinsky gave his name as Count Puslovsky and identified him as a poet. Dzerzhinsky even quotes Blyumkin's words:

Several days or perhaps a week before the assassination, I learned from Raskolnikov and from Mandelstam (who works in Lunacharsky's office in Petrograd) that this person Blyumkin would permit himself to say things like, 'People's lives are in my hands – I sign a piece of paper and two hours later a human life is over. Here, take this Count Puslovsky that I've got in jail – a poet, a great cultural treasure – I'll sign his death warrant, but if you want him alive, I'll let him live,' and so forth. When Mandelstam, who was outraged at this, started to protest, Blyumkin threatened him that if he told anyone about him, he wouldn't stop at anything to get back at him.'

Mandelstam told his wife that he then went at once to Larisa Reysner[10] (not Kameneva) in order to get word through her to Dzerzhinsky, who – by all accounts, even Ivanov's – immediately took steps to restrain Blyumkin.

The restraint was exceedingly mild. Dzerzhinsky says that Blyumkin was temporarily relieved of his duties. He used his new-found leisure to participate in a plot by the Left SRs to disrupt the peace concluded between Germany and Russia at Brest-Litovsk. This was to be done by murdering the head of the German mission at that conference and now the ambassador in Moscow, Count Wilhelm von Mirbach-Harff. Blyumkin and his confederate Andreev went to the German embassy, housed in the former Berg mansion on Denezhny Pereulok, early on the afternoon of 6 July 1918 and gained entrance with passes bearing the forged signature of Dzerzhinsky. An eye-witness account[11] of the rather slovenly murder that ensued somewhat tarnishes Blyumkin's reputation as a terrorist. Sitting a few feet from the hapless Mirbach, he fired three shots point-blank and...missed. The count managed to scamper across the immense room and practically out the door before Andreev dispatched him with a single shot in the back of his head. Two grenades were exploded to cover their escape, which they made through a window.

Though Blyumkin was sentenced to death, he was later pardoned and even resumed his career in the Cheka. At later encounters with Mandelstam he made a sort of ritual of flashing his pistol and threatening revenge. Accounts of these incidents can be found in the memoirs of his widow, his friend Ehrenburg, and others. The feud now strikes me as rather less terrifying than it once did. Besides, given Blyumkin's skill with his weapon, Mandelstam seems to have been in little danger. Blyumkin was executed in 1929 for complicity in a Trotskyist plot, and Mandelstam, who hated the idea of capital punishment, was sickened by the news.[12]

VII

Mandelstam evidently went off at once on one of his innumerable flights to the Crimea. Vera Arturovna Sudeykina, then the wife of the artist Sergey Sudeykin and now the widow of Igor Stravinsky, knew Mandelstam well. It was her house – and vineyard – that provided the background for one of Mandelstam's most magnificent poems, No. 92. In December 1966 the poet Yevtushenko called on her and her husband in Hollywood, and Robert Craft, the meticulous Boswell and musical aide of Stravinsky, was there to put down her picture of Mandelstam in the Crimea in 1918. The date is not further specified:

> Mandelstam was always ardent and always hungry, but as everyone was hungry at the time, I should have said even hungrier than other people. Having very few clothes, he parsimoniously hoarded the most presentable ones, which included an emergency shirt, as he called it, and a pair of almost-fully-soled shoes. Once he called on us wearing a raincoat and nothing else, then paced up and down by our cupboard the whole time like a peripatetic philosopher, not to keep warm but to find out – sniffing like a Platonic philosopher – whether our larder had any food. I also remember a train trip with him to Simferopol. The cars were so crowded with soldiers and refugees that babies sleeping on the floor were helmeted with pails to keep them from being accidentally crushed by people struggling to push through. I sat between Mandelstam and Sudeykin, who dressed me like a Moslem woman on account of the soldiers.[13]

VIII

Mandelstam now vanishes for a time. There are various accounts of his whereabouts, but none seem reliable. It was, after all, one of the most tumultuous periods, for the Left SR revolt against the Bolsheviks that had been heralded by the murder of Count Mirbach now erupted in at least twenty-three cities of central Russia, and Yaroslavl was completely under their control. The next firm date comes from the most reliable of all sources, Nadezhda Yakovlevna. In March 1919, she told me, Mandelstam went to Kharkov in the Ukraine, his reason being the availability of food there. 'The difference in prices was so great,' she told me

> that the money on which one starved in Moscow was enough to afford luxury in the Ukraine. He got a good deal of paper roubles somehow and moved to Kharkov, where he lived for a month or so on what would barely have bought bread in Moscow. And then when he came to Kiev he was still 'full of gold' and could feed me pastries.

At this point my narrative of Mandelstam's life directly adjoins that of the lady to whom this book is dedicated. In Kiev, that spring of 1919, they became 'man and wife' – a relationship formalized a few years later – and from then until another May, that of 1938, they were practically never apart. And the brief periods of separation were filled with Mandelstam's letters to her, now published in the third volume of the New York edition, letters of an unexampled tenderness and solicitude. Nadezhda Yakovlevna's memoir *Hope Against Hope*, to which I have often referred already, is in its own right so great a monument to the human spirit that

I sometimes think of it as only incidentally a record of the poet Mandelstam's works and days. But it is also that. While it concentrates principally upon the last four years of his life, there are numerous flashbacks dealing with the whole period of their life together.

IX

In Kiev Mandelstam lived at the Hotel Continental. His artistic life was centered in a basement club on Nikolaevsky Street with the curious name of 'Khlam,' an acronym made up of the initials of the Russian words for 'artists, writers, actors, musicians,' which came out to be identical with the word for 'rubbish.' This was Nadezhda Yakovlevna Khazina's milieu. A student of art herself (in the studio of Alexandra Exter), her friends in 'Khlam' included Ilya Ehrenburg and his future wife, Lyuba, who, like Yevgeniya Borisovna Gronfeyn, the future wife of Isaac Babel, was also an art student. The artist Alexandr Tyshler was there, and so was Valentin Iosifovich Stenich (real name: Smetanich), the future translator of James Joyce and John Dos Passos into Russian. Yury Terapiano, the poet, also knew Mandelstam in 'Khlam' and has left memoirs of the experience.[14]

He soon found a job through a certain Zubkov, the Commissar in charge of Sobes (a portmanteau word, the expansion of which means 'social maintenance'), which was an organization similar to Lunacharsky's Narkompros.

> And then something very comical happened [Nadezhda Yakovlevna told me]. He got my friends, the artists, and Ehrenburg to come to work there. And he kept me as his private secretary. Led me around by the hand – we were already man and wife by that time. But Ehrenburg demanded that I really be an actual secretary and wanted me to do something for him. But Osia wouldn't have it, wouldn't allow it.

What happened when General Denikin's White Army briefly drove the Red Army out of Kiev and occupied the Ukrainian capital was not, however, so comical. Living in the hotel that housed the government offices and himself employed in a government agency, Mandelstam was naturally regarded as a Bolshevik. Being Jewish was no help. From Nadezhda Yakovlevna's house in Lipki (Linden Trees), a central (and posh) quarter of the town, they watched in horror as the Whites sought out Bolshevik sympathizers in such scenes as the following, given in her words:

> Across from the Duma – we lived opposite the Duma – there was a mob and they were catching people, women for the most part, and beating them savagely and killing them on the spot. They were looking for some 'Bolshevik Rosa' – somebody they'd dreamed up. I don't know – perhaps there was such a person – but anyway that was the reason given for beating

and killing several dozen people in front of our very eyes. It was terrifying. An insane mob. Osip Emilevich wasn't terribly eager to stay in Kiev after that. He left with some actors and made his way via Kharkov to Koktebel. I didn't go with him. I was simply afraid, so I stayed behind.

The terror of such bestial scenes caused Mandelstam to write of Kiev as the Viy, a hideous Ukrainian legendary monster (who provides the title for one of Gogol's most famous stories). He recalled these events of 1919 in what is probably the last poem he ever wrote, dated May 1937:

> Как по улицам Киева-Вия
> Ищет мужа не знаю чья жинка,
> И на щеки ее восковые
> Ни одна не скатилась слезинка.
>
> Не гадают цыганочки кралям,
> Не играют в Купеческом скрипки,
> На Крещатике лошади пали,
> Пахнут смертью господские Липки.
>
> Уходили с последним трамваем
> Прямо за город красноармейцы,
> И шинель прокричала сырая:
> —Мы вернемся еще, разумейте!

As someone's wife, I don't know whose, looked for her husband down the streets of Kiev, the Viy, not even one teardrop rolled down her waxen cheeks.

Gypsy women are not telling pretty girls' fortunes, the violins aren't playing in Kupechesky Park, on the Kreshchatik horses have fallen dead, and the genteel upper-class quarter, The Lindens, smells of death.

The Red Army soldiers went straight out of town on the last streetcar, and an overcoat, wet with blood, shouted: 'We'll be back again, understand!'

Nadezhda Yakovlevna told me that the wife in this poem was Lyuba Ehrenburg, frantically searching for her husband, who had gone out into the street after the official curfew. It is the only poem that seems to have derived – and very belatedly, at that – from the Kiev of 1919, a period that was in general unproductive. Only two poems, Nos. 105 and 106 are dated 1919. The first was certainly written in Kiev (Terapiano recalls the occasion itself – adding that the last two lines were furnished by the poet Makkaveysky), but they are both informed by the atmosphere of the classical and Christian world of the Crimea, to which Mandelstam was headed.

X

5 December 1919. Mandelstam had already been in Feodosia for five weeks when he wrote to Nadezhda Yakovlevna, in Kiev, the first of his extant letters to her. It tells one something of their life together that the first sentence would have been equally suitable for the last letter in 1938.

My dear child!

There is almost no hope that this letter will reach you. Kolachevsky is going to Kiev tomorrow via Odessa. I pray God you will hear what I say: my child, I can't do without you, and don't want to. You are my whole happiness, my dear one – that's as plain as God's daylight to me. You've become so close to me that I'm always talking to you, calling you, complaining to you. You are the only one I can talk to about everything, everything. My poor darling! You are 'kinechka' to your mother and you're my 'kinechka' too. I am glad and I thank God that He gave you to me. With you nothing will be frightening, nothing painful.

Your little paw, like a baby's, all black from the charcoal, your blue smock – it's all memorable to me, I haven't forgotten anything.

Forgive me for being weak and for not always being able to show how much I love you.

Nadyusha! If you were to turn up here right now I would burst out crying from happiness. My little animal, forgive me! Give me your forehead to kiss – your round little forehead, like a baby's. Daughter, sister – I smile with your smile and hear your voice in the silence.

Yesterday, without meaning to, I thought to myself 'I must find it' – using the *feminine* form of 'must' – for you, that is, you said it *through* me. We're like children, you and I – we don't look for big words but say whatever we have to.

Nadyusha, we're going to be together no matter what, I'll find you and live for you because you give me life without even knowing it, my darling, 'by your immortal tenderness.'

Nadenka! I got four letters all at once, on the same day, only just now… I sent many telegrams, called.

There's only one route open from here now: Odessa – still closer to Kiev. I'm leaving in a few days. Write me in care of Mochulsky at the Odessky Listok [Odessa Sheet]. Maybe I'll get through from Odessa. Somehow, somehow I'll reach you[…].[15]

XI

Whether he ever went to Odessa I don't know. If he did, he soon returned to the Crimean seacoast and stayed there until the summer of 1920 in the company of his brother Alexandr, Ilya Ehrenburg, his usual hosts Maximilian Voloshin and his mother, and a number of people such as Andrey Sedykh, Em. Mindlin, the Sudeykins, and others who have left a rather large fund of memoirs of Mandelstam at this period. The most interesting memoir of all is the poet's own 'Feodosia,' composed as a sort of appendage to his autobiographical *Noise of Time*.[16] Like most of his autobiographical writing, it focusses on other people rather than on himself. There are charming miniatures of Alexandr Alexandrovich Sarandinaki, the Harbor Master, of Colonel Tsygalsky, an officer in Wrangel's Volunteer Army (White), and of an artist named Mazesa da Vinci. But of Mandelstam himself we learn only incidentally and *en passant.* He does not even mention, for example, the presence of his brother Alexandr, whose existence, like that of his other brother Yevgeny, also failed to leave any trace in *The Noise of Time.*

Mandelstam's connection with the personages of the memoir is usually slight. The Harbor Master provided him with an asylum for the night in his marvelous office, glistening with maritime instruments and imposing charts and documents. Mandelstam himself is the 'bird' of the chapter entitled 'The Old Woman's Bird,' for another of his many temporary dwellings was a room in the quarantine quarter, where his aged hostess ministered to him with such daily and dainty cleanings and feedings that he felt like some caged canary. His presence is only implied in the chapter devoted to Colonel Tsygalsky, 'Barmy Zakona' (The Royal Mantle of the Law), and in the last, 'Mazesa da Vinci,' he is altogether absent. In his status as an outsider one can discern a leading theme of the early poetry: that of the loneliness and solitude of the artist. 'Feodosia' also represents another instance of what one might term the controlling metaphor of all Mandelstam's art – the clash of two particular opposites: the frail and beautiful with horror and death. It is a theme that unites the four portraits, where one central trait, gentleness, is constantly felt to emerge in vivid contrast against the background of war and death in the beleaguered little port city. Harbor Master Sarandinaki combines in his person both the powerful 'civic god of the sea' and the gentle soul of a 'sea kitten.' The military officer Colonel Tsygalsky symbolically houses in his quarters both the bedraggled eagle of the Volunteer Army and his own demented sister, whom he nurses and for whom he has a touching solicitude. The artist Mazesa, who himself added the feminine ending to his name, is portrayed as a sort of Renaissance genius *manqué*, more native to the gentle Florence of the painter whose name he assumed than to ravaged Feodosia.

He was almost entirely without means and depended for food and lodging on the kindness of the many intellectuals gathered in Feodosia at the time – another reason for his comparing it to Renaissance Florence. The cultural and artistic life of the little port seems rather to have been quickened than retarded by the dislocations of the Civil War. Mandelstam was a contributor to *Kovcheg* (The Ark), an almanac published by a group of poets in Feodosia in 1920. The literary society FLAK, whose initials stood for *Feodosiiskii literaturno-artisticheskii kruzhok* (Theodosian Literary and Artistic Circle), continued to hold its Saturday night meetings, at which Mandelstam occasionally gave readings. The president of FLAK was Mikhail Vasilevich Mabo, the director of the Azov Bank, mentioned in 'Feodosia' as one of those who gathered daily in Harbor Master Sarandinaki's observatory for the purpose of reading their own poetry and plays. Mabo – or Mabeau, as he spelt his name in the emigration, or Mabo-Azovsky, to give him his *nom de plume* – emigrated to America, where he published a brief memoir of Mandelstam, Voloshin, and other intellectuals whom he had known in Feodosia. It contains a description of one of Mandelstam's readings at a meeting of the society. Under the impression of the poet's general helplessness and unprepossessing presence, Mabo feared that the occasion would turn out to be a fiasco, but he found, as did many others, that Mandelstam underwent a remarkable transformation when he stood before an audience to recite his poetry.

> He came out onto the stage with his head lowered and had the appearance of such a queer fellow. But when he had begun to read he was instantly transformed, just as if he had caught fire with some holy flame...And when he left the stage, accompanied by stormy applause, he was a totally different man.[17]

But life in wartime Feodosia was not all devoted to poetry readings. Sudden and unexplained arrest by the naturally nervous agents of General Wrangel was a daily occurrence. Memoirists such as Terapiano and Odoevtseva mention Mandelstam's earlier arrest or detention in Kiev – for some petty speculation in foodstuffs, for having turned up in the former apartment of a Bolshevik official, and so on – but there is no confirmation of this, however plausible it may be. He was arrested by the Whites in Feodosia, however, and the charge was serious enough.

> Nadezhda Yakovlevna: 'Just before he left Feodosia, some woman working in a Bolshevik underground organization approached him and asked him to take some paper with him, two sheets of white paper. He took them, and right away, in an hour, he was arrested. But on the way to prison he managed to destroy those sheets of paper...'
> Ehrenburg: 'When Wrangel's men arrested Osip Emilevich Mandelstam, Voloshin immediately set out for Feodosia. He returned in a gloomy mood and told us that the Whites regarded Mandelstam as a dangerous criminal. They declared that he was pretending to be mad: when they put him into solitary confinement, he began to knock on the door, and when the guard asked him what he wanted, he replied, "You must let me out – I'm not made for prison." When he was being questioned, Osip Emilevich interrupted the interrogator: "Tell me, do you release those who are innocent or not?" I can understand that in 1919 in the counter-intelligence such words sounded fantastic, and that a White officer might take them as an attempt to feign mental illness; but if you think about it – forget about tactics, even about strategy – was there not in Mandelstam's behavior a deeply human truth? He did not try to prove his innocence to the hangman but just asked the straightforward question – was there any point in his talking at all? He told the jailer that he was "not made for prison"; that is childish and at the same time – wise.'[18]
> Nadezhda Yakovlevna: 'They let him go. Ehrenburg writes that it was Voloshin that got him out, but that's wrong. Voloshin arrived after he'd already been set free. It was Colonel Tsygalsky, the one in *The Noise of Time*, that got him out. Voloshin was late, that's all.'

In the Crimea in 1920 there were many preparing, like Harbor Master Sarandinaki himself, for the 'joyous flight across the Atlantic' to escape the consequences of 1917. Did Mandelstam also contemplate an escape from what he was later to call the 'black velvet of Soviet night'? The evidence is frail. Mabo, who helped Mandelstam materially with food and shelter, recalled his having often expressed a desire to flee such scenes as he had witnessed in Kiev and perhaps also the 'time of silence' that he had foreseen that New Year's Eve of 1916. It was his penniless condition, Mabo thought, rather than any lack of desire, that caused Mandelstam to remain. But we are now in possession of a fact that Mabo and most of Mandelstam's friends lacked at that time: they knew nothing of his attachment to Nadezhda Yakovlevna Khazina.

Whatever the reason for his remaining, Mandelstam and his brother Alexandr set out that August for what was to prove an adventurous trip back to Moscow. Three years later, he published an account of the first stage of their journey. Entitled 'Mensheviks in Georgia,'[19] the article contains only one sentence alluding to his stay in the Feodosia jail:

> Iphigenia's homeland lay exhausted under the soldier's heel. And I had to look at the beloved, dry, wormwood hills of Feodosia and at the Cimmerian hills from the window of a prison and to stroll about a burnt-out little courtyard where some terrified Jews had been gathered into a tight little bunch and the mutinous officers hunted for lice in their field shirts...

He and his brother managed to board a small, flat-bottomed Azov barge, crowded to the rails with deck passengers consisting of the multinational rabble that was abandoning the Crimea, and, after a trip of seven days across the Black Sea, arrived in Batum – 'the only air-hole for the Crimea.' At this time (1918–21) Georgia was an independent republic under a government composed largely of Mensheviks. Batum was a nightmare of intrigue, espionage real and imagined, arrests, and deportation back to Feodosia. The latter was especially dangerous, since the counter-intelligence of the Volunteer Army, closely cooperating with the counter-intelligence of the Mensheviks in Georgia (according to Mandelstam), regarded it as irrefutable evidence of complicity with the Bolsheviks. Persons sent back to Feodosia were shot at once.

Here is the translation of part of Mandelstam's account:

> Three days after arriving I became involuntarily acquainted with the military governor of Batum. We had the following conversation:
> 'Where did you come from?'
> 'The Crimea.'
> 'You can't come to us.'
> 'Why not?'
> 'We have too little bread.'

Suddenly he explained: 'We live so well that if we were to permit it everyone would come here.'

That marvelously, astonishingly naive, classical sentence became deeply impressed in my memory. The little 'independent' government that had grown up on someone else's blood wanted to be bloodless. They hoped to go down in history pure and safe, hemmed in by threatening powers, to become something like a new Switzerland – a neutral plot of ground, congenitally 'innocent.'

'You will have to go back.'

'But I don't want to stay here – I'm going to Moscow.'

'No matter. We have a rule: everyone goes back where he came from.'

The audience was terminated. During our conversation some suspicious-looking people had been poking about the room and now, pointing greedily and excitedly in my direction, they were trying to convince the governor of something. In the stream of incomprehensible words, one could always be made out: Bolshevik.

People were lying on the floor. It was crowded as a hen-house. An Austrian prisoner of war, a sailor from Kerch, a man who had incautiously wandered into the Soviet mission, a bourgeois from Constantinople, a demented young Turk who kept scrubbing the floor with a tooth brush, a White officer who had fled from Gandzha. The French mission went the officer's bail. The Turk was given his freedom to the accompaniment of kicks. The rest were to go to the Crimea. There were a lot of us. We were given nothing to eat, as in an Oriental prison. A few had money. The guards would kindly go after bread and grapes. The door would be opened to admit a sturdy, ruddy-faced tavern keeper with a tray of Persian tea... One was released. Once again he blundered into the Soviet mission and on the following day he came back to us. It was like a farce, like some operetta. Jokingly, facetiously, people were being dispatched to where they would be killed – because, for the counter-intelligence in the Crimea, deportation from Georgia was supremely incriminating evidence, an unmistakable brand.

I went into the city to fetch some bread with a companion who was also my convoy. His name was Chigua. I fixed his name in my memory, for that man saved my life. He said that we had two hours' time, that I might make enquiries and appeals and so on, and that we could go wherever I wished. And he added, furtively, 'I like the Bolsheviks. Are you a Bolshevik, by any chance?' We two – I a rather ragged customer with a look of having done some time at hard labor and with one trouser leg ripped open, and my guard with his rifle – wandered about the little toy streets past coffee houses with orchestras, past Italian offices. There was an aroma of strong Turkish coffee, and from the cellars came the smell of wine. We wandered into editorial offices and trade union headquarters, spreading panic as we went, and knocked at the doors of peaceful houses, led thither by fantastic addresses. We were invariably kicked out. But Chigua knew where he was taking me, and a certain person in one print shop clapped his hands together and made a telephone call. He got in touch with the civilian governor-general. The order came to appear at once with my guard. The old Social Democrat was embarrassed. He apologized. The military authority acted independently of the civil. Nothing to be done. I was free. I could smoke English tobacco and go to Moscow.[20]

The road to Moscow lay through Tiflis, where there was a Soviet embassy. Mandelstam and his brother at once boarded the train which begins its trip of 327 versts to the Georgian capital by crawling northward along the coast to Supsa, where it turns inland to the east through the great fertile plain of the Rion.

By the time the Ehrenburgs arrived (having escaped from the Crimea on a salt barge which nearly sank during a storm on the Black Sea), Mandelstam was thoroughly at home in Tiflis. He had made the acquaintance of two remarkable Georgian poets, Paolo Yashvili and Titsian Tabidze, who provided refuge for homeless Russian poets and writers in Georgia much as Voloshin had done in the Crimea, and during the next two weeks the Ehrenburgs and the Mandelstams passed the time largely in their company.[21] According to one journal,[22] Mandelstam and Ehrenburg gave readings of poetry in Tiflis, but the travellers' main occupation while waiting for the appropriate papers to come from the Soviet embassy appears to have been eating. Under the tutelage of the Georgian poets, the Russians left the opulent table of one 'dukhan' only to commence the following meal in another and thus to repair the damage suffered by their appetites in the starved Crimea. Ehrenburg describes their lodgings, which were less sumptuous:

> Paolo settled us in a grimy old hotel. There were no rooms to be had in the city, and we all had to fit into one room of the hotel: the Mandelstam brothers, Lyuba, Yadviga[23] and I. Osip Emilevich declined the use of a bed – he was afraid of bedbugs and germs. He slept on a high table. When day began to break I would see his profile above me. He slept on his back, and he slept with an air of great solemnity.

Finally the call came from the embassy. Ilya Ehrenburg was appointed a 'diplomatic courier' and given some sealed mail bags to deliver to the Foreign Office in Moscow. The others – Mandelstam and his brother Alexandr, Ehrenburg's wife and daughter, and an anonymous comrade returning from England – were designated in the covering document as 'accompanying' the courier, while a Red Navy man and a young actor of the Moscow Art Theater were named as his 'guard.' The independent republic of Georgia was one of the few nations with whom the Soviet government maintained diplomatic relations at the time, and it was far from sure just how fastidiously the Georgians themselves would respect the immune status of the courier and his seven companions. The trip took eight days and combined intense boredom (Mandelstam recited poetry to relieve this) with various delays and adventures. At Mineralnye Vody a more serious guard of Red Army men with machine guns joined the group. Mandelstam was terrified at the sight of such weapons, but when things came to an actual clash with a contingent of Whites who had torn up the tracks and fired on the train (it was pulled by an armored locomotive), Mandelstam was beside himself and conceived the plan of hiding out in the hills with Lyuba Ehrenburg until the danger had passed. She declined, evidently feeling more secure in the train.

6

From the insane ship to hunchbacked Tiflis

Mandelstam had not been in Moscow long before he had another of his slapstick encounters with Blyumkin, an incident witnessed by Ilya Ehrenburg.[1] Mandelstam was eating in the buffet of the Press House when suddenly Blyumkin popped up from a neighboring table, aimed his pistol at his favorite enemy, and shouted that he was going to shoot him that minute. Mandelstam screamed. The pistol was knocked from Blyumkin's hand and the affair ended as usual, bloodlessly. Mandelstam left for Petersburg, or Petrograd, as it temporarily was.

Life in the desolate, hungry city – no longer even the capital – was dispensed in rations.[2] Nadezhda Yakovlevna cherishes the story of Mandelstam's clothing ration, which had, like many another slip of official paper, to be signed by Maxim Gorky. The ragged clothes that had sufficed in the warm south could not be relied upon in a northern winter, so Mandelstam asked for a sweater and a pair of trousers. In the immemorial manner of bureaucratic chieftains, Gorky allowed half the request, the sweater, but cancelled the trousers, saying something to the effect that Mandelstam deserved no more.

But if Gorky withheld trousers, he provided shelter. He had organized a sort of hostel for homeless writers and intellectuals known as the *Dom iskusstv* (House of the Arts) or, by the inevitable acronym, as *Disk*. It was located in one of the most sumptuous private houses of Petersburg, the former Yeliseev mansion (No. 59, Moyka) on the corner of Nevsky Prospekt and the Moyka Canal. Most of the outstanding writers and artists of the time found shelter in this extraordinary literary dormitory. Olga Forsh has left a fascinating (though imaginatively transformed) picture of the society in Disk in a book called *Sumasshedshii korabl'* (The Insane Ship)[3] – an image of the house itself. Outwardly, the conditions of life were bleak. But Andrey Bely's witticism that the triumph of materialism had abolished matter is indicative not only of the hardness of life: it conveys the almost frivolous intellectual zest that sustained the artists of Petersburg in the absence of more material comforts. All memoirists of the period are at one in this: that the reigning mood was not one of despair but rather of a desperate gaiety. In the house of a fortune deriving from produce, wine, and groceries, the spacious kitchen with its gleaming copper pots and pans (the former staff remained) now provided an ample and warm setting for what amounted practically to an uninterrupted symposium. The participants were such writers as Viktor Shklovsky, Marietta Shaginyan, Bely, Nikolay Klyuev, Yevgeny Zamyatin, Mikhail Slonimsky, Lev Lunts, Mikhail Zoshchenko, Yevgeny Shvarts, Vladislav Khodasevich, Olga Forsh, and many others. There was naturally no single controlling aesthetic or literary tendency.

The central part of the Yeliseev mansion, with its palatial rooms and large halls opening onto the canal, was separated by a solid wall from a smaller section with three façades, where the windows gave onto Bolshaya Morskaya Street, the Nevsky and the Moyka. Mandelstam had a room in this less sumptuous wing, at the end of a corridor on the third floor. This strangely crooked hall led past the rooms of Khodasevich, Lozinsky, Forsh, and Nadezhda Pavlovich, among others, to Mandelstam's even stranger room. The shape, dictated by the curved outer wall and the eccentricities of the corridor, consisted mostly of angles, none of the walls being perpendicular to any other. Khodasevich, as I have already said, found the space satisfyingly like the character of its inhabitant. Viktor Shklovsky saw his fellow tenant in slightly different terms:

> His somehow feminine dissoluteness and birdlike frivolity were not completely devoid of any system. He has the true habit of the artist, and an artist lies in order to be free in the only affair that concerns him; he is like the monkey who, according to the Hindus, does not talk so that he will not be forced to work.[4]

The almost frenzied mood of desolate merrymaking that reigned among the passengers on the insane ship can be seen in another incident. In the midst of their real deprivations, when the actual necessities of life were often wanting, the poets and writers of Petrograd arranged a fancy-dress ball. It took place on 11 January 1921 in the 'school of rhythm' on the Millionaya. Nadezhda Pavlovich describes some preparations for it in her memoir of Blok:

> Someone succeeded in getting the theater of opera and ballet (formerly the Mariinsky) to lend us the masquerade costumes. They were fairly well rumpled and had to be repaired and ironed. The ironing board was set up in my long, narrow room. The servants in the House of the Arts were the former footmen and doormen of the Yeliseevs. That evening someone asked the old footman Yefim where Mandelstam was, and he got a very recherché answer: 'Mr Mandelstam is in Mrs Pavlovich's room ironing a toad.' This was later repeated everywhere.[5]

But literary evenings, one may be sure, were more commonplace. At one of them, held in the Poets' Club on 21 October 1920, Mandelstam read his poem on Venice (No. 110), a masterpiece of visual splendor. The opulent phonetics and the brilliant imagery of glass, mirrors, candles and the green Adriatic must have contrasted about as strangely with the daily life of its first audience as the *bal masqué*.

Веницейской жизни мрачной и бесплодной
Для меня значение светло.
Вот она глядит с улыбкою холодной
В голубое дряхлое стекло.

Тонкий воздух кожи. Синие прожилки.
Белый снег. Зелёная парча.
Всех кладут на кипарисные носилки,
Сонных, тёплых вынимают из плаща.

И горят, горят в корзинах свечи,
Словно голубь залетел в ковчег.
На театре и на праздном вече
Умирает человек.

Ибо нет спасенья от любви и страха:
Тяжелее платины Сатурново кольцо!
Чёрным бархатом завешанная плаха
И прекрасное лицо.

Тяжелы твои, Венеция, уборы,
В кипарисных рамах зеркала.
Воздух твой гранёный. В спальне тают горы
Голубого дряхлого стекла.

Только в пальцах роза или склянка—
Адриатика зелёная, прости!
Что же ты молчишь, скажи, венецианка,
Как от этой смерти праздничной уйти?

Чёрный Веспер в зеркале мерцает.
Всё проходит. Истина темна.
Человек родится. Жемчуг умирает.
И Сусанна старцев ждать должна.   (1920)

Of the gloomy, fruitless life of Venice
the meaning is clear to me.
See where it peers with its cold smile
into the blue, decrepit glass.

Subtle leather smell. Dark blue veins.
White snow. Green brocade.
Everyone put in sedans of cypress wood,
taken warm and sleepy from his cloak.

And candles burning, burning in their baskets
like the dove flown back into the ark.
On the stage and in the idle
assembly, man is dying.

For there's no salvation from love and terror:
Saturn's ring is heavier than platinum!
The executioner's block and the beautiful face
are both veiled in black velvet.

Heavy are thy garments, O Venice,
thy mirrors in cypress frames.
Thine air has facets, and in the bedrooms thaw
mountains of blue, decrepit glass.

Only, fingers hold a rose or phial –
green Adriatic, farewell!
Why are you silent? Say, Venetian lady,
how does one evade this festive death?

Black Vesper flits in the mirror.
All passes. Truth is dark.
Man is born. Pearl dies.
And Susanna must await the elders.

Alexandr Blok was in the audience. Later, he went home to make the following note in his diary.

> The high point of the evening was Osip Mandelstam, who arrived from a stay in Wrangel's prison. He has grown greatly. At first one can't bear to listen to the sing-song that is common among Gumilyov's set, but one gradually gets used to it. He is clearly an artist. His poetry arises out of dreams, extremely original dreams, which lie wholly within the realm of art.[6]

Sitting next to Blok on the same occasion was Nadezhda Pavlovich, who has recorded her impressions not only of Mandelstam but of Blok's reaction to Mandelstam.

> The most interesting evening was the one at which Osip Mandelstam gave a public reading – the first since his return to Petrograd.
> He brought some magnificent poems, and Blok listened to him with great interest, especially to his poem about Venice, which recalled to Alexandr Alexandrovich his own Venetian impressions.
> Mandelstam's face was not striking on first glance. Thin, with slight, irregular features, he reminded one in his whole aspect of the people in Chagall's paintings. But then he began to read, in a sing-song way and slightly rocking to the rhythm of the verse. Blok and I were sitting side by side. Suddenly he touched my sleeve softly and with his eyes pointed toward the face of Osip Emilevich. I have never seen a human face so transformed by inspiration and self-forgetfulness. Mandelstam's homely, insignificant face had become the face of a seer and prophet. Alexandr Alexandrovich was also astonished by this.[7]

Mandelstam had one love affair that lasted – that with Nadezhda Yakovlevna. But both before and after his meeting her he was capable of many other love affairs that were, though seemingly intense, transient and without consequence. Without consequence in life, that is, for they left their traces in his poetry. In Petrograd in the autumn of 1920 Mandelstam fell deeply, and briefly, in love with Olga Nikolaevna Arbenina, a beautiful actress of the Alexandrinsky Theater.[8] Anna Akhmatova, who played the role of confidante in Mandelstam's several affairs, told me in 1962 that everything in his poetry having to do with the theater in Petersburg is linked by some strand or another to Arbenina. Three poems at least, Akhmatova said, belong entirely to her: Nos. 119, 120 and 122. Like the poem to Tsvetaeva discussed below (p. 221), the first is a 'love poem' only very indirectly and only, perhaps, to those who wish to read that through the historical myth that encloses it: the Greek attack in the Trojan horse against Priam's city, to recover Helen. The second is an everyday interior scene – a poem made of a kitchen conversation. The third, addressed, like the second, to a woman, is more conventionally a 'love poem,' the love in this case being disappointed. (I shall discuss all three in greater detail in analyzing *Tristia*.[9])

It was in another institution organized by Gorky, the publishing house *Vsemirnaia Literatura* (Universal Literature), that Mandelstam found an opportunity to make some money by translating. Gorky's plan was to enrich and enlarge proletarian culture by providing Russian versions of foreign literature and also, of course, to give employment to starving writers. Mandelstam despised translation, especially translation in verse, even though Innokenty Annensky, a poet revered by Mandelstam and himself a masterful translator, had urged him to practise that discipline as a means of learning verse technique. Nadezhda Yakovlevna, who told me this fact, continued:

> So he tried to translate Mallarmé, and he came out with a line of such unheard-of stupidity that he laughed over it the rest of his life:
>
> I molodaia mat', kormiashchaia so sna
>
> [which means: 'And the young mother, nursing as she wakes from sleep' – the joke being that *so sna* 'from sleep' is phonically identical to *sosna* 'pine tree' and the phrase following the comma might also mean 'the nursing pine tree' – C.B.]. So ever afterwards when I had to jump on him for translating so badly, I'd say 'nursing pine tree!' Or he would say it himself: 'another nursing pine tree!'
>
> I'll tell you another funny thing that happened with translations [she went on]. This was much later. In Voronezh, he and I translated some Maupassant. I think he did 'Yvette.' I took the manuscripts to Moscow and sat down to correct them and proofread what the typist had done, and suddenly I realized that some sort of butler was talking in the story. There wasn't any in the text. I thought it must be another edition. Took another edition out: no butler. Then it dawned on me what had happened. Mandelstam hadn't even translated – he'd described one of the illustrations! There was an illustration in the book showing some sort of very dignified butler. I mean, he was *so* bored by translation that he couldn't even read the text!

Like it or not, in the decade following, Mandelstam was to be heavily, and on one occasion grimly, involved in the labor of turning French, German, even English works into Russian. The art of translation has had a strange, dual fate in Russia. On the one hand, there have been translators of genius, like Zhukovsky, one of the greatest poets of the Golden Age, who was almost exclusively a translator, or Pasternak, whose versions of Shakespeare are works of original genius. Partly because of this, no doubt, Russia has produced brilliant critics and theoreticians of translation – the greatest of them all being a Leningrad scholar of the present day, Yefim Etkind. On the other hand, translation has acquired a bad smell as a sort of intellectual Siberia to which writers whose own work is politically suspect are banished. In this respect, translation is like that other asylum for writers in disgrace, children's literature. For Mandelstam, translation was at first a means of earning the money to live on, but as the 1920s wore on it became increasingly his first exile. During the long period when Mandelstam's name dropped from public view – roughly from the early 1930s until the late 1950s – one line in Kozmin's dictionary of Russian writers was widely credited as true, there being little information to the contrary: 'From 1923 on occupied himself almost exclusively with translations' (p. 178). The general acceptance of this has been a source of bitterness to those who knew something of the real work that Mandelstam was accomplishing in the 1920s and 1930s.

When the Guild of Poets was first organized some four years before the war, it was a non-partisan group – or more precisely, it was a multi-partisan group – and included Blok, Klyuev, and Alexey Tolstoy as well as Gumilyov, Akhmatova, and Mandelstam. But it quickly developed into the stronghold of Acmeism alone. No one denies that the Guild was the creature of Nikolay Gumilyov, and when he left for the war it was, as we have seen, left leaderless and consequently disbanded. Toward the end of 1920 a second Guild of Poets was established in Petrograd by Gumilyov, who declared that it would be like the original, that is, non-Acmeist, Guild, and invited Vladislav Khodasevich to join. Khodasevich agreed, but before going to the organization meeting he dropped in to see Mandelstam, his neighbor in the House of the Arts. Why had Mandelstam said nothing about the revival of the former Acmeist group, Khodasevich wanted to know. Mandelstam laughed,

'But because there is no Guild. Blok, Sologub, and Akhmatova have all refused...Gumilyov only wants to play at being chairman. He likes playing with toy soldiers. And you got in. There is no one there except the Gumilyovlings [Gumiliata].'
'But, forgive me, what are you yourself doing in such a Guild?'
'I am drinking tea with jam.'[10]

90

Mandelstam's relationship with Gumilyov was no doubt rather complicated. In daily life, they appear to have been on a very friendly footing and to have treated each other with great mutual respect. But this could hardly have been the case in their artistic life. Gumilyov, a born teacher and critic, had been immensely useful to Mandelstam at a crucial period in the younger poet's life, but for all their shared 'Acmeism,' they were too different as poets to have enjoyed much mutuality. Georgy Ivanov quotes Mandelstam as having said, 'I struggle with him as Jacob struggled with God.' And he asserts that their relationship with each other in artistic matters was the purest 'love-hate.' *Se non è vero, è ben trovato.* Adamovich reports another revealing remark:

> Mandelstam was very friendly with him, loved him, and valued his opinions, although he was unable to overcome his indifference to what Gumilyov wrote. I remember exactly, word for word, one of his remarks about Gumilyov's poetry: 'He has come so far out of the woods that there are no trees left.' It was clear that Gumilyov's plastic and somewhat insipid 'perfection,' deriving in the best instance from Théophile Gautier, struck Mandelstam as insufficient, as having been achieved too easily.[11]

We shall know a good deal more about Mandelstam's feelings for Gumilyov if and when his memoir of the Acmeist syndic ever comes to light. Anna Akhmatova writes that Mandelstam dictated it to her in 1925, but I know nothing more about it.[12] In the meantime, there is his letter to her, written from Yalta on 25 August 1928 – that is to say, just after the seventh anniversary of Gumilyov's execution, a fact which could hardly have failed to influence the writer's feelings:

> You must know that I have the capacity for carrying on imaginary conversations with only two people – with Nikolay Stepanovich and with you. My conversation with Kolya has never been interrupted and will never be interrupted.[13]

What would have become of Gumilyov as a poet will never be known. His conception of poetry was evidently undergoing an interesting change at about this time, but there was no 'late' Gumilyov, as there was no 'late' Lermontov. He was a young man of 33 on the day in August 1921 when the Cheka arrested him for complicity in the so-called Tagantsev plot to overthrow the Bolshevik power. My colleague Nina Berberova had met Gumilyov a short while before when she entered a group of young poets organized by him under the name *Zvuchashchaia Rakovina* (The Sounding Shell). She recalls strolling with him about the streets of Petrograd on 3 August and places the time of his arrest on the next day. Efforts to gain his release led to nothing. He was shot by a firing squad some three weeks later (the exact date is still in the files of the secret police – and so, perhaps, is the poetry that Gumilyov said, in a letter to his wife, he was writing in prison). An amazing assortment of people were wiped out by the same firing squad on the same charge – 61 in all –

including former officers like Gumilyov, but also simple sailors, writers, scholars, workers, and even their wives.

Mandelstam had so great a horror of violence and above all of execution that even the death of his old tormentor Blyumkin, who was shot for his Trotskyist activities, sent him into a sick depression. His reaction to Gumilyov's fate can only be imagined.

He was spared at least the proximity of the slaughter, for he had left Petrograd in early March 1921 and travelled via Moscow to Kiev, where he rejoined Nadezhda Yakovlevna Khazina, from whom he was never again to be separated for long. By June of that year they had set out together for Tiflis, travelling, as I have already mentioned, under the protection of Mandelstam's former assistant in Narkompros and now head of the evacuation of the Caucasus, Lopatinsky. Mandelstam wrote to Nadezhda Yakovlevna's mother as they were on the way to assure her that all was well, that Nadya was eating properly, and that letters might reach them at the central evacuation office in Rostov. He closed with a paragraph that opens an immense perspective into what might have been a possible future for him:

> Before leaving, we'll submit the application to the Lithuanian Mission. The grounds (my papers) have been acknowledged as *sufficient*. It will take a month and will go through automatically while we're away.[14]

He was thinking of applying for Lithuanian citizenship. His having been born in Warsaw and his father's origin from Kurland were a help. The Symbolist poet Yurgis Baltrushaitis, a Lithuanian himself and that country's ambassador in Moscow from 1921 to 1939, had urged him to take the step, and now Mandelstam was evidently on the verge of doing so. It is worth noting that this was before the arrest of Gumilyov. For some reason, he changed his mind. 'You can't escape your fate,' Nadezhda Yakovlevna writes as she laconically closes the books on that future, 'and better not to try.'[15]

The Mandelstams lived in the railway car of Lopatinsky's train, which evidently made its way by such lurches as the times allowed. In Baku they encountered Mandelstam's early mentor Vyacheslav Ivanov, and at some point or other Sergey Gorodetsky, the co-chairman of Acmeism and its earliest apostate (he lost no time denouncing the executed Gumilyov), came to visit them in their car. There was always something of the stage Russian about Gorodetsky. In speaking of another such type, Bezymensky, Mandelstam called them strongmen who lift cardboard weights. Gorodetsky brought not only his bluster but also bottles of wine and little goblets to drink it from. Nadezhda Yakovlevna, meeting him for the first time, found him distinctly unprepossessing. She told me something that seems revealing not only about Gumilyov and Gorodetsky, but also about the literary 'schools' of the time:

From the very beginning, even though he was still a young man, he made the immediate impression on me of being a senile idiot. I kept asking Mandelstam why they had associated themselves with such an idiot, and he explained that Gorodetsky had been very popular at the time, and that was what Gumilyov wanted. It was a political move of Gumilyov's, so to speak, to take into the group where there were only young poets at least one who was already popular.

In Tiflis they lived for a while with Sergey Bagdatev, a prominent Bolshevik in the Causasus, but were soon without shelter again when for some reason everyone in the building was transferred elsewhere. Mandelstam was turned away from the local House of the Arts, which was for Georgian poets. The formerly cordial relationship with Tabidze and Yashvili was not resumed, though Mandelstam was friends with many younger Georgian poets of the same group, known as the Golubye Rogi (Blue Horns). He continued to translate for his daily bread. He translated some of the Blue Horns poets themselves (Nos. 464, 465) as well as the Georgian classic Vazha Pshavela – working, of course, from literal Russian versions since he knew no Georgian. He was so taken with Pshavela that for once he drew great satisfaction from the task of turning a foreign poem into Russian. His version of the long narrative poem 'Gogotur and Apshina' (No. 466) is regarded by Georgians adept in both languages as a great triumph.[16]

Mandelstam always held to one and the same idea – that he mustn't live in 'literature,' not depend on 'literature.' He was forever wanting to acquire some profession for himself. But it was always pure fantasy. He went to the Tsentrosoiuz [the main consumers' cooperative organization – C.B.] in Batum at about this time and tried to get a place there in the cooperative.[17] But instead of a job they proposed that he give a lecture on Blok, which he did. Blok had just died.[18] That ended that connection.

Returning to Tiflis, Mandelstam went to the legation of the Russian Republic where Legran, who had been a schoolmate of Gumilyov's in the Tsarskoe Selo Gymnasium, was ambassador. It was Legran who informed him that Gumilyov had been executed. Nadezhda Yakovlevna was present:

I recall hearing at that moment something that I was later to hear over and over through the years. Legran's wife said, 'I never did like Gumilyov.' So that method of saying farewell to those who perished had already begun even then. Probably she really didn't like him.

The effort to settle in Georgia was a failure. Russians in general were *personae non gratae*, and refugees from the Civil War like Mandelstam and his wife, who were little better than beggars in their ragged clothes, were especially unwelcome. At the end of 1921 the pair went back to Batum – where they ran across the young Mikhail Bulgakov, as ragged and hungry as they – and from there set out on the steamer *Dmitry*, bound for the Russian port of Novorossiisk. The eve of the New Year, ·1922, found them in one of the ports of call, Sukhum. A woman who had formerly been a nursemaid but was now the commissar in charge of the *Dmitry* took them under her protection and gave them sleeping space on the floor of her cabin. The refuge was godsent. The human cargo of the ship was a terrifying rabble composed mostly of Red Army soldiers who had just been discharged. Nadezhda Yakovlevna, who had witnessed the White atrocities in Kiev, was later to call this her most vividly horrible impression of the Civil War. All the filth, violence and menace seemed to concentrate itself in one particular episode – an epileptic seizure that overcame one of the men. When the Mandelstams were able to set foot on Russian soil once again, Novorossiisk seemed to them like home. They found a place to stay the night in a newspaper office. Mandelstam soon found employment there. A short while later, the paper transferred him to Rostov, where a number of his articles appeared in the newspaper *Sovetskii Iug* (The Soviet South), some of them later being republished in the central press.

The fugitive pieces of journalism that Mandelstam turned out in various remote provinces of Russia have been only partly recovered. Of those we have, some are now interesting chiefly for having been written by Mandelstam. Others retain an intrinsic interest. The witty and high-spirited article on Batum provides not only a fascinating picture of that town but also allows one to infer from it Mandelstam's own recent life there. His picture of the Tsentrosoiuz, for instance, strikes one differently when one recalls his own efforts to use it as an escape from hated 'Literature.'

Batum is like something you could hold in the palm of your hand. You don't have any sense of the limits or distances of it. You run around in it as you might run around in a room, and what is more the air is always sort of steamy, the way it is in a room. The mechanism of that little, almost toy-like city, which present conditions have raised to the status of a kind of Russian profiteering California, is unusually simple. There's one main-spring – the Turkish lira. The lira must change its value overnight, when everyone's asleep, because people wake up in the morning to find a new rate of exchange for the lira and no one knows how it happened. The lira pulses in the blood of every Batumian, and the people who announce the next morning's rate are those who sell you your breakfast roll.

These are very calm, polite, pleasant Turks, who sell a traditional lavash made from very clean fresh American wheat. In the morning bread costs ten lira, in the afternoon fourteen, that evening eighteen, and the next morning, for some reason, twelve.

As for occupations, the Batumians have absolutely none. A man's natural condition counts as trade. Soviet workers stand out against the background of the native population for two things: their having no lira and their association with black bread, the existence of which has never registered on the retina of a single Batumian. [. . .]

The reigning language in Batum is Russian. Even the most inveterate foreigners start speaking Russian the day after they arrive. This is all the more amusing since there are practically no Russians in Batum, and for that matter Georgians themselves are not numerous. It's a city with no nationality: the people there lost it chasing after easy profits.

Here's an incident that shows how profoundly estranged Batum is. In the largest local moviehouse an Italian film set in Russia is showing; and the title alone is worth the price of admission – 'Wanda Warenida'! In this flabbergasting scenario Russian women walk about as if they were Turkish – in black veils – which they take off only inside the house. The Russian 'princes' prance about in operatic costumes right out of *A Life for the Tsar* and go riding in troikas equipped with English harness, while the sleighs themselves look like complicated Scandinavian Viking ships.

I was in the audience. No one in that packed auditorium was astonished or laughed. Everyone apparently found it completely natural. And it was only when the Italians showed a Russian wedding with the young pair being led into the church wearing some sort of huge crowns that a few Red Army men in the audience couldn't take it any longer and began hooting.

Emigrants from the Crimea are extremely common in Batum at the moment. The Crimea has now got very poor, it's hard to manage there, and so every time the *Pestel* docks it unloads a cargo of refugees from Feodosia, Yalta, and Sevastopol. They first wander uncertainly along Greek Street but after a few days they sprout their feathers and become citizens of the free city.

The pleasantest things in commercial Batum are the houses of commerce themselves. There is a comeliness and culture in them that is lacking in the precocious Italian and other European business firms, where the presiding atmosphere is vain bustling and an unpleasant predatory spirit. There is one point in which the commerce of the Orient leaves that of Europe simply nowhere: commerce is not merely an apparatus of distribution – it is a social phenomenon, and you sense in the customs of Oriental commerce a respect for the human being, who is not simply to be robbed and eaten with kasha.

Twilight comes, but Batum doesn't want to go to bed. Until late at night an unbroken avalanche of people in festive mood goes back and forth along Marinskaya Street. You sense that everyone in the crowd has 'closed a deal' and is now reaping the fruits of his commercial subtlety. The brilliantly lit stalls and gateways are filled with fruit and with that joy of the southern winter, mandarin oranges. Some enterprising dirty-faced brats dance the *lezghinka* and then throw themselves right under the feet of passers-by, who become terrified and have to buy their way out with some small tip. The crowd is so lively that its loud joyous racket comes up to the fourth floor and lulls your first sleep.

And at that hour entire blocks of the city are dead as a desert. Those are the special blocks of shops near the sea. Whole streets of them, extinguished, in darkness, with shutters locked tight by heavy iron padlocks.

Only watchmen wander about with their unremitting rattles guarding the sleeping billions. Through some of the iron shutters, though, one can see light, for people also live in the shops. The fact is that there are no apartments in Batum. There is not even a 'housing crisis.' That has been eliminated in a very simple way: the lack of rooms is so totally irrevocable that no one would ever take it into his head to go look for one. If you are a newcomer to Batum they don't ask where you live, they ask where you spend the night. People are so afraid of these homeless new arrivals that there isn't a single coffee-house where you can leave your baggage from the station: the proprietors are sure that you mean to come back and spend the night – and that they dread like the plague.[19]

Another article in *Soviet South* reveals that the inspiration of editors does not vary greatly with time or country. It is the usual commemorative bit on a notable anniversary. Entitled 'The Bloody Mystery-Play of 9 January,' it appeared in the issue for 22 January (the dates are the same, the first being Old Style and the second New).[20] This dealt with the event that had triggered the 1905 Revolution: the massacre in Petersburg of the procession led by the priest Gapon to demand from the Tsar a redress of various grievances. Mandelstam's article is as fervently revolutionary as the context demanded. More characteristic of him is his depiction of the event as a stage spectacle, specifically as a religious mystery, and one that had to obey the stern necessity imposed by the very geography of its stage, the ineluctably centripetal force of the street-plan of Petersburg.

He was also writing articles of a more literary nature during his stay in Rostov. One of them was printed under the title 'A Letter about Russian Poetry' in the Rostov newspaper *Molot* (The Hammer).[21] The title was almost a traditional one for such survey articles as this, but in recent years it had become associated most closely with the name of Nikolay Gumilyov. At any rate, the partisan anti-Symbolist zeal of Mandelstam's piece recalls the pre-war heyday of the 'schools' battle in Petersburg. The Symbolists, Mandelstam wrote, had turned out to be like those grandiose buildings erected for international exhibitions and, immediately afterwards, taken down and carted away. For the Symbolist Blok, however, Mandelstam reserved the highest possible praise: his poetry was the standard by which Russian poetry was to be measured.

'It will always be a curious and mysterious question, where the poet Blok came from,' Mandelstam wrote. 'Who were your people?' – this question, asked by one of the damned in the *Divine Comedy*, was to strike Mandelstam with especial force when he wrote his essay on Dante, for it was the one that he himself was forever asking in his critical writing. His intuition of the essential wholeness of a cultural tradition demanded an answer. His own response to the question of Blok's origin came in another essay written to commemorate the first anniversary of his death in 1922 and published in the August issue of Isay Lezhnev's journal *Rossiia* (Russia).[22]

'A Letter about Russian Poetry' contained brief genealogies of other Russian poets. One of them, that for his close friend Akhmatova, is strikingly insightful. It has been often quoted as an example of how Mandelstam can enclose a brilliant critical aperçu in a few seemingly casual phrases:

> Akhmatova brought into the Russian lyric all the enormous complexity and wealth of the nineteenth-century Russian novel. If it weren't for Tolstoy's *Anna Karenina*, Turgenev's *Nest of Gentlefolk*, all of Dostoevsky and even some of Leskov, there would be no Akhmatova. Akhmatova's origins lie completely within Russian prose, not poetry. She developed her poetic form, keen and original, with a backward glance at psychological prose.

Another essay in *The Hammer* suggests some of the reasons why Mandelstam was not so warmly received by the poets of Tiflis as he formerly had been. In 'Something about Georgian Art,'[23] he took them all to task for what he pictures as little better than their toadying to European poetry, filling their own verse with the images of Paris while ignoring what Mandelstam himself found to be the brilliant images of their native Georgia. Margvelashvili, recalling the episode in 1967, writes that his countrymen were so incensed by Mandelstam's reading them a lesson in patriotism that they replied in a polemical article of their own.[24] I have not seen it, but I can well imagine that they found ammunition to defend themselves in Mandelstam's own poetry, filled as it is with the images of Western culture from Antiquity to his own day.

In Rostov the Mandelstams made the acquaintance of a surgeon, a certain Professor Trinkler from Kharkov, who had been provided a private lounge-car to come to Rostov to perform an operation, no doubt on a prominent Bolshevik. Kharkov was about half-way to Kiev and Nadezhda Yakovlevna's parents, whom they were hoping eventually to rejoin. Professor Trinkler kindly took them aboard on his return trip and even put them up in Kharkov, where they remained for a while. They met a number of young writers in Kharkov – Grigory Nikolaevich Petnikov and Valentin Kataev among them – and found the atmosphere intellectually stimulating. Nadezhda Yakovlevna recalls that it was in Kharkov that they first heard of Freud, Spengler, and Einstein's theory of relativity. They were greedy for such conversation after the skimpy mental regimen of remote Georgia.

It was in Kharkov that Mandelstam wrote one of the most important of his critical essays, 'O prirode slova' (On the Nature of the Word).[25] The sister of the Premier of the Ukraine, Kristian Georgievich Rakovsky, had organized a small private publishing house in Kharkov under the name *Istoki* (Sources) and commissioned Mandelstam to write the essay, which appeared as a separate booklet, and also a memoir of the literary life in Petersburg. Before this latter work could be brought out, the publishing venture failed, and Mandelstam's first artistic prose was thus lost. It was entitled 'Shuba' (The Fur Coat) and contained reminiscences of life in the House of the Arts in Petrograd. Nadezhda Yakovlevna recalls that parts of it did appear in some newspaper in Kharkov, but as of this writing, it has not been recovered.

The Mandelstams stayed in Kiev for only a few days, but it was long enough to tidy up one aspect of their relationship: they got married. Their union was always a *mariage d'amour*, but on the occasion of its official registration it was a *mariage de convenance* in the strictest sense – the train compartment that they had managed to get for the trip to Moscow could only be occupied by a provably married couple. 'So we nipped into the ZAGS (Registry Office),' Nadezhda Yakovlevna said. Years later, after Mandelstam's posthumous rehabilitation, the official record proved to be useful again, for the legal status of his widow made it possible for her to be recognized as his heir and thus receive the occasional few roubles when some outlying journal published a poem or two.

The journey back from the periphery to the center had taken in all some two months, for they arrived in Moscow in the early spring of 1922. For a period of two weeks they could find nowhere to live. Nikolay Gudzy, later a prominent scholar and historian of Russian literature, put them up for a few days, and they finally managed to get a room in the House of Herzen, an institution at No. 25 Tverskoy Boulevard that sheltered writers much as the soon-to-be defunct House of the Arts had done in Petrograd. They lived there until August 1923.

The wing of approaching night

The work that had accumulated since 1916 now constituted a second book of poems, which was published this year under rather mysterious circumstances. In Leningrad on a visit, Mandelstam arranged to sell them to a certain Blokh, whose publishing house, Petropolis, carried 'Petersburg–Berlin' as the place of publication, it being the practice to bring out Russian books in the West to gain international copyright protection. Mandelstam received a small advance but returned to Moscow without settling many important matters such as the sequence of the poems or even...the title. Undismayed, the casual Blokh asked Mikhail Kuzmin to think up a title, which he did – happily, I think – by naming it *Tristia* after one of the greatest poems in it. Blokh then took the manuscripts off to Berlin and printed an edition of 3,000 copies, the poems being more or less randomly placed in an approximate chronological sequence. With his customary editorial fastidiousness he allowed the book to appear with the wrong date (1921) on the cover, though the title-page bore the correct 1922. In a rather complicated review the Futurist poet and critic Sergey Bobrov managed first to dismiss everything that Mandelstam had written up to this point (along with the whole of Acmeism) and then to conclude with high praise for his new work, stopping just short of comparing him to Pushkin.[1]

The early 1920s and in particular the year 1923 saw the beginning of Mandelstam's fall from grace. It was very gradual and to those not in the know almost imperceptible, but that was when it began – not in the 1930s. I have found that a number of Russian dissidents are eager that this fact should be understood, for it was the fate of others besides Mandelstam, and in 1966 when the novelist Sholokhov dutifully attacked the already condemned Sinyavsky and Daniel by saying that the camps were too good for such traitors and that 'in the Twenties we should have known what to do with them,' the remark was received almost with relief, as though Sholokhov had finally blurted out an inconvenient truth: that was when the repressions began that culminated in the bloodbath a decade and a half later. Mandelstam's name, which at the very beginning of the 1920s had figured on many prominent mastheads, began to vanish from them now as though at some signal. He was still received in the vestibules of power. He could enlist Bukharin's aid in quashing some charge that had been brought against his brother Yevgeny, for instance,[2] but in 1922 he could not help the homeless Khlebnikov find a room. This was a bitter defeat, for the 'Acmeist of Acmeists' was a tremendous admirer of the Futurist Khlebnikov. He took him to Nikolay Berdyaev, who was, before his exile that same year, acting head of the Writers' Union, and screamed at him that his protégé was a 'great Russian poet,' to the intense pleasure of Khlebnikov but to no avail. The room in question went to D. Blagoy. Shortly thereafter, Khlebnikov and his great friend, the artist P. V. Miturich, set out for Astrakhan, but on the way Khlebnikov died an agonizing death from some obscure malady (28 July 1922) in a small village.

Mandelstam's efforts on his brother's behalf took him to Nikolay Bukharin for the first time. Bukharin, who was later on to be Mandelstam's protector in many ways, also attempted to aid him on this occasion by printing some of his work in *Izvestia*, of which he was then editor. He asked him for a poem, saying, 'It's important that you be seen to be with us.' Mandelstam at first said that he had nothing, and then reluctantly gave the paper No. 130 ('Kak rastet khlebov opara' [When the leavened dough of loaves rises]) – principally, Nadezhda Yakovlevna told me, because it pleased him that a poem referring to the cherubim should appear in the government newspaper. For some reason, the poem appeared in a facsimile of Mandelstam's own handwriting.

It was at this period that non-literary tactics began for the first time to be used in literary disputes: such is Nadezhda Yakovlevna's rather understated formulation. According to her, Osip Brik, the brilliant theoretician of Formalism, maintained a sort of salon that operated as a listening post for the Cheka. Brik and the erstwhile Futurists gathered about the short-lived journal *Lef* (1923–5) were particular opponents of Mandelstam and all he stood for. Art for them was a product like any other which had to satisfy the demands of a market, the market in this case being the State itself. How this belated Futurist doctrine struck Mandelstam, the greatest of the Acmeists, or how it would have struck the recently deceased Blok, greatest of the Symbolists, can be easily imagined. It should be emphasized that the most conspicuous poet associated with *Lef*, Vladimir Mayakovsky, was not a party to this early persecution of Mandelstam, for whom he seems always to have nourished a peculiar fondness. At the famous Yeliseev store he once leaned across a counter to greet Mandelstam with a stentorian shout: 'Like an Attic soldier enamoured of his enemy!' But the disputes were no longer literary only, nor were they carried on in Mayakovsky's crude but open-hearted and upright way.

In the autumn of 1923 Mandelstam and his wife managed a brief holiday at a sanatorium in Gaspra, a Crimean spa famous for the ailing Tolstoy's having been taken there in 1902. The KUBU had now acquired it as a rest home for the professors and other intellectuals in its charge. Mandelstam used the respite to write a work that had been commissioned by Isay Lezhnev, the editor of *Rossiia* (Russia). *Shum vremeni* (The Noise of Time) is the autobiographical work from which most of our knowledge of his early life comes.

One day while they were there, Abram Efros, an art historian and translator and, as it turned out, a rather sinister practical joker, arrived with the news that Mandelstam had been investigated *in absentia* by a commission of the Herzen House and censured for his rude behavior in demanding less noise in the hallways. Outraged that his affairs should be thus examined and judgment passed without his even being heard, he fired off a telegram to the Writers' Union renouncing his room. With this hasty and over-sensitive reaction to what in fact turned out to be pure fabrication, Mandelstam inaugurated what Nadezhda Yakovlevna called the 'fantastic homelessness' that was to be the normal condition of their life from then on. Some ten years later they were once again lodged in the Herzen House, but the sordid provocation to which they were then subjected had nothing of the joke about it. See Chapter 8, under the date 1932.

When he returned to Moscow, he spent fruitless months of the northern winter looking for a room. They stayed for a while with his brother Yevgeny. On finally discovering a place to live he wrote an ecstatic letter to his father in Petrograd: 'Our own kitchen...firewood...quiet – in a word: paradise.' But not all of the letter seems to justify the word:

> What am I doing? Working for money. The crisis is serious. Much worse than last year. But I've already caught up. Getting more translations, articles, and so on... 'Literature' is loathesome to me. My dream is to chuck all that filth. The last work I did for myself was in the summer. Last year I was still able to do a lot of work for myself. This year – nothing...[3]

Lezhnev rejected *The Noise of Time*. It was scarcely 'what the age demanded,' and besides, as Nadezhda Yakovlevna notes, Lezhnev had written his own *Noise of Time* along the correct lines: the story of a poor Jewish youth who grows up to accept Marxism. Nikolay Tikhonov, a poet very much under the influence of the Acmeists but later on one of the government's most reliable utensils, also rejected Mandelstam's book. He too had written 'correct' memoirs, about his experiences with Gorky. So for the time being Mandelstam's manuscript was left on his hands, an unsalable literary property when he badly needed the promised fee. The magazines suddenly had no further use for his services to poetry, for his ideological unacceptability had been channeled through such organs as Osip Brik's salon to the center, whence it was relayed in various imperatives to the editorial offices of Moscow and Petrograd. Nikolay

Ivanovich Bukharin, closest to the ideological center of all Mandelstam's well-wishers, edited *Prozhektor* (The Searchlight), but was unable to help. He said, 'I cannot publish you – give me some translations.' Vladimir Narbut, Mandelstam's fellow Acmeist from the early days and now head of the publishing house *Zemlia i Fabrika* (Land and Factory) said nearly the same: 'Osip, I cannot print your work – give me translations.' Nadezhda Yakovlevna, from whose conversation I quote the above, continued: 'There had probably been some decision at the top – in the Central Committee or the Ministry of Culture or God knows where – wherever it is that ideology comes from – that divided writers into "ours" and "theirs." Mandelstam and Akhmatova turned up in the extreme category of "theirs."'

The effort mentioned above to free his younger brother from the grasp of the Cheka led Mandelstam from Bukharin to one further interview with the head of the secret police, Felix Dzerzhinsky. Nadezhda Yakovlevna sees this episode in 1922 as Mandelstam's first real awakening to what the future was likely to be. He lost no time in putting his vision of that future, though in rather oblique terms, into an essay that was published early the next year (20 January 1923) in Alexey Tolstoy's newspaper *Nakanune* (On the Eve), which appeared in Berlin. It seems to me an essential exhibit in any discussion of Mandelstam's attitude toward the revolution. It is brief enough, and important enough, to give here in full translation:

HUMANISM AND THE PRESENT
(1923)

There are epochs which contend that they care nothing for man, that he is to be used like brick or cement, that he is to be built with, not for. Social architecture is measured by the scale of man. At times it becomes inimical to man and feeds its own grandeur on his debasement and nullity.

Assyrian prisoners swarm like baby chicks under the feet of a huge emperor; warriors, personifying the hostile might of government, kill bound pygmies with long spears; and Egyptians and Egyptian builders treat the human mass as a material of which there must be a sufficiency and which must be delivered in any desired quantity.

But there exists a different social architecture of which man is also the scale and measure, but which builds for man rather than with him. Its greatness rests not on the nullification of personality but on the highest form of expediency consistent with its needs.

Everyone senses the monumentality of the forms in the social architecture that is approaching. The mountain cannot yet be seen, but already it casts its shadow upon us and we – unaccustomed to monumental forms of social life, trained in the governmental and legal flatness of the XIXth century – we move about in this shadow with fear and bewilderment, unsure whether this is the wing of approaching night or the shadow of our native city, which we must enter.

Simple mechanical enormity and bare quantity are inimical to man, and it is not a new social pyramid that attracts us, but social Gothic: the free play of weights and forces, a human society conceived as a complex and dense architectural forest, where everything is appropriate, individual, and every particular detail echoes in unison with the whole mass.

The instinct for social architecture – i.e. for structuring life in grandiose monumental forms, seemingly far beyond the immediate needs of man – is profoundly inherent in human societies and is not dictated by idle whim.

Renounce social architecture and you will demolish the simplest, the most universally unquestioned and most necessary of structures: man's house, the human dwelling.

In countries subject to earthquakes the people build flat houses, and the tendency toward flatness, the renunciation of architecture, runs from the French Revolution through the entire legal life of the XIXth century, which spent its whole existence in the tense expectation of some subterranean jolt, some social blow.

But the earthquake did not spare even the flat houses. The chaotic world burst in – both into the English 'home' and the German 'Gemüt.' Chaos sings in our Russian stoves, it bangs with our dampers and oven doors.

How is one to guard the human dwelling against the terrible tremors, how to ensure its walls against the subterranean shocks of history? Who would dare say that the free house of man should not stand upon the earth, its best ornament and the stablest thing known?

The legal creations of recent generations have proven powerless to protect that which they arose to serve, over which they struggled and philosophized vainly.

No laws about the rights of man, no principles of property and inviolability can any longer ensure the human dwelling, they no longer save the house from catastrophe, they afford neither assurance nor security.

The English, more than anyone else, are hypocritically concerned about the legal guarantees of personal liberty, but they forget that the concept 'home' originated many centuries ago in their own country as a revolutionary concept, as the natural justification of the first social revolution in Europe, of a deeper type and one more akin to our time than the French.

The monumentality of the approaching social architecture results from its mission to organize the world's economy on the principle of universal home-life to meet the needs of man, widening the scope of his domestic freedom to world proportions, fanning the flame of his individual hearth to the size of a universal flame.

The future is cold and terrifying for whoever fails to understand this, but the inner warmth of the future – the warmth of practicality, thrift, and teleology – is just as clear for the contemporary humanist as the heat of today's hot stove.

If the social architecture of the future does not have as its basis a genuinely humanistic justification, it will crush man as Assyria and Babylonia crushed him.

The fact that the values of humanism have become rare, have been, so to speak, taken out of circulation and are now latent, is by no means a bad sign. Humanistic values have merely withdrawn, concealed themselves, like gold currency, but like the gold reserves they secure the entire traffic in ideas of modern Europe, and their control is all the more powerful for being latent.

The transition to gold currency is the business of the future, and we shall see the replacement of temporary ideas – paper notes – by the gold coinage of the European humanistic tradition, and the splendid florins of humanism will ring not against the archeologist's spade but in the light of their own day and, when the moment has come, will be the hard cash that passes from hand to hand.[4]

It is a moving essay. One sees in it the attempt of a doomed intellectual humanism seeking not to adjust its moral values to those of the revolution but rather to assert them one last time, as though by casting the future in certain words one could make it come out that way. It is desperate writing, and the author of it was demonstrably ambivalent toward his subject, a fact that can be very graphically shown by comparing the images at the end of this piece with the same images at the end of 'The Horseshoe Finder' (No. 136), a poem written that same year. In the article, there is an air of hope about those coins of humanism that will be resurrected for their new currency; in the poem, the speaker compares himself to just such an unearthed coin, scarred by the teeth of time, and so worn as to be utterly insufficient even for himself (see below, p. 287). Mandelstam's mind declared itself in images, which had for him a life of their own, and were never mere decorations. One may be sure that the diametric opposition of these identical images, used at the same period, bespeaks a profound indecision of spirit. The 1920s, an era normally contrasted to the 1930s in a favorable light as relatively free, were for Mandelstam oddly more melancholy than the age when his reasons for grief would be apparent to everyone.

He wrote little poetry now, and was on the verge of a time when he would write none. The twenty poems that he gathered together under the rubric '1921–1925' in his last collection are analyzed below in Chapter 14. It was a low output even for a poet who was never at any period grossly prolific. The paucity no doubt derives in part from the increasing reluctance of editors to violate ideological directives by printing him; but partly it must have come from the confusion of soul that one senses in the writing demanded of him. *Buria i natisk* (the title of the essay means 'Storm and Stress' and is a *calque* of the German *Sturm und Drang*) appeared in the first issue of *Russkoe iskusstvo* (Russian Art) for 1923 and is a brisk summary of the recent history of Russian poetry.[5] But among the brilliant aperçus there are passages that can hardly fail to strike the reader familiar with Mandelstam's life and opinions as unsettling. He attacked the work of Anna Akhmatova, for instance, who was perhaps more kindred to him in spirit than any other person except his wife. Her work was a 'vulgarization of Annensky,' and contained not 'the real past' but merely 'yesterday.' 'This "yesterday" is easily understood poetry, a hen-house with a fence, a cosy little corner where domestic fowl cluck and peck about. This is not work done upon the word but rather respite from the word.' Though certain later phrases of the essay seem slightly to soften this judgment, it was certainly understood by Akhmatova herself as a harsh 'revaluation' of her work. And in *Russian Art*'s second issue that same year Mandelstam dealt Akhmatova another glancing blow by calling her work a kind of 'stylitism of the parquet.' The neatness of such wounding phrases normally tempts a lesser sort of critic than Mandelstam. Akhmatova writes in her memoir of him that they never discussed his published opinions of her work – neither these nor those in which he praised her.[6]

Anna Akhmatova was not the only old friend to be critically revalued by Mandelstam. He wrote a number of such literary surveys in the early 1920s. Two of them, both dealing with the literary life of Moscow, appeared in Lezhnev's journal *Rossiia*.[7] The treatment given Marina Tsvetaeva seems even today to be slightly shocking – or perhaps it is even more shocking, for we now have a better idea of her genuine stature as a poet.

> For Moscow the gloomiest sign of all is Marina Tsvetaeva's madonna-like handicraft, which echoes the dubious solemnity of the Petersburg poetess Anna Radlova. The worst thing in literary Moscow is its female poetry. The experience of recent years has shown that the only woman to have entered the circle of poetry with the rights of a new muse is the Russian science of verse created by Potebnya and Andrey Bely and strengthened by the Formalist school of Eykhenbaum, Zhirmunsky and Shklovsky.

He went on:

> The tastelessness and historical falsity of Marina Tsvetaeva's poetry about Russia – pseudo-national and pseudo-Muscovite – is infinitely beneath the poetry of Adalis, whose voice occasionally attains masculine strength and truth.

His praise was reserved for the Futurists, though the context makes it appear that he was praising them rather for being male than for being Futurist. Nevertheless, what he had to say about Mayakovsky is rich in perspectives on the situation in which he found himself:

> Mayakovsky is working at the elementary and enormous problem of 'poetry for everyone, not for the elite.' Of course, the *ex*tending of poetry's base proceeds at the expense of its *in*tensity, its content, its poetic culture. Wonderfully well-informed about the wealth and complexity of world poetry, Mayakovsky, in establishing his 'poetry for everyone' has had to turn his back on whatever was incomprehensible, i.e. whatever presupposed in the listener the slightest education in poetry. But to address, in poetry, an audience totally unprepared for poetry is just as ungrateful a job as sitting on a tack. The reader who is absolutely unprepared will be absolutely

perplexed; or else poetry, if it is divorced from any culture whatever, will altogether cease to be poetry and then, by a strange trait in human nature, will become accessible to a limitless circle of readers. But Mayakovsky writes poetry and very cultured poetry: an elegant song-and-dance man whose stanza breaks up into ponderous antitheses, is saturated with hyperbolic metaphors and sustained in monotonous short *dol'niki* [accentual lines]. Mayakovsky has absolutely no business impoverishing himself. He runs the risk of becoming a poetess, which has already half happened.

The second of the two articles was also sharply polemical, the target now being the new writers of prose, which at about this time began to replace poetry as the most favored literary vehicle. What angered Mandelstam was the raw, uncooked nature of the prose, which largely dispensed with plot, offering in its stead *byt* (a Russian word meaning, roughly, the ordinary, fair-to-middling aspects of daily life). *Byt* made its way into the new prose in the form of actual documents, bits of newspaper reportage, telegrams, literal reproductions of current slang and small talk. Mandelstam called such writers eclectic in the most literal sense.

> Why was it precisely the Revolution that proved to be favorable to the rebirth of Russian prose? Precisely because it prompted the type of the anonymous prose writer, the eclectic, the collector – not a creator of verbal pyramids out of the depths of his own spirit but one of Pharaoh's modest slave-drivers, overseeing the slow but sure construction of actual pyramids.

(The reader who recalls the essay on 'Humanism and the Present' will not fail to see that these images of Egyptian tyranny over the human spirit are another index to the ambivalence in Mandelstam's own soul, like the images of recovered coins.)

In the summer and autumn of 1923 Mandelstam wrote a number of articles in a rather popular vein for the magazine *Ogonek*. Two of them related to the theme with which we have just been dealing, namely, the fate of Russian culture in the years following the Revolution. No such high-sounding name is given to his mission in the pages of *Ogonek*, to be sure, but it is nevertheless clear, beneath the witty surface of the writing, how serious was his concern over the attempts then being made to make practising poets and artists of the throngs of peasants and workers who were attending lectures and practical classes in verse technique almost before they themselves had learnt to read. The two articles had the general title 'Armiia poetov' (The Army of Poets).[8]

The French managed these things better, he wrote. In the French Gymnasium students are thoroughly drilled in verse technique and awarded prizes for academic poems, the result being that they are relieved to be done with poetry as soon as they get out of school and can devote themselves to some serious occupation. But in Russia the enforced idleness of the last few years and the collapse of education had produced as one unhappy result a generation of versifiers whose mania for writing verse amounted to a disease. There was an epidemic. The capitals were being engulfed by a flood of unspeakably bad verse from the provinces as well as from within their own limits. The real target of Mandelstam's attack was, of course, not so much the deluded would-be poets as it was the philistine assumption that poetry and literature in general, unlike such pursuits as engineering, called for no special gift and no special preparation. Two years before, Alexandr Blok had concluded his great speech in celebration of Pushkin (13 February 1921) with what he called (adopting at the end of his talk that Pushkinian gaiety which he had praised at the beginning) three 'gay truths of common sense.'

> There are no special arts. One should not give the name of art to what is not called that. In order to create a work of art, you have to know how to do it.[9]

That, in sum, is what Mandelstam affirmed over and over again in the early 1920s, as he sought to defend the beleaguered art of poetry. Behind the comic thumbnail sketches of importunate poetasters in the second part of his article on the army of poets we can discern scenes of real life. In his memoir 'Kak ia ne stal poetom' (How I did not become a Poet), V. Kaverin records with outright gratitude his (at the time) painful interview with Mandelstam in the Petrograd House of the Arts. Viktor Shklovsky, whom Kaverin had cornered in the gymnasium, did not even stop exercising on a bicycle machine when the neophyte poet read his poems, and he sent him away with a withering dismissal: 'Not funny... elementary.'

> But I was still not reconciled to my fate. I went to Osip Mandelstam with my poems. Where and when did this conversation take place? Did it last long? I was so agitated that my memory has retained nothing except what was said by Mandelstam. It had seemed that one would need hours, perhaps years, to enter the separate world of his poetry, but I had flown across that distance in a few split seconds. And there, in the depth of what he was saying, following the flight of his thought, I gained my first intimation of the fact that poetry does not exist for itself alone, and that if it does not strive to express life, to give it lasting form, no one has any use for even the cleverest gathering of rhymed lines. Mandelstam spoke to me sternly, with conviction and passion. There was no room for irony. It was important to him that I stop writing verses, and what he was saying was a defense of poetry against me and against those tens and hundreds of young men and women who were amusing themselves with the game of words.[10]

Nikolay Chukovsky, who did eventually become a poet, had a similar experience in the summer of 1922. Mandelstam came across the young man one morning asleep on a park bench, penniless and exhausted. He had been trying to sell copies of an almanac that he had published with disastrous results. Mandelstam asked to hear some of his work.

I recited the most recent of my poems, recited them carefully and exactly as he himself and all the Acmeists recited, that is to say, laying great stress on the phonic and rhythmic side of the verse, not on the sense of it. Mandelstam listened attentively, his face showing neither approval nor disapproval. When I had finished one poem, he nodded his head and said, 'More.' And I recited some more.

When I had read everything that I could, he said, 'It doesn't matter how gutta-percha a voice you read those poems in – they are still bad.'

That was his final judgment. Never again did he ask me to recite any of my poetry.[11]

But, like Kaverin, Chukovsky recalls this severe sentence with gratitude and with great respect, for, as the rest of his memoir reveals, Mandelstam was characteristically able to separate his estimate of the poetry from his estimate of the poet. He treated the stranded youth with great kindness, even going to the length of helping him dispose of the ill-fated almanac.

Of the more or less hack journalism that Mandelstam turned out in the early 1920s no single piece is so striking today as a brief interview published in *Ogonek* (23 December 1923). Like Mandelstam, the young Annamese revolutionary leader Nguyen Ai Quoc was in his early thirties. But he was a member of the Comintern and was later to become known to the entire world under his Party name, Ho Chi Minh.

Many people, when they hear about this interview today, tend to laugh at the slightly comic effect of such an extraordinarily improbable juxtaposition of personalities. But it was also a juxtaposition of two fates that have come to force themselves upon our consciousness as emblematic. And so it is not only sensational but poignant. It is moving to reflect upon this conversation (in French) between two young men in Moscow who looked into the future to the year 1947 – about as far distant from them in one direction as it is from us in the other – and imagined, one fervently and the other with a gentle complaisance, a Congress of the International. Neither Mandelstam nor, in fact, the Comintern itself would last that long.

But Ho Chi Minh would outlive the despised French masters of his native country to confront another army that was for the most part not yet born in 1923. It would probably be best to seek no further significance in this brief episode – which, in any case, I give here in full translation. Some of the lessons of history are mute, or they are muffled in what Mandelstam calls 'the oceanic silence of universal brotherhood.'

[INTERVIEW]

'And how has Gandhi's movement been reflected in Indochina? Haven't any of the reverberations, any echoes, reached there?' I asked Nguyen Ai Quoc.

The wing of approaching night

'No,' answered my companion. 'The Annamese people – peasants – live buried in the profoundest night, with no newspapers, no conception of what's happening in the world. It's night, actual night.'

Nguyen Ai Quoc is the only Annamese in Moscow and represents an ancient Malaysian race. He is practically a boy, thin and lithe, wearing a knitted woolen jacket. He speaks French, the language of the oppressors, but the French words sound dim and faint, like the muffled bell of his native language.

Nguyen Ai Quoc utters the word 'civilization' with disgust: he has traveled the length and breadth of practically the whole colonial world, been in northern and central Africa, and he's seen his fill of it. In conversation he often uses the word 'brothers.' His 'brothers' are the Negroes, Hindus, Syrians, Chinese. He wrote a letter to the Frenchified Negro, René Maran, author of the densely exotic *Batouala* to ask him a question point-blank: did or did not Maran wish to aid the liberation of his colonial brothers? René Maran, crowned by the French Academy, answered reticently and evasively.

'I come from a privileged Annamese family. In my country such families don't do anything. The young men study Confucianism. You know, Confucianism is not a religion but rather a study of moral practice and decent behavior. In its very foundation it presupposes a "social world." I was a boy of about thirteen when I first heard the French words for liberty, equality, and fraternity...for us, you see, every white man is a Frenchman. And I wanted to learn something about French civilization, to explore what lay concealed behind those words. But the French are training parrots in the native schools. They hide books and newspapers from us and ban not only modern writers but even Rousseau and Montesquieu. What could I do? I decided to leave. An Annamese is a serf. We are forbidden not only to travel but even to move about at all inside the country. The railroads have been built for "strategic" purposes – the French don't think we're yet grown up enough to use them. I managed to get to the coast and...just left. I was nineteen. The elections were going on in France. The bourgeois were slinging mud at each other.' A spasm of almost physical revulsion passes across the face of Nguyen Ai Quoc. Normally wan and dull, his face suddenly lights up. He squints his large liquid eyes and stares at one with the penetrating gaze of a blind man.

'When the French came, all the decent old families scattered. The bastards who knew how to worm their way into favor grabbed the abandoned houses and estates. Now they've grown rich – a new bourgeoisie – and they're able to bring their children up in the French way. If any boy in my country goes to school to the Catholic missionaries it means he's just trash, scum. They pay money for that. So they go, the morons, and it's just the same as joining the police or the militia. Catholic missionaries own a fifth of our whole country. No one but the concessionaires can compete with them.

'What is a French colonizer? Oh, what an untalented, limited type that is. His first concern is to make arrangements for his relatives. The next is to grab and steal as much and as quickly as possible, and the aim of his whole policy is – a little house, "one's own little house" in France.

'The French are poisoning my people. They've made the use of alcohol obligatory. We take a little rice of good quality and make a nice liquor – for when friends come or for some family celebration of ancestors. The French took bad, cheap rice and distilled barrels of liquor from it. No one wanted to buy theirs. There was a surplus of liquor. So the governors were directed to make an obligatory apportionment of it on a per capita basis and they forced people to buy liquor that nobody wanted.'

I had a vivid image of the way these gentle people, with their love for tact and moderation and their hatred of excess, had been made to drink hard liquor. Nguyen Ai Quoc's whole presence was imbued with an innate tact and delicacy. European civilization works with bayonet and liquor, hiding them under the soutane of a Catholic missionary. Nguyen Ai Quoc breathes culture, not European culture, but perhaps the culture of the future.

'In Paris now there's a group of comrades from the French colonies – five or six men from Cochin China, the Sudan, Madagascar, and Haiti – who are publishing a little magazine called *Pariah* devoted to fighting the French colonial policy. It's a very small magazine. All the staff make up the cost of publishing it out of their own pockets – instead of receiving an honorarium.'

A bamboo cane with an appeal carved on it went around surreptitiously from village to village. It was replanted from one place to another – and a secret agreement was made. It cost the Annamese dearly. There were executions. Hundreds of heads rolled.

'The Annamese have no clergy and no religion in the European sense. The cult of ancestors is a purely social phenomenon. There are no priests. The eldest member of the family or the village elder performs the memorial rites. We know nothing of priestly authority.

'Yes, it's interesting how the French authorities taught our peasants the words "Bolshevik" and "Lenin." They began hunting down Communists among the Annamese peasantry at a time when there wasn't a trace of a Communist. And that way they spread the propaganda.'

The Annamese are a simple, courteous people. In the nobility of his manner and in the dim, soft voice of Nguyen Ai Quoc one can hear the approach of tomorrow, the oceanic silence of universal brotherhood.

There's a manuscript on the table. A calm, businesslike report. The telegraphic style of a correspondent. He's indulging his fancy on the theme of a Congress of the International in the year 1947. He sees and hears the agenda, he's present, taking down the minutes.

When we were saying goodbye Nguyen Ai Quoc recalled something. 'Oh, yes, we had one other "rebellion." It was led by a minor Annamese prince named Zjuntan. Against the deportation of our peasants to the slaughter in France. Zjuntan escaped. He's now in exile. Say something about him, too.'

In 1923 Mandelstam republished both his collections of poetry in new editions. *Tristia*, which had come out the year before in an unsatisfactory form, was now retitled *Second Book*; *Stone*, now in its third edition, bore the subtitle *First book of poems*.

The Futurist Bobrov, as I have mentioned, greeted the first (Berlin) edition of *Tristia* in extremely positive terms. It tells one something of the literary (and not only literary) struggles of the time that when the Symbolist Valery Bryusov now reviewed *Second Book* in the pages of the same journal he attacked both the Acmeist Mandelstam and his Futurist admirer.[12] But the attacks were different, for that upon Mandelstam was ideological. Bryusov's review is not so much a review as it is a subtle *donos*, an act of political informing. When one considers his infinitely superior gift as a poet, Bryusov is an even more distasteful personality than Sergey Gorodetsky. His embrace of Bolshevism and the new order of things was more fervent by far than that of Mayakovsky, the unofficial poet-laureate of the Revolution, and his personality incomparably more devious.

The obliquities of his article require a certain translation into straightforward language. He invents the name 'Neo-Acmeist' for 'certain circles' (not further specified) by whom Mandelstam had been made 'exceedingly famous,' and designates him as their teacher. The one theme running throughout the review is the existence of this new school, an amalgam of several circles. What had taken place, that is to say, was the rebirth of a literary group associated in the public and official mind with Nikolay Gumilyov, an executed conspirator against the regime. All of the faults in Mandelstam's book – and Bryusov finds little else – are the faults of 'Neo-Acmeism' generally. The poets whom Bryusov puts into his imagined school were Igor Shisov, Sergey Zelenetsky, Nikolay Berner, E. Novskaya, and Pavel Antokolsky. Except for the last one, these are complete nonentities. No one without access to a large research library today could possibly discover the identity of these utterly unknown people, Mandelstam's 'disciples.' According to Nadezhda Yakovlevna, however, they were 'the most compromising people he could think of.'[13] It was to be understood that Mandelstam was not an isolated antagonist of the 'new reality' – he stood at the head of a concerted effort. What Gumilyov had been, Mandelstam now was.

The details of Bryusov's attack on *Second Book* are enough to make one wring one's hands, for he was, after all, neither uncultured nor ungifted. The first charge of all is that Mandelstam's book does not belong to the present age (read: is 'out of step with modernity' – a commonplace meaning, roughly, 'class enemy'). This he substantiates by pointing to the excessive reference to the classical world and to things foreign generally – a strange recrudescence of xenophobia in a man whose best books bore titles like *Chefs d'oeuvre*, *Me eum esse*, *Tertia vigilia*, *Urbi et orbi*, *Stephanos*, and *Mea*. 'All of modernity,' he sums up unambiguously, 'must absolutely be clad in the garments of past ages.'

Having attacked Bobrov for quoting only four of Mandelstam's poems,

Bryusov contents himself with one, No. 112. In order to understand the tone of the attack on Mandelstam by one of the most influential and able poets of his day, one ought first to read the poem:[14]

Когда Психея-жизнь спускается к теням
В полупрозрачный лес, вослед за Персефоной,
Слепая ласточка бросается к ногам
С стигийской нежностью и веткою зеленой.

Навстречу беженке спешит толпа теней,
Товарку новую встречая причитаньем,
И руки слабые ломают перед ней
С недоумением и робким упованьем.

Кто держит зеркало, кто баночку духов—
Душа ведь женщина,—ей нравятся безделки,
И лес безлиственный прозрачных голосов
Сухие жалобы кропят, как дождик мелкий.

И в нежной сутолке не зная, что начать,
Душа не узнает ни веса, ни объема,
Дохнет на зеркало, и медлит передать
Лепешку медную хозяину парома.

When Psyche – Life herself – goes down among the shades,
to the half-transparent forest, following Persephone,
a blind swallow throws itself at her feet
with Stygian tenderness, and a green twig.

Shadows come thronging out to meet the fugitive,
their new companion, to greet her with cries, laments,
and wring their frail hands before her
to show how confused they are, how full of timid hope.

One holds out a mirror, another a phial of perfume –
the soul is feminine, after all, fond of trifles –
and the dry complaining falls like fine rain
on the leafless forest, the transparent voices.

Not knowing what to do in her confusion, how to start,
the soul loses what sense she had, once, of weight and size.
She breathes on the mirror. She's afraid to hand
the Master of the ferry his fee, the copper lozenge.

Of this exquisite poem, Bryusov says that it is an unscientific (read: non-Marxist) approach to the whole question of the afterlife and will scarcely satisfy the demands of up-to-date readers. What is more, the facts of mythology – if one must have mythology – are themselves inaccurate: Persephone did not as a rule accompany the souls of the departed on their journey to Hades. Having thus demolished the poem, Bryusov asks what is left? Merely a series of pretty pictures. 'Pictures for the sake of pictures!' he exclaims (read: *l'art pour l'art*, &c. &c., but by now the reader himself can supply the enciphered message).

I discuss below, as I have mentioned, the poems that Mandelstam isolated as a sort of 'third book' under the rubric '1921–1925.' In the chapter devoted to them I treat them from the point of view of certain formal features, but several of them can be discussed here, in the narrative of his life. First among these is No. 140 ('1 January 1924'), the very title of which seems to plead for our reading it in its temporal context.

Like one or two others, 140 is a sort of milepost in the oeuvre. It belongs with Nos. 251 and 260, poems of the early 1930s, on several grounds. They are all plainly autobiographical in content, revelatory as the snapshots in an album, though the scenes of his personal life and opinions are set, as they always are in Mandelstam, in the long perspectives of history and culture. Certain formal features also unite them into a kind of subgroup. They tend to be longer than the average, and formally rather lax and dilatory. They are cityscapes, the city being the implacable Moscow where he could never, try as he might, find a home either in the spiritual or in the most abjectly literal sense.

No. 140 and those associated with it have a common theme that lies behind the surface fiction of aimless wandering in the city: loss and the anguish occasioned by loss, the loneliness of the solitary figure in a great crowd. For Mandelstam the loss was precisely of that which alone sustained him, the word, as he called it. Under another aspect, it is the loss of Self, which he did not distinguish from his art. In a year's time, the loss foreseen here would become actual, and last for five years.

[140.] 1 ЯНВАРЯ 1924

Кто время целовал в измученное темя—
С сыновней нежностью потом
Он будет вспоминать, как спать ложилось время
В сугроб пшеничный за окном.
Кто веку поднимал болезненные веки—
Два сонных яблока больших—
Он слышит вечно шум, когда взревели реки
Времен обманных и глухих.

Два сонных яблока у века-властелина
И глиняный прекрасный рот,
Но к млеющей руке стареющего сына
Он, умирая, припадет.
Я знаю, с каждым днем слабеет жизни выдох,
Еще немного,—оборвут
Простую песенку о глиняных обидах
И губы оловом зальют.

О глиняная жизнь! О умиранье века!
Боюсь, лишь тот поймет тебя,

В ком беспомóщная улыбка человека,
Который потерял себя.
Какая боль—искать потерянное слово,
Больные веки поднимать
И с известью в крови, для племени чужого
Ночные травы собирать.

Век. Известковый слой в крови больного сына
Твердеет. Спит Москва, как деревянный ларь,
И некуда бежать от века-властелина...
Снег пахнет яблоком, как встарь.
Мне хочется бежать от моего порога.
Куда? На улице темно,
И, словно сыплют соль мощеною дорогой,
Белеет совесть предо мной.

По переулочкам, скворешням и застрехам,
Недалеко, собравшись как-нибудь,
Я, рядовой седок, укрывшись рыбьим мехом,
Всё силюсь полость застегнуть.
Мелькает улица, другая,
И яблоком хрустит саней морозный звук,
Не поддается петелька тугая,
Всё время валится из рук.

Каким железным, скобяным товаром
Ночь зимняя гремит по улицам Москвы.
То мерзлой рыбою стучит, то хлещет паром
Из чайных розовых—как серебром плотвы.
Москва—опять Москва. Я говорю ей: «здравствуй!
Не обессудь, теперь уж не беда,
По старине я уважаю братство
Мороза крепкого и щучьего суда».

Пылает на снегу аптечная малина
И где-то щелкнул ундервуд;
Спина извозчика и снег на пол-аршина:
Чего тебе еще? Не тронут, не убьют.
Зима-красавица и в звездах небо козье
Рассыпалось и молоком горит,
И конским волосом о мерзлые полозья
Вся полость трется и звенит.

А переулочки коптили керосинкой,
Глотали снег, малину, лед,
Всё шелушится им советской сонатинкой,
Двадцатый вспоминая год.
Ужели я предам позорному злословью—
Вновь пахнет яблоком мороз—
Присягу чудную четвертому сословью
И клятвы крупные до слез?

The wing of approaching night

Кого еще убьешь? Кого еще прославишь?
Какую выдумаешь ложь?
То ундервуда хрящ: скорее вырви клавиш—
И щучью косточку найдешь;
И известковый слой в крови больного сына
Растает, и блаженный брызнет смех…
Но пишущих машин простая сонатина—
Лишь тень сонат могучих тех.   (1924.)

Once you've kissed exhausted time on the top of his head
you'll remember later – like a son, tenderly –
how time lay down to sleep
in the wheaten drift outside the window.
Once you've raised the enflamed eyelids of the age –
two large, sleepy apples –
you will hear ever afterwards the noise of the roar
made by the rivers of the waste, dishonest times.

The despot age has two sleepy apple eyes
and his earthen mouth is beautiful
but when he dies he will fall
on the numbing arm of his aging son.
I know that with each day life's breath grows weaker.
A little more and they'll cut off
this simple song of earthen wrongs
and seal my lips with tin.

O earthen life! O dying age! I am afraid
that the only one to understand you
will be the man whose smile is helpless,
who has lost himself.
What pain – searching for the lost word,
lifting painful lids,
with quicklime in the blood
gathering night grasses for someone else's tribe.

The age. The layer of lime in the sick son's blood
hardens. Moscow sleeps like a wooden casket.
There's nowhere one can run from the despot age…
The snow smells of apples, as in the old days.
I want to escape from my own house,
but where? It's dark in the street,
and my conscience gleams in front of me, white,
like salt scattered on the pavement.

A passenger like any other, in my sleazy coat,
I've somehow got ready to go. Not far –
along back lanes, among the starling houses and thatch,
forever trying to button the lap robe.

One street after another flashes by.
Frozen runners crunch on the snow like an apple.
The buttonhole is too tight, won't give,
keeps slipping out of my hands.

Through the streets of Moscow winter night
clangs like iron hardware.
It bangs on the door like a frozen fish, billows
from the glow of tearooms in steam, silvery, like the scales
Moscow is Moscow again. I say Hello to her,   of a roach.
don't judge too harshly, it's all right now,
I never stopped respecting the kinship
of hard frost and pike's justice.

The raspberry globe of the pharmacy burns on the snow,
someone's typing on an Underwood,
the sleigh driver's back, the snow knee deep:
what more do you want? They won't touch you, won't kill you.
Beautiful winter. The goat sky
has crumbled into stars and is burning with milk
and the whole lap robe rubs and rings
like horsehair against the frozen runners.

And the alleys were smoking like kerosene stoves,
swallowing the snow, the raspberry, the ice.
They keep forever flaking like a Soviet sonatina
when they remember nineteen twenty.
Could I possibly ever betray to gossips –
the frost is smelling of apples again –
the oath I swore to the Fourth Estate,
vows solemn to the point of tears?

Who else will you kill? Who else praise to the stars?
What lie will you think up next?
That's the Underwood's cartilage: quick, tear out a key –
you'll find it's a pike's small bone.
And the layer of lime in the sick son's blood
will melt, there'll be a burst of blessed laughter. . .
But the typewriters' little sonatina
is no more than a shadow of those sonatas, the great ones.

Like many other poems in Mandelstam, this one has a doublet, No. 141, and the doublet, owing to the fame of its first two lines, is probably better known than the longer and, no doubt, original member of the pair. '1 January 1924' was written at Christmas-time in Kiev, writes Nadezhda Yakovlevna, where they were visiting her parents. It is one of the two poems in her experience that Mandelstam composed without his customary nervous pacing about. She says nothing of the composition of No. 141, which is simply dated '1924.'

Нет, никогда ничей я не был современник,
Мне не с руки почет такой.
О как противен мне какой-то соименник,
То был не я, то был другой.

Два сонных яблока у века-властелина
И глиняный прекрасный рот,
Но к млеющей руке стареющего сына
Он, умирая, припадет.

Я с веком поднимал болезненные веки—
Два сонных яблока больших,
И мне гремучие рассказывали реки
Ход воспаленных тяжб людских.

Сто лет тому назад подушками белела
Складная легкая постель,
И странно вытянулось глиняное тело,—
Кончался века первый хмель.

Среди скрипучего похода мирового
Какая легкая кровать.
Ну что же, если нам не выковать другого,
Давайте с веком вековать.

И в жаркой комнате, в кибитке и в палатке
Век умирает—а потом
Два сонных яблока на роговой облатке
Сияют перистым огнем.   (1924.)

No, never was I anyone's contemporary –
not for me such honor.
O how despicable that namesake of mine.
That wasn't me, that was someone else.

The despot age has two sleepy apple eyes
and his earthen mouth is beautiful,
but when he dies he will fall
on the numbing arm of his aging son.

Along with the age I raised my own painful lids –
two large sleepy apples –
and the thundering rivers told me the course
of the inflamed quarrels of men.

A hundred years ago the light folding bed
was white with pillows,
and the earthen body strangely stretched upon it:
the age's first drunkenness was ending.

What a light bed it was
amid the creaking of the world's campaign.
Well, if we're not to hammer out another,
let us live this age we've got.

> And now the age is dying in its overheated room,
> its hooded cab, its tent – and afterwards
> two sleepy apples shine on their corneous wafer
> with feathery flame.

Unlike English, with its prohibition against the 'double negative,' Russian demands a negative for each negative idea. An imitation of the Russian grammar would be approximately:

> No, never, not no one's contemporary was I,
> not for me such honor.
> O how despicable to me's that sort of namesake of mine.
> That wasn't me. That was someone else.

The negatives are clotted together as far forward in the opening sentences as they can come. This, and the percussive syntax of the short, stabbing sentences, recalls Dostoevsky's underground man and his snarling recusancy. It is the verbal equivalent of bared teeth, and it is the most salient instance of the other theme in these poems: defiance of the 'new reality.' It is intermittent and not fully sustained – how could it have been? – but it is there all the same. The sense of loss is recumbent, sick, dying. But the questions in the first poem jerk one alert no less than the defiant opening of the second: 'Could I ever possibly betray to shameful malignant gossip...the great oath I swore to the Fourth Estate?' (The translation is more narrowly literal.) And: 'Who else will you kill? Who else praise to the stars? What lie will you think up next?' The questions are undirected. They swim past the consciousness in this poem along with the typewriters and the traditional signs of pharmacies, objects like any other, but in the mid-1920s their first readers understood them at once, and were apprehensive for their author.

To discuss in detail the other poems that belong to this type of the autobiographical survey would carry us into the 1930s, a decade that lies beyond the scope of this book. Besides, they are too long. But the point seems to me worth making that after the various tragedies that befell Mandelstam during the last half of the 1920s, he returned not only to the general tone and form of these works but even to certain of the phrases and images. And in picking up where he had left off five years before, he neither apologized nor altered his behavior, to paraphrase a line of No. 251. When the critic Nikolay Ivanovich Khardzhiev heard Mandelstam recite these poems one evening in 1932, he wrote to his friend Boris Eykhenbaum that they were 'terrifying exorcisms.'

No. 251 (which contains the poem erroneously separated as '223' in the first edition of Vol. I) is another ambulatory poem. The solitary wanderer is the same lost consciousness as before. The first verse paragraph presents a line or two of the speaker's physical presence:

Еще далеко мне до патриарха,
Еще на мне полупочтенный возраст,
Еще меня ругают за глаза
На языке трамвайных перебранок,
В котором нет ни смысла, ни аза:
—Такой, сякой!—Ну чтож, я извиняюсь,
Но в глубине ничуть не изменяюсь...

I've still got a long way to go before I'm a patriarch.
I'm still of an age that gets no respect at all.
I'm still berated behind my back
in the language of streetcar squabbling
where there's not the slightest grain of sense:
'So and so!' – Well, so what, I say 'excuse me'
but in my heart of hearts I don't change at all.

And the second introduces the loose method of this poem, which, like
the others, consists of an inventory of certain disjointed scenes and
experiences:

Когда подумаешь, чем связан с миром,
То сам себе не веришь: ерунда.
Полночный ключик от чужой квартиры,
Да гривенник серебряный в кармане,
Да целлулоид фильмы воровской...

When you think what it is that connects you to the world,
you can't believe yourself – it's such nonsense:
a little midnight key to someone else's apartment,
a silver coin in your pocket,
and the celluloid of a cops & robbers film.

Trying constantly to think of something for which he might develop an
enthusiasm, the speaker takes his 'effete' walking stick and goes out to
experience the trifles that connect one with the world. He listens to
'sonatas in the back alleys' (a direct echo of '1 January 1924'), licks
his lips at the street peddlers' stands, leafs through books and concludes
that he is 'not alive, and still – alive.' The final lines convey the anguish
of his loneliness:

И до чего хочу я разыграться,
Разговориться, выговорить правду,
Послать хандру к туману, к бесу, к ляду,
Взять за руку кого-нибудь:—будь ласков,—
Сказать ему,—нам по пути с тобой...

How I long to get caught up in the game,
be lost in conversation, tell the truth,
evaporate this gloom, send it to hell,
take someone by the hand and say: 'Be kind.'
To tell him: 'I'm going the same way as you.'

119

That was finished in the early fall of 1931. In the spring of the following year Mandelstam wrote 'Midnight in Moscow' (No. 260). It is another such spasmodic panorama of city scenes blent with historical perspectives – his own and those of the age. To cite one line, it is a kind of 'catching time by the tail.' Even more than the preceding poem, it is reminiscent of '1 January 1924' and of its doublet, No. 141. It is the dialogue into which it enters with those works of 1924 that chiefly justifies our discussing it here.

The refusal to betray the 'oath sworn to the Fourth Estate' (No. 140) is affirmed once again:

> Для того ли разночинцы
> Рассохлые топтали сапоги, чтоб я теперь их предал?
> Мы умрем, как пехотинцы,
> Но не прославим ни хищи, ни поденщины, ни лжи!

> Is that what the *raznochintsy* stamped
> their cracked boots for – that I might now betray them?
> We'll die like the infantry,
> but we won't praise the plundering, the day-labor, the lying!

And the famous opening lines of No. 141, written eight years earlier, are now flatly contradicted, the result being a new kind of defiance:

> Пора вам знать, я тоже современник,
> Я человек эпохи Москвошвея,
> Смортите, как на мне топорщится пиджак,
> Как я ступать и говорить умею!
> Попробуйте меня от века оторвать!—
> Ручаюсь вам, себе свернете шею!

> It's time you knew: I'm also a contemporary,
> I belong to the age of the Moscow Garment Combine.
> Look how this jacket bunches on me,
> how I'm able to walk and talk!
> Just try to tear me away from the age –
> I promise you, you'll sprain your neck!

As his widow was to write some thirty years later, 'the "sick son of the age" suddenly understood that it was he who was healthy.'[15]

8

1925–1938:
Silence, prose, arrest, exile,
sickness, death

The detailed narrative of Mandelstam's life ends with 1925. The three collections of his poetry that he was able to see through the press had now been written, and, for a while, he could write no more. Poetry returned in the 1930s, and those poems deserve a book for themselves. As for the account of his last years, that forms the core of one of the greatest books of our era, Nadezhda Mandelstam's *Hope Against Hope.* This chapter is an outline for the reader who wishes to know the bare facts of the poet's remaining thirteen years.

Mid-1920s

The beginning of the poetic silence coincides with the onset of the heart trouble that was to plague Mandelstam intermittently with other ailments from then on.

Latter half of the 1920s

He lived mostly by translations. A partial catalogue may be found in the bibliography in vol. iii of the New York edition. His wife, whose knowledge of foreign languages was equal to his own – and in the case of English, much superior – collaborated in this work to such an extent that it is safer to regard all of it as in one degree or another a joint effort.

1925 Winter

They move to Leningrad (Morskaya Street) to be near Mandelstam's father, who was ill and in the hospital. Later they move to Tsarskoe Selo (now called Detskoe Selo, i.e. Children's Village) and live in the pension kept by a man named Zaytsev. Anna Akhmatova, from whom Mandelstam has lately been somewhat estranged, moves there with Nikolay Punin and settles in the same pension. She and Nadezhda Yakovlevna become friends. 'She often told me that her new friendship, the second friendship, with Osip Emilevich came about through me – or rather, thanks to me.'

At about this time Mandelstam fell in love with Olga Vaksel, about whom little is known except that she later emigrated to Norway, where she died. He wrote a number of poems to her: Nos. 198, 314, 315, and 316. His affair with her, though evidently brief, was very serious. Nadezhda Yakovlevna told me: 'It was the one occasion in our life when we were on the verge of getting a divorce.'

1925 Spring

Nadezhda falls ill with tuberculosis. They plan to move to Yalta for the sake of her health. She goes first, Mandelstam remains behind to arrange translation work. The first sizable group of Mandelstam's letters derive from this period. He arrives only in mid-November.

1926 February

Mandelstam is back in Moscow and Leningrad looking for work (translations, reviews). His letters to Nadezhda in Yalta are numerous (fifteen from this month alone) and filled with great tenderness.

1926 Spring

They return to Tsarskoe Selo.

1926 Fall

Still ailing, Nadezhda goes south again, first to Koktebel, then to Feodosia. Mandelstam remains in the north for the usual reasons. He lives in Tsarskoe Selo at several addresses. One apartment is in a wing of the Large Palace. He then moves to another in the building that had formerly housed the famous lycée attended by Alexandr Pushkin. Akhmatova recalls that he disliked the idea of living there. See letters 39–48 in vol. III.

1926 Winter

Nadezhda returns in December.

1927

Not one letter survives from his year, which is creatively a kind of blank in the poet's life. He was engaged in literary hack work, pure and simple. It required restless travelling about to Leningrad and Moscow and endless red tape with publishers' contracts.

1927 Summer

Vladimir Narbut, Mandelstam's fellow 'Acmeist' and now an editor in the publishing house *Zemlia i fabrika* (Land and Factory), proposes that Mandelstam edit a Russian translation of Charles de Coster's novel *La Légende de Thyl Ulenspiegel et de Lamme Goedzak*. Mandelstam got a contract for 'revising' the translation, which paid more than editing. Gorlin, an editor at *Gosizdat* (State Publishing House) for whom Mandelstam often worked, advises him against becoming involved with the project. The reason: A. G. Gornfeld, an influential critic whose translation of de Coster, along with one by V. Karyakin, is to be revised, looks upon de Coster as his personal property. The event proves Gorlin's warning to have been well founded.

1927 Fall

The Mandelstams go to Sukhum and Armavir in the Caucasus to visit his brother Alexandr. Nadezhda Yakovlevna:

> On the boat we met some very high-ranking military men. Mandelstam was struck by the brilliancy and snobbery of those men. I don't remember their names – they were probably the generals who were later wiped out. One of them said a marvelous thing that Mandelstam remembered and repeated everywhere: 'In order to command a post, you've got to have a portrait.' Good, no?

From the 'Chronicle' of literary news in the periodical *Na literaturnom postu* (On Literary Guard), no. 21, p. 81; 'Osip Mandelstam is writing a novel. Preparing a collection of articles on literature and art. Getting together a collected edition of his poetry for the State Publishing House.' Only the novel is mysterious. Perhaps what is meant is Mandelstam's often announced (and finally dropped) work on the death of the Italian soprano Angiolina Bozio (1830–59). Paragraphs from it appear to have found their way into his novella *Egipetskaia marka* (The Egyptian Stamp), which appeared the following year. See New York edition, II, 560ff., and my *Prose of Osip Mandelstam* (Princeton, 2nd edn, 1967), pp. 200f.

1927 Winter

The winter of 1927–8 was spent in Tsarskoe Selo.

1928

Judging by publication alone, this year was the height of Mandelstam's public career. The following books appeared: *Stikhotvoreniia* (Poems) in an edition of 2,000 copies. *O poezii* (On Poetry), a collection of his criticism: 2,100 copies. *Egipetskaia marka* (The Egyptian Stamp), containing the autobiographical *Shum vremeni* (Noise of Time), first published in 1925.

1928 Spring

Mandelstam learns that five elderly bank clerks have been arrested on some charge or other and are to be shot. Horrified, he runs about among government offices trying to save them. The decisive move was to send N. I. Bukharin a copy of *Poems* with an inscription which Nadezhda Yakovlevna remembers as approximately: 'every line in this book argues against what you plan to do.'

Nadezhda Yakovlevna is once more in Yalta on account of her illness.

1928 Summer

25 August. From Yalta Mandelstam writes a brief letter to Anna Akhmatova shortly after the anniversary of Gumilyov's execution: 'My conversation with Kolya [Nikolay Gumilyov] was never broken off and never will be.'

While in Yalta they learn that Narbut has been removed from the Communist Party, which he joined shortly after the Revolution, and from his post at the head of the Land and Factory publishing house. His replacement is a certain Ionov. The change will be disastrous for Mandelstam. Gorlin's warning to stay away from the revision of de Coster's *Ulenspiegel* now proves well grounded. The sordid mess drags through the next year and into 1930; here it is in outline:

In accordance with his contract Mandelstam revised two earlier translations of de Coster's novel, one by Gornfeld (under the pseudonym B. Yu. Korshan) and one by V. N. Karyakin. When the work now appeared Mandelstam was horrified to find his name alone on the title page with no mention of those whose translations he had revised. Mandelstam himself is the first to advise Gornfeld of the error and offers by telegram to recompense him. He also demands at once that the publisher paste in a note on the title page to set things right.

This Ionov refuses to do, though a pro-forma correction does appear in the newspaper *Vecherniaia Moskva* (Evening Moscow). Gornfeld suggests in an article that Mandelstam is little better than a petty thief and Mandelstam, infuriated, writes a blistering reply, whereupon the whole matter becomes a *cause célèbre* that flares up periodically for the next year and a half. One of the most odious figures in the history of Stalinist journalism, David Zaslavsky, now joins the fight with articles denouncing Mandelstam and hinting broadly at outright plagiarism. Prominent Moscow writers publish a letter in his defense. The case is finally adjudicated in several courts. Mandelstam is subjected to endless gruelling and exhausting interrogations, which cover his entire lifetime and seem for some reason to concentrate on the period of the Civil War. The upshot is that a commission of FOSP (Federation of Soviet Writers' Organizations) finds him morally to blame for the fact that the publisher failed to make an agreement with the earlier translators. The foregoing is the more or less public record, but the campaign against Mandelstam was private as well. Payment due him for other such hackwork was withheld on one technicality or another. The need for money was never greater: Nadezhda, ill with tuberculosis, had just undergone an appendectomy in Kiev. But he becomes practically unemployable. The Mandelstams' protector, Nikolay Bukharin, learns to what extent it is an organized campaign to 'remove' Mandelstam (the anti-Semitic overtones cause them to refer to it later as their 'Dreyfus Case') and orders it stopped. Through S. I. Gusev, head of the Press Department of the

Central Committee, Bukharin arranges for them to be sent out of harm's way on a trip to Armenia. See my note on and translation of Mandelstam's *Chetvertaia proza* (Fourth Prose) in *Hudson Review* (April 1970), 49–66.

1928/9

In the midst of the above affair they have lost the apartment in the lycée of Tsarskoe Selo and moved to Moscow, where Mandelstam finds work on the newspaper *Moskovskii Komsomolets* (Moscow Komsomol Member). Now homeless, they live in a room in the flat of Mandelstam's brother Alexandr.

1930

In the early spring of this year they leave for Sukhum where they spend some two months recuperating in a rest home belonging to the Central Committee. Mandelstam is physically and mentally exhausted. His revulsion against 'Literature,' writers as a class, and officialdom generally has never been more intense than now in the aftermath of the 'Dreyfus Case.'

1930, 1 May

This holiday finds them in Tiflis. Shortly thereafter they go to Erivan and begin the travels about Armenia that will later be recorded in Mandelstam's *Puteshestvie v Armeniiu* (Journey to Armenia). While there, Mandelstam dreams of getting an ordinary job – anything, just so it has nothing to do with Literature. He announces to a group of local writers that the formula, 'National in form, Socialist in content,' is stupid and illiterate. It is Stalin's prescription for correct writing. Thereafter his acquaintances are almost exclusively scientists, especially biologists. The trip lasts about eight months.

At the end of their stay in Armenia Mandelstam writes *Chetvertaia proza* (Fourth Prose), a highly stylized reflection of the events of 1928–9 and his seething fury at what was happening. It has never been published in the USSR. The ejaculation seems to have made poetry possible once again: he wrote his first poem in some five years (No. 202, dated October 1930, Tiflis) and the poems of the cycle 'Armenia' (Nos. 203–215). The order of the poems as printed in the New York edition unfortunately obscures the right sequence.

1930 Late fall

They leave for Moscow, then go to Leningrad, where Mandelstam hoped to settle, but an official of the writers' organization, the poet Tikhonov, decides otherwise: 'Let him go to Moscow – Leningrad writers don't want him here.' It was a question of getting a room and some work. Tikhonov controlled both.

1931 January

The last two poems that Mandelstam was ever to write in his city read
like the valedictions that they finally proved to have been:

223

Помоги, Господь, эту ночь прожить:
Я за жизнь боюсь—за Твою рабу—
В Петербурге жить—словно спать в гробу.

Give me help, O Lord, to live through this night
for I'm terrified for my life, Your slave:
living in Petersburg is like sleeping in a grave.

224

Мы с тобой на кухне посидим.
Сладко пахнет белый керосин.

Острый нож, да хлеба каравай...
Хочешь, примус туго накачай,

А не то веревок собери
Завязать корзину до зари,

Чтобы нам уехать на вокзал,
Где бы нас никто не отыскал.

You and I will sit for a while in the kitchen
The kerosene smells sweet.

A sharp knife, and a big round loaf of bread...
Pump the primus stove high if you like,

Or else gather some string
to tie up the basket before dawn,

So that we can leave for the station
where no one would ever find us.

1931, 15 January

Mandelstam's birthday. He jots down the following in a notebook:
'In January I turned 40. I've reached the age of the rib and the demon.
Constant searching for some shelter, unsatisfied hunger for thought.'
(*Voprosy literatury* (Problems of Literature), 4 (1968), 184.)

1931, March/April

By about this time they are in Moscow. Between 17 and 28 March
Mandelstam writes one of his most dangerous poems, No. 227, known
familiarly as 'The Wolf.' His favourite and almost his only associates
are again the biologists.

1931 Summer

They receive humiliatingly squalid rooms in Dom Gertsena [Herzen's House], which belonged to the Writer's Union, on Tverskoy Boulevard, no. 25, where they are to live until the fall of 1933. Great difficulty finding work. Nadezhda takes a job for the first time, on the newspaper *Za kommunisticheskoe prosveshchenie* (For a Communist Education). Mandelstam writes *Journey to Armenia*. His favorite reading is now Dante.

1932

Though this year is in most respects practically a blank (there are no letters at all, and in her outline of the principal events of their life together, Nadezhda Yakovlevna omits 1932 altogether), it contains an episode that contributed directly to Mandelstam's first arrest and to his eventual downfall. *Hope Against Hope* begins with a sentence that must rank as one of the greatest opening sentences of all time – 'After slapping Alexey Tolstoy in the face, Mandelstam immediately returned to Moscow' – but neither in that book nor in anything else that she has written does she describe the events that led to such a scene. This has not prevented the story from being told in one way or another. In an ill-natured article in the New York émigré paper *Novoe russkoe slovo* (New Russian Word) for 27 February 1966, Gleb Glinka supplies one wildly erroneous account. Yelena Tager's account in *Novyi zhurnal* (New Review), no. 81 (1965) is far more accurate but deals with the aftermath rather than the events themselves. Here is the story as I received it from Nadezhda Mandelstam:

In the house of the Writers' Union on Tverskoy Boulevard the poet and his wife had received three small rooms in a rather dirty and unkempt wing of what had once been a grand Moscow residence, the House of Herzen. In another entrance of the same wing lived the writer Sergey Petrovich Borodin (b. 1902; until 1941 he used the pseudonym of Amir Sargidzhan) and the woman with whom he cohabited, one Tatyana Dubinskaya. Their apartments were entirely separate, with no common kitchen, etc., as has been reported.

> Evidently Sargidzhan and his wife had been set to watch us, and they made constant attempts to trap us. His wife especially kept after me to meet some foreigners. That was very dangerous at the time – the winter of 1932–3. Ten times a day they would both come in to see us, the moment someone else dropped in on us. It's clear that some record was being kept of who visited us. The conversations about foreigners went like this: I absolutely had to meet So-and-so because he would give me some stockings. You could get things from foreigners, they could pass things to you, and so on. It was to me that she was forever coming with that sort of thing – she was a very low type. Osya understood right away that one couldn't talk in the presence of Dubinskaya and Sargidzhan.

Well, the dramatic episode itself happened like this. We were standing outside in the courtyard. She walked past and said something impudent. I can't even remember now what it was, but. . . [What did it refer to? = C.B.] Just like that, apropos of nothing, just shrugged her shoulders and said something. Mandelstam told me to go to our place and not speak to her. We went in and locked the door. Then a minute later there was a scream from the courtyard: 'Mandelstam insulted me!' Sargidzhan came bursting in. . .or rather he didn't burst in, but I opened the door. . .and he hit me. He hit me very hard. He stormed about in the room for a second and ran out. That's all.

What happened next was that the neighboring district court refused to hear the case. We simply wanted to bring him to court, and he'd have had to pay a fine or something for making that scandal. But evidently the district court had been warned not to take the case.

Mandelstam then took his complaint to the Writers' Union itself, and the 'court' that finally tried Sargidzhan was a so-called 'comrades' court,' and amounted to a kind of hearing conducted by the Union itself. The president of this tribunal was Alexey Nikolaevich Tolstoy, a nobleman of the ancient family, a very gifted writer, and one of the most serviceable instruments of the new government. The proceedings were conducted more or less as a trial. Character witnesses were heard. A great number of writers signed a statement on behalf of Sargidzhan, asking that he not be mistreated. Nadezhda Yakovlevna continued:

The sentence that they finally decided on was very strange: they said that the whole affair was a survival from the bourgeois system and that both sides were equally to blame. The crowd that was at the hearing raised an absolutely wild commotion and threw the judges out. The judges took refuge in a little room. The crowd of writers stood there shouting and making a fuss and wouldn't let them out for hours. Finally Alexey Tolstoy came out and they fell upon him shouting. As he forced his way through the crowd he said, 'Leave me alone, leave me alone! I couldn't do anything! We had our orders!' And that was the end of the first episode.

The second episode was the slap in the face. Mandelstam thought the man ought not to have obeyed the orders. Not such orders. That's the whole story.

It is not quite the whole story, to be sure, but the second part of it took place in the spring of 1934.

There's one footnote [she went on]. For one solid month after that Sargidzhan sat in his room and didn't come out. He would come out only very late at night. That often used to be done here – an order would come down that a person who had made a scandal should sit at home and not show himself, not give rise to any talk. One full month he sat there. After the Zhdanov episode Akhmatova was ordered to sit at home for one month. Nobody believed her when she said that, but I knew: Sargidzhan also had to sit at home for a month not going out anywhere.

I've tried to understand why that story with Sargidzhan took place. Probably his job was – in addition to the job of direct surveillance – the job of everyday compromise. It was necessary that a man have a bad reputation. The people had to be prepared to understand that this man is not respectable. That was done very often. One of the most famous cases of everyday compromise was that of the well-known doctor, Dr Pletnyov. He was accused of having bitten his nurse. Photographs, portraits, pictures of the old ottoman, of the nurse. An awful row. That was all done shortly before he was arrested. That's the way public opinion was made to understand that you couldn't have any respect for this man. And probably Sargidzhan had some such job to do. But Sargidzhan was simply – a cad. He overdid it a little bit. Temperament. In any case, it is likely that he was ordered to beat up a woman. It's much more likely that he himself was supposed to get beaten up, or something like that.

He lives in Tashkent. Nowadays he complains to everyone that people don't speak to him after that affair with Mandelstam. And he's forever saying that if only he'd understood, he would...and so on. So evidently the thing did after all sour his life a little.

The above incident strikes me as without doubt the most significant event of Mandelstam's life in 1932. Weight is lent to this view by noting that the Sargidzhan affair, like the earlier 'Dreyfus Case,' had as one of its worst results the drying up of poetry, this time for almost a year. There are no poems dated between August 1932 (No. 266) and May 1933 (No. 267).

1932, 10 November

An 'evening' of Mandelstam's poetry takes place on the premises of the *Literaturnaia gazeta*. Shortly afterwards, the critic and close friend of Mandelstam, Nikolay Ivanovich Khardzhiev, writes to the famous scholar Boris Eykhenbaum the following, which is quoted without permission:

Mandelstam is the only consolation. He is a poet of genius, of valor, a heroic man. A gray-bearded patriarch, Mandelstam presided as shaman for two and a half hours. He recited every poem that he had written (in the past two years) in chronological order!

They were such terrifying exorcisms that many people took fright.

Even Pasternak was afraid – he lisped: 'I envy you your freedom. For me you are a new Khlebnikov. And just as alien to me as he is. I need non-freedom.'

Khardzhiev indicates that during the question period poets who had a cosier relationship with the new regime questioned Mandelstam sharply.

And Mandelstam called them 'Chicago' poems (American *publicity* 'poetry'). He answered them with the haughtiness of a captive emperor – or captive poet.

1933, 14 March

Boris Eykhenbaum, the recipient of Khardzhiev's letter, gives a talk on Mandelstam's poetry, calling it 'the rebirth of Acmeism, bypassing Futurism.' (*Den' poezii* (Day of Poetry), 1967, pp. 167f.)

In the early spring of 1933 Mandelstam was also able to give readings of his poetry at other evenings in Moscow and Leningrad. Yelena Tager remembers one of them for which there had been no announcements, no posters, no publicity whatsoever. But the hall was filled, the aisles were full, the doors jammed. 'Loyalists' were of course present and during the question period handed down notes to the stage.

> One note was clearly meant as a provocation. Osip Emilevich was asked to express his opinion about contemporary Soviet poetry and evaluate the older poets who had come down to us from before the Revolution.
>
> A thousand eyes watched as Mandelstam turned pale. His fingers crumpled the note into a ball. A poet was undergoing public interrogation and had no means of avoiding it. Most of the audience, of course, were simply curious, nothing more, but there were those who turned pale themselves.
>
> Mandelstam strode up to the edge of the stage, his head thrown back as always, his eyes ablaze. 'What do you want from me? What sort of answer?' Then he said, with an adamant, melodious voice: 'I am Akhmatova's contemporary.' And there followed thunder, a squall, a storm of applause. (*Vozdushnye puti* (Aerial Ways), IV (1965), 51f.)

Writing in 1962, Anna Akhmatova recalls the year 1933:

> At that time, Osip Emilevich was met in Leningrad as a great poet, persona grata, and so on; all of literary Leningrad went to pay its respects to him at the Hotel d'Europe...and his arrival and his evenings were events long remembered, remembered even today. (*Aerial Ways*, IV (1965), 35.)

1933 Spring and Summer

The Mandelstams are in the Crimean town of Stary Krym.

Poetry returns in May (No. 267).

Journey to Armenia appears in *Zvezda* (Star), No. 5. This will be his last appearance in the Soviet press for over thirty years, and the last in his lifetime.

1933, 30 August

Pravda for this date carries an article reviewing the first seven issues of *Zvezda* for 1933. In an article entitled 'Teni starogo Peterburga' (Shades of Old Petersburg), S. Rozental singles out *Journey to Armenia* for special attack. It is a collection of fancy phrases, and Mandelstam, like a typical Petersburg snob, overlooks the new achievements of Socialism in Armenia, etc.

1933 Fall

With Bukharin's help they get an apartment in Moscow in the Prechisten-
skaya quarter: no. 5 Nashchokinsky Pereulok, Apt. 26. The street was
later renamed after Furmanov. This grim dwelling in the midst of the
willing toadies of official literature elicited from Pasternak the insensitive
remark: 'Now you've got an apartment – you can write poetry.' In
response Mandelstam wrote 'The apartment is quiet as paper' (No. 272),
a poem of barely controlled fury.

1933/4 Winter

According to Anna Akhmatova, Mandelstam's usual confidante, he was
in love at this time with the poetess Maria Petrovykh. (*Aerial Ways*, IV
(1965), 28.)

1934, 10 January

Poems on the death of Andrey Bely.

1934 Spring

The final episode of the Sargidzhan affair is played out in Leningrad.
In the editorial rooms of the Writers' Publishing House Mandelstam
walks up to Alexey Tolstoy and, to the utter stupefaction of all present,
slaps the enormous man across the face, saying, 'I have punished the
hangman who ordered the beating of my wife!' Yelena Tager, arriving
seconds later, meets Mandelstam and Nadezhda Yakovlevna fleeing the
scene. Inside, witnesses of the outrage are still frozen in attitudes of
horror, like the last tableau of Gogol's *Inspector General*.

Tager writes that Tolstoy, in spite of being urged to do so, refused
to bring charges against Mandelstam. For perfectly obvious reasons,
nevertheless, rumor has persistently associated the name of Tolstoy with
what happened next.

1934, 13 May

The beginning of the end: agents of the secret police come at night to the
apartment on Nashchokinsky Pereulok, seize Mandelstam, and search
their effects. The immediate cause of this first arrest seems to have been
a poem (No. 286) derogatory of Stalin. He is imprisoned and interrogated
in Moscow, then sentenced to three years exile in Cherdyn, a small town
near the upper reaches of the river Kama and to the north of Solikamsk.
Nadezhda goes with him. The detailed account of this period is to be
found in the opening pages of her memoir *Hope Against Hope*.

In Cherdyn he attempts suicide by throwing himself from a hospital
window.

The sentence is somewhat softened by Stalin's personal order. They are allowed to choose residence in some town of European Russia, excluding most of the principal cities. They select Voronezh.

May 1934 – May 1937

The sentence of exile. Mandelstam is on the brink and sometimes over the brink of insanity. Nadezhda's presence is an absolute necessity: when she is absent for even a short while he is attacked by sick dread, breathlessness, fainting.

August 1935 – Dec. 1936

No poems at all for some 16 months.

1936 Summer

With the aid of money sent by Akhmatova, Pasternak and others the Mandelstams manage a few weeks of rest in Zadonsk. News comes of the murder of Kirov in Leningrad. The stage is set for the Great Purge.

1936/7 Winter

As an exile, Mandelstam is practically unemployable. The occasional job, such as writing a radio script on the youth of Goethe, is the only work he can get. During this last winter not even the dirtiest hackwork is available during the increased 'vigilance.' They depend upon the generosity of friends.

1937, 12 Jan. – 14 Feb.

As a last desperate measure of salvation, Mandelstam tries to write an adulatory 'ode' to Stalin. It will not come. In its stead come many other poems. (See *Hope Against Hope*, Chap. 43, and my article 'Into the Heart of Darkness: Mandelstam's Ode to Stalin,' *Slavic Review*, 4(1967), 584–604.)

1937 April

Nadezhda goes to Moscow. Mandelstam begs his mother-in-law to stay with him in an effort to stave off the unendurable attacks of anxiety and shortness of breath that come when he is alone.

He writes to Korney Chukovsky for help: 'There is only one man in the world that one can and must turn to in this matter.' He pleads with Chukovsky to save him by writing to that one man and to persuade others to write.

1938 May

The last surviving poem (No. 395) bears this date.

1938, 16 May

End of the sentence of exile.

1938 Summer

They lose the apartment. Nadezhda had managed to keep her permit to live in Moscow by regularly renewing her papers there rather than in Voronezh. Now the tenant, who wants the rooms for himself, denounces her to the local police, who cancel her registration. From now on they live in various small towns in the Moscow region. Friends give them money.

Lakhuti, an official of the Writers' Union arranges for Mandelstam to make a visit to the construction site of the White Sea Canal, hoping that he will produce poems in celebration of it. Mandelstam brings back one characterless little poem, a description of the landscape, which Nadezhda destroys after his death.

1937 Fall

Mandelstam has one or two heart attacks. Stavsky arranges for him and his wife to stay two months at a sanatorium in Samatikha, about 25 versts from the station of Charusta on the Murom railroad line. They are to remain there while the general question of Mandelstam's suitability as a writer is thrashed out.

1938 March

They arrive in Samatikha.

1938, 30 April

The order for Mandelstam's arrest (No. 2817) is issued on this date.

1938, 2 May

The morning after the May Day celebrations in the sanatorium the secret police come for Mandelstam for the second and last time. He is driven away in a truck.

For several months Nadezhda Yakovlevna stands in line at the Lubyanka to transmit parcels and money on those days when prisoners whose names begin with 'M' are dealt with.

1938, 2 August

Mandelstam is sentenced to five years hard labor for counterrevolutionary activities. He is transferred to Butyrki Prison, where convoys await shipment to the camps.

1938, 7 September

He is sent to a transit camp near Vladivostok to await shipment to a permanent camp.

1938, c. 20 October

Mandelstam's last writing – a scrap of paper addressed to his brother Alexandr and Nadezhda asking for money and warm clothes.

1938, 27 December

The official date of Osip Mandelstam's death. A package sent in response to the letter was returned owing to 'death of addressee.' Two years later (in June 1940) Alexandr received official notice that death occurred on 27 December 1938 as a result of 'heart failure.'

9

The romance of the precise

The romance of the precise is not the elision
Of the tired romance of imprecision.
It is the ever-never-changing same,
An appearance of Again, the diva-dame.

WALLACE STEVENS

I

Better to admit it at once: the topic of this chapter, Mandelstam and
Acmeism, is like a theme assigned by one's composition teacher, and
inspires the same feeling, a certain weariness of the spirit. No wonder
that we – or I at any rate – shrink from it. Writing about an ism has an
air of unreality. In one sense an ism is like a fist, ephemeral. When the
blow has been struck the hand drops its imitation of the cudgel and
resumes its more specific functions – pointing, moulding, caressing. In
another sense, it is as enduring as human nature itself, of which after
all it is merely a concentrated and specialized manifestation. As material
for thought, it offers little resistance, which fact has, sadly enough, made
the ism rather more than less eligible as the subject of numerous theses.

But, running from it, I was pursued by it, in the form of an opportune
passage from Hazlitt's *Table Talk* in Herbert Read's old anthology *The
Knapsack*, taken out into the park at noon:

> A really great and original writer is like nobody but himself. In one sense,
> Sterne was not a wit, nor Shakespeare a poet. It is easy to describe second-
> rate talents, because they fall into a class, and enlist under a standard: but
> first-rate powers defy calculation or comparison, and can be defined only
> by themselves. They are *sui generis*, and make the class to which they belong.

This strikes me as applying pregnantly to Mandelstam. He was a great
and original writer. For very various reasons he nevertheless enlisted himself under a standard with some lesser talents. And as he grew in stature and
power, he did not so much leave the movement as simply cause it to be
coterminous with himself. To write of Mandelstam and Acmeism is to
follow a narrow stream near the point where it rises, through its brief
career as a river, to the point where its waters mingle indistinguishably
with those of a great inland sea. To trace it beyond that would be to
write the story of the sea.

For Mandelstam at one stage of his life as a poet Acmeism was vitally
important; at no stage was it totally without importance. Akhmatova
felt the same – about her great friend as about herself. To the day of her

death she would become incensed at the suggestion, then becoming more and more frequent, that Acmeism was 'merely' a later Symbolism, that it had never been more than a slogan. Like Mandelstam, she was remarkably unsentimental. That she should have insisted upon the relevance of Acmeism in 1966 cannot be left out of account. At the very least, it prompts one to wonder what that relevance might have been.

Nor would Mandelstam ever renounce Acmeism. It was one of the friends that he would not abandon in their distress. In her memoir of him, Akhmatova wrote:

> There in Voronezh he was forced by people whose motives were not very pure to give a talk on Acmeism. What he said in 1937 ought not to be forgotten: 'I renounce neither the living nor the dead.' Asked to define Acmeism, Mandelstam answered: 'a longing for world culture.'[1]

This public lesson in loyalty contains probably the widest definition the movement ever received. The narrowest was that contained in the 1913 manifestations of Gumilyov and Gorodetsky, where one is reminded of the cut-and-dried quality of Pound's *Donts for Imagists*. But neither terminus of this range is qualified for full credence. Both were shots in a polemic, one of them desperate and one, by comparison, almost for fun, but polemics nonetheless, where everything is slightly off balance and extreme. And they appear at the extreme limits of Acmeism in time – or even beyond those limits: Gumilyov's was a recipe for what did not yet exist, Mandelstam's a memorial for what was mostly over. For rhetoric, both prophecies and eulogies vie with polemics.

I shall not, then, undertake any more than the merest outline of Acmeism in order to have a frame to which one might refer. Readers wishing a fuller treatment of this subject may consult Sam Driver's succinct article or William Chalsma's doctoral dissertation.[2]

II

A small notebook belonging to Gumilyov and filled with jottings made in London in 1917 has survived.[3] There among the laundry lists, bits of poems and articles, addresses and appointments for lunch, and the enigmatic 'Kate Syrett/278 Bd Raspail/Paris,' one finds endlessly tantalizing fragments: 'The Poetry book-shop/Southampton-St./nr. Theobald's Rd....*The New Age*/38 Cursitor St./Chancery Lane/Le journal le plus éclairé de l'Angleterre/To-Day/19, Adam street. Adelphi ...Gordon Bottomley/W. H. Davies/Rupert Brooke/Lascelles Abercrombie/F. S. Flint...' and so on.

What is this? A roster of people to read and places to visit, no doubt, a 'must' list for a visiting man of letters extending his acquaintance with literary London; not, probably, people he expected to meet. Brooke had died two years earlier in the Aegean. Whether the others were in London at that moment I don't know. One may doubt whether, with that address, he even found the Poetry Bookshop, then located at 35 Devonshire Street. But he must have done so. It was at the time the central gathering place not of a narrow coterie but of English poets generally – and not only English, for the Italian Marinetti and the American Frost could have been found there on one occasion or another. Surely the Russian Gumilyov put in his appearance. He certainly met Arundel del Re, an Italian journalist and critic whom Harold Monro, the proprietor of the Poetry Bookshop and a doyen of the literary world of the Georgians, had brought to England as a protégé and who was at various times an editor of *Poetry Review* and *Poetry and Drama*. Del Re, the occasional contributor of a 'Letter from London' to *Apollon*, was a natural contact for Gumilyov. The author of a valuable memoir of the period, 'Georgian Reminiscences,' he knew everyone there was to know. First among them, most certainly, was a man whose name does not occur in Gumilyov's notebook, the ubiquitous Ezra Pound, about whom del Re wrote:

> A true poetic genius and a born leader, there has been no really new and vital movement in English poetry since 1910, upon which he has not exercised a clearly marked influence either directly or indirectly, for his personality is probably the most remarkable (that of Robert Bridges excepted) that has appeared in English poetry during the present century.[4]

There has been practically no dissent from these opinions of del Re. The question whether Gumilyov ever encountered Pound in person is therefore really not to the point, for his influence was in any case unavoidable. As for the other man whom one's imagination yearns for Gumilyov to have met, T. E. Hulme, a writer of considerable influence upon Pound himself, he was away in the trenches, where he died that same year.

The reason for bringing up these personal matters of 1917 is not, I regret to say, to answer any questions, but to point the direction in which many absorbing questions lie. For the fact is that some four or five years earlier, and apparently independently of each other, Gumilyov and his associates, on the one hand, and Pound and Hulme and their associates, on the other, had invented or re-invented more or less the same thing. The points of similarity between the goals of the Anglo-American Imagists and those of the Russian Acmeists are so striking that they tease the mind almost intolerably. They had rediscovered the viability in their own age of the kind of poetry advocated by Théophile Gautier – whom both Pound and Gumilyov, incidentally, explicitly hailed as their preceptor. Gumilyov is in fact the translator of Gautier's *Emaux et camées* into Russian. Many other things besides common paternity could of course be cited as leading two sets of young poets toward ideals of precision, balance, hardness, and an almost brutal immediacy and masculinity. A half-century of Darwinism had really only just begun to percolate into that subsoil of culture whence poetry springs. The triumphant machine argued for a new functionalism. In the first year of the new century Henry Adams had contrasted the new mechanical culture with the old in the opposition of the Dynamo and the Virgin: 'All the steam in the world could not, like the Virgin, build Chartres,' he wrote.[5] But the Acmeists quickly saw that the machine had its organic beauty no less than the cathedral. The machine has been so preempted by the Futurists, who made a cult of it, that it seems time to reassert its obvious importance for the Imagists and the Acmeists. Undoubtedly the most important common pressure upon them was the necessity to rebel against a generation of 'fathers' who themselves had much in common. The reigning poets in both countries were utterly self-indulgent and had little truck with the grit and resiliency of the real. The faint pastel hue of the Edwardians and Victorians was no less infuriating to Pound than the effete otherworldliness of the Russian Symbolists was to Gumilyov.

On top of it all, there was certainly *some* degree of contact. Arundel del Re's communications from London were by no means the only channel at the disposal of the Petersburg intellectuals for knowing what was going on in the literary world of England and the West. The literary and art journals of St Petersburg were notably international in outlook and, what is more, in actual coverage. I should think it indisputable that the Russians knew a good deal more of what was going on in Europe than that the reverse were true. Besides, very little 'contact' is really needed among genuine poets. A sentence or two, or a poem, if apprehended by artists ripe to receive their message, can spark a poetic revolt. In 1962, reminiscing about his old schoolmate, Victor Zhirmunsky picked up an open book from the table on the porch of his summer house, sniffed it, and slammed it shut. That, he told me, was all Mandelstam required in order to possess the contents more securely than any doctoral candidate in the subject.

But the question how and whether the Acmeists and Imagists had any knowledge of each other will have to be examined in greater detail in some other place. The point to be made here is simply that readers with some knowledge of what the Imagists demanded in poetry already know a good deal of the Acmeist program.

III

For the finer details of that, we must go to what the Acmeists themselves demanded. Gumilyov's manifesto, entitled 'Acmeism and the Heritage of Symbolism,' appeared in the first issue of *Apollon* for 1913. As befits a manifesto, it is rude, extreme, and in several places it must seem to us now faintly silly. It breathes a zoological hatred not so much for the Symbolists, who are declared dead anyway, as for the Futurists and the Ego-Futurists, whom Gumilyov calls, as if he were just back from one of his African safaris, 'hyenas that always follow after the lion.' He explains the name Acmeism as coming from the Greek ἀκμή, which he defines as meaning 'the highest degree of something, the prime, the time of flourishing.' Andrey Bely, in his memoirs *The Beginning of the Century*, reports that he himself invented the name – and meant it satirically, of course – in a conversation with his fellow Symbolist Vyacheslav Ivanov, and that Gumilyov defiantly accepted it. Gumilyov mentions another name, Adamism, for which Mandelstam says Gorodetsky was responsible, but whoever invented it, it never took hold.[6] Then come the tenets of the new movement, which I shall outline here.

The first position contains a word that is strangely symbolic of the whole spirit of the school: равновесие 'equilibrium'. The new movement would demand 'a greater equilibrium of forces and a more exact knowledge of the relationships between subject and object.' Whatever the latter may mean, the call for balance bespeaks not only the relative sanity of official Acmeism, but also that other face of sanity, its moderate not to say middling quality. As a principle, 'equilibrium' has a low power of suggestion concerning what to write about. It expresses an attitude toward a theme, a treatment of material, but not the theme or the material themselves. There is a notable exception to this, however, and one of great interest for the work of Osip Mandelstam. For equilibrium does suggest not only an 'architecture' of the poem but real architecture itself as a subject. But I shall speak of this in greater detail in the section on 'Animated Temples' (below pp. 183–94).

Acmeism derives, Gumilyov continues, not from Teutonic sources (mystical, Romantic) but from the Mediterranean (Romance clarity). See Ezra Pound's infatuation with the Troubadours and Provence.

Some of Gumilyov's declarations have a kind of minuteness that seems beneath the scale of this clarion document. Acmeists were to strive towards the liberation of meter, for example, by dropping syllables, a free distribution of the stress, rethinking the syllabic system of versification. As it turned out, metrical innovation was far more characteristic of the Symbolists than of the Acmeists, who were for the most part content with the Russian prosodic tradition as they inherited it.

Acmeism will be marked by bright irony as opposed to despairing German seriousness. They will accept the symbol – as what modern poet would not? – but would not sacrifice to it the poet's other means of affecting his reader. It illuminates some of the difference between Symbolism and Acmeism that Alexandr Blok, the best of the Symbolists and for many the greatest Russian poet of this century, would be horrified at this notion that a poem might be so calculated for its effect rather than simply accepted by the poet as a thing donated to him by his talent and the language. That Osip Mandelstam, the greatest of the Acmeists and for many the greatest Russian poet of this century, should largely agree with Blok on this point illuminates the trivialness of labels.

Some of Gumilyov's merely rhetorical jabs, nearly devoid of all objective meaning, have become the best known relics of his article. He said it is more difficult to be an Acmeist than a Symbolist just as it is more difficult to build a cathedral than a tower. But his self-congratulation was really meant to convey a private joke in the word 'tower,' which was the nickname of Vyacheslav Ivanov's apartment, one of the headquarters of Symbolism and, if Bely is to be believed, the birthplace of the name if not the substance of Acmeism. One of the principles of the new school, he continued, was always to follow the line of greatest resistance, another phrase born from the general metaphor of building, the resistance intended being that of the poetic material. It recalls (or rather predicts) Mandelstam's promise at the end of 'Notre Dame' to create beauty from the same 'cruel weight' as could be seen in the Gothic structure.

What salvages Gumilyov's article from being merely a bit of partisan breast-beating is the occasional deeply felt paragraph, the cosmic insight that jostles prescriptions for metrical novelty.

> But to rebel in the name of other conditions of existence here where death exists is as strange as for a prisoner to break down a wall when there's an open door in front of him. Here ethics becomes aesthetics...Here death is the curtain dividing us, the actors, from the spectators, and in the inspiration of our performance we despise all cowardly peeping to know what will come next.

If Gumilyov's posture was often merely a pose, there were postures into which he grew, which became his in earnest. He was in fact neither terrified nor enchanted by death. He did not court death in his Hemingwayesque life of safaris and war, nor did he flee it when, with his New Testament and his Homer, he waited for it before the Bolshevik firing squad. He rather accepted it in the spirit of Tolstoy's 'Three Deaths' and with somewhat greater composure than the author of that story himself. The sentence next following after those I have translated should be read in the light of these reflections: 'As Adamists, we are to a certain extent forest animals, and in any case we will not relinquish the animal part of our nature in exchange for neurasthenia.' His interpretation of that element of the school summed up in its other name lies not in human but in pre-human, primitive nature, in that part of nature that does not thinly intellectualize about the next world, since, after all, the door leading to it is available.

Symbolism had exerted its strongest efforts in the direction of the Unknown. What was to be the Acmeist attitude? The Acmeist was to be conscious of the unknown, but since it was *ex hypothesi* unknowable, he would, in effect, have the common decency not to gossip about it. That is what he meant, but not his phrase. It seems appropriate here, however, for I think that the flirtation carried on by Symbolism with mysticism, theosophy, and the occult had offended two of the strongest traits in Gumilyov's character: his genuine and traditional piety, and his devotion to the gentleman's code. I do not think it an accident that in this paragraph he twice represents the unknowable as ladies – as the dead ladies in Villon's ballade and as the 'beautiful lady' Theology. The term 'beautiful lady' (прекрасная дама) is another of the personal jabs, this time at Blok, who had made the phrase his own in the title of a collection of his poems. But it is also indicative, I think, of Gumilyov's gentlemanly distaste for careless talk about the intimacies of the spiritual life. If, in his ideal commonwealth, the Church would have been separate from the State, she would have been even securer from the tampering of Literature.

The manifesto concludes with a genealogy: the ancestors of Acmeism. There were four, each of them a 'cornerstone of the Acmeist building' (the architectural metaphor is ubiquitous among these builders of poems), and the special contributions from each member of the unusual company deserve mention.

> Shakespeare showed us the inner world of man; Rabelais – the body and its joys, wise corporeality; Villon told us of a life without a trace of self-doubt, though aware of everything – both God and vice, both death and immortality; for this life Théophile Gautier found fit garments of impeccable forms.

Equipped with his knowledge of human psychology and physiology, the Acmeist was to 'adjust' – not in gloomy resignation, but joyfully – to reality, and in the strictness of self-imposed forms write balanced, clear poems about it all.

IV

In the same issue of *Apollon* and immediately following Gumilyov's article was the manifesto of Sergey Gorodetsky. One of the differences between Symbolism and Acmeism is that the Acmeists – to begin with, at least – structured their organization with something like the clarity called for in poems. As a matter of fact, Gorodetsky attributed the demise of Symbolism in part to the lack of one acknowledged leader. There were three 'syndics' of Acmeism, to use their own term: Gumilyov, Gorodetsky, and – to the extent, by no means total, that a closely allied discussion group known as the Guild of Poets was identified with Acmeism – D. Kuzmin-Karavaev, a lawyer and historian who never played a great role and had nothing whatsoever to do with the early theoretical formulations.

As for Gorodetsky, he had the vicious nature of the typical extremist. The most fervid and partisan advocate of Acmeism is precisely the one who first recanted, and who renounced not only the dead but also the living. After Gumilyov's arrest for complicity in a counterrevolutionary plot in 1921, Gorodetsky hastened to denounce him, though such denunciations were by no means so *de rigueur* then as they later became; and later, when such words could easily amount to a kind of verbal homicide, he declared that Anna Akhmatova had gone over to the camp of the class enemy. His voluminous poetry, unlike that of his former associates, is today unread. I shall comment briefly and with distaste upon his manifesto, which cannot, however, be completely ignored, especially as it contains several of the most widely known slogans of the new school.

Ironically enough, the two best-known of these appear in nearly every account of the movement and transmit Acmeism from one age to the next in the voice of its earliest apostate:

> The battle between Acmeism and Symbolism – if it is a battle and not the occupation of an abandoned fortress – is first of all a battle for *this* world – for its sounds, its color, its forms, weight, and time – for our planet Earth.
>
> For the Acmeists the rose has again become beautiful for itself alone, for its petals, scent and color, and not for its supposed likeness to mystical love or anything else.

Gorodetsky touches upon the obligatory 'equilibrium' ('Art is above all a condition of equilibrium') and the architectural figure ('The Symbolists tried to build their verbal monument with no attention to the laws of weight but dreamed of holding it together with nothing more than wires of "correspondences"'). His manifesto is chiefly distinguished from the others by its personal reference. He begins with an extended list of grievances against the Symbolists, whom he names by name; and he concludes by extolling the virtues, exemplary for Acmeism, of Zenkevich, Narbut, Gumilyov, and Akhmatova. Aside from these passages, his article represents little more than a rephrasing of the credo contained in Gumilyov's.

V

In Gorodetsky's rota of enemies and (at the time) friends, Mandelstam is absent. He was soon enough to replace Gorodetsky forever at the head of the movement, but at the moment when the school was *in statu nascendi* Mandelstam was insufficiently prominent to be one of the vendibles in the Acmeist vitrine. Nevertheless, he wrote his own manifesto, of which the history is rather curious. So far as can now be determined, it was never published until his colleague Vladimir Narbut printed it in his Voronezh journal *Sirena* in 1919. At that time the title of it, 'The Morning of Acmeism,' seemed strangely anachronistic. When I published the first translation of it in *The Russian Review* (No. 1, 1965) I made a good deal of the implied challenge in the date of publication, which since no other date was then available, was also taken as roughly the

date of composition. To announce the 'morning' of Acmeism then was
to insist that 1919 was not, as it was widely held to be at the time, rather
more the 'morning after.' It now appears that Mandelstam's article was
written at about the same time as Gumilyov's and Gorodetsky's. Why
it was not published then is not known. No doubt Mandelstam, even
though his first book was published later that same year, was still too
neophyte a poet for his name to shed any lustre upon a new venture.
The editors of his collected works have suggested that Gorodetsky
evidently had some objections to it, but they do not say what these were.[7]
Obviously, as it was not published when the school was being formed,
it could not have had much effect on the larger public conception of
Acmeism. Just as obviously, though, since it must evidently have been
known among those of the inner circle, who did not depend in the tight
little world of Petersburg writers upon publication for their knowledge
of what was afoot, it must have been a statement of some moment.
However that may be, our subject is Mandelstam, not Acmeism, so I
shall give his brief manifesto in full translation.[8]

THE MORNING OF ACMEISM

A.

Given the enormous emotional excitement associated with works of art, it
is desirable that talk about art be marked by the greatest restraint. The
huge majority of people are drawn to a work of art only insofar as they
can detect in it the artist's world view. For the artist, however, a world
view is a tool and instrument, like a hammer in the hands of a stonemason,
and the only thing that is real is the work itself.

To be – that is the artist's greatest pride. He desires no other paradise
than existence, and when he hears talk of reality he only smiles bitterly,
for he knows the endlessly more convincing reality of art. When we see
a mathematician produce the square of a ten-figure number without
thinking about it we are filled with a sort of astonishment. But too often we
fail to see that a poet raises a phenomenon to its tenth power, and the
modest exterior of a work of art often misleads us concerning the monstrously
condensed reality that it possesses. In poetry this reality is the word as such.
Just now, for instance, while I am expressing my thought in the most exact
way that I can, but certainly not in a poetic way, I am speaking essentially
with the consciousness, not with the word. Deaf mutes understand each
other perfectly and railroad signals perform their extremely complicated
function without any recourse to the word. Therefore, if one is to regard
the sense as the content, then one must regard everything else in the word
as a simple mechanical appendage that only impedes the swift transmission
of the thought. 'The word as such' was slow aborning. Gradually, one
after the other, all the elements of the word were drawn into the concept
of form; only the conscious sense, the Logos, is still to this day regarded
erroneously and arbitrarily as the content. There is nothing but detriment
for Logos in this needless honor; Logos requires only to be on an equal

143

footing with the other elements of the word. The Futurist, since he could not manage to cope with the conscious sense as creative material, thoughtlessly threw it overboard and repeated essentially the same crude error as his predecessors.

For the Acmeists the conscious sense of the word, the Logos, is just as splendid a form as music is for the Symbolists.

And if, among the Futurists, the word as such is still creeping on all fours, in Acmeism it has for the first time assumed a more dignified vertical position and entered upon the stone age of its existence.

B.

The sharp edge of Acmeism is not the stiletto nor the sting of Decadence. Acmeism is for those who, seized with the spirit of building, do not cravenly renounce their own gravity, but joyously accept it in order to awaken and use the forces architecturally sleeping in it. The architect says: I build – that is to say, I am right. For us the consciousness of our rightness is dearer than all else in poetry, and – scornfully discarding the jack-straws of the Futurists, for whom there is no pleasure more exquisite than hooking a difficult word on the tip of a knitting needle – we are introducing the Gothic into the relationships of words, just as Sebastian Bach established it in music.

What sort of idiot would agree to build if he did not believe in the reality of his material, the resistance of which he must overcome? A cobblestone in the hands of an architect is transformed into substance, and the man who does not hear a metaphysical proof in the sound of a chisel splitting rock was not born to build. Vladimir Solovyov experienced a special kind of prophetic horror before gray Finnish boulders. The mute eloquence of the granite mass disturbed him like an evil enchantment. But Tyutchev's stone, which, 'having rolled down from the mountain, lay in the valley, torn loose of its own accord or thrown down by a sentient hand,' is the word. In this unexpected fall the voice of matter sounds like articulate speech. This challenge can be answered only with architecture. Reverently the Acmeists pick up this mysterious Tyutchevian stone and lay it in the foundation of their building.

The stone thirsted, as it were, for another existence. It was itself the discoverer of the dynamic potential concealed within it – as if it were asking to be let into the 'groined arch' to participate in the joyous co-operative action of its fellows.

C.

The Symbolists were not good stay-at-homes, they liked to make journeys; but they did not feel well, did not feel quite themselves in the closet of their own organisms and in the universal closet which Kant constructed with his categories.

The first condition of successful building is a genuine piety before the three dimensions of space – to look upon them not as a burden or unlucky accident but as a God-given palace. Really, what is one to say about the ungrateful guest who lives off his host, makes use of his hospitality, and all the while despises him in his soul and thinks only of how to outwit him? It is possible to build only in the name of the 'three dimensions,' since they are the condition of all architecture. That is why an architect has to be a good stay-at-home, and the Symbolists were poor architects. To build means to fight against emptiness, to hypnotize space. The fine arrow of the Gothic belltower is angry, for the whole idea of it is to stab the sky, to reproach it for being empty.

D.

The particularity of a man, that which makes him an individual, is tacitly grasped by us and forms part of the far more significant concept of the organism. Acmeists share their love for the organism and organization with the physiologically brilliant Middle Ages. In its chasing after refinement the nineteenth century lost the secret of genuine complexity. That which in the thirteenth century seemed the logical development of the concept of organism – the Gothic cathedral – now has the aesthetic effect of something monstrous; Notre Dame is a festival of physiology, its Dionysian debauch. We do not wish to divert ourselves with a stroll in the 'forest of symbols,' because we have a more virgin, a denser forest – divine physiology, the boundless complexity of our dark organism.

The Middle Ages, defining in its own way the specific weight of a man, felt and acknowledged it for each man completely regardless of his merits. Men were styled Master readily and with no hesitation. The humblest artisan, the very least clerk, possessed the secret of impressive grandness, of the devout dignity so characteristic of that age. Yes, Europe has passed through a labyrinth of delicate open-work culture, when abstract being, totally unornamented personal existence, was treasured as a sort of heroic accomplishment. Hence the aristocratic intimacy which united all people and which is so alien in spirit to the 'equality and fraternity' of the French Revolution. There is no equality, no competition – there is the complicity of those united in a conspiracy against emptiness and non-existence.

Love the existence of the thing more than the thing itself and your own existence more than yourself: that is the highest commandment of Acmeism.

E.

A = A: what a splendid theme for poetry! Symbolism languished and longed for the law of identity; Acmeism makes it its slogan and offers it instead of the dubious *a realibus ad realiora.*

The ability to feel surprise is the poet's greatest virtue. But how then is one not to be surprised by that most fruitful of all laws, the law of identity? Whoever has been seized with reverential surprise before this law is undoubtedly a poet. Thus, having acknowledged the sovereignty of the law of identity, poetry receives life-long feudal possession of all that exists without condition or limitation. Logic is the kingdom of the unexpected. To think logically means to be continually amazed. We have come to love the music of proof. For us logical relationship is not some ditty about a siskin but a choral symphony with organ, so difficult and inspired that the director must exert all his powers to keep the performers under his control.

How persuasive is the music of Bach! What power of conviction! One must prove and prove endlessly: to accept something in art on faith alone is unworthy of an artist, it is easy and tiresome...We do not fly: we ascend only such towers as we ourselves are able to build.

F.

The Middle Ages are dear to us because they possessed to a high degree the feeling of boundary and partition. They never mixed various levels, and they treated the beyond with huge restraint. A noble mingling of rationality and mysticism and the perception of the world as a living equilibrium makes us kin to this epoch and impels us to derive strength from works which arose on Romance soil around the year 1200. And we shall prove our rightness in such a way that the whole chain of causes and consequences from alpha to omega will shudder in response; we shall learn to carry 'more easily and freely the mobile fetters of existence.'

VI

Enough has been said about the manifestoes of Gumilyov and Gorodetsky to make unnecessary any comment on the obvious similarities between those and Mandelstam's article. The differences are more striking and more interesting.

I think that the most impressive difference on first reading is that it is harder to understand. That may be due in part to Mandelstam's always rather demanding prose style, but it is also due to another of the important differences, namely, that his manifesto is on a considerably higher level of abstraction and theory than either of the others. Later, in his essay 'On the Nature of the Word,' he was to complain about the scantiness of the leaders' theory. There is no prescription for the treatment of syllables in prosody, as in Gumilyov's piece, and, except for a footnote on Vyacheslav Ivanov, there is none of the personal reference to be found in Gorodetsky's. In spite of the occasional dig at the Futurists and Symbolists, it really makes, in sum, a rather unpartisan impression. Though we may never know exactly when this was written or why it was not published at the moment when it had its greatest actuality, one may surmise, I think, that its difficulty and its detachment might easily disqualify it from sharing the dais at the grand opening of a school.

For all its brevity, Mandelstam's article contains a world view of considerable scope and order. He is concerned to fix and identify certain ultimate realities which, taken together, will provide the background for the sort of poetry Acmeists wish to write. He begins with the ultimate reality of the poem, its basic unit the word, and moves from a description of that through a doctrine of the poem, of man, of the universe itself, and of the principle, the law of identity, cementing the whole together. Though one should never forget Mandelstam's cautionary remark at the beginning – that a world view for an artist is 'true' only in the sense that an artisan's tool is 'true,' i.e. if it works, if it permits the writing of poems – I think that this philosophical statement is important enough to examine at some length. He was probably in his early twenties when he wrote it, but I do not think that he ever changed his mind concerning the basic principles of it. Nor do I think that the basic principles according to which he wrote poems changed so much as is sometimes supposed. There would often appear to be, in his later work, a striking lack of such 'Acmeist' merits as order, clarity, logic, equilibrium, and so on; but it seems unfair to invest these words with one's own, rather than Mandelstam's, definition and then to find them inapplicable to him. What follows is therefore a commentary on 'The Morning of Acmeism.'

The article, which is no less than a world view, begins by telling us to disregard, or at least not to overestimate, the world view in a poem. Mandelstam must slightly 'dethrone' the philosophy of a poem, to which too much attention has been paid, and calls it merely a tool or implement. The essence of the poem is the 'word,' its language (by a tradition-hallowed synecdoche in Russian, 'word' stands for language generally). The ultimate reality of the poem, the word is a complex of many parts, which, however, have in a poem no independent existence and which cannot be divided into 'form' and 'content.' The sense of a word enters into its form; its consonants and vowels are a part of the content. The Futurists think that they can ignore one element, the sense, and build poems with such depleted words but they cannot. It should be noted that when Mandelstam uses the phrase 'word as such,' which one normally associates so closely with the Futurists, he means something rather different.[9] I think that in emphasizing the complexity of the 'condensed reality' in a word, he refers to its polysemous, ambiguous nature in a poem and therefore also means something quite different from what the Acmeists generally are thought to have called for: plain, no-nonsense words that denominate things in good burgherly fashion and have done with it.[10] The burden of the first section is that the word is a complex of interdependent parts. It seems pertinent at about this point to recall the formula of Basil Bunting to which Ezra Pound gave such prominence in his *ABC of Reading*: *Dichten = condensare*.

The poem, the larger whole composed of the word as just described, will also be a structure of interrelated, interdependent parts, like a Gothic cathedral. That is what is meant by the assertion that the Acmeists will introduce the 'Gothic' into the relationships of words. The poem as a whole will work, will function, and, like a good building, will not collapse. That is the 'rightness' or correctness that the Acmeists value in their work. It should be noted that the author of *Stone* (1913) lost little opportunity to refer to that material in his manifesto. Two literary allusions and the general metaphor of architecture provide occasions for bringing it in. Solovyov, a poet and philosopher of great importance for the Symbolists, felt a superstitious fear before massive gray stones; but Tyutchev's stone, which seems like a live thing with its own will, is a better image for the word in the poem. The word is a stone. The poem is a structure of words that support and oppose each other, as a cathedral is a structure of stones that support and oppose each other. In a sense, the best commentary on this is Mandelstam's own poem 'Notre Dame' (No. 39).

The poet does not any more make the rules by which his materials combine than the architect invents other dimensions or other forces than gravity and the weather. The world is what it is, and poetry is a part of it. This is a polemic with the Symbolists, who thought themselves endowed with means of getting outside of space-time into 'other worlds.' One of the strongest traits in Mandelstam's nature as a poet is this sense of the immanence of poetry in experience. In the present early statement, as in his latest declarations on the matter, he held with extraordinary tenacity to the view that he was the discoverer (or the recipient) of his poems, or of the occasions when poems were possible. The notion of the poet as a law unto himself, as a being free to create and dispose of his material without regard for what that material itself and the world around it wanted, was utterly abhorrent.

The doctrine of man, and of man in society, is a background to the kind of poetry that Acmeists wish to write. More than that, it greatly resembles the doctrine of the word and the poem and is no less stretched upon the controlling metaphor of the Gothic cathedral. What is important in a man is not his individuality in the sense of what is special and different about him, but his individual share in what is common to all men: his participation in existence. Man is a system of functioning parts and is the essential reality of a larger system of functioning parts, society. For man, read word; for society, poem. If the Symbolists had typically been egocentric, the Futurists were, in public appearances perhaps more than in their actual poetry, egomaniacs. The Acmeists might easily have seen themselves as surrounded by poets bent on a kind of apotheosis of the Self. It seems natural, therefore, that a theorist of Acmeism should plead for a supra-personal view of the human community as the only view that would further the sort of objective poems he wished to write.

Mandelstam's specific rejection of the ideals of the French Revolution provides a target for all the detractors of Acmeism, who never ceased referring to the elitist, anti-democratic tone that they found in gatherings presided over by Gumilyov and in public pronouncements of the group. No doubt the Acmeists often gave good grounds in their actual behavior for these charges of exclusiveness and hauteur; establishing a school and gaining public recognition for it demanded its measure of showmanship, and though the Acmeists never went so far as the Futurists with their painted faces and outré costumes, they undoubtedly elected along with a name deriving from ἀκμή the aloof pose that befitted it. But nothing could be further from the mark than to accuse Mandelstam of actually holding any such views about man in society. Nothing in his behavior or in anything that he wrote could justify it; and this section of his manifesto is no basis, either. The badge of his aristocracy is simple existence, and the nobility is the nobility conferred upon every man by his participation in the larger enterprise of humanity. In Acmeism, or at least in Mandelstam's conception of it, there is a contradictory blend of aristocracy and democracy, a simultaneous cult of nobility and humbleness; and this provides an easy target for those who wish to single out only the first term. But the 'acme' towards which men and poets were to strive was never, in his view, something that could be bequeathed; it could only be attained by relentlessly perfecting one's own skills, by knowing one's trade. Hence the great emphasis upon the nobility of labor, hence the name 'Guild of Poets' for the poetry discussion group affiliated with Acmeism (and often misconstrued as being identical with it), and hence the emphasis upon a Medieval pride in artisanship.

The 'logic' of the Acmeist aesthetic, and world view, rests upon a fairly unassailable basis, the Law of Identity itself, A is A. This is meant of course to strike at the root of the Symbolist method, the 'correspondences' themselves, which might be most simply expressed as A is Something Else. And it is essentially only the formulaic expression of Gorodetsky's more discursive, and more famous, sentence about the rose. It might seem that mystical knowledge of arcane things would lead to astonishment; the calamity of Symbolism was that any charlatan could pretend to such powers, and the result was not surprise but mere tiresomeness. Reality is the only permanent novelty. This section contains the one personal reference in Mandelstam's article (in his footnote), and it should be noted that the person is the Symbolist *maître* Vyacheslav Ivanov, whom Mandelstam had idolized two or three years earlier. But Ivanov frames the section, for it opens with his formula *a realibus ad realiora* and ends with his apartment, the same Tower mentioned by Gumilyov. In a later and somewhat securer statement, discussed below, Mandelstam balanced all this by acknowledging Acmeism's debt to Symbolist ideas and specifically to those of Vyacheslav Ivanov.

The last section adds nothing new to the argument and is a sort of coda. But those themes of the article that it touches upon in a few scant words are of central importance. If one had to settle upon one phrase to describe the Acmeist ideal, one could, I think, do worse than: the world as a living equilibrium. Reduce it further, as Mandelstam later did, and the word would be: organic. The physiology of the Gothic cathedral was no doubt endlessly fruitful as an inspiration, but I think that Mandelstam hints in the very words of this last section at another great idea, one of the most persistent of the Middle Ages and the Renaissance, the 'Great Chain of Being.' The Acmeists were, I think, if one can use without pejorative sense a word that would gratify their detractors, encomiasts of the *status quo*. Their ideal was the real, after all, and whether conceived of as a 'living equilibrium' or as a 'great chain of being,' it had to be conceived of as a system of fixed relationships beneath the lovely mutability of appearance. A commentary upon the whole Acmeist world view might be found in one of the most famous embodiments of the 'great chain' ideology, Ulysses' 'degree' speech from Act I, Scene 3, of *Troilus and Cressida*:

> The heavens themselves, the planets, and this centre
> Observe degree, priority, and place,
> Insisture, course, proportion, season, form,
> Office, and custom, in all line of order:
> And therefore is the glorious planet Sol
> In noble eminence enthron'd and spher'd
> Amidst the other; whose med'cinable eye
> Corrects the ill aspects of planets evil,
> And posts, like the commandment of a king,
> Sans check, to good and bad: but when the planets
> In evil mixture to disorder wander,
> What plagues, and what portents, what mutiny,
> What raging of the sea, shaking of earth,
> Commotion in the winds, frights, changes, horrors,
> Divert and crack, rend and deracinate
> The unity and married calm of states
> Quite from their fixture! O! when degree is shak'd,
> Which is the ladder to all high designs,
> The enterprise is sick.

The occasion for this speech in the play is military and political, but the *status quo* of Mandelstam was the *status quo* of culture – and of culture in a supra-national, broadly human sense. The Acmeists wanted the world to hold still long enough for them to catch a likeness of it. They gave the world a sitting, and sought to capture the beautiful dependency of parts in unison. It is easy to confuse this with a *status quo* in the political sense, but it is also simple-minded to do so. The old revolutionary Ho Chi Minh died as I was writing this, and I was reminded of Mandelstam's interview with him in Moscow in 1923.[11] It is an opportune rebuttal to any view of Mandelstam's attitude as political, let alone reactionary. What appealed to him was the orderliness of traditional Annamese culture: 'I had a vivid image of...these gentle people, with their love for tact and moderation and their hatred of excess.' He saw in the figure of Ho Chi Minh 'the approach of tomorrow, the oceanic silence of universal brotherhood.' It was wholly in his character to respond warmly to a vision of the cultural balance that had existed before the advent of the hated French colonials, the balance *in statu quo ante*, and to sympathize with its restoration through socialist revolution. If that is reaction, it is reaction of a most unconventional kind.

VII

The topic of this chapter is Mandelstam and Acmeism, not Mandelstam's poetics generally. Were it that, it would sprawl beyond the edges not only of such an outline as this but perhaps of the book as well. It would have to take account of the greater part of what he wrote in prose and also of many poems. With some of his maturest utterances on the matter – with the essay on Dante, for instance, which is at least as much about himself as it is about Dante, and with the fundamental credo of the *Vos'mistishiia* – we shall deal later.[12]

For the moment it remains to look at other writings bearing specifically upon his conception of Acmeism. *The Morning of Acmeism*, dating from about 1913 and published in 1919, is the central document: not only was Acmeism its declared, and only, subject, but it was conceived at the moment when Acmeism was enjoying the greatest relevance and actuality that it ever had. But it is framed in time by two works, the essay on Villon of 1910 and the essay 'On the Nature of the Word' of 1922, which will repay examination.

The essay on Villon is interesting for its date alone, for the earliness of the time when Mandelstam was giving expression to some of the fundamental canons of Acmeist taste. This is not to say that its subject, who was after all declared by Gumilyov to be an Acmeist ancestor, is without interest. It was not published in *Apollon* until a few months after Gumilyov had already announced in those pages the school and its genealogy, but it was written three years earlier. Not that Mandelstam was the only Russian poet obviously pleading at this time for a move away from Symbolism in the Acmeist direction: Mikhail Kuzmin's essay 'On Beautiful Clarity' appeared in 1910, and one can glean more than a few 'Acmeist' positions (as well as many contrary utterances) from Gumilyov's own writings of that same year.

Villon's eligibility as an Acmeist is immediately declared. He was, Mandelstam begins, like an earlier appearance of Verlaine: both had revolted against an 'artificial, hothouse' poetry (understand: Symbolism). About half the essay is given over to details of Villon's life, which Mandelstam narrates with indulgent amusement. There is a remarkable characterization of the lyric poet as a type:

> His revolt is more like a case at law than a rebellion. He succeeded in uniting in one person both plaintiff and defendant. Villon's relationship

with himself never exceeded certain bounds of intimacy. He is tender, attentive, concerned for himself, but no more so than a good lawyer is for his client. Self-compassion is a parasitical feeling, pernicious both for the soul and the organism. But the dry, juridical mercy which Villon shows himself turns out for him to be a source of good cheer and of an unshakeable faith in the justice of his 'case.' An extremely dissolute, 'amoral' man, like a true descendant of the Romans, he lives completely in the world of legality and cannot imagine any relationships outside of jurisdiction and norm. A lyric poet is by his very nature a bisexual creature, capable of dividing endlessly for the sake of his internal dialogue. No one has ever so clearly exhibited this 'lyrical hermaphroditism' as Villon. What a varied selection of enchanting duets: the embittered one and his comforter, mother and child, judge and accused, man of property and beggar...

And there is even a forestalling of certain phrases of Gumilyov's manifesto ('Villon distinctly realized the abyss between subject and object') and of that passage in his review of Mandelstam's first book where he praises him for having become an Acmeist by renouncing the moon for more mundane affairs ('The moon and other neutral "objects" were irreversibly excluded from his poetic usage. On the other hand, he comes to life at once when the talk gets round to roast ducks in sauce...').

But it is in the final paragraphs of the essay, where the topic is the physiology of the Gothic, that one gets a true foreglimpse of the Acmeist manifesto – and not only of that. But of that principally. Identical phrases were lifted from the Villon essay for the manifesto:

The physiology of the Gothic – such a thing existed, and that is precisely what the Middle Ages are: a physiologically ingenious age – took the place of a world view for Villon and recompensed him many times over for his lack of any traditional link with the past...What, if not architectonics, explains the miraculous equilibrium of the stanza in which Villon entrusts his soul to the Trinity through the Virgin Mary...The man of the Middle Ages thought himself just as indispensable and as joined to the universal building as any stone in a Gothic structure...Without being conscious of it, the medieval man regarded the unadorned fact of his own existence as service, as a kind of feat.

The essay on Villon is Mandelstam's earliest effort in prose. This makes it all the more impressive that it should have contained *in nuce* one of his last poems. In comparing the fluent dynamism of a Gothic cathedral to that of an ocean surge he anticipated No. 374 ('Я видел озеро'), a poem then twenty-seven years in the future. He also anticipated one much nearer at hand – 'Notre Dame.' For a commentary on both of these, see below, pp. 186, 192.

In 1928 when Mandelstam gathered eleven of his critical essays into the book *On Poetry*, he put the Villon piece, for all its priority in time, in the last place. He also dated it (which he did for only one other essay in the collection) as if calling attention to the time when he had first argued many of the positions that were later to solidify, for a time at least, into the doctrine of a school.

VIII

In 1910 Mandelstam was a nineteen-year-old student of philosophy and Old French in Heidelberg, school and Paris then behind him; in 1913, the supposed date of the manifesto, he was a young man, already a poet of some narrow renown, the author of a first collection of poems, in St Petersburg; in 1922 he was a poet of much wider fame, the author of two books and numerous essays, much in demand, married, and, not least, the survivor of a war, a revolution and a civil war – upheavals that had gravely imperilled the values informing his literary views. The last date is the date of 'On the Nature of the Word.' Mandelstam published it first as a separate booklet in Kharkov, in the Ukraine. The cover bore an epigraph from a poem by Gumilyov, shot the previous year by a Bolshevik firing squad; but this, like much else besides, had to be removed by the time the essay appeared in the 1928 edition. In that collection it is still roughly twice as long as any other essay, and its central position also underscores its central importance. If the word, as Mandelstam had reiterated by printing his manifesto in 1919, is the ultimate reality of the poem, then the essay on the nature of the word will be pivotal in a book entitled *On Poetry*.

In preparing the essay for its 1928 publication, Mandelstam had to omit more than the epigraph: he had to omit all reference to Acmeism, which was by then as officially dead as Gumilyov. This explains the omission of so important an essay as 'The Morning of Acmeism,' which as a bugle call of 1913 would, anyway, have lacked immediacy at the end of the 1920s. The Villon essay, it is true, was included and contained much of the manifesto, as we have seen. The essay on the nature of the word also contained the stamps and stubble of Acmeism, but in 1928 it would have required a very astute reader to recognize them. The reason why Mandelstam's Acmeism had absolutely to be shielded from a Soviet audience will emerge from a consideration of what, by 1922, it had become. For it was half poetics, and half moral force.

The dimensions of the essay (rather long for Mandelstam) make it eligible as a separate booklet, and so do its concerns. It leads up to the definition of Acmeism at the end, but along the way it deals with several matters and a number of Russian authors (Khlebnikov, Andrey Bely, Chaadaev, Rozanov, Balmont, and Annensky – a poet revered by the Acmeists and regarded by them and others as a chief inspirer of their program) which to explore here would be impossible. Our topic is Mandelstam and Acmeism. If we permitted ourselves to be controlled by Mandelstam's own tendency – which was, I think, as official Acmeism

disintegrated, more and more to identify the term with his own poetic –
then we should find this note expanded to the size of a book.

The general argument of the essay is to answer the question whether
there exists one isolable entity called Russian literature, stretching from
the Igor Tale to Khlebnikov; and, if there is, by what it is united. The
answer, not in itself astonishing, is that the Russian language is the
unifying force. Had the argument stopped there we should have been
left with an overly complicated statement of a textbook commonplace.
It doesn't, of course, and the heart of the essay is a discussion of the
nature of language (the 'word') and how, if that is the unifying principle
of an historical phenomenon extending across centuries, one is to conceive
of it as linking the beginning with the latest terminus. For this purpose
Mandelstam calls upon a philosopher who profoundly influenced his
view of the world, Henri Bergson. He makes this explicitly clear:

> In order to salvage the principle of unity in the whirlwind of changes and
> in the ceaseless flow of phenomena, modern philosophy in the person of
> Bergson, whose profoundly Judaic mind is gripped by an insistent need for
> practical monotheism, offers us a doctrine concerning the system of
> phenomena. Bergson regards phenomena not in the order of their sub-
> ordination to a rule of temporal sequence, but, as it were, in their spatial
> extent [or perhaps, to keep it closer to Bergson's terminology, in their
> 'duration']. He is interested exclusively in the internal linkage of phenomena.
> This linkage he liberates from time and considers separately. The phenomena
> that are thus interlinked form as it were a kind of fan, the panels of which
> one can unfurl in time, but at the same time it lends itself to a rolling
> up that the mind can comprehend.

The connection between Bergson and Mandelstam is a topic that would
repay extensive study; for the moment the briefest mention must suffice.
It is enough to quote a few sentences to demonstrate how Bergson's
very style has been absorbed into the depiction of the language, a kind of
durée made palpable and present:

> To return to the question whether Russian literature is one and if so what
> is the principle of its continuity, we discard at the very outset the theory
> of improvement [i.e. progress]. We shall be speaking only about the inner
> connection of phenomena and we shall try first of all to discover criteria
> of possible unity, a pivot that will enable us to unfold in time the various
> and scattered phenomena of literature.
>
> As the criterion of unity for the literature of a given people, of the
> relative unity, we can recognize only the language of the people, for all other
> indications are themselves relative, temporary and derivative.[13] But language,
> though it does change, does not for a single minute harden at rest, from one
> point to another, each of them blindingly clear to the mind of philologists;
> and within the bounds of all its changes it remains an unchanging magnitude,
> a 'constant,' remains internally one.

The pages of Bergson will furnish any number of passages to set beside these.

The central part of Mandelstam's essay is a hymn to the Russian language of such extraordinary power and such brimming love as to make other much anthologized encomia, such as that by Turgenev, seem feeble valentines. Nowhere does the Russian language emerge with such physicality of being. His own pages often testify to his sense of the language as an almost tangible presence, and in this essay, aided by Bergson's image-laden conception of time, he literally bodies forth the Russian language as a 'turbulent sea of events' in which Russian history and culture are awash. Useless to seek to pin Mandelstam's picture of the language like some butterfly in a case: it will not hold still, and it undergoes metamorphosis before one's very eyes. Is it a sea? It is flesh, sounding and speaking flesh, endowed with the secret of free embodiment, hence 'Hellenistic.' And so on. It must be intuited, after all, not known. What emerges, however, is a powerful 'feel' of the Russian language as an ambience with a being of its own, which – and the polemical points rest upon this – must be respected. Bad poets violate the nature of the word, 'apply it' to this or that purpose; good poets cooperate. We come thus to Acmeism, for which he has a new name – the 'organic school.'

As applied to the word, such an understanding of verbal concepts opens broad new perspectives and allows one to envisage the creation of an organic poetics – not legislating in character, but biological...having all the traits of biological science.

The task of creating such a poetics was assumed by the organic school of the Russian lyric, which grew out of the creative initiative of Gumilyov and Gorodetsky at the beginning of 1912, and officially included Akhmatova, Narbut, Zenkevich, and the author of these lines. The very small literature about Acmeism and its leaders' miserliness regarding theory make the study of it difficult. Acmeism arose out of repulsion: Away from Symbolism, Long live the living rose! – such was its original slogan. Gorodetsky in his time attempted to inoculate Acmeism with a literary world view – 'Adamism' – a sort of doctrine about a new earth and a new Adam. The attempt was unsuccessful, Acmeism did not concern itself with a world view; it brought with it a number of new tastes, much more valuable than ideas, and above all the taste for an integral verbal conception, the image, understood in a new organic way. Literary schools do not live by ideas but by tastes. To bring with oneself a whole heap of new ideas but not new tastes means not to create a new school but only to start a polemic. On the contrary, it is possible to create a school on the basis of taste alone, without any ideas whatsoever. It was not the ideas but the tastes of the Acmeists that proved to be lethal for Symbolism. The ideas turned out to be in part taken over from the Symbolists, and Vyacheslav Ivanov himself did much to further the construction of Acmeist theory. But see what a miracle resulted: for those who live within Russian poetry a new blood began to flow through its veins. It is said that faith moves mountains, but I say that as regards poetry it is taste that moves mountains. Owing to the fact that in Russia at the beginning of this century there arose a new taste such massifs as Rabelais, Shakespeare, and Racine were removed from their places and came to us for a visit. The lifting power of Acmeism in the sense of its active love for literature, for its difficulties, for its burden, is extraordinarily great; and the lever of this active love was precisely this new taste, the manly will [to create] a poetry and poetics in the center of which stood man, not flattened into a lozenge by pseudo-Symbolist horrors, but as the master of his own house; a genuine Symbolism, surrounded with symbols, that is to say, with utensils, possessing verbal concepts as its own organs.

More than once in Russian society there have been moments of ingenious reading in the heart of Western literature...The Acmeist wind turned the pages of the classics and the romantics, and they fell open at the very place that was most needed by the age. Racine opened at *Phèdre*, Hoffmann at the *Serapion Brothers*. The iambics of Chénier came to light, and the *Iliad* of Homer. Acmeism is not only a literary but also a social phenomenon in Russian history. In Russian poetry there came along with it a rebirth of moral force. Bryusov said, 'I want the free ship to sail everywhere; and I shall praise equally both the Lord and the devil.' This wretched 'nothingism' will never be repeated in Russian poetry. The social inspiration of Russian poetry has up to now reached no further than the 'citizen,' but there is a higher principle than that of 'citizen,' – the concept of 'man' [the Russian word here means *vir*, not *homo*].

The new Russian poetry, as distinct from the old civic poetry, must educate not only citizens, but also 'men.' The ideal of absolute manliness was prepared for by the style and the practical demands of our epoch. Everything has become heavier and more massive; therefore man also must become harder, since man must be the hardest thing on earth – he must be to it what the diamond is to glass. It is the conviction that man is harder than everything else in the world that makes for the hieratic, that is to say, the sacred character of poetry.

The age will cease its noise, culture will fall asleep, the people will be regenerated after having given over their best energies to a new social class, and all this current will draw after it the fragile ship of the human word into the open sea of the future, where there is no sympathetic understanding, where sad commentary replaces the fresh wind of the enmity and the sympathy of contemporaries. How is it possible to fit out this ship for its long voyage if one does not supply it with everything that will be necessary to such a distant and such a valuable reader? Once more I shall compare the poem to the Egyptian ship of the dead. All the needs of life have been stored, nothing has been forgotten in that ship. But I see the possibility of numerous objections and the beginning of a reaction to Acmeism in this, its initial formulation, like the crisis of pseudo-Symbolism. Pure biology is not suitable for the construction of a poetics. The biological analogy is good and fruitful, but to apply it consistently would mean to create a biological canon, no less crushing and intolerable than that of pseudo-Symbolism. 'The rational abyss of the Gothic soul' [a phrase from Mandelstam's poem 'Notre Dame'] peers out of the physiological conception of art. Salieri merits respect and fervent love. It was not his fault that he heard the music of algebra just as powerfully as he heard living harmony.

In the place of the romantic, the idealist, the aristocratic dreamer about the pure symbol, about an abstract aesthetics of the word, in the place of Symbolism, Futurism and Imaginism, has arrived a living poetry of the word-object; and its creator is not the idealist-dreamer Mozart, but the stern and strict artisan Salieri, reaching out his hand to the master of things and material values, to the builder and creator of the concrete world.

If you discount more or less random utterances like that remark in 1933 about the longing for world culture, this essay was the last thing Mandelstam had to say about Acmeism as he understood it. In my view, it was a useful thing, one that provides a way of looking not only at Acmeism but at any ism. It is a question of taste, pure and simple, though one must understand the taste in question to be fashioned out of moral no less than aesthetic predilections.

I should like to conclude by saying that one of the best ways to grasp Acmeism, or any other ism, or what there is to grasp of them, is to examine the worst poems of the minor poets of the movement. They tend to be parodies, which are revealing and edifying. In Auden's 'Daydream College for Bards' the curriculum would include 'no books of literary criticism, and the only critical exercise required of students would be the writing of parodies.'[14] I think that some isms only exist for the purpose of rearing a generation of students, who learn by parodying its requirements and then, when they have learnt their trade, go on to do their own work, to which, if they are geniuses, the ism has no relevance aside from the genealogical; but if they are ungifted they never leave school and go on parodying it or themselves or something else forever.

Consider Zenkevich, a minor poet who went on to become a carpenter of translations. Take Georgy Ivanov during his minor – i.e. Acmeist – period, before he 'left school.' Take Gorodetsky, a minor poet who became a non-poet. Take that noble and tragic minor poet Gumilyov, whose future – possibly brilliant, possibly as a great poet – was denied him. At their weakest, their most school-conscious moments, they show us the skeletal structure of Acmeism. Their 'thing' poems posit mere subjects of such tedium that one is not inclined to wait for the predication. Their 'brute' poems become catalogues from a biology text. Their vigorous and manly poems inspire the feelings that come from watching some sports-minded curate at his calisthenics.[15]

Ivanov's early poems are as acmeist as anything ever written, and they are nearly too boring to read. There is evidently nothing of himself in them. They were written to the recipe of Acmeism but without the slightest moral conviction. When he found (in exile, in Paris) his real voice, his actual passion, he wrote moving poems of great power. There isn't a trace of Acmeism in them – neither of the early nor of the later,

Mandelstamian, variety – for they are totally immoral, that is to say, immoral from the point of view of Acmeism. Acmeists like Mandelstam and Akhmatova could be pessimistic about their personal fate or even about the 'age,' but the vision of a world devoid of all moral sanctions is utterly foreign to them. They were not profound philosophers on this point. They accepted a traditional humanistic code, not less traditional for its being so seldom observed, of ordinary decency. It was ultimately the morality of the New Testament and the middle class. In respect of the former, it was primitive and free of doctrinal accretions; in respect of the latter, it was untouched by either the philistine or the hypocritical. The entire credo can be put without undue simplicity in the terms familiar to children: one should tell the truth, pay honest debts, help the unfortunate, never steal or kill, refrain from excess, love others, life itself, and God. To celebrate as Ivanov did the opposite of these things in poetry, however one conducted one's life, was, for the Acmeists, unthinkable.

10

'Stone'

For the listener, who listens in the snow,
And, nothing himself, beholds
Nothing that is not there and the nothing that is.
WALLACE STEVENS, 'The Snow Man'

I. MANDELSTAM'S BOOKS OF POEMS

Here is a brief indication of the collections of his own work made by Mandelstam himself. It is not a full bibliographic account. That is readily available in the third volume of the New York edition (and the reader ought to consult the bibliography of the 1955 edition as well, for it helpfully shows which poems were where). There is another, far more intimate story of Mandelstam's attitude toward the groupings of his work, both public and private, in the memoirs of his widow.

Mandelstam published two books of poetry, or two and a half, or three, depending upon how you wish to regard a special section of poems that appeared in the collection of 1928. The first was *Kamen'* (Stone), the second *Tristia*. And when these appeared under their original titles within the collection *Stikhotvoreniia* (Poems) of 1928, Mandelstam printed twenty poems under the rubric '1921–1925.'

These books appeared in various editions, under various names, and – what is somewhat more surprising and confusing – with a varied composition of poems. A poem of one collection can wander dreamily and without much apparent reason into the other. Thus 'Nashedshii podkovu' (The Horseshoe Finder), a poem of 1923, was attached to the edition of *Stone* that appeared that year. It also turned up in the edition of *Tristia* of that year. Finally, it found its chronological home in the third section of *Poems* under its correct temporal rubric – '1921–1925.' And there were a number of other such nomads, but this slight shifting about was confined to the periphery: the fundamental stock of poems remained largely constant and the identity of the books was never seriously altered. I expect that while Mandelstam was much concerned over the fundamental character of his books, he would willingly concede this or that to the exigencies of publishers and the book trade. The easiest way to grasp how and when his books appeared is to put them on a chart under their real names.

    1913   *Stone*
    1916   *Stone*
    1922   *Tristia*

1923   *Stone* (Subtitled: First Book of Poems)
        Tristia (Actual title: *Vtoraia kniga*, i.e. *Second Book*)

1928   *Stone*
        Tristia   Sections of a book entitled *Poems*
        1921–1925

Strictly speaking, Mandelstam published five other books of poems between the two books of 1923 and the collection of 1928. Four of them were little books for children – delightful, and repaying study, no doubt, but not to be treated by me – and the other was a translation of slight value. I shall deal with the individual editions of the fundamental books in the sections where I discuss them as a whole. During the years when he was bringing out these five books he was supporting himself by many exertions of a similar kind. We know only a portion of the many works of prose that he translated or edited, but it should be noted that among the authors who reached their Russian audience through the efforts of Osip Mandelstam were Upton Sinclair and...Captain Mayne Reid. The legend that he had abandoned poetry and become a translator was launched at about this time.

It remains to add a word about the collections that never saw the light of day during his lifetime. One should remember, incidentally, that the legend I mention had some basis in fact. As I have mentioned already, Mandelstam was poetically silent for five years, from 1926 to 1930. And there was another such period during the Voronezh exile – from August 1935 to December 1936: sixteen months. It is hardly necessary to add that no poem is known to have been written between the spring of 1937 and his death in December 1938.

In speaking of Mandelstam's private collections one is therefore speaking of the poems written from 1930 to 1937. These fall into two groups.

The first, called 'New Poems,' existed in two notebooks, called simply 'First Notebook' and 'Second Notebook,' and contained the work from 1930 to 1934. The *originals* of these had been confiscated by the police at the first arrest. What now exists are the poems of that period that were reconstituted from memory and written down in Voronezh.

The second group contained the poems of 1935 to 1937, which were written down in three notebooks, called, respectively, 'First,' 'Second,' and 'Third Voronezh Notebook.'

It must be perfectly obvious that what information I have on the matters immediately preceding comes in its entirety from the one person who could have told me, Nadezhda Yakovlevna, who was herself the amanuensis of all the texts from 1930 to 1937. Her account of the origin of that rich fund of poetry, and of the nature of its first storehouse, is the fullest and the only authoritative account that we shall ever have, and it is now available in her published memoirs.

That was what Mandelstam published while he was alive, and those were the general contours of what he wrote but could not publish. There is yet a third level, the level of the 'author's last wish,' that is to say, those revisions of already published work that Mandelstam wished to make. To this level we have scarcely begun to penetrate, and we shall not fully know it until those conditions that impede intellectual commerce in the world have improved. But I should like to suggest it here if only to indicate how much is left to be done before we have a clear idea of what Mandelstam wished to remain as the work of his pen.

Natalia Yevgenevna Shtempel, whose kindness to the Mandelstams in Voronezh was so sustaining, to whom some of his most beautiful lines were addressed, and who helped save much of his work from destruction in the Hitler war, once showed me her copy of the 1928 collection *Poems*. In Mandelstam's own hand there were many alterations, each of them signed with his initials, the letter 'V' for Voronezh, and the date ('37') – a formal and deliberate procedure that gives his emendations a certain weight. On page 64, for example, the poem entitled '1913' (No. 57) was cancelled entirely and the cancellation signed by the author. Were I the editor of his work, I should certainly not eliminate it from *Stone* on that account: no one, not even the author, can change the fact of its having been there. But I should note the disavowal. And what is more to the present point, if I were writing a history of the book, I should be uncomfortably aware that my knowledge of the cancellation had come to me haphazardly, that there must be entirely too much of which I was unaware, and that all accounts of the history of Mandelstam's books must at the moment be tentative and sketchy.

II. SEASHELL

Since there was something troublesome, anyway, about the titles of Mandelstam's books, it is perhaps excusable to consider still other titles for them. It is an aid to summing up impressions and, half-serious though it may be, it does force one to sort out some of the multifariousness of the book. What else might the first collection, *Stone*, have been called?

The most obvious alternative title is one that the book did in fact bear at one stage in its prehistory: *Rakovina*, the first meaning of which is 'seashell.'[1] This evidently derives from the poem (No. 26) of that name, though I think it better to avoid any too automatic assumption that the poem, because it once furnished the name for the book, is therefore of peculiarly emblematic significance, a succinct statement, say, of the whole. Mandelstam did conceive of a book of poems as a distinct whole, a stage of his work with its own individual character and not simply a fortuitous gathering of what had accumulated. This might lead one to look for a poem that expresses that uniqueness more completely and sharply than others. Whether 'The Seashell' does so will appear from what follows.

But quite apart from its attachment to a certain poem, the word *rakovina* is eligible on its own independent merits as the title of a collection, especially if the collection be that of a man recently (in fact, in mid-book) associated with the school of Acmeism. The actual etymology of the word seems in dispute,[2] but historical accuracy is quite beside the point, for every Russian will immediately associate the first part of *rakovina* with *rak*, which means 'crawfish' or 'shellfish'; and for the Acmeists, with their pronounced animalism, the crustaceans seemed low on a satisfyingly remote rung of evolution. The shell is appealing on many other grounds as well. As a beautiful, patterned object of sculptural form, an object produced by an animal and in comparison with the animal himself, vastly more permanent, it easily furnishes an emblem of poetry, as the Acmeists and many others conceived it. Its link with the sea summons up the classical world of the Mediterranean, and its auditory associations – the sounding, musical overtones of seashell – make it a powerful echo of the Hellenic past to which Mandelstam was so powerfully attracted.

In his book *Men Without Art* (1934) Wyndham Lewis presents what he calls 'the theory of the External, the Classical, approach in Art.' That is in the chapter entitled 'Mr Wyndham Lewis: "Personal-Appearance" Artist.' Objecting to the 'jelly-fish' contours of certain forms of art – he instances Joyce's *Ulysses* and Rodin's 'cleverly dreamified stone-photographs of naked nature,' – he writes: 'To put this matter in a nutshell, it is *the shell* of the animal that the plastically-minded artist will prefer. The ossature is my favorite part of a living animal organism, not its intestines.'

This may be in one of Lewis's favorite idioms, that of the crank pamphlet, but it is nevertheless an opportune statement of the grounds on which a shell might appeal to an artist who was an Acmeist *in posse* long before becoming one in fact.

But if the automatic assumption that the poem, because of its lending its title to the book, recapitulates the book in little is to be avoided, nevertheless there may be some presumption of a thematic link between the poem and the book as a whole. Here is the poem:

> Быть может, я тебе не нужен,
> Ночь; из пучины мировой,
> Как раковина без жемчужин,
> Я выброшен на берег твой.
>
> Ты равнодушно волны пенишь
> И несговорчиво поешь;
> Но ты полюбишь, ты оценишь
> Ненужной раковины ложь.

Ты на песок с ней рядом ляжешь,
Оденешь ризою своей,
Ты неразрывно с нею свяжешь
Огромный колокол зыбей;

И хрупкой раковины стены,
Как нежилого сердца дом,
Наполнишь шопотами пены,
Туманом, ветром и дождем...   (No. 26, 1911.)

Perhaps I am not necessary to you,
Night; out of the universal gulf
Like a shell without pearls
I am cast up on your shore.

You froth the waves indifferently
And obstinately sing.
But you will love and know the worth
Of the lie of the useless shell.

You will lie down on the sand beside it
Will cover it with your chasuble
You will bind to it inseparably
The enormous bell of the billows.

And the walls of the fragile shell,
Like the house of an empty heart,
You will fill with the whispers of foam,
With fog, wind and the rain...

It is perhaps good to begin with a poem that is not terribly demanding.
This beautiful little lyric is a slight thing in several ways, but, like many
of the early poems of *Stone*, it is a slight thing exceedingly well done –
one is reminded of T. S. Eliot's remark about the early poems of Blake,
that they were 'quite mature and successful attempts to do something
small.' The symbolism of the poem – and it should be noted that it *is*
a Symbolist poem in a rather emphatic way – is hardly novel. The
dominance of hushing sibilants in a poem about the waves of the sea is
more or less *de rigueur*. The figure of the 'house of an empty [or literally,
untenanted] heart' recalls Pushkin's renowned image of the dying Lensky.
And the very neatness of that clipped epigrammatic ending – three words
in identical cases, in an iambic tetrameter line with a missing accent on
the third foot (statistically the commonest variation in Pushkin) – also
makes it seem that the Master's finger was holding the knot for Mandelstam to tie.

In one respect 'The Seashell' is wholly typical of Mandelstam's early
poems (and perhaps of the early poems of most modern poets) in that
it is about poetry. The poet is a shell, and the other person in this implied
dialogue (actually a lyric monologue, of course) is the world, in the

figure of night. The poet of this poem is, typically for Mandelstam, not the poet–maker but the poet–instrument, not the creator of his poems but the receiver and transmitter of them. The shell is night's creature. It is fragile and empty and passive where the world is overpowering and irresistible, but, without it, the world would lack a coherent voice. There is, therefore, underneath the fragility and the assertion of uselessness a rather considerable touch of arrogance, or at least of serene self-confidence. The 'lie' of the poet will be loved, for he will, after all, be the instrument of nature's grandest effects.

The one other theme that ought to be mentioned is the contrast seen in the two 'persons' of the poem. That contrast is one that appears almost to have obsessed Mandelstam, for it is present in his earliest work and in nearly everything that he wrote, whether in poetry or prose, for the rest of his days. It was, if anything was, the master metaphor of his entire *oeuvre*, and since it will become a great deal clearer after rather than before reading many poems, I shall only mention it here. It is the contrast of the fragile versus the huge, weak vs. strong, passive vs. active, and...but once the general semantic juxtaposition is clear, it is pointless to comb the thesaurus for antonyms. Given the 'key' of this fundamental dichotomy, the reader can extend it for himself. The metaphor is that of victim and oppressor, and in poetic terms these can be represented in an endless number of ways: the mouse and the lion, the reed and the oak, the flute and the organ. It is the clash of whatever is hot, oily, mammoth, and cruel with whatever is cold, clean, petite and meek. Mandelstam returned so persistently to this clash and to the terror inherent in it that I think it must be partly to blame for the distorted image of him (discussed above in Chap. 2) left by the memoirists. Consciously or not, they read their awareness of this controlling metaphor into their perception of the man in life, where he was always assigned the role of the fragile victim.

To be sure, it would require a peculiarly antiseptic kind of criticism to treat this ever-present juxtaposition as divorced from Mandelstam's idea of himself. No doubt in the inwardness of his poetic imagination, Mandelstam often did feel himself identified with the delicate, helpless, passive victim of a crushing reality. But there is a great difference between what a man is and what his imagination suggests to him, and we are now concerned with the imagination.

III. SILENCE

There is another poem that might have furnished a title for the first book, and that is 'Silentium' (No. 14). It never in fact did, so far as I know. But silence itself, muteness, tongue-tie – this is a central theme of Mandelstam's earliest poems. As a theme it tempts one to grand flights of interpretation. Did the all-pervasive master metaphor, by which qualities immediately summon forth the juxtaposition of their diametrical opposites, suggest this? If poetry itself is a constant concern, this *eo ipso* suggests not-poetry, or silence. The effort to impose upon words the order of a poem suggests the tangling and stuttering of not-order, of tongue-tie. Speech: muteness. Silence is the limitless, the unfathomable and ubiquitous ambience against which speech has its momentary being: it is the death of which poetry is the life. To follow this train to an *O Altitudo* of conjecture might lead one to dalliance with notions of the death-wish – for silence is no mere theme in these poems, it is the consummation devoutly to be wished, the goal of the lyric ego. And perhaps that would not be wrong. But I don't know, for I lack any information on the point other than that in the poems themselves. And the evidence of the poems is simply that Mandelstam used a persistent cluster of ideas, a cluster for which we might adopt the title 'Silentium,' as the occasion for some of his best poetry. Here is the poem, dated 1910, that bears that title:

Она еще не родилась,
Она и музыка и слово,
И потому всего живого
Ненарушаемая связь.

Спокойно дышат моря груди,
Но, как безумный, светел день,
И пены бледная сирень
В мутно-лазоревом сосуде.

Да обретут мои уста
Первоначальную немоту,
Как кристаллическую ноту,
Что от рождения чиста!

Останься пеной, Афродита,
И слово в музыку вернись,
И сердце сердца устыдись,
С первоосновой жизни слито!

It has not yet been born,
it is music and the word,
and thereby inviolably
bonds everything that lives.

The breast of the sea breathes tranquilly
but the day is brilliant, like a fool,
and the pale lilac of the foam
lies in a bowl of cloudy blue.

May my lips acquire this
primeval quietness
like a crystal note
congenitally pure.

Mandelstam

> Remain foam, Aphrodite;
> and return to music, word,
> and heart, be ashamed of heart
> when blent with life's foundation!

The first word is something of a problem, though it never was until a friend of mine, Richard McKane, presented it to me in a translation different from the one I had always mentally been using. The word is a Russian pronoun that can mean 'it' or 'she' depending upon the antecedent, which is of course the problem. The 'it' of my translation means 'silence'; the 'she' of his meant 'Aphrodite.' I discover from this provocative conflict what provocative conflicts are best at disclosing, namely, the assumptions that I had made without being really aware of them. 'Silentium' is a neuter noun in Latin, but its Russian equivalent, *tishina*, is feminine, to which one refers by the feminine pronoun. That is one assumption, that Mandelstam had *named* his poem 'Silentium' but had thought of its subject, 'silence' or *tishina*, in his native Russian. The other assumption is much broader and involves my whole conception of his image of silence as something that pervades and unites everything in existence. That seems to me fundamental. It seems, incidentally, to underlie the image of silence in the next poem (No. 15) as the element through which the midnight birds fly. McKane evidently thought that the reference was to Aphrodite, who is after all the principal feminine person (and noun) in the poem and who has in fact, in the poem's chronology, not yet been born, for the speaker asks her to 'remain foam.' But is she the other things represented by those predicative nominatives? Is she both 'music' and 'the word'? Is she that which connects all living things? Love?

Finally, I am not sure, nor do I believe that anyone ought to be. The argument from the gender of a word that remained merely latent, *tishina*, is not, now that I am aware of having made it, unassailable. It is – I hesitate to say, knowing that some readers detest even innocent puns – the *argumentum ex silentio*, a feeble one at best. But the problem, if it is a problem, lies more in the translation than in the original, it being one of the penalties of speaking English that one *must* resolve an ambiguity of which the Russian reader may hardly be aware. In English the Russian *ona* is *either* 'it' or 'she'; it cannot, as in Russian, be *both* it and she.

As often happens, there are some obvious and some unexpressed links with other poems nearby. In 'Silentium' there are links to 'The Seashell,' the obvious ones being the sea images. But there is another, more concealed link, and that is the subliminal image of Botticelli's 'Birth of Venus' – Aphrodite being wafted over the sea on a seashell – that glimmers through these lines.

The silence of the title is not, of course, merely the absence of sound. Mandelstam was the Russian master of blooding abstractions, and his silence is a hypostasized something, almost substance. It is the primal state, the condition preceding even creation itself, the Background against which all communication takes place, both music and the word, and is therefore the link between them, as between the calm sea and the lunatic brilliance of the day. The longings of the speaker of the poem – a poet, again – are universal in scale: to go beyond statement, to achieve a mute art, a 'meaningless' art, like that of architecture and sculpture, to be, finally, fused with the first principle of life. The last two lines can challenge interpretation, I think, but it would be wrong to see the last line with its immortal longings as merely another instance of 'one must end somehow.' It becomes clearer the more one studies Mandelstam how persistently he felt poetry to be immanent in nature, to *be* there in the silence, a presence with which he could be 'fused' by his gifts. Poetry was not an occasion for sentiment, for 'heart,' there being something infinitely 'beyond all this fiddle,' as Miss Moore has memorably said. Little wonder that Mandelstam could be brutal when confronted by tyro versifiers for whom poetry was merely a fashionable instance of the main chance.

I think that the poem tugs one in two ways. On the one hand there is the polarity of coolness, the glacial museum-like fixity that so struck Mandelstam's first readers, especially those who found it all too chilly for comfort. There is the pale lilac and the crystal note and the generalized stasis of the whole. On the other hand, there is a suggestion that the condition back into which the poet invites the ordered world to collapse is a condition of infinite rawness, of chaos, in fact. According to one version Aphrodite was born of chaos. And the foam, according to another, is the foam (*aphros*) that gathered around the severed penis of her father Uranus, which had been cut off by his son Cronos.

So much for what the book might have been called. *Rakovina* may have seemed rather too similar to the title of Gumilyov's 1910 collection *Zhemchuga (Pearls)*. Or perhaps by 1913 it simply seemed too conventionally pretty. Or perhaps its other meaning ('wash-basin') made it seem, on the contrary, too prosaic. *Silentium*, as I said, was not, so far as I know, ever a possible title, but if there are good reasons why it might have been (its powerful thematic resonance), there are better reasons – its abstractness, its echo of Bryusov's pretentiously classical titles, *Me eum esse*, *Stephanos*, and so on – why it might not have been. The fact is that the first book came out as *Kamen' (Stone)*. And this proved so satisfactory that the second book, *Tristia*, a name not of Mandelstam's invention, was first announced as *Vtoroi Kamen' (Second Stone)*. If the aim was taciturnity *cum* Dinglichkeit, it must be admitted that *Stone*, the grand mute of imagery, is solidly concrete as well.

IV. PATTERNS, VISUAL AND KINETIC

The Imagists in London were absorbed with the reproduction in poems of clear, sharply defined visual patterns. So were the abstractionists, like David Bomberg and Wyndham Lewis, of the closely allied Vorticist movement. The most famous poem of Amy Lowell, who so identified Imagism with herself that Pound regarded it finally as 'Amygism,' is entitled 'Patterns.' And several of the earliest poems of Mandelstam remain in the mind as indelible traceries of visual patterns. Usually, the patterns mean poetry itself. Here is No. 6:

> На бледно-голубой эмали,
> Какая мыслима в апреле,
> Березы ветви поднимали
> И незаметно вечерели.
>
> Узор отточенный и мелкий,
> Застыла тоненькая сетка,
> Как на фарфоровой тарелке
> Рисунок, вычерченный метко,
>
> Когда его художник милый
> Выводит на стеклянной тверди,
> В сознании минутной силы,
> В забвении печальной смерти.   (1909.)

> On the pale blue enamel
> conceivable in April
> the birches raised their branches
> and vespered imperceptibly.
>
> The fragile netting froze
> the pattern fine and small
> like the design on porcelain
> plates – precisely drawn
>
> when the courteous artist limns it
> on the firmament of glass,
> conscious of his passing power,
> unmindful of sad death.

In seeking to characterize the Russian text of this poem one is conscious of skirting the phrase 'hauntingly beautiful,' and of regretting the great pity of the trite phrase: that it sometimes seems the only right thing to say. Seldom in his career did Mandelstam match, and never, I think, did he exceed the sheer verbal beauty of this brief lyric, the harmonies of which hover in the mind's ear once it has been read. It is difficult to believe that an eighteen-year-old poet could achieve such mastery, such lofty 'incorrectness' as the verb of the fourth line, or such restraint as the epithet for death, the simple word for 'sad.'

This combination of transparent, almost *naïf* clarity with the infinitesimal syntactic jolt must have been what struck many of Mandelstam's first readers. The verb *vecheret'* is normally impersonal and intransitive, and occurs almost exclusively in the third person singular (meaning 'it is drawing toward evening') so that one would expect here *vecherelo*. The rhyme demands *vechereli*, however, which is plural rather than singular, so that, as one of the happy heuristic gifts of rhyme, one gets the birch trees themselves as subject. I thought that to have them 'vesper' would convey some of the faint oddity in this usage. It is scarcely enough of a case to base the charge of 'Russian Latin' upon, but it is a minor item in the account.

From a picture of nature, the birches lifting their branches against a pale April sky in the evening, one moves to an image of a concrete human craft, the design on porcelain, and thence to a third step that Mandelstam makes appear both easy and inevitable, the identification of the two images in the glass sky of the third stanza. We conclude with a long thought, the longest and most persistent thought of the early poems, and an eternal theme: the fleeting power of the artist and the permanence of his work in the face of death. It will not be overlooked, I suppose, that the poet as the earthly artist of porcelain verse and God as the divine artist of birch patterns against the sky are involved in the ultimate identification of the third stanza. Beneath the frailty of these lines there is, as there was in 'Seashell,' more than a touch of iron confidence.

Mandelstam's most famous poem, the one that springs to the mind of the ordinary literate Russian when his name is mentioned, was written that same year and involves another pattern traced on glass.

Дано мне тело—что мне делать с ним,
Таким единым и таким моим?

За радость тихую дышать и жить,
Кого, скажите, мне благодарить?

Я и садовник, я же и цветок,
В темнице мира я не одинок.

На стекла вечности уже легло
Мое дыхание, мое тепло.

Запечатлеется на нем узор,
Неузнаваемый с недавних пор.

Пускай мгновения стекает муть—
Узора милого не зачеркнуть.   (No. 8, 1909.)

A body's given me – what shall I do with it,
so one and so my own?

For the quiet joy of breathing and living
tell me whom I am to thank?

169

Mandelstam

I am the gardener, I am the flower too.
I am not lonely in the prison of the world.

Already on the windowpanes of eternity
my breathing, my warmth, has settled.

A pattern is imprinted on it
but lately can't be recognized.

Let the moment's dross flow down:
the gentle pattern cannot be effaced.

Anthology pieces sometimes assume such an importance in the consciousness of readers that they come to stand, whether they are really representative or not, for all of a writer's work. But of Mandelstam's early work, at least, this poem is perfectly typical. The miniature form, the delicacy and quietness of manner, the faintly self-assertive solipsist who speaks the lines, even much of the diction – all can be found in many other lyrics of this period. Since it is one of the most familiar of his poems, it is certainly one that underlies many remarks about the 'strangeness' of Mandelstam's language. In Russian, the line 'so one and so my own' trembles, as I suppose it does in English, on the verge of the comic. In fact, one of Mandelstam's funniest little ephemera rests upon this single joke:

Не унывай,
Садись в трамвай,
Такой пустой,
Такой восьмой...   (No. 423, c. 1915.)

Don't be glum,
Get on the tram:
So desolate,
So...number '8'.

There is something, in fact, about the entire first stanza that is ludicrous, that lends itself to mockery, even. A critic unfriendly to Mandelstam did not fail to note that his whole problem, the incorporeality of his verse, rested upon his not knowing what to do with his body. If it takes a certain effort to arrive at this realization of its comic potential, it is probably because of the seductive music of the lines, the plaintive music of the repeated / o mni tela...o mni dela / followed by the single stressed vowel / i i i i / of the second line.

Nor is this the only 'strangeness' in his most famous poem. The fifth line

Я и садовник, я же и цветок

strikes many Russian readers as not quite Russian, as either a Jewish or at any rate a very local locution. The purist version would be

Я сам садовник, я же и цветок.

170

The original first line and the form in which many Russians of that day still remember and recite it was also unidiomatic and strikingly peculiar:

Имею тело... (I possess a body...)

Mandelstam himself altered this to the version printed above, which is more normal.

The theme of the poem, as it eventuates, is the same as the theme of many others of this time: *ars longa, vita brevis*. For all its fragility, or because of it, the pattern left by the poet's breath upon the windowpanes of eternity will endure. And the note of arrogance that must underlie such an assertion is there: it is not to be obliterated.

So much to suggest the frequent reference to visual pattern, which the reader of Russian will easily discover for himself among the poems of *Stone* (and among those not included in his books, such as No. 147, which, in the manuscript of Pushkinskii Dom is dated 1909 and reads like a variant of No. 6). These visual patterns are actually not so important, I think, as a rather less obtrusive but more affective kind of pattern – the pattern of regular motion, kinetic patterns, the hypnotic, lulling periodicity of some mechanical contrivance or natural process. The swing of a pendulum. The back and forth of a swing. The waves of the sea. The very iteration of the human heartbeat itself. Sometimes these things blend, as in the line

Спокойно дышат моря груди

The breast of the sea breathes tranquilly.

Always they are blent with the mesmeric action of the fundamental beat of poetry, the meter. Sometimes it is the beat of poetry alone that accomplished the effect, as in the almost hallucinating poem that begins

Сегодня дурной день

Today is a bad day

where the single strange pattern $\_\acute{}\_\_\_\acute{}\acute{}$ is repeated through sixteen lines.[3]

Whatever the agent, the result is a dreamlike state, a suspension of the active grasp of the mind and a substitution for it of the mind as a tablet, as passive recipient of sensation. The real poet may have made his poems, may have fashioned them with deliberate art, but the speaker of the poems is anything other than maker: he is a kind of conduit of the world, of the throbbing, pulsing, irresistible rhythm of the world. That is the burden of many of the early poems of *Stone*.

Я качался в далеком саду
На простой деревянной качели,
И высокие темные ели
Вспоминаю в туманном бреду.   (No. 4, 1908.)

I was swinging in a distant garden
on a simple wooden swing
and remember the tall dark firs
in hazy delirium.

The swing not only comes back through the delirium but was partly the original occasion of it. It very frequently happens that images and words become associated with each other in Mandelstam's poems and thereafter recur together. The association can be natural or quite arbitrary and personal. An instance of the latter kind can be seen in this poem and in No. 20, written three years later. There is presumably nothing in nature that necessarily links the ideas of dark fir trees and rocking motion. But in No. 4 the verb for 'swing' and the noun for 'a swing' (both beginning with the root *kach-*) became allied with 'dark firs.' We therefore read in No. 20:

Горячей головы *качанье*
И нежный лед руки чужой
И *темных елей* очертанья
Еще невиданные мной.

The rocking of a fevered head
and gentle ice of another's hand
and outlines of the dark fir trees
that I have still not seen.

Consider the similar, though rather more conventional association of the words for pendulum (*maiatnik*) and fate or fateful (*rok*, *rokovoi*) in the poem just mentioned, *Segodnia durnoi den'*, and in the one to be discussed below, No. 12.

The trance-like state of No. 10 arises from the 'ebbing and flowing' of a weaver's hands at the loom:

На перламутровый челнок
Натягивая шелка нити,
О пальцы гибкие, начните
Очаровательный урок!

Приливы и отливы рук—
Однообразные движенья,
Ты заклинаешь, без сомненья,
Какой-то солнечный испуг,

Когда широкая ладонь,
Как раковина пламенея,
То гаснет, к теням тяготея,
То в розовый уйдет огонь!

Of which the prose sense is:

O lithe fingers, drawing threads of silk onto the mother-of-pearl shuttle, begin the entrancing lesson! The ebbing and flooding of the hands are monotonous motions; you conjure up without a doubt a kind of sunny fright, when the broad palm, glowing like a shell, now dims as it draws towards the shadows, now goes off into roseate fire!

A poem of the following year, *Kogda udar s udarami vstrechaetsia* (No. 12, 1910), appears to have been remotely inspired by Poe's 'The Pit and the Pendulum,' but as often happens when Mandelstam made use of earlier works of art, the reference is oblique, fragmentary and atmospheric rather than particular. There is simply a nameless terror in the poem, fear without an object, or with objects that dissolve and reappear in other guises. The pendulum swings menacingly above the speaker of the poem who is pinned beneath it, unable to 'meet, to arrange things' or to avoid the suggested blow. Finally, the pendulum seems to weave sharp patterns

Узоры острые переплетаются

and the poem ends with the mention in the last two lines of poisoned darts in the hands of brave savages, who appear to have burst in as his consciousness crosses the line between sanity and hallucination. There the poem now ends, trailing aposiopetically off with a dribble of dots...
It is dramatically more effective than the version printed up to the collection of 1928, where there was an additional stanza making the savages more explicitly present and therefore rather weaker in power of suggestion.

V. THEATER OF INTERRUPTED WORDS

A poem from the latter half of *Stone* provides a phrase to describe several characteristic poems of the first half. It is No. 64, written in 1914, and the phrase occurs in the last stanza:

> Что делать вам в *театре полуслова*
> И полумаск, герои и цари?

> What is there for you, heroes and kings, to do
> in a *theater of broken words* and partial masks?

The last word in the Russian phrase that I have italicized means literally 'half word.' It occurs in expressions meaning 'to catch on quickly' (i.e. having heard only half a word) and 'to stop abruptly' (halfway through an utterance). Both these uses, combined with the word 'theater,' convey a sense of those poems in *Stone* that seem most to deny the general title of the book, for they are little wisps of incomplete speech, fragile dramas that stop short with suggesting a scene and an action – anything but stone. And nothing that Mandelstam wrote could be more opposed to the spirit of the poem from which I take the phrase itself, incidentally, for it is a poem that looks back with nostalgia to the plays of Ozerov, to their fulness and explicitness, the proper stage for kings and heroes. But that, I repeat, was a poem from the latter half of the book – in fact, from a period later than its first edition – and the distinction is an important one.

Since their very essence is brevity, the three poems that I shall cite can all be quoted in full. The first is the very first poem in *Stone*:

Звук осторожный и глухой
Плода, сорвавшегося с древа,
Среди немолчного напева
Глубокой тишины лесной...   (1908.)

In translating these four lines, I thought it historically and suggestively right to string the poem out in the leggy style of some of the English *Imagistes*, of whose work it reminds me. The very appearance of the poem when printed thus seems to transmit better than precision could the fragmentary quality of the Russian. Here, at any rate, it is:

The sound
careful and mute
of a fruit
        broken loose
from a tree
amid the ceaseless melody
of the wood's
deep hush...

It is all subject, without predicate. The subject is a lonely sound, itself merely tentative amid the enclosing silence of the forest, into which the poem trails off...It thus not only posits a subject, a thing any poem might do, but also enacts it, which few poems do. Marina Tsvetaeva, one of the few people to have noticed this poem, was struck precisely by the gestural identity of the poem with its object: the stanza, she said, *is* that falling fruit.[4]

Curiously enough, Mandelstam's prose (*The Noise of Time*) begins with the same enigma-word as his poetry, *glukhoi*: 'Ia pomniu khorosho glukhie gody Rossii...,' 'I remember well the remote and desolate years of Russia...,' to quote my own 1965 translation of the prose ('remote and desolate' here do the work of 'mute' in the poem above). It has been noted that this beginning echoes certain beginnings by Alexandr Blok, e.g.

Рожденные в года глухие
Пути не помнят своего

Those born in remote and desolate years
do not remember their own path

and:

В те годы дальные, глухие,
В сердцах царили сон и мгла

In those distant, remote and desolate years
dream and the mist held sway in hearts.

The first is from a poem of 1914, the second is the opening of the second chapter of *Vozmezdie* (Retribution), like Mandelstam's *Noise* a work of autobiography. But I think these echoes rather less relevant when we observe that it was in some measure also self-quotation. Individual words, as we shall often see, had their own biographies for Mandelstam. They had their own 'life and contacts.' His repetitions of words are almost never to be encountered without some trace of their milieu being repeated also. When his first work of prose, significantly entitled *Noise*, came out in 1925, it did not lack the debut-word of 1913 – *glukhoi*.

The commonest meaning of the word is 'deaf,' but it vaguely means many other things – one of them being, as it chances, 'vague' itself. Said of a place, it is 'solitary,' 'god-forsaken,' 'overgrown'; of a wall, 'blank'; of a rumor, 'vague'; of a season, 'dead'; of a sound 'mute,' 'hollow.' Through its various senses runs the notion of blockage and impediment, the result of which is silence.

Mandelstam was an aural poet. He heard his lines and took them down, having wrested them from silence, from what he could not, at first, hear. Perhaps that accounts in some way for the importance of silence, of muteness in his work, especially in his earliest work. The poems came from silence where they were perfect; such is his Platonic notion. Should they not aspire to that condition? Not, of course, to non-existence (he did not conceive of his poems as ever having not existed), but to that first and ultimate stasis, concealed and perfect, from which he brought them forth. If they often explicitly did that in the course of his first book, it seemed almost predictable from the first four lines.

The next scene in Mandelstam's mute theater is, for him, tolerably hectic. There are three syntactic wholes in the four short lines of No. 3, as if he were trying to compensate for the want of predication in the first poem. But it is really no less fragmentary. The sound of the girl leaving in her light shawl is as lost and lonely as that of the nameless fruit, and as cautious.

> Из полутемной залы, вдруг,
> Ты выскользнула в легкой шали—
> Мы никому не помешали,
> Мы не будили спящих слуг...   (1908.)

> From the half-darkened hall, suddenly
> you slipped out in your light shawl –
> We did not bother anyone,
> we did not wake the sleeping servants...

175

The broken soliloquy of No. 19, written two years later, is perhaps more characteristic:

> Душный сумрак кроет ложе,
> Напряженно дышет грудь...
> Может, мне всего дороже
> Тонкий крест и тайный путь.　　　　(1910.)

> A sultry twilight covers the couch,
> the breast breathes tensely...
> Dearest of all to me, perhaps,
> are the slender cross and secret path.

It seems worth remembering that these fragments, these mere relics of some action, some momentary sensation or reflection, were being cultivated at about the same time in London. Consider Ezra Pound's

Gentildonna

> She passed and left no quiver in the veins, who now
> Moving among the trees, and clinging in the air she severed,
> Fanning the grass she walked on then, endures:
> Grey olive leaves beneath a rain-cold sky.

or:　　　　　　　　### The Jewel Stairs' Grievance

> The jewelled steps are already quite white with dew,
> It is so late that the dew soaks my gauze stockings,
> And I let down the crystal curtain
> And watch the moon through the clear autumn.
> 　　　　　　　　　　　(from the Chinese of Rihaku)

For the last poem, Pound provided a note of interpretation. Had Mandelstam been equally seized with a passion for teaching his readers, he might have told us something of that penumbral hall and twilit couch, but of course he wasn't and didn't. The curtain falls as quickly as it rose, and there is no program.

VI. DOWN FROM THE TOWER

As I pass from the poems written during the first five years of Mandelstam's career, I discover in myself a feeling of relief which I think ought to be admitted and understood. For all their individual beauty, for all the astonishment still to be felt at such stanzas as

> И стоит осиротелая
> И немая вышина,
> Как пустая башня белая,
> Где туман и тишина.　　　(from No. 21, 1911.)

> And there stands an orphaned
> and mute height
> like an empty white tower
> where fog and silence are.

there is still a thinness about them that, taken in quantity, becomes wearying. Nothingness as a subject has its severe limitations. The absence of sight, sound, and even of the Self can – and did – furnish a lyrical ground productive of excellent verse, but it is a soil that is quickly depleted of its meager nutrients. Moreover, I think that the reader must inevitably sense a basic flaw in the consciousness out of which the poems are written. The lines assert fragility and a longing to sink, to expire, to be mastered by some stronger will and...vanish. But the poems have a permanence that can be sensed in their masterful technique. It is not necessary to specify or argue the point in detail now. Every reader who can sense the quality of a Russian poem will know that these are whatever is the opposite of temporary. Not all of them have been engraved in the stone walls of Moscow prisons, but their permanence is of the order of those lines that have.

What is more, the speaker of the poems is secure in his awareness of the fact, and this, too, is a contradiction. One becomes quickly aware that the voice uttering these poems is quite clearly that of an 'Alice,' to use Auden's marvelous term. It is very Alice, this fastidiousness, this dainty swoon, this polite despair. And yet one is just as quickly aware that the whole Alice tonality is a sort of trick; to be more precise, it is a gambit, a shrewd surrender of material in the expectation of gain. For the speaker ends his poems too often with very confident assertions of superiority and determination – specifically, determination to outlast the ages

> Узора милого не зачеркнуть.

Perfectly reasonable objections might be raised to all this. Such a poem as No. 11, beginning

> Ни о чем не нужно говорить

which, for all its brevity, is full of an oceanic vigor of life, some force that seems to spring from the primal energy of creation, is a poem with an irresistible animality about the dolphin plunge of its last two lines:

> И плывет дельфином молодым
> По седым пучинам мировым.

> And swims like a young dolphin
> about the gray deeps of the world.

Furthermore, to cite the presence of some trick or contradiction in the personality of the poems would seem to betray an ignorance of the fact that illusion is the basis of all art, that the persona is inevitably a trick.

The answer to the first is that I am speaking now of the overall impression made by the work of five years, not about individual poems. The answer to the second is that illusion can be accomplished with greater or lesser skill; the trick can be adroit or clumsy. In his later work Mandelstam achieved a mastery over the lyric ego and brought its parts into a superior harmony. Contradictions remained, as they must in any human enterprise, but they were in the first place no longer trivial or obvious (i.e. predictable and therefore poetically less effective): they were profounder paradoxes that speak to us of the condition of man, of his fundamental quandary.

And the result, I think, is that the poems simply strike one as more serious, more deliberate, and of heightened consequence. The greater confidence that comes with greater mastery is evident throughout, and the presumption of permanence is vastly stronger when the poem itself is not obliged to assert it. That the poems are more serious and the voice more assured is a fact attested to by the admission into the surface of the poem of an occasional gleam of wit – something almost totally absent from the more youthful works.

Gumilyov reviewed *Stone* when it first appeared, and when the edition of 1916 came out he greeted it once again in the pages of *Apollon*.[5] He had not changed his mind. In particular, he agreed with himself about precisely where the book divided in two – the point separating the earlier 'Symbolist' poems from the later 'Acmeist' poems. It was a poem of six lines written in 1912:

> Нет, не луна, а светлый циферблат
> Сияет мне, и чем я виноват,
> Что слабых звезд я осязаю млечность?
>
> И Батюшкова мне противна спесь:
> «Который час?» его спросили здесь,
> А он ответил любопытным: «вечность». (No. 31.)

> No, not the moon – the tower clock's bright dial
> is shining at me. How am I guilty
> if the feeble stars strike me as milky?
>
> And Batyushkov repels me with his bile:
> 'What time is it?' they asked him here, and he
> Replied to them one word: 'Eternity.'

Gumilyov was an acute critic. His reviews of current poetry were very brief, usually, and like all periodical criticism, generally had to be written on first acquaintance. Nevertheless, most of his judgments stand. He seems to me to have been generally right in this case; but with the greater space at my disposal, I shall propose certain limitations. Given the utterly contingent nature of all 'turning points' in art, this is better than most. It is not abrupt. There are 'Acmeist' notes in the foregoing poems and 'Symbolist' notes in those that follow, but this poem, by and large, is the boundary.

As it chances, it is also a poem that provides one with certain reassuring parallels in places where the parallels matter. I have already mentioned that in his essay on Villon Mandelstam had portrayed him as an Acmeist *avant la lettre* (which in some sense he certainly was, having been appointed a forefather by Gumilyov). But Mandelstam specified the turning point in Villon's career – his discovery of his own 'Acmeism,' as it were – at that moment when he expelled the *moon* from his poetry in favor of such tangible and sublunary delights as roast duck in sauce.[6] And the *Imagistes* of London would also cite T. E. Hulme's dethroning of the *moon* as the very first instance of the kind of poetry they championed. Like Mandelstam, he also dethroned the stars, calling them 'wistful' instead of 'feeble.' His poem of seven lines is entitled 'Autumn.'

> A touch of cold in the Autumn night –
> I walked abroad,
> And saw the ruddy moon lean over a hedge
> Like a red-faced farmer.
> I did not stop to speak, but nodded,
> And round about were the wistful stars
> With white faces like town children.

The negative particle with which Mandelstam's poem begins seems a good opener for a statement rejecting one poetic mode for another, the conventional moon for a plain clockface with its exceedingly prosy, non-Russian name. I think that its meaning, if it were possible to reduce it to prose, would be approximately this. I will not call that a moon when I can see that it is only a clockface on the tower; and if the weak gleam of the stars seems just milky to me, with no other symbolic value, that is what I will call it. I dislike the haughtiness of those who can't give a straight answer to the simplest question and, when asked what time it is (as, for example, on the above clockface) reply with some thundering abstraction like 'eternity.'

But it seems to me that there might be other reasons for the negative, that the poem is by no means very clear in its present form, and that, as is common in the study of Mandelstam, we can best understand it not in isolation but in the context of the poems near it.

I have no other evidence for this than what is on the page, but it seems to me that this rather tremendous occasion, the marker delimiting Mandelstam's earlier from all his later manner, is actually a fragment – the remnant of a sonnet. Its outward form is clearly that of a sestet (there are three rhymes in the pattern aaB ccB, but no two of his sestets have the same pattern). And while it might be mentioned that he wrote several other poems beginning with the same 'nyet,' the negative is, after all, a standard transition from the thought of the octet to the traditionally opposed thought of the sestet. Perhaps even stronger than the purely formal evidence is the fact that the poem is thematically linked with the three that follow, especially the one that follows next, and they are all sonnets – a form very little practised in Russia and almost never by Mandelstam. These three, plus No. 173, a poem of 1913 which he never reprinted in his collections, are all that he wrote, so far as I know.

Typically for this poet, it is also closely linked with those that precede it (thus further frustrating any desire to see it as a clean break with the first part of the book).

Я ненавижу свет
Однообразных звезд.

I hate the light
of the monotonous stars.

That is the beginning of No. 29. 'Am I therefore to blame...?' one imagines the dialogue as continuing through the pivotal No. 31. And there are numerous other points in the everlasting colloquy of Mandelstam's poems with each other, but one despairs of tracing them all.

The bond with those that follow is easier to manage, and more rewarding. No. 32 looks to me like the achieved sonnet of which No. 31 is – what? – the variant, or sketch, or remnant. In 32 'eternity' does in fact 'chime on its stone clock,' thus making Batyushkov's answer the literal truth, to which the speaker of the poem must take an attitude like that in 31 but different from it.

Perhaps the reading of the sonnets will be more productive if I say beforehand what it is, besides their form, that holds them together and relates them to the foregoing poem. There is a sense of menace in them all, a pervasive sick peril. The menace is the one final menace in poems or in life: death itself. But its several realizations derive from only one metaphor behind the poems. That metaphor is spatial: a great *height* above an *abyss*, into which the speaker might *fall*. This inspires great *fear*, for the fall would be into an endless temporal space, *eternity*. The words that I have italicized here are those that occur twice or three times in the poems.

The metaphor is realized differently in the three poems. It is perhaps most clearly to be seen in 32 and 34. In 33, the basic metaphor really occurs but once (though very explicitly) – in line 8. As for the rest of the Casino poem, the void is a panorama of the sea, and the scene evokes an emotion that seems to derive not so much from menace as from a comfortable enjoyment of the visual images presented in the lines. Line 8 is, however, in the poem. No matter what emotions are felt by the speaker who walks through these landscapes from the vicinity of the belltowers, to the casino on the dunes, to the monastery with its oppressive ceilings, he never escapes from an awareness of the 'desarts of vast eternity.' A sense of that emptiness, the last of them says, is fear itself.

These poems about structures – towers, casinos, monasteries – are in fact also poems about the structure of poetry, or of a possible world for poetry. That world consists of the things that oppose the fear of the

void and bring solace. Richard Wilbur takes a line from Thomas Traherne
for the title of his famous lyric 'A World without Objects is a Sensible
Emptiness,' but he warns 'the tall camels of the spirit' back from the
desert, back from the search for some absolute and mystical brightness
of the sun, back to the light shining from the things of this world: 'lamp-
shine blurred in the steam of beasts.' The conclusion and the impulse
toward it are those of Mandelstam's new manner. But the world without
objects is for him a place of terror, the equivalent of death. The stopgaps
against emptiness are the flight of the swallow, or of the gull, or of the
belltower itself, where the eternity of Batyushkov's answer is no longer
an abstraction but the actual stroke of the stone clock. They are the ray
of light on the crumpled tablecloth, the wine in its decanter, the wood
burning in the fireplace. The anguish of eternity is eased by the transitory,
the evanescent, by things temporary but actual which, when caught in
poetry, endure. Many essentials of Acmeism were memorably conveyed
by Mandelstam in the first poems that he wrote under the sway of its
doctrine.

ПЕШЕХОД

Я чувствую непобедимый страх
В присутствии таинственных высот,
Я ласточкой доволен в небесах
И колокольни я люблю полет!

И, кажется, старинный пешеход,
Над пропастью, на гнущихся мостках
Я слушаю, как снежный ком растет
И вечность бьет на каменных часах.

Когда бы так! Но я не путник тот,
Мелькающий на выцветших листвах,
И подлинно во мне печаль поет;

Действительно, лавина есть в горах!
И вся моя душа—в колоколах,
Но музыка от бездны не спасет!   (No. 32, 1912.)

The sort of translation that I have been offering the reader never looks
so naked as when it is put in some strict form, like that of the sonnet;
but it is easier to follow that way. This is the meaning of No. 32:

PEDESTRIAN

I feel an unconquerable fear
in the presence of mysterious heights.
I am glad of the swallow in the sky
and love the belltower's flight.

And I, like an ancient walker
above the abyss on a dubious board,
seem to hear the ball of snow as it grows
and eternity striking on a clock of stone.

So be it. But I am not that wayfarer
briefly seen on faded leaves,
and genuine sadness sings in me.

There is indeed an avalanche in the hills
and all my heart is in the bells,
but music won't save you from the abyss.[7]

КАЗИНО

Я не поклонник радости предвзятой,
Подчас природа—серое пятно.
Мне, в опьяненьи легком, суждено
Изведать краски жизни небогатой.

Играет ветер тучею косматой,
Ложится якорь на морское дно,
И бездыханная, как полотно,
Душа висит над бездною проклятой.

Но я люблю на дюнах казино,
Широкий вид в туманное окно
И тонкий луч на скатерти измятой;

И, окружен водой зеленоватой,
Когда, как роза, в хрустале вино—
Люблю следить за чайкою крылатой!   (No. 33, 1912.)

CASINO

I hold no brief for preconceived joy.
There are some times when nature's a grey spot.
When, faintly drunk, I'm doomed to know
the colors of a meager life.

The wind is playing with a shaggy cloud,
the anchor's sinking to the ocean floor,
and, lifeless as a sheet, my soul
hangs above the damned abyss.

But I love the casino on the dunes,
the panorama from the misty window,
the fragile ray of light on the rumpled tablecloth.

And with the greenish water all around,
when the wine lies in its crystal like a rose,
I love to trace the winged gull in flight.

Паденье—неизменный спутник страха,
И самый страх есть чувство пустоты.
Кто камни к нам бросает с высоты—
И камень отрицает иго праха?

И деревянной поступью монаха
Мощеный двор когда-то мерил ты,
Булыжники и грубые мечты—
В них жажда смерти и тоска размаха...

Так проклят будь готический приют,
Где потолком входящий обморочен
И в очаге веселых дров не жгут!

Немногие для вечности живут,
Но если ты мгновенным озабочен—
Твой жребий страшен и твой дом непрочен!

(No. 34, 1912.)

Falling never fails to go with fear
and fear itself's the fear of emptiness.
Who throws us stones down from the heights,
and does a stone deny the yoke of dust?

And you once measured out the cobbled court
with the wooden footfall of a monk.
Paving stones and crude daytime delusions
contain the thirst for death and wide expanse.

So let the Gothic refuge be accursed
where the ceiling tricks you as you enter
and no merry wood is burning in the hearth.

Few devote their lives to eternity
but if the passing moment causes you distress
your fate is awful and your house won't last.

VII. ANIMATED TEMPLES

Can we compose a castle-fortress-home,
Even with the help of Viollet-le-Duc...?

STEVENS, 'Notes toward a Supreme Fiction'

In his talk before the Russian student group in Heidelberg on 10 February 1910, Aaron Steinberg had quoted Verlaine's much-quoted line 'de la musique avant toute chose.'[8] It was of course one of the slogans that the Russian Symbolists had embroidered on their banner along with Goethe's 'Alles Vergängliche ist nur ein Gleichnis,' and, in the discussion that followed the lecture, it was one of the things that Mandelstam chose to comment upon.

He had no objection, he said, to 'music' in poetry, but it must be music transformed into *architecture*; and he cited what Eckermann reported Goethe to have said of architecture, that it is 'eine erstarrte Musik.' A poem should stand like a work of the builder's art, its structure clear, its central form distinguishable from the elaborations upon it. It was evidently the Gothic that Mandelstam had in mind. Steinberg remembers that he attributed Goethe's famous remark – wrongly, but understandably enough – to his equally famous celebration of the Strasbourg cathedral.

Mandelstam was often enough called the last of the Acmeists. It sometimes strikes me that he was also the first. He repeatedly anticipated – as in this remark of 1910, and above all in his essay on Villon, written that same year – the Acmeist manifestoes of three years later. What is more, he anticipated Mikhail Kuzmin's essay 'On Beautiful Clarity,' often regarded as a kind of Acmeist manifesto *avant la lettre*, and even made use of the same architectural metaphor that Kuzmin was to employ. Kuzmin's essay appeared only in the fourth issue of *Apollon* for 1910.

Mandelstam and architecture: the conjunction is very familiar. In the *Journey to Armenia* he wrote that as a child he had not gone berrying or mushroom gathering, for he preferred

> Gothic pinecones and hypocritical acorns in their monastic skullcaps. I would stroke the pinecones. They would bristle. They would try to convince me. In their shelled tenderness, in their geometrical absent-mindedness, I sensed the rudiments of architecture, the demon of which would accompany me all my life.[9]

Accompany him it did, and it played an enormous role, but I sometimes think that it has accompanied his subsequent reputation rather too closely, too jealously excluding many of the other demons that swarmed after him. The name Mandelstam seems automatically to drag behind it some reference to poems about architecture, which is misleading and, worse than that, reductive. It therefore seems worth mentioning before broaching the theme itself that there are really not all that many poems about buildings in his collected works, and also that many other poets of the time – Gumilyov and Benedikt Livshits, to name only two – were drawn to this subject.

Still, there can be little doubt that among Mandelstam's early work certain poems on famous buildings made the strongest impression on his contemporaries and continue to exert the same fascination today.

The first architectural poem is that on the Hagia Sophia (No. 38), written in 1912. There had been towers and buildings in earlier poems, but there they had been rather decorative or incidental.

> И стоит осиротелая
> И немая вышина,
> Как пустая башня белая
> Где туман и тишина. (No. 21.)

> And there stands an orphaned
> and mute height
> like an empty white tower
> where the fog and silence are.

The empty house in No. 26 is perhaps more functional as an echo of Pushkin's famous metaphor at the death of Lensky:

> И хрупкой раковины стены,
> Как нежилого сердца дом,
> Наполнишь шопотами пены,
> Туманом, ветром и дождем...

> And the walls of the fragile shell
> like the house of an uninhabited heart
> you will fill with the whisperings of foam,
> with fog, wind and the rain.

Mandelstam had made Villon a patron saint of Acmeism before Gumilyov conferred the title upon him officially (and upon Rabelais, Shakespeare, and Gautier) in his manifesto. Villon had irreversibly excluded from his poetic usage, Mandelstam wrote, 'the moon and other neutral "objects"' in revolt against the conventions of the 'powerful rhetorical school, which one might with full justice regard as the Symbolism of the XVth century.' Instead of the moon, roast ducks in sauce – as succulent a touch of Acmeism as the oysters on the bed of ice in Akhmatova's plate. In 1912, Mandelstam himself writes:

> Нет, не луна, а светлый циферблат   (No. 31.)
> сияет мне...

> No, not the moon, but a bright clockface
> is shining at me...

And we have no less an authority than Gumilyov's that this renunciation of the moon for the mundane face of a tower clock marks Mandelstam's entry, or at least his reception, into Acmeism. By the time he wrote 'Hagia Sophia' (No. 38) that same year the lesson of specificity had been learned. Not only is it about a specific building but the lexicon – apses, exedrae, pendentives – is architectural in an emphatically special, even professional, sense. He was Acmeist in spades.

> Айя-София—здесь остановиться
> Судил Господь народам и царям!
> Ведь купол твой, по слову очевидца,
> Как на цепи подвешен к небесам.

> И всем векам—пример Юстиниана,
> Когда похитить для чужих богов
> Позволила Эфесская Диана
> Сто семь зеленых мраморных столбов.

> Но что же думал твой строитель щедрый,
> Когда, душой и помыслом высок,
> Расположил апсиды и экседры,
> Им указав на запад и восток?

Прекрасен храм, купающийся в мире,
И сорок окон—света торжество;
На парусах, под куполом, четыре
Архангела прекраснее всего.

И мудрое сферическое зданье
Народы и века переживет,
И серафимов гулкое рыданье
Не покоробит темных позолот.

HAGIA SOPHIA! Here did God decree
that nations and their emperors should stop!
In fact, as one who saw it said, your dome
depends as though from Heaven by a chain.

All ages take example from Justinian's
when from her shrine in Ephesus Diana
allowed the plunder of one hundred seven
green marble pillars for the gods of others.

But what was in your lavish builder's thought
when he from heights of spirit and design
distributed the apses and exedrae
and showed them which was East and which was West?

A splendid temple bathing in the world:
its forty windows are the jubilee of light.
On pendentives beneath the dome the four
Archangels dim in splendor all the rest.

Now will this building, spherical and wise,
outlast the ages and the people in them.
Nor shall the hollow sobs of seraphs warp
or craze the dark occasions of the gilt.

For reasons that I hope to make clear in a moment, it will be simpler to discuss many things in the above poem after having read the poem 'Notre Dame' (No. 39), which is, if anything, even better known, and which follows next in the collection *Stone*.

Где римский судия судил чужой народ—
Стоит базилика, и радостный и первый,
Как некогда Адам, распластывая нервы,
Играет мышцами крестовый легкий свод.

Но выдает себя снаружи тайный план:
Здесь позаботилась подпружных арок сила,
Чтоб масса грузная стены не сокрушила,
И свода дерзкого бездействует таран.

Стихийный лабиринт, непостижимый лес,
Души готической рассудочная пропасть,
Египетская мощь и христианства робость,
С тростинкой рядом—дуб, и всюду царь—отвес.

Но чем внимательней, твердыня Notre Dame,
Я изучал твои чудовищные ребра,
Тем чаще думал я: из тяжести недоброй
И я когда-нибудь прекрасное создам.

The prose sense of this poem is the following:

In the place where a Roman judge judged an alien people there stands a basilica, and the light groined arch – joyful and first, as Adam once was – plays with its muscles as it spreads out its nerves.

But the secret plan is revealed from without: here the strength of the saddle-girth arches has taken care that the ponderous mass not crush the wall, and the battering-ram of the bold vault is idle.

An elemental labyrinth, an inscrutable forest, the Gothic soul's rational abyss, Egyptian might and Christian modesty: next to a reed – an oak, and everywhere plumb is king.

But the more attentively, O stronghold Notre Dame, I studied thy monstrous ribs, the more frequently I thought: some day I too will create beauty from cruel weight.

We may pass quickly beyond the immediate similarities – that the two poems are both pictures of famous churches, with considerable attention to architectural detail – to the less obvious. Both begin with the same words – *sudit'* 'to judge, decree' and *narod* 'people, nation' – as if they had both sprung from a single source – the idea, say, of the cathedrals as embodiments of some historic jural impulse binding men into communities. Such pairs, and even triplets, of poems are common in Mandelstam. Both of them seem triumphs (in differing degree) of the Acmeist aesthetic: they are pictures of objects, presentational with graphic intensity. In 'Hagia Sophia' Mandelstam insists upon the precision of the numerals – 107, 40, 4 – of all grammatical categories the most traditionally 'unpoetic,' and of the recherché technical terms as earnests of utter veracity and professionalism in representation. Both poems are 'logical' and conclude with the slight flourish of a demonstration; verbs in the future tense declare a moral sublimate that seems to have derived from the elements of the poem.

But if these objects stand before us in the present moment of contemplation, they are also presented in the perspective of history. Again: if they seem great stolid impassive massifs of stone, they are also, examined more closely, compact of movement. It is precisely the dynamism of these portraits that strike me as their strongest quality – dynamism in time but even more compellingly dynamism in space. 'Frozen music': Goethe's phrase must have been marvelously pregnant for Mandelstam. Music is movement or nothing. The epithet 'frozen' provides an instance of that Cusan *contradictio in adjecto* to which Mandelstam was in thrall. In the essay already mentioned he had proposed a variation of Verlaine's line as a suitable slogan for Villon,

Du mouvement avant toute chose!

but, as is often the case in his literary studies, he might have been speaking of his own practice, for his pictures are never still. These cathedrals are not static and finished entities. They are processes.

We see Notre Dame, especially, 'with the ferocious eye-measure of a simple carpenter' (No. 48) as stress and counter-stress, as weight and support, as thrust and opposition. We see it, that is to say, as its builders themselves saw it, in their terms – not 'literature' but a real structure locked in battle with gravity and the weather. The movement of Hagia Sophia is more grandiose, less subject to the pull of mere earth, and it is a movement of the whole. In a beautiful image (suggested perhaps by the word for 'pendentive,' which is also the common word for the sail of a ship), the great temple 'bathes in the world' – René Magritte might have painted it.[10] The movement of Notre Dame, however, is that of the parts composing the whole. It is an organism. It is, in fact, a man, Adam himself, with a Gothic soul and monstrous ribs. This is that 'celebration of physiology, its Dionysian debauch' ascribed to the same cathedral in Mandelstam's Acmeist manifesto, 'The Morning of Acmeism,' which is so closely linked to this poem that it might almost be read as a commentary upon it:

> The stone thirsted, as it were, for another existence. It was itself the discoverer of the dynamic potential concealed within it – as if it were asking to be let into the 'groined arch' to participate in the joyous cooperative action of its fellows.

Just such a celebration of the physiology of Gothic could be found in Auguste Rodin's *Les cathédrales de France* (1914), which, had it been published earlier than it was, might almost have been seen as an inspiration for this poem. As it was, I think it must have inspired others. It reads in part like an Acmeist tract – a hymn to the truth, logic, proof, balance, and above all, the honest workmanship of the Gothic. Nadezhda Yakovlevna told me that Mandelstam, especially during his last years, had it with him constantly.

In order to comment upon a statement made at another level by these 'architectural' poems, it will be useful to read 'The Lutheran' (No. 37), which, though not architectural itself, seems to me to belong with 'Hagia Sophia' and 'Notre Dame.' It immediately precedes them in Mandelstam's first book.

Я на прогулке похороны встретил
Близ протестантской кирки, в воскресенье.
Рассеянный прохожий, я заметил
Тех прихожан суровое волненье.

Чужая речь не достигала слуха,
И только упряжь тонкая сияла,
Да мостовая праздничная глухо
Ленивые подковы отражала.

'Stone'

А в эластичном сумраке кареты,
Куда печаль забилась, лицемерка,
Без слов, без слез, скупая на приветы,
Осенних роз мелькнула бутоньерка.

Тянулись иностранцы лентой черной,
И шли пешком заплаканные дамы,
Румянец под вуалью, и упорно
Над ними кучер правил в даль, упрямый.

Кто б ни был ты, покойный лютеранин,—
Тебя легко и просто хоронили.
Был взор слезой приличной затуманен,
И сдержанно колокола звонили.

И думал я: витийствовать не надо.
Мы не пророки, даже не предтечи,
Не любим рая, не боимся ада,
И в полдень матовый горим, как свечи.   (1912.)

Out for a walk, I met a funeral
On Sunday last, beside the Lutheran church.
An absentminded stroller, I observed
The stern distress of those parishioners.

The foreign language failed to filter through
And nothing glistened but the fragile bridles
Or dim reflections from the horses' hooves
Among the vacancy of Sunday sidewalks.

But in the carriage's resilient twilight
Where sadness, hypocrite, asylum sought,
Without a sign of greeting, wordless, tearless,
The boutonnière of autumn roses sat.

The foreigners in sable ribbon went
Behind on foot with ladies weak from weeping,
Their ruddy faces under veils. Intent,
Implacable, the driver kept advancing.

No matter who you were, departed Lutheran,
Your funeral was easy, debonnaire.
A decorous tear befogged the vision duly
And proper bells rang in the autumn air.

My thoughts were plain. No need for eloquence.
We neither prophets nor forerunners are,
Do not fear Hell, would not for Heaven repent:
Our candles make the noon crepuscular.

It seems to me that these three poems, taken together, form one whole:
a triptych of the religions of Europe – Protestant, Orthodox, and Catholic.
The statement of the poems about these creeds is not without its interest.

The Protestant poem is of course dictated to a great extent by its obvious predecessor, Fyodor Tyutchev's poem on the same subject. The scene – and, by extension, the religion itself – is remorselessly everyday. The mode of the poem is narrative. It seems deliberately to open with one of the most tradition-bound openings of that genre, the tried and true pedestrianism of, for example, Auden's 'As I walked out one evening...' The speaker has a reality not present in the speakers of the others, not even in 'Notre Dame,' where the speaker brings himself in for the finale. He is, though, even more of an outsider than the normal casual onlooker at a funeral procession, for the mourners are foreigners. There is, moreover, a bourgeois tone to the proceedings, and the observer looks upon the bourgeois world with the usual irony of the artist. The conclusion – and note that it is, as in the other poems, a real conclusion, which Mandelstam stresses by using one of the tags of logical transition hallowed in the tradition of Russian verse ('And I thought...') – the conclusion is one of mere indifference and non-involvement. The 'we' is a kind of ventriloquism and does not include the speaker, who is merely voicing the thought of his subjects, who shine futilely in the drab noonday of their faith, the appropriate occasion of which is a burial, a leavetaking like that in Tyutchev's poem. But Tyutchev's notation of the unadornment of Lutheranism is almost sympathetic when compared with Mandelstam's reduction of their ritual to veils and boutonnières.

The Orthodox poem is all dazzle and richness, a Derzhavinian 'feast for the eyes.' The splendor and color of this visual celebration betoken a mysterious union of gorgeousness and wisdom. There is a sense of mystery, but the elements of the mystery are outwardly simple: the massive size and weight of the dome and its apparently unsupported hovering over the vast interior of the cathedral. The intricacy is the intricacy of elaboration and number: one hundred and seven, forty, four. Though the speaker of the poem, as in 'The Lutheran,' directly addresses his subject with the personal pronoun, he himself scarcely exists in the dialogue and seems to have vanished in the spectacle of green and gold, in the jubilee of light.

Intricacy is the essence of the Roman Catholic 'Notre Dame,' which is all system, of no color at all. The building is held together by a physiological cunning, like the nerves and muscles of Adam. It is anthropological, of this world, with the gravity of which it wrestles, whereas the Hagia Sophia is divine. Here, the subject of the verb *sudit'* is the Roman judge: there, it was God. The 'Morning of Acmeism' to the contrary notwithstanding, there is something not entirely 'joyous' about this 'joyous cooperative action.' Notre Dame is a scene of assault and resistance. It is a harmony, or peace, but it is the peace of the stalemate and the stand-off, the result of balanced opposition, an equilibrium with the constant threat of sudden imbalance. For if the Hagia Sophia depends as by a chain from Heaven, Notre Dame depends as a conclusion from its premisses: it hangs over a 'rational' abyss by the uncertain cord of human reason. Hagia Sophia is filled with the peace that passeth understanding, for its joyousness and beauty have no taint of the rational. Notre Dame is a maze, a forest, an abyss, a fortress – in short, one of the monsters produced by the dream of reason. The word *Sophia*, by that reverberative process so familiar in Mandelstam, produces *seraph*s and *sph*eres; but Notre *Dame* is perversely seen as A*dam* (which rhymes in Russian pronounciation). To all the other clashes in this microcosm of man, Mandelstam seems to insist upon that between male and female nature.

The conclusion of 'Notre Dame' has been complained of. I myself disliked it on first reading the poem. It not only seems tacked on in the spirit of 'one must end somehow,' but there is also a kind of stout-hearted quality, a serviceable optimism, that does not seem justified by anything in the poem. To quarrel with it is not altogether easy, for there is an obvious – if not, for the poem itself, very relevant – appeal in this prescient statement by the young poet who would in fact impress the world as having created sublimity from most ungrateful materials.

But does not the ending seem more appropriate when we read it in the context of this triptych? The pridefulness of this speaker who suddenly thrusts forward his individuality at the end of the poem seems not unconnected with what has preceded it. He has 'studied' the building and his rational conclusion, conveyed in the neat equilibrium of a ratio itself (the more attentively : the more often), seems satisfyingly final.

Or so, at least, one may argue, as if argument might compel liking, which of course it can't. Hagia Sophia in its beautiful ignorance is the proper gem and center of this triptych. It transcends whatever role it may have had as thesis, as illustration, and Notre Dame, great poem that it is, somehow doesn't quite. I feel that the ending is to blame. It is the something too much, the overstatement, the slight excess of which Hagia Sophia is innocent. The poem had made, had powerfully made, its point before that.

The figure of Notre Dame turned up in later poems and in concealed ways. There is an unmistakable verbal echo of lines 3 and 4 in the same lines of No. 61, the poem from which the title of this chapter comes. It is another architectural poem about, as it chances, another church, the Kazan Cathedral on the Nevsky in St Petersburg.

> На площадь выбежав, свободен
> Стал колоннады полукруг—
> И *распластался* храм Господень,
> Как *легкий крестовик*-паук.

А зодчий не был итальянец,
Но русский в Риме; ну так что ж!
Ты каждый раз как иностранец
Сквозь рощу портиков идешь;

И храма маленькое тело
Одушевленнее стократ
Гиганта, что скалою целой
К земле беспомощно прижат!   (1914.)

Prose translation:

When it had run out onto the square the semicircle of the colonnade became free, and the Lord's temple crawled about like a light garden spider.

And the architect was not Italian but a Russian in Rome; but what of that! You walk through the grove of porticos each time like a foreigner.

And the little body of the temple is a hundredfold more animated than the giant that is helplessly pressed, like an entire cliff, to the earth.

Not only do the italicized words recall the similar or identical words of 'Notre Dame,' but the comparison in the last stanza of the light Kazan Cathedral with the nearby St Isaac's Cathedral, 'pressed to the earth,' seems to echo the contrast between the lighter-than-air Hagia Sophia and Notre Dame, struggling against the tug of gravity.

In order to discuss the last appearance of Notre Dame in Mandelstam's poetry we must go far beyond the boundaries of *Stone*. He was nearing the end of his three-year ordeal in the Voronezh exile and was less than a year from his death in the camp. There is a poignancy to the very tense of the verbs in this poem, which, with the exception of the last two, are all in the past. The poem is not, like 'Notre Dame,' a notation of immediate vision. It is rather like the assembled shards of some fragmented dream, important pieces of which are missing. Here is No. 374.

Я видел озеро, стоящее отвесно,
С разрезанною розой в колесе
Играли рыбы, дом построив пресный,
Лиса и лев боролись в челноке.

Глазели внутрь трех лающих порталов
Недуги—недруги других невскрытых дуг,
Фиалковый пролет газель перебежала,
И башнями скала вздохнула вдруг.

И влагой напоен, восстал песчаник честный,
И средь ремесленного города-сверчка
Мальчишка-океан встает из речки пресной
И чашками воды швыряет в облака.   (1937.)

I think that it will be more economical of space, and perhaps a bit clearer, to comment upon this poem line by line as I give the prose sense of it.

1   I saw a lake standing plumb [or sheer; the adverb *otvesno* recalls the noun *otves* 'plumb' of 'Notre Dame' and is the only noticeable verbal link to the earlier poem. The comparatively flat façade of the cathedral is seen as the surface of a lake.]

2–3   Fish, having built [themselves this] freshwater house, were playing with a sliced rose in a wheel [the famous rose window of the West front; the word *igrali* 'playing' is the past tense of a verb that occurred in the present in 'Notre Dame' – a less conspicuous but perhaps a significant echo.]

4   and the fox and the lion struggled in the boat.

5–6   Within three baying portals peered the ailing unarchenemies of other unopened arches [Verses of dense phonetic and semantic wordplay. The translation attempts only one pun: the word *nedugi* can mean both 'ailments' and 'non-arcs.' Transliteration may be more revealing: *glazeli vnutr' trekh laiushchikh portalov | nedugi – nedrugi drugikh nevskrytykh dug.* The picture is the familiar three portals of Notre Dame, each portal filled with the voussoirs of successively smaller arches leading to the sculptured tympanum.]

7   A gazelle was running across the flight of violets [The gazelle was engendered by, or engendered, the first word in the transliteration above, 'peered.' The word *polet* 'flight' is used in architectural parlance for the distance spanned by an arch. The gazelle and the adjective *fialkovyi* 'violet' convey the delicacy of elements of the Gothic. The translation makes rather clearer than the original what I take to be a concealed reference to Eugène *Viollet*-le-Duc, the architect who restored Notre Dame in 1846–79.]

8   And suddenly the rock sighed with towers [the two towers]

9   And, drunk with moisture, the honest sandstone rose up

10   And in the midst of the chirping artisan-city [or literally: the artisan cricket-city]

11   the *gamin* ocean [i.e. a mischievous lake] rises up from the freshwater river

12   and hurls cups of water at the clouds.

For all its transformations, it is still Notre Dame with its rose window, its three portals and two towers, its zoological *chimères*, its stone, its river, and its sprawling 'cricket' city of Paris, busy with its crafts.

But if the earlier portrait of Notre Dame was a structure of stone and depended upon the commonplaces of commentaries on the Gothic, this is a structure of words, and depends upon the Russian language, upon the poet's lashing his language into the skewed shape of his vision. Images slur into images, the visual puns seconded by those of the words. Notre Dame is now the surface of a lake, now the water beneath it, now a ship upon it, now the rock cliff rising above it. But being the Seine, it is also itself. The animals are the decorations of its sculptured façades and also those on the Ark that sails this flood. The image of the ship may be the only one prompted by earlier sources, for the cathedral as viewed from the east, where one can see the delicate wooden mast-like spire, has been compared to a ship in full sail – as theologians of the Middle Ages liked to call the Church herself a ship making for safe harbor.

The rose window and the towers of Notre Dame pursue Mandelstam in other poems, as in No. 373 ('Ia proshu, kak zhalosti i milosti'), which was begun a day earlier but finished on the same day as No. 374, but this was the last poem devoted to her alone. In Mandelstam's last memorial of the great church that he first looked upon as a young man in Paris in 1907, Notre Dame is 'changed, changed utterly.' But one should follow with the next line of Yeats's poem: 'A terrible beauty is born.' For if his eye revised the elements of his loved Gothic, the terrible beauty of this poem must slightly revise for us our apprehension of that earlier ending: the promise to create splendor from cruel weight.

VIII. THAT HAS SUCH PEOPLE IN'T

As one reads further in *Stone* the clockface of No. 31 seems to have been anything other than the moon. It was more nearly the sun. The sun now bursts hard, clear and brilliant upon a scene of frost and pellucid air. The outlines of St Petersburg etch themselves upon the retina with a lasting clarity. When the sun had burnt off the murk, one could suddenly see perspectives that had been obscured. The perspectives were spatial: the actual Admiralty sat like a rook in the capital at the end of its boulevards.[11] And they were temporal: real human figures – real at least to the extent of having real names like Bach and Luther and Eugene Onegin – begin to lend scale to the historical vistas that will henceforth define a certain 'now' in Mandelstam's poems, to replace the dubious 'always / never' of the former manner. When he inscribed a copy of the 1913 edition to Anna Akhmatova with the phrase 'bursts of consciousness in the swoon of days,' he was hardly describing what we now consider the second part of the book, much of which was not there in the first edition. Had it been there, the phrase would not have fitted.

There is humor. The year 1913 may have been the last year of what the nineteenth century had meant when it said 'Europe,' but Mandelstam was twenty-two, was tasting his first acclaim as a poet, and perhaps most important of all, he had depleted his first vein of inspiration, survived the depletion, and discovered another that was even better. The humor is often explicit, but more often it springs from an intangible sense of elation, a gaiety of language, that would never be absent from his poems again. There would be somber poems, some of them unrelieved. But by 1913, after practically no discernible apprenticeship – and an apprenticeship, at that, which would have adorned the *floruit* of lesser poets – Mandelstam had discovered for himself the truth in Pushkin's line

Мне грустно и легко; печаль моя светла

I am sorrowful and easy; my sadness is luminous

half of which he appropriated for himself in a poem (No. 80) at the end
of his first book:

> Да будет в старости печаль моя светла
>
> May my sadness in old age be luminous.

The secret of luminous sadness is implicit in the gaiety of language, and
the gaiety is there in the profoundest tragedies, as Yeats knew in 'Lapis
Lazuli':

> They know that Hamlet and Lear are gay;
> Gaiety transfiguring all that dread.

Like all true humor, it is self-deprecatory – the humor of maturity and
of artistic awareness. The celebrations of Russian grandeur, the evidence
of which was everywhere in the city of St Petersburg, swell with a kind
of imperial ecstacy. There are lines for which the word 'thrilling' is not
inappropriate: they recall at times one of the pinnacles of all Russian
poetry, the exordium of Pushkin's *Bronze Horseman*, which was celebrating
the same thing. But these grand flights, these 'tootings at the weddings
of the soul,' could hardly be read for themselves alone were it not for the
relief they gain from certain poems near them, poems in which a fatuous
Englishman at his tennis and an urchin buying an ice-cream from a street
vendor are celebrated with equal and exquisite pomp.

Some of the humorous poems are practically nothing more than verbal
toys, though they are elegant toys. Here is a short poem that describes
the final curtain of a Wagnerian opera and the scene of the departing
crowd. The dominant pattern of the line is comic in itself –

$$ \_ \; ' \_ \_ \_ ' \_ \_ \; \| \| \; \_ ' \_ ' $$

– with the break being very pronounced and the last two beats percussive.
The diction, meanwhile, tugs one towards the general lugubriousness
that satire always detects in the patrons of art (the ponderous opera, the
heavy furcoats, the marble stairs) and towards the flying Valkyries, the
singing violins, the idiot in the gallery (for which the Russian, following
the French, is the diminutive of 'paradise'), and the drivers outside
dancing around their fire. My translation aims to compensate for its
want of exactness by keeping some of the rhythm.

> Летают Валькирии, поют смычки.
> Громоздкая опера к концу идет.
> С тяжелыми шубами гайдуки
> На мраморных лестницах ждут господ.
>
> Уж занавес наглухо упасть готов;
> Еще рукоплещет в райке глупец;
> Извозчики пляшут вокруг костров.
> Карету такого-то! Разъезд. Конец.　　　(No. 55, 1913.)

With Valkyries winging it, and singing strings,
The opera ponderously folds up and dies.
On travertine staircases the gentry's things
Are brought them by liverymen with sleepy eyes.

The curtain has pointedly come down for good.
Some fool in the gallery still shouts Bravo.
The cabbies are capering to warm their blood.
The carriage for So-and-so! That's all. Let's go.

The next year Mandelstam wrote a poem about the moon which is
even more of a verbal toy and comes about as near as anything in Russian
to being the purest fluff. But the nonsense of it must have appealed to
him, for he returned to it over a period of years, leaving an expanded
variant of it dated '1914–1927.' It is a very ungrateful business to translate
such fragile whimsey as this, but a prose trot might gesture toward the
meaning of it.

> ...На луне не растет
> Ни одной былинки;
> На луне весь народ
> Делает корзинки—
> Из соломы плетет
> Легкие корзинки.
>
> На луне—полутьма,
> И дома опрятней;
> На луне не дома—
> Просто голубятни.
> Голубые дома—
> Чудо-голубятни...   (No. 58, 1914.)

Translation: On the moon there doesn't grow a single blade of grass; on
the moon the entire population make baskets – weave light baskets out of
straw. On the moon it's semi-dark, and the houses are tidier; there are
no houses on the moon – only pigeon-houses. Light-blue houses – marvelous
pigeon-houses.

The expanded version adds the information that there are no roads
on the moon, only benches, across three of which one leaps at every
step; that there are light-blue fishes, but since there is no water, the
fish do not swim, but fly...and so on.

Most noticeable of all, I think, is that what had been the barren world
of Mandelstam's book now suddenly flourished with a human population.
Some of the persons referred to are historical: Justinian, Peter the Great,
Verlaine, Socrates, Luther, J. S. Bach, Isaiah, E. A. Poe, Charles Dickens,
Anna Akhmatova, Rachel (i.e. Élisa Félix), Ovid, Sumarokov, Ozerov,
Napoleon, Metternich, Beethoven, Flaubert, Zola, Cicero, Homer, Julius
Caesar, Augustus, Racine, and others. Some are fictional: Eugene Onegin,

Eugene (the hero of Pushkin's *Bronze Horseman*), Ulalume, Oliver Twist, and Dombey and his children, among others. There are generalized portraits of human types, all of them thoroughly literary – the human artifacts of certain identifiable cultural milieus. 'The Old Man' (No. 40) traces a few events in the day of its eponymous subject who, though he is no one in particular – simply a besotted but appealing old reprobate – is placed for us by looking like Verlaine and leading the home life of Socrates. 'Abbé' (No. 74) is a sketch of the, as the poem has it, inevitable cleric in the novels of Flaubert and Zola. He is an ineffectual, good-natured priest caught between his religion and the petty distresses and pleasures of the world. I asked Anna Akhmatova whether there might not have been some real event behind this embryonic narrative. She replied that it was 'pure literature.'

And Mandelstam tried his hand at several other typological studies. There is the scatter-brained American girl 'doing' Europe, the 'eternally young' Englishman performing the ritual of lawn tennis, and the actors in a deliciously trite film melodrama. Other poems convey crowd scenes with a firm directorial hand: the drunken and multinational rabble of a basement dive, the gentry in their elegant suburbs and at the opera, and a party of Lutheran bourgeois at a funeral.

Mandelstam's interest in the cinema was evidently very great, as he referred to it several times in his poems and even more often in his prose. Not surprisingly, the figure of Chaplin appealed to him immensely, as it did to a great many Russian writers and artists of the time. But I think that ideas inspired by the technique of the cinema, rather than by its content, were of even greater moment. His enormous debt to Bergson will, I believe, become clearer when it is further explored. But it is already clear that Bergson's fondness for cinematic analogies and metaphors greatly reinforced a similar fondness in Mandelstam and provided him with the vehicle for one of his most important statements on poetic technique (in the essay 'Talking About Dante'). This is reason enough for looking at his first tribute to the movies. But there are other reasons, namely, that it is in many ways a typical poem of the period and that, in the Russian original, the rhythms of the poem ape the shadowy flickerings on the screen with spasmodic hilarity.

КИНЕМАТОГРАФ

Кинематограф. Три скамейки.
Сентиментальная горячка.
Аристократка и богачка
В сетях соперницы-злодейки.

Не удержать любви полета:
Она ни в чем не виновата!
Самоотверженно, как брата,
Любила лейтенанта флота.

А он скитается в пустыне—
Седого графа сын побочный.
Так начинается лубочный
Роман красавицы-графини.

И в исступленьи, как гитана,
Она заламывает руки.
Разлука. Бешеные звуки
Затравленного фортепьяно.

В груди доверчивой и слабой
Еще достаточно отваги
Похитить важные бумаги
Для неприятельского штаба.

И по каштановой аллее
Чудовищный мотор несется,
Стрекочет лента, сердце бьется
Тревожнее и веселее.

В дорожном платье, с саквояжем,
В автомобиле и в вагоне,
Она боится лишь погони,
Сухим измучена миражем.

Какая горькая нелепость:
Цель не опрадывает средства!
Ему—отцовское наследство,
А ей—пожизненная крепость.   (No. 50, 1913.)

CINEMA

A cinema. Three benches.
A fever of sentimentality.
A rich aristocratic lady
In the nets of a wicked rival.

The flight of love cannot be stopped:
She's absolutely blameless!
She loved an ensign of the fleet
Like a brother, selflessly.

But he's adrift in some wilderness –
The natural son of a greying count.
And so begins the shilling love
Affair of the lovely countess.

And like a gypsy in a frenzy
She begins to wring her hands.
The moment of parting. Maniacal bangs
From the racked pianoforte.

In her feeble, trusting bosom
There's enough left-over daring
To pilfer certain crucial papers
For the enemy headquarters.

And down the lane of chestnut trees
Speeds the monstrous motorcar.
Projector chirps and hearts do flips
With mounting alarm and gaiety.

In a travelling dress, with a *sac-voyage*,
In automobile and railway car,
It is only pursuit that frightens her,
Exhausted by a dry mirage.

But how preposterously the end
Leaves all the means unjustified!
He got his noble patrimony
But she – got life, not matrimony.

Nor should one omit two other categories of human reference in the poems of 1912–15. Mandelstam now dedicated certain poems to people with whom he had recently become acquainted. The dedicatee has, of course, no part in the poem itself, but his name does stand at the beginning of it, providing us with something that the author wished us to know, and it cannot be wholly irrelevant. It surely counts for something that in the 1916 edition of *Stone* Mandelstam dedicated his first sonnet to Mikhail Lozinsky, the publisher of *Giperborei* (Hyperboreus) and a staunch Acmeist partisan (especially since the poem was evidently written under the influence of a poem by Andrey Bely dedicated to Valery Bryusov). The poem 'Petersburg Stanzas' carries a dedication to Nikolay Gumilyov, the chief syndic of the Acmeists.

The most original human reference of all is that concealed in the history of the poem, unknown to the reader, and therefore obviously without the least aesthetic consequence. But not without interest to those studying the poet as well as his poems. If the figure with the 'alarmingly red mouth and the fringe of hair falling over his eyes' in No. 43 is indeed Georgy Ivanov – and it has been twice alleged that it is – then we glimpse, however remotely, one facet of an early friendship. Even more intriguing is the use to which Mandelstam put a Petersburg happening in No. 47:

Мы напряженного молчанья не выносим—
Несовершенство душ обидно, наконец!
И в замешательстве уж объявился чтец,
И радостно его приветствовали: «просим!»

Я так и знал, кто здесь присутствовал незримо:
Кошмарный человек читает «Улялюм».
Значенье—суета, и слово—только шум,
Когда фонетика—служанка серафима.

О доме Эшеров Эдгара пела арфа,
Безумный воду пил, очнулся и умолк.
Я был на улице. Свистел осенний шелк,
И горло греет шелк щекочущего шарфа... (1912.)[12]

We cannot bear strained silence –
The faultiness of souls is offensive, after all!
The reader had been confused when he first appeared
And was gleefully greeted with cries of 'Please!'

I knew it, I knew who was invisibly there:
A man out of a nightmare was reading 'Ulalume.'
Meaning is mere vanity and the word is only noise
While phonetics is the seraph's handmaiden.

Edgar's harp would sing of the House of Usher,
The madman drank some water, blinked, and said no more.
I was on the street. The silk of autumn whistled
And the silk of a tickling scarf warmed my throat.

As I was reading Mandelstam's poems one day with the late Artur Lourié, he told me the story behind this one. The reader of Poe's work was Vladimir Pyast, and the incident is from real life. Pyast, who wrote one of the best memoirs of the literary scene of the time – *Vstrechi* (*Meetings*), 1929 – was a minor poet and a great admirer of Poe, whom he translated. The epigraph of his first book of poems – *Ograda* (*Fence*), 1922 – comes from the same poem that he was reading that evening, 'Ulalume':

> Here once, through an alley Titanic
> Of cypress, I roamed with my Soul –
> Of cypress, with Psyche, my Soul.

He was wildly eccentric. He wore trousers of the loud checked pattern usually known as 'kopperfil'dy' after the Dickens character (and once affected by Mandelstam) but, by Pyast's acquaintances, as 'pyasty.' And he was periodically mad. The poem records an occasion when the fit of insanity came upon him as he was declaiming his favorite author. He drank from the glass of water on the rostrum, suddenly stared at the audience, and fell mute as a stone. The hall emptied in silent embarrassment.

As an example of the portraiture of historical personages I shall quote Mandelstam's poem on Bach, No. 45:

БАХ

Здесь прихожане дети праха
И доски вместо образов,
Где мелом Себастьяна Баха
Лишь цифры значатся псалмов.

'Stone'

Разноголосица какая
В трактирах буйных и церквах,
А ты ликуешь, как Исайя,
О рассудительнейший Бах!

Высокий спорщик, неужели,
Играя внукам свой хорал,
Опору духа в самом деле
Ты в доказательстве искал?

Что звук? Шестнадцатые доли,
Органа многосложный крик,
Лишь воркотня твоя, не боле,
О несговорчивый старик!

И лютеранский проповедник
На черной кафедре своей
С твоими, гневный собеседник,
Мешает звук своих речей.   (1913.)

BACH

This parish is the progeny
Of dust. No images, but boards
Whereon the numbers only of
The psalms of Bach appear in chalk.

What discordancy is there
In boisterous taverns and in church!
But like Isaiah you exult,
O hyperreasonable Bach!

Can it be true, great quarreller,
Playing your grandsons your chorale,
That you in fact were searching for
The spirit's cornerstone in proof?

And what is sound? The semiquavers,
The organ's sesquipedalian shriek
Are only your muttering, nothing more,
You unmanageable old man!

And now the Lutheran preacher from
The blackness of his pulpit box
Has mixed his words with those of his
Impatient interlocutor.

This picture of Bach is verbal in more ways than one. It presents him as a talker – specifically, as a reasoner, arguer, logician of the organ. Even the epithet *nesgovorchivyi* 'intractable' or 'unmanageable' conveys in its root that he cannot be *talked* into compliance. In a sense, therefore, the poem is also a continuation of the argument against the Symbolists,

201

who had sought to turn language into music. Here Mandelstam was doing what he did much more explicitly in his Acmeist manifesto, where he spoke of 'introducing the Gothic into the relationships of words, just as Sebastian Bach established it in music.' He was countering the demand for music in words by concentrating upon the verbal, logical qualities in music – the discursive reasoning of it.

In the essay on Dante, Mandelstam returned to the idea of the 'verbal organ' in a passage that seems appropriate to this poem:

> Long before Bach and at a time when large monumental organs were not being built yet, and there existed only the modest embryonic prototypes of the future marvel, when the chief instrument was still the zither, accompanying the voice, Alighieri constructed in verbal space an infinitely powerful organ and was already delighting in all of its imaginable stops and inflating its bellows and roaring and cooing in all its pipes.

That, however, is an aspect of the poem that comes after some reflection upon it. What chiefly strikes one, I think, is the relationship between the speaker of the poem and his subject. This relationship emerges not only directly from what is said but also by implication from the manner of its saying. The language of the poem is, oddly enough, a good deal gayer than that in 'Cinema' or 'Tennis,' where the frivolity of the theme alone sufficed. There, the wit lay in treating nameless figures of fun with an absolutely straight face. But Bach was much too important to Mandelstam for solemnity. The relationship between speaker and subject is therefore that quintessentially Acmeist relationship – the domestic. Bach is a familiar. One may speak of his grandsons and his 'muttering.' One may call him 'old man' and tease him with a slightly outlandish superlative form like *rassuditel'neishii*, the quality of which I have tried to convey with 'hyperreasonable.' One may treat him, that is, with the sincerest respect of all, that from which love has banished any taint of fear.

This domestication of the heroes of the past was Mandelstam's habitual way of paying them homage. It was, after all, his feeling of kinship with them that drew him to them in the first instance. Adulation has probably never been more comfortable and unconstrained. Mandelstam did not deal with Dante as a person in the poems, though he was mentioned often enough. But in the great essay on Dante his effort in dealing with the central figure of the *Divine Comedy* is to cut through the accumulated clichés, especially those that would dehumanize him through some form of apotheosis, and see Dante in his social and physical reality.

> Dante is an impoverished descendant of an ancient Roman line. He is an internal *raznochinets*. Not courtesy but something completely opposite is characteristic of him. One has to be a blind mole not to notice that throughout the entire length of the *Divina Commedia* Dante does not know how to behave, he does not know how to act, what to say, how to make a bow.

This is not something I have imagined; I take it from the many admissions that Alighieri himself has strewn about in the *Divina Commedia*. The inner anxiety, and the heavy, troubled awkwardness which attend every step of the unselfconfident man, the man whose upbringing is inadequate, who does not know what application to make of his inner experience or how to objectify it in etiquette, the tortured and outcast man – it is these qualities that give the poem all its charm, all its drama, and they are what create its background, its psychological ground.

In the 'Ode to Beethoven' (No. 72) the speaker of the poem comes to terms with another 'terrible' figure by similar means – by bearding him in his lair, as it were, to express a tender affection for him.

> Бывает сердце так сурово,
> Что и любя его не тронь!
> И в темной комнате глухого
> Бетховена горит огонь.
> И я не мог твоей, мучитель,
> Чрезмерной радости понять.

> The heart's occasionally so stern
> That even in love you daren't approach it;
> And even in the darkened room
> Of deaf Beethoven a fire burns.
> Nor was I capable, tormentor,
> Of grasping your excessive joy.

But then we are shown Beethoven as a 'marvelous pedestrian' who 'strides headlong, his green hat in his hand' as he absentmindedly makes his way to a piano lesson. 'With whom,' the speaker asks, 'can one more deeply and completely drain the whole cup of tenderness?'[13] Other figures who are treated with this same mingling of profound esteem and easy familiarity are the biologist Lamarck and the great poets Batyushkov and Ariosto.

In all of these human portraits there is a peculiar doubleness that strikes me as intriguing. Consider that there is always someone else in the poem. There is the central figure, but there is always one other. There is Bach, but there is – almost inevitably, it seems, once you begin to observe this phenomenon – also Isaiah. This happens in the slightest poems. If Luther occupies No. 42, there will be, and is, room for the Apostle Peter. In the eight lines of 'Akhmatova' there is room for the actress Rachel (Élisa Félix) in her greatest *rôle*, Phèdre.

Is this nothing more than the old fundamental act of poetry, the making of one thing into another? The distances between the terms of these juxtapositions are truly immense: between the Verlaine and the Socrates of No. 40, the Martin Luther and the Apostle Peter of No. 42, the Ovid and the Scythian of No. 60, but it is upon such distances that the terms of metaphor plume themselves. Is there no further *comment* involved?

Let me propose that there might be some, that, for example, the prophet Isaiah in the generally stern picture of Bach might lend not only his fervent accusatory presence but also his traditional suggestion of New Testament compassion. Bach's familial tenderness might thus be suggested twice. In the poem on Petersburg the Eugene (Onegin) who is mentioned first is the blasé snob of Pushkin's novel-poem, the emblematic hero of the official Petersburg, but the second Eugene, the hero of *The Bronze Horseman*, adds his wretched poverty and madness to the portrait of the capital.

I think that the doubleness at which I am trying to get through these questions is a feature of more than the human portraits. It is something that links together all the pictorial poems in *Stone* from 1912–13 on. They are transparent. One's attention is called to them, one focusses upon them, and...they vanish at once. But the point is that they vanish to reveal something else. Bach is faintly suggested, we see him in his family circumstance, chalking the psalm numbers on the board; but then Bach evaporates and we are left, really, with the idea of a logical, argumentative, organic art. Lamarck appears even more briefly, then vanishes to reveal (or metamorphoses into) the general idea of the order of animate nature, and Man's place in that order.

The same is true of the pictures of buildings; it is true of the 'pictures' of *Dombey and Son* or Racine's drama or the poems of Ossian. It may be that the sameness I am seeking to pin down is a sameness that inheres in the very nature of poetry itself, namely, that poems are always about something else. The buildings, books and men in Mandelstam's poems are themselves and...cultural emblems. The scope, the range of cultural suggestiveness is immense in Mandelstam's poems: perhaps that is the distinctive feature of them. If it is a commonplace that poems are about more than one thing at a time, it is not a commonplace that poems should have the weight and significance of his. The raising of a phenomenon to the tenth power, he called it in his Acmeist manifesto. He does indeed raise it, and the rate of acceleration is very fast.

But it would be a great mistake to suppose that the original phenomenon is lost, that the Admiralty is there merely to seed some cloud of geopolitics and start it raining. No, the Admiralty remains vividly before us in all of its precise details. But the whole suddenly discloses to us more than the sum of its parts, and we find that we are not looking at the Admiralty but at the idea of the Admiralty. The poem, we finally realize, is not about the Admiralty, but about what the Admiralty was about. This is what gives one the sense that the poems take the place of their subject, like Stevens's poem that 'took the place of a mountain.' They present them not only externally but also 'sympathetically,' from their own and their creators' point of view.

If this is true of a poem like 'The Admiralty' that 'accurately' pictures

its subject, it is also true – perhaps even truer – of poems that distort the
subject. Take for example the poem on Dickens's *Dombey and Son*

ДОМБИ И СЫН

Когда, пронзительнее свиста,
Я слышу английский язык—
Я вижу Оливера Твиста
Над кипами конторских книг.

У Чарльза Дикенса спросите,
Что было в Лондоне тогда:
Контора Домби в старом Сити
И Темзы желтая вода.

Дожди и слезы. Белокурый
И нежный мальчик Домби-сын;
Веселых клерков каламбуры
Не понимает он один.

В конторе сломанные стулья,
На шиллинги и пенсы счет;
Как пчелы, вылетев из улья,
Роятся цифры круглый год.

А грязных адвокатов жало
Работает в табачной мгле—
И вот, как старая мочала,
Банкрот болтается в петле.

На стороне врагов законы:
Ему ничем нельзя помочь!
И клетчатые панталоны,
Рыдая, обнимает дочь.   (No. 53, 1913.)

DOMBEY AND SON

I never hear the English tongue –
More piercing than a whistle –
But I see Oliver Twist among
His heaps of office ledgers.

What was it like in London then?
Consult the works of Dickens:
The yellow water of the Thames
And Dombey's office in the City.

Showers of rain and tears. A blond
And gentle boy – old Dombey's son.
And all but he can understand
When the accountants make a pun.

The office holds some broken chairs,
The shillings and the pennies thrive,
And figures of the fiscal years
Swarm like bees above a hive.

However: dirty lawyers' stings
Still function in the smoke and mist.
See where the wretched bankrupt swings
And dangles like a length of bast.

There's nothing for it. All in vain.
The law's on the opponents' side.
And so in tears the daughter clings
To trouser legs in checkered plaid.

This poem is clearly not 'about' the novel. If it were, why should it begin with Oliver Twist? Why should it seem almost perversely to misrepresent the novel, portraying old Dombey as a suicide when in fact the book ends in the sentimental glow of Dombey reconciled with the daughter whom he had neglected and surrounded by his grandchildren? The answer, it seems to me – if we wish to say that the poem is about anything other than itself – is that the poem is about what the novel was about. Dickens created a long, complex fable of which the subject is a certain quality of life in a certain place at a certain time. Mandelstam did not know this life at first hand but only through the novels of Dickens and others. Nevertheless, his poem is about that same quality of life, not about the novel. Our thinking about the relationship of the poem to the novel is hampered by the irrelevant fact that both are made of language. But the poem is just as radically independent of the novel as would be, say, a sequence of gestures by a dancer in a solo ballet called 'Dombey and Son.' There may be no suicide in the novel, but that noose answers the requirements of the poem, as the dancer's leaps and grimaces would answer the requirements of the choreography (which no one would ever dream of attacking for being unlike the novel – as one Soviet critic has attacked the poem). The noose comes from the same phonic impulse – the clustering of consonants in the vicinity, especially the consonant *l* – that produced the words for 'haze,' 'dangle,' 'bankrupt,' and so on.

11

'Phaedra'

In trying to bring the commentary on *Stone* to a conclusion I found myself in a familiar quandry, for, as usual, one cannot divide Mandelstam up into separate convenient pieces – especially when the pieces are in some way contiguous. His poems won't stay apart. And now, neither will his books. *Stone* concludes with No. 81 and *Tristia* opens with No. 82, both of them poems on the same play of Racine, the *Phèdre*. Each contains a translation of one line spoken by the heroine in her first scene:

> Que ces vains ornements, que ces voiles me pèsent.

In the 1923 edition of *Stone* Mandelstam further cemented the end of the first book to the beginning of the second by inserting between these two poems a translation into Russian alexandrines of the first 22 lines of *Phèdre*. (In the New York edition this poem is now No. 460.)

I propose to treat these two poems together and in some detail. They are interesting in themselves, for one thing; but there are several other reasons for a close examination. In one of its aspects, Mandelstam's poetry was certainly what Zhirmunsky called it (in the phrase of Schlegel), *die Poesie der Poesie*, and it is worthwhile knowing how the poet appropriated for his own purposes the work of earlier writers. The most direct way of doing this (if we disregard the method of Jorge Luis Borges' character Pierre Menard, the *author* of the *Don Quixote*) is to translate the earlier writer's words into one's own language. Another way is to write an ekphrastic poem about one's perception of the earlier work – that is No. 81. A third way, that of No. 82, is to write as it were from *inside* the other work. To be sure, this metaphoric expression is merely another way of putting the idea of writing about one's perception of the work. One is still doing that, but the difference that is brought about when the perception is from within the play itself rather than from the other side of the footlights makes an enormous difference in the poem that results.

Here is the text of No. 81.

Я не увижу знаменитой "Федры",
В старинном многоярусном театре,
С прокопченной высокой галереи,
При свете оплывающих свечей.
И, равнодушен к суете актеров,
Сбирающих рукоплесканий жатву,
Я не услышу обращенный к рампе
Двойною рифмой оперенный стих:

—Как эти покрывала мне постылы...

Театр Расина! Мощная завеса
Нас отделает от другого мира;
Глубокими морщинами волнуя,
Меж ним и нами занавес лежит.
Спадают с плеч классические шали,
Расплавленный страданьем крепнет голос
И достигает скорбного закала
Негодованьем раскаленный слог...

Я опоздал на празднество Расина!

Вновь шелестят истлевшие афиши,
И слабо пахнет апельсинной коркой,
И словно из столетней летаргии—
Очнувшийся сосед мне говорит:
—Измученный безумством Мельпомены,
Я в этой жизни жажду только мира;
Уйдем, покуда зрителы-шакалы
На растерзанье Музы не пришли!

Когда бы грек увидел наши игры...   (1915.)

I shall not, in an old many-tiered theater,
see the famous *Phèdre*
from the high smoke-blackened gallery
by the light of guttering candles.
Nor shall I, indifferent to the vanity of actors
gathering in their harvest of applause,
hear the line feathered with its coupled rhyme
and flung across the footlights:

– How repellent are these veils to me...

Racine's theater! A mighty drapery
divides us from another world.
A curtain waving in deep folds
lies between it and us.
Classical shawls fall from shoulders,
a voice dissolved by suffering grows in strength
and, scorched with indignation, Racine's style
achieves through pain the point of tempered steel.

208

I've missed Racine's solemnity!

Disintegrating posters rustle once again
and one can faintly smell the orangepeel
and my neighbor says, as though he'd just
come to from a hundred years of lethargy:
– Exhausted by the madness of Melpomene,
I thirst in this life for peace alone;
let us leave before the jackal audience
arrive to tear the Muse to tatters!

If a Greek should see our games...

The very form of the first line immediately recalls a poem written the previous year:

> Я не слыхал рассказов Оссиана...   (No. 67, 1914.)

> I did not hear the tales of Ossian...

And the essential argument of the two poems is the same, namely, the apparent paradox: although I did not hear the recitations of Ossian nor sit in Racine's audience, nevertheless both the bardic landscape of Scotland and the 'other world' of classical French tragedy are or can be present to me now. The Ossian poem, in fact, reads in some ways like a commentary upon both of the *Phèdre* poems, but of that, more later.

It is perhaps even more striking to note that lines 14–17 are in some sense practically a variant of the short poem on Akhmatova (No. 59), also written the year before:

> В пол-оборота, о печаль,
> На равнодушных поглядела.
> Спадая с плеч, окаменела
> Ложно-классическая шаль.
>
> Зловещий голос—горький хмель—
> Души расковывает недра:[1]
> Так—негодующая Федра—
> Стояла некогда Рашель.

> Half turning round, O sadness,
> she glanced at the uncaring crowd.
> The pseudo-classical shawl
> falling from her shoulders turned to stone.

> The dire voice, hopelessly intoxicating,
> unfetters the depths of the soul:
> thus Rachel used once to stand –
> an indignant Phèdre.

The Rachel in question is the actress Élisa Félix (1820–58), whose stage name was Rachel and whose most triumphant *rôle* was that of Racine's tragic heroine. But apart from the mention of Phèdre, there is also the same shawl falling from the same shoulders, the same voice, the same indignation. It is another case of an earlier poem being consumed by a later one, and metabolized by it.

Let us return to the first poem on *Phèdre*. It is written in unrhymed iambic pentameter verse – the verse of Pushkin's Shakespearean play, *Boris Godunov*, and the typical meter of Russian verse plays. This meter is appropriate to a poem which aims at creating the atmosphere of a dramatic performance, the impression made upon an audience by Racine's tragedies. The perspective is entirely that of the spectator and listener. It becomes rather Flemish in the intimacy of its details: the smells and the sounds of one spectator's immediate vicinity. All of the details selected by his attention justify the negative in the first line, for they are all hindrances. He is in a blackened, rustling, guttering, annoying world where all conspires to prevent his seeing the play, for which he has come too late, which he will neither see nor hear. Only the second hemistich of one of Phèdre's lines –

Que ces vains ornements, que ces voiles me pèsent –

can be heard, though it is easy enough to hear four affectedly theatrical lines from the neighbor, who is clearly one of the indifferent ones. A heavy curtain strangely closes off the stage in the very midst of the action, at the moment when the heroine herself is speaking. That curtain is of course not the actual curtain of the theater but the curtain of time and of the profoundly different tradition that governed the conventions of French seventeenth-century theater. I think it possible also to see the curtain 'waving in deep folds' as an image suggesting the majestic verse of Racine's twelve-syllable line. The controlling emotion of the man who speaks the poem is very similar to the emotion of the single line from the play that is quoted: the desire to break through the veils, curtains, shawls, draperies – many fabrics were spun out of Phèdre's *voiles* – that impede a violently felt wish. In her case, the veils summarize the impossible position of being unable either to declare her love for her stepson Hippolyte or to escape from it. She is caught in a sensual passion that is sumptuous like her veils and, like them, an entangling torment. In the case of the speaker of the poem, these textile images convey all the barriers of time and cultural distance, as well, perhaps, as those of his immediate circumstance, that prevent or impede the direct perception of Racine's imagined world.

I have said, however, that the argument here is the same as that in the Ossian poem, namely, that although one may never have heard the tales of Ossian, nevertheless the whole atmosphere of his world is available. Racine's world is distinctly not available in No. 81. Is this a contradiction? I think it is not, but then I must repeat what the reader is forever in danger of forgetting, that I do not think the argument of the poem ends with that poem or even, in the present case, with that book. It continues in *Tristia*. Before going to that, it is time to look at the Ossian poem.

Я не слыхал рассказов Оссиана,
Не пробовал старинного вина—
Зачем же мне мерещится поляна,
Шотландии кровавая луна?

И перекличка ворона и арфы
Мне чудится в зловещей тишине,
И ветром развиваемые шарфы
Дружинников мелькают при луне!

Я получил блаженное наследство—
Чужих певцов блуждающие сны;
Свое родство и скучное соседство
Мы презирать заведомо вольны.

И не одно сокровище, быть может,
Минуя внуков, к правнукам уйдет,
И снова скальд чужую песню сложит
И как свою ее произнесет.   (No. 67, 1914.)

I have not heard the tales of Ossian,
have not tasted of that ancient wine –
why, then, does my fancy seem to see
a glade, and the blood on Scotland's moon?

And in the dire silence I seem to hear
the calling back and forth of harp and raven
and all the wind-whipt scarves of the retinue
are flashing in the moonlight.

I've come into a blessed legacy –
the roaming visions of another's bard;
we've clearly got a patent to despise
our own propinquity and boring neighborhood.

And this may not be the only treasure, either,
to skip the grandsons and descend to their sons,
and another skald will write the song he's come by
and sing it then as if it were his own.

It is the last two stanzas that provide what strikes me as a kind of commentary on the two Phèdre poems. The third stanza even confers the right to be contemptuous of one's boring neighbor (and all he stands for), but it is the last that shows the way out of the contradiction, that leads out of the predicament of the spectator and into the solution of the first poem of *Tristia*, which follows:

—Как этих покрывал и этого убора
Мне пышность тяжела средь моего позора!

    —Будет в каменной Трезене
    Знаменитая беда,
    Царской лестницы ступени
    Покраснеют от стыда,

      •   •   •
    •   •   •

    И для матери влюбленной
    Солнце черное взойдет.

—О если б ненависть в груди моей кипела—
Но видите—само признанье с уст слетело.

    —Черным пламенем Федра горит
    Среди белого дня.
    Погребальный факел чадит
    Среди белого дня.
    Бойся матери ты, Ипполит:
    Федра—ночь—тебя сторожит
    Среди белого дня.

—Любовью черною я солнце запятнала...

      •   •   •

    —Мы боимся, мы не смеем
    Горю царскому помочь.
    Уязвленная Тезеем
    На него напала ночь.
    Мы же, песнью похоронной
    Провожая мертвых в дом,
    Страсти дикой и бессонной
    Солнце черное уймем.   (1916.)

– How heavy to me amid my shame is the splendor
of these veils and this attire!
    – In stone Troezen there will be
    a famous misfortune;
    the steps of the royal stairs
    will turn red from shame.

      •   •   •
    •   •   •

    And for the enamored mother
    a black sun will rise.
– O, if it were hate that boiled in my breast –
but you see that the confession flew of itself from my lips.
    Phaedra burns with a black flame
    in broad daylight.
    A funeral torch smoulders
    in broad daylight.

Fear thy mother, Hippolytus:
Phaedra, the night, is watching you
in broad daylight.
– With my black love I have besmirched the sun
[Death will cool my ardor from a pure phial.]
   – We're afraid, we dare not
   ease this royal grief.
Stung by Theseus, the night
has assaulted him.
And with our funeral song
as we follow the dead home,
we shall cool the black sun
of a wild, unsleeping passion.

Is this Racine's *Phèdre*, or Mandelstam's? But the question is too limited. Why should one exclude the predecessors of Racine – Euripides and Seneca – from the question of proprietorship? The answer is that it is Mandelstam's remaking, within the infinitely stricter terms of the lyric, of the old story of helpless incestuous love.

I do not mean to suggest that he has remade the story indifferently from all of the three sources: it is specifically Racine's version that he has 'sung as if it were his own.' Mandelstam doubtless knew Euripides' *Hippolytus*, though there is good reason to suppose that he never read it in the Greek. Much more likely is that he knew the Russian translation made by the revered Innokenty Annensky, which appeared in the *Journal of the Ministry of Public Education*, nos. 340 and 341 for 1902, but a reading of that does not suggest his specific familiarity with it, for he took nothing from it for his poem. His Latin was a good deal better than his Greek, but Seneca's *Phaedra* does not seem to have furnished anything. In Euripides, Phaedra hangs herself, and in Seneca she flings herself upon a sword; but in Racine she takes poison, as in Mandelstam's cancelled line 21. That Racine's version is the one to have shaped his conception of the story can also be seen from an earlier draft of the poem on Anna Akhmatova (No. 59), where the epithet for Phaedra was the Russian word for 'poisoner' *otravitel'nitsa*.

The imagery of light and heat – specifically that of the sun, Phaedra's forebear – inheres in her story, and is therefore present in each version of it. But no one made so deliberate and extensive a use of it as Racine, who threads it obsessively through the whole texture of his play. Annensky, in his translation of Euripides, often uses the Russian for 'sun' where the original has φάος (line 57) or φέγγος (line 178) or some other word for 'daylight,' 'brightness,' and so on. On the other hand, when the Greek provides him with the actual word for 'sun' he will ignore it, preferring to convey the sense by periphrasis:

Вы, светлые лучи!...И ты, земля!

shouts Hippolytus when the nurse discloses Phaedra's guilty love for him, but the Greek reads, in line 601:

$$\dot{\omega} \ \gamma a \hat{\imath} a \ \mu \hat{\eta} \tau \epsilon \rho \ \dot{\eta} \lambda \acute{\iota} o v \ \tau' \ \dot{a} v a \pi \tau v \chi a \acute{\iota}$$

Again, in translating line 617, he renders the Greek for 'light of the sun' with the Russian for 'rays of the heavens.' He did not, therefore, seek to make the word for 'sun' unusually prominent in his version; and it does not, in fact, stand out.

Mandelstam's poem is built very simply. There are three translated passages, each originally consisting of a rhymed couplet of Russian alexandrines (iambic hexameter divided by a caesura after the third foot). Each is followed by a passage of seven or eight lines in a shorter meter: the first and third are trochaic tetrameter, and the central passage consists of four-beat and three-beat accentual lines in alternation.

The translated passages are the easiest to deal with. The first is based upon the same line from the lips of Phèdre that we have already seen in the last poem of *Stone*:

> Que ces vains ornements, que ces voiles me pèsent.

In this poem he expands it to the length of a couplet, managing thereby to include all of Racine's line plus some material of his own:

> – How heavy to me amid my shame is the splendor
> of these veils and this attire!

The second translated passage comes from the mouth of the other principal protagonist, Hippolytus. Only the first of the two lines

> – O, if it were hate that boiled in my breast

is in any sense a translation, and, at that, it falls short even of the relative exactitude of lines 1–2. The only speech by Hippolytus that seems to underlie this one is line 56 in Racine's play:

> Si je la haïssais, je ne la fuirais pas.

He is speaking to his confidant Théramène about his own forbidden love for Aricie. As for the second line of this couplet, line 12

> but you see that the confession flew of itself from my lips

there is no specific original in Racine. Furthermore, the punctuation would seem to indicate that it is not meant to be read as direct speech at all; but punctuation, generally speaking, is a treacherous guide in the poems of Mandelstam as we now have them. As a summation of the play, of course, rather than as a translation, the meaning of the line is more than obvious, for the *Phèdre* is constructed on the classical scheme of primary and secondary *avowals*, first to the confidant and then to the principal; and in each case the avowal of love is wrested from the speaker by some power beyond his control. The line in question is closely followed in the same scene (Act I, Scene 1) by Hippolyte's timid avowal of his illicit passion for Aricie. Phèdre's own words when she is confessing her love to Hippolyte may seem even closer to the words of Mandelstam:

> Que dis-je? Cet aveu que je te viens de faire,
> Cet aveu si honteux, le crois-tu volontaire?   (693–4.)

The last couplet is now defective since Mandelstam cancelled the second line (21), which I have nevertheless given above in square brackets:

> [Death will cool my ardor from a pure phial.]

In any case, neither line qualifies as 'translation' in the literalist sense of the term at all, for no single utterance of the original can be adduced as the model for Mandelstam's words. The translations in the poem thus become less and less literal – more and more original with Mandelstam himself.

But how willingly one foregoes literalness now in the song that a Russian poet has taken as his own, for no other line, whether translated or not, so succinctly conveys the whole atmosphere and the tragedy of *Phèdre*:

> – With my black love I have besmirched the sun.

And few lines open such vistas into an imagery of which we have not seen the last in the pages of Mandelstam. Phèdre's tragedy is her guilty (black) love for Hippolyte and the twisted crimes against her husband, her stepson, and her own essential nobility into which this passion betrays her. But the fatal taint is in her blood. She is, in the words of the exquisite line, 'fille de Minos et de Pasiphaé.' Minos is not only the violent king of Crete but also the judge of the Underworld. Pasiphaé is not only the mother of the Minotaur through having coupled with the bull (enticed, in the marvelous phrase of Robert Lowell's translation, by his 'magnetic April thunders'), but also the daughter of the Sun. Phèdre is compounded explosively of black and red, of guilt and rectitude, of passion and noble reason. There is no escape – not even in death itself, for she would then come before her terrifying father to be judged – nor any place in this world, for the Sun, her even more terrifying grandfather, searches out everything with his light. And with her black love she has soiled the Sun.

The line, while not precisely a translation, uses elements that are among the commonest leitmotifs of Racine's play. Throughout, the word *flamme* is used, as it commonly is, for 'love' or 'passion.' (Mandelstam approximated it most closely with the word *pyl* of line 21). And it is juxtaposed everywhere to the opposing notions of darkness and blackness. One of the clearest precedents for Mandelstam's line comes in Phèdre's speech to Oenone when she first confesses her 'black love' for Hippolyte:

> Je voulais en mourant prendre soin de ma gloire,
> Et dérober au jour une flamme si noire.   (309–10.)

And in her dying speech, Phèdre says to Theseus:

> Le ciel mit dans mon sein une flamme funeste.   (1625.)

But the exact phrase 'black love' itself occurs in the words of Theseus about his son Hippolytus:

> Pour parvenir au but de ses noires amours,
> L'insolent de la force empruntait le secours.   (1007–8.)

As for the second part of the line, that sums up the often repeated words of the play which convey, in various forms, the idea of soiling, besmirching, blackening that which was pure and undefiled. The last words of Phèdre provide an example:

> Et la mort, à mes yeux dérobant la clarté,
> Rend au jour, qu'ils souillaient, toute sa pureté.   (1643–4.)

And the verb *noircir* in this sense is common; cf. lines 893, 1314, 1428, and elsewhere.

In Mandelstam's poem the three passages in a shorter meter all depend upon the contrasting imagery of light and dark, red and black, day and night. None of these lines is a translation in the ordinary sense, and it tells us something about translation in the ordinary sense when we realize that it is precisely in these passages that Mandelstam leads us into the poetic core of Racine's tragedy, the core in which the fable itself has been burnt away to leave a residue of incandescent essential words: *soleil, jour, noircir, flamme, rougir, sang, funeste*. He disposes of these elements now with a proprietary hand. The song is wholly his own, and he has made a Russian chorus (his closest approach to the ancient sources of Racine) to comment upon the tragedy. The compression has a purely Mandelstamian, modern multivalence. The steps leading to the royal palace in Troezen will 'redden with shame.' The verbal phrase derives from the word 'rougir' that occurs throughout *Phèdre*, where, of course, it always means human blushing as a token of shame. But in Mandelstam the reddened steps also call up an image of blood-splashed stairs and foreshadow the violence and death with which the tragedy ends.

It was a similar kind of compression that led Mandelstam to fuse the notions of heat, light, passion, on the one hand, and cold, dark, shame, on the other, into the single image of the black sun. Again, the phrase is a replica not of any single verbal original in Racine but of the central moral conflict of the play. It is, to be sure, much more than that, for the image of the black sun is very widespread and ancient in literature and must surely derive from man's original terror at the sight of the solar eclipse. In the Paris of the 1920s Harry Crosby's famous avant-garde publishing venture, of which Mandelstam could not have been unaware, was called the Black Sun Press. That derived in all probability from the famous sonnet by Gérard de Nerval, 'El Desdichado' ('Je suis le ténébreux, – le veuf, – l'inconsolé'), which contains the lines:

> mon luth constellé
> Porte le soleil noir de la Mélancolie.[2]

Which was no doubt even more familar to Mandelstam. But the question where he got the image is, since it cannot be decided, anyway, rather trivial. What strikes me as worth noting is that it answers precisely the kind of demand that he was making upon his imagery elsewhere in this poem: that it should strike to the metaphoric core of Racine's play and, by a process of fusion and compression, make it new, make it, that is, his own. It was his luck or genius to draw for his purpose upon one of the grand commonplaces of poetic art and thereby make it a striking novelty. In the next 'choral' speech the identical procedure enabled him to take one of the plainest phrases in Russian (*sredi belogo dnia* 'in broad daylight') and cause it to glitter with diamond brightness as the refrain.

The two poems on *Phèdre* are among the earliest works of Mandelstam in which it is possible to trace a poetic process that he was later to single out for much praise – above all in his great essay on Dante. Put in the simplest possible terms, it might be called the transformation of imagery. This means the gradual breeding of one image out of another by a process of association, the association being of all possible kinds. But this will be discussed later. For the time being, it will suffice to point out the workings of this metonymic process in the *Phèdre* poems.

I have already mentioned the textile stuffs that are generated by the mention of Phèdre's veils in the first poem (No. 81). These produce the drapery, curtain, and shawls that follow. These are immediately burnt away by a few lines that depend upon the white-hot processes of smelting and forging. But decay claims it all in the sibilant whispering of the final passage with its tattered posters, torn Muse, and lethargic neighbor, who surfaces with 'oof!' (in *ochnuvshiisia*) from a century of dullness.

The process in the first poem of *Tristia* (No. 82) is more sophisticated – one of the reasons, I think, for its not being in the earlier book.

The contrast that will control the poem is suggested first in the sixth line: 'will turn red from shame.' It is fully realized in the image of the black sun (line 10), which I have discussed. (I know nothing, by the way, of the missing lines 7 and 8.) And then the black sun spawns the imagery that will march through the poem to its last line. But perhaps my figure of marching is wrong. Perhaps I should use Mandelstam's figure of the airplane that releases another, which in turn releases another, and so on. Or the source, I think, of Mandelstam's image: Henri Bergson's figure of the artillery shell that bursts into fragments, which then burst into further fragments...In any case, the point is that the black sun furnishes us (line 13) with 'guilty love,' put literally, after Racine, as 'black flame.' After the refrain this has become, in line 15, a funeral torch. The black sun in ancient usage was the opposite of the sun of day, i.e. it was the night. And that is what Phèdre herself becomes in line 18: she is the night, and immediately says: 'With my black love I have soiled the sun.'

Night 'falls' in Russian as it does in English, and to 'fall upon' is to attack. The night, the black sun, that has overcome Hippolytus, falls also upon Theseus, the hapless mourner of two deaths at the end of the tragedy. The black sun that arose in the first choral speech, gleamed darkly amid the broad daylight of the second, now lights the funeral of the last. In the final line, it is extinguished. The Russian verb *uniat'*, meaning 'to calm, cool, assuage,' has seldom had so sinister a meaning as here, where it refers to the death of Phèdre by her own hand, the final 'cooling' of her hot passion, for in this transformation of imagery, she has become the black sun, the night.

12

Three poems of 'Tristia'

The book that begins with a poem written from inside another man's work, Racine's *Phèdre*, also bears the title of another man's book, Ovid's *Tristia*. The title itself was supplied without consulting the author by another writer, Mikhail Kuzmin; and according to Nadezhda Yakovlevna, the MS was taken away to Berlin by the publisher, who brought it out in 1922 in a form that was unsatisfactory to the poet himself. Put in this way, these facts make it seem that Mandelstam had rather less than full charge of his career at the moment when his talent was manifesting itself more and more phenomenally.

The facts may be put in a different light, of course. Writing from 'inside' the earlier work of art was Mandelstam's way of making not only a comment upon that work but also an utterly new poem of his own. *Tristia*, though it may have been selected by Kuzmin rather than Mandelstam, was hardly a haphazard or an unlikely choice, for it was already the title of one of the best poems in the book. The geographical and historical connotations of the title were apt, for Mandelstam had brought the manuscript back with him from the shore of the Black Sea to the metropolis; Ovid's laments had been written from his exile in the same place to an audience in Rome. Furthermore, the author could not have been all that displeased with the title. After banishing it in favor of the colorless name *Second Book* of 1923, he restored it for the collected edition of 1928, and the evidence is that from its first appearance the book always went by the name of *Tristia* when he referred to it.

The question of the form of the collection is somewhat more difficult to deal with. Mandelstam favored the principle of chronological order, and the rather chaotic order of the Berlin edition could hardly have pleased him. He had rather more control over the next version, *Second Book*, but so had the Soviet censor. According to Nadezhda Yakovlevna, *Second Book* was put together from memory alone, and there are numerous departures from the order finally determined in the 1928 edition, the last one that Mandelstam was able to see through the press.

In that last edition, where the size of *Tristia* had to be accommodated to the requirements of a larger collection, a number of poems had obviously to be excluded on grounds that had little to do with the author's final estimate of them. Perhaps some were excluded because Mandelstam no longer wished them to appear, but one can never be sure. Insofar as they were able, the editors of the New York edition have followed the principle of chronological order, and they have restored to *Tristia* those poems that were in its first two editions. A certain degree of arbitrariness is inevitable, and so is human error, but it seems to me clear that the New York edition is the best – that is to say, closest to Mandelstam's own wishes – of all the editions of *Tristia*.

In one sense of the term, *Tristia* is a less conspicuously structured book than *Stone*, for there is no sharp dividing line within it between one manner and another. To be sure, the 1923 edition (and only that one) contained two poems written that year that seem abruptly new when one comes upon them in the context of *Tristia*. These are No. 136, 'The Horseshoe Finder,' and No. 137, 'The Slate Ode.' When Mandelstam last saw them through the press, they were relegated to their chronological place in the third section of the collection of 1928.

Tristia consists of the poems written between 1916 and 1920 (No. 124, dated 1921, appeared only in the first edition). The first edition contained the most poems (46) and the third the least (38); the second edition had 43 and so has the New York edition. Mandelstam dates ten poems as having been written in 1916, nine in 1917, four in 1918, three in 1919, and sixteen, equal to the output of the previous turbulent three years, in 1920.

It is Mandelstam's most 'classical' book, if one takes the term to mean simply reference to the culture of Greece and Rome. It differs from the 'Roman' *Stone*, however, in referring almost exclusively to the classical world of Greece – a fact which should not be obscured by the slight irony of its bearing a Latin title.

The general emotional tone of *Tristia* is well conveyed by the title, however, and it seems to me among the more substantial generalities that one can in fact speak of emotional tone as a distinguishing characteristic of *Tristia*. In the several voices of these poems we discern an emotional motivation that is at once more mature, serious, and credible than what has gone before. The sadness of the poems is luminous, but it also is, or is made with consummate art to seem, more genuine and therefore more moving than the often frail and 'artistic' despair of the early poems of *Stone*.

In time, the book embraces the end of the First World War, the Revolution, and the Civil War – events that put an end to the old world forever. The world of Petersburg, in particular, and all that the city and its culture had meant for Mandelstam vanished. Gumilyov was shot, the Acmeists scattered. 'Petropolis,' as he said in one of the most famous poems of *Tristia*, was dying. Mandelstam called the city by its Greek name, as Derzhavin and others had done: it was a way of seizing upon what must have struck him as all that remained of the devastated, hungry capital – the idea of it.

THREE POEMS OF *TRISTIA*

I wish now to consider three early poems of *Tristia* – numbers 85, 118, and 86. The numbers alone make it clear that the order in which I mean to take them up is an unusual one. It violates chronology: 85 and 86 are dated 1916, but 118 is dated 25 November 1920.

This, however, is the order in which Mandelstam himself last published them (1928). The editors of the New York edition assume, not entirely without reason, that Mandelstam, in spite of his preference for a chronological arrangement, put 118 among the poems of an earlier date for purposes of 'camouflage.' I think that in addition to this there might be other and more cogent explanations. But that is an argument best pursued after having read the poems.

No. 89   On the sledge

На розвальнях, уложенных соломой,
Едва прикрытые рогожей роковой,
От Воробьевых гор до церковки знакомой
Мы ехали огромною Москвой.

А в Угличе играют дети в бабки,
И пахнет хлеб, оставленный в печи.
По улицам меня везут без шапки,
И теплятся в часовне три свечи.

Не три свечи горели, а три встречи—
Одну из них сам Бог благословил,
Четвертой не бывать, а Рим далече,—
И никогда он Рима не любил.

Ныряли сани в черные ухабы,
И возвращался с гульбища народ.
Худые мужики и злые бабы
Переминались у ворот.

Сырая даль от птичьих стай чернела,
И связанные руки затекли;
Царевича везут, немеет страшно тело—
И рыжую солому подожгли.   (1916.)

On a sledge overlaid with straw,
Ourselves but partly covered by the fateful bast,
We rode through immense Moscow
From the Sparrow Hills as far as the familiar little church.

221

But in Uglich children play at knucklebones
And there's a smell of bread left in the oven.
I am conveyed about the streets bareheaded
And in the chapel three candles glimmer.

Not three candles burning, but three meetings –
And one of them had God's own blessing on it;
There is to be no fourth, and Rome is far away –
And Rome He never loved.

The sledge dove into the black ruts
And people were returning from the open place for strolling.
Thin mouzhiks and cross old women
Shifted at the gate from foot to foot.

Raw distance seemed to blacken with the flight of birds
And bound hands went numb.
They're bringing the Tsarevich, the body numbs with terror,
And now the amber straw's been set on fire.

If the poem on *Phèdre* that opens *Tristia* is a considerable advance over the poem on *Phèdre* that closes *Stone*, I think it true that this is an even 'newer' work, less like any earlier poem.

For anyone seeking a prose sense, a scenario, it is in my estimation almost incoherent. As it chances, however, the poem is unusually seductive in this regard, so that even those who would ordinarily not think of demanding such 'sense' from a poem nevertheless seek it here. The reason for this becomes clear, I think, if one isolates certain words and phrases: Sparrow Hills...Moscow...Uglich...Not three candles burning, but three meetings...there is to be no fourth...Tsarevich.

One need not be particularly acute in Russian history to sense the abundance of historical reference in these words. In fact, the Western reader's acquaintance with the opera *Boris Godunov* will practically suffice. The poem is redolent of old Muscovy – of its topography, history, and above all of its ideology. This, together with the poem preceding, represents the entry into Mandelstam's work of Moscow, a city that now joins the Petersburg and Rome that had dominated his first book. 'Rome is far away' now in every sense, and the Sparrow Hills (today the Lenin Hills and the site of Moscow University) have replaced the seven. *Rus'ju paxnet* (it smells of ancient Russia), to quote the words of Pushkin at the beginning of *Ruslan and Ljudmila*: the sledge, the straw, the bast matting, the little church (familiar, to say the least), immense Moscow, the game of 'babki,' and so on.

The particular episode in Russian, or Muscovite, history to which the poem chiefly refers is that called the 'Time of Troubles,' especially the events concerning Tsar Boris Godunov. It will be recalled that Boris was appointed by the dying Ivan IV as guardian to the heir, Ivan's son

Fyodor, upon whose death Boris was elected Tsar. He is suspected of having contrived the murder of another of Ivan's sons, the Tsarevich Dimitry, who died mysteriously in the town of Uglich.

In Russian, 'Uglich' is as familiar a name, and almost as fraught with historical meaning, as 'Runnymede,' say, or the 'Alamo.' Perhaps it would be more revealing to say that it has the associative weight of the phrase 'a butt of malmsey,' the instrument by which Richard III also rid himself of a political rival. The phrase reminds one too that Russians generally remember the events of Godunov's reign from Pushkin's 'Shakespearean' play.

The two capitals of Moscow and Petersburg represent a familiar polarity in Russian culture, the former standing for everything that is old, native, quintessentially Russian, the latter, Peter's city, 'the most intentional city in the world,' in Dostoevsky's memorable phrase, for what is new and Western. Moscow stands for Russian piety, Petersburg for eighteenth-century scepticism and reason. All the homely touches of the poem, therefore, belong to the realm of Moscow: it is the home not only of the church but of the kitchen. Its flat immensities and its raw distances (those of Petersburg being very 'cooked' indeed) form the natural setting for a kind of herd life: flocks of birds and that other essential character from the drama of Boris, the *narod*, or people. Another touch of antiquity can be felt in the phrase, 'Not three candles burning, but three meetings.' In the earliest period of Russian letters, this negative parallelism, as Roman Jakobson has called it, was a much cultivated and essentially Russian device of rhetoric. It consists of a kind of unmasking of a metaphor: There was X. It was not X – it was Y.

The three meetings were therefore three candles burning in the Russian chapel. What were the three meetings themselves? The answer is unmistakable from the phrase that follows soon after: there is to be no fourth [meeting]. This is a part of the medieval Muscovite ideology known as 'The Third Rome' from its central element. The formulaic expression is that of a monk from Pskov named Filofey (Philotheus) who wrote to Vasily III of Moscow: Два Рима падоша, а третий стоит, а четвертому не бысти. 'Two Romes have fallen, but the third stands, and there is to be no fourth.'

It was a device for national self-congratulation and self-justification by which the hierarchs and rulers of Moscow legitimized their aspirations. Essentially, it held that Moscow was the third and last center of Christian holiness and divinely ordained political power. It was the third meeting. The first had been Rome, but that had fallen and its religion become corrupt and secular. The second was Byzantium, but its piety had been compromised by its overtures at a reconciliation with the Western Church, and besides, the Turks had captured Constantinople in 1453 and made the holiest shrine of the Eastern Church, the Hagia Sophia, into a mosque.

Thus had legitimacy descended to Moscow by its gradual forfeiture in the places where it had formerly resided.

Legitimacy – what ought by right and custom to be the case – is therefore an underlying theme of the poem, one to which many separate strands lead. Perhaps it is *the* underlying theme. The opposing theme is violence, by which legitimacy is forever threatened. The background of Boris, like that of Moscow, is drenched in blood. The touches of domesticity and innocence in the poem – the 'legitimacy' of the straw, the little church, the children at their play, the bread – are threatened by the mere proximity of the black ruts, the cross old women, the bound hands, and the straw set afire at the end.

Consider how the themes of legitimacy and violence are compounded in one of the subtlest lines of the poem:

> Четвертой не бывать, а Рим далече

> There is to be no fourth, and Rome is far away

This is the line that most unequivocally reveals the presence of the Third Rome theme in the poem, but I think that the educated Russian ear will detect yet another subtext beneath it:

> Иных уж нет, а те далече

> Some are gone already, and those [who remain alive] are far away.

The line is from the last stanza of Pushkin's *Eugene Onegin*. It is conspicuously similar in grammatical form, with identical punctuation, and the same conjunction joining two phrases, the first of which is negative and the second affirmative. The last word, also identical, is the relatively rare form for 'far away.' It is a concealed lament for Pushkin's friends who were exiled and executed for taking part in the Decembrist Revolt of 1825, an attempt to introduce the legitimacy of a constitution into the Russian form of autocracy.

The atmosphere of threat and violence is there in the explicit forms that I have suggested and in this concealed but still effective form. It is there also, I think, in the very grammar of the Russian language. For instance, the Russian way of saying 'I am conveyed...' is to use an active verb form that means 'they take me,' the actual pronoun being tacitly understood. But its force is there as the agent of the action and it causes one to question, if only subliminally, who it might be. Who, for that matter, is the 'I' who is being taken about the streets bareheaded? In the next to last line the identical verbal form has 'Tsarevich' as its object, but there seems little support elsewhere in the poem for identifying the speaker with the Tsarevich himself. The same way of expressing the passive makes the final ominous line even more ominous: the Russian says 'they have set fire.' And the object is again ambiguous. Is the straw the same straw of the first line? The poem does not provide the information to answer the question with assurance.

One of the oppositions throughout the poem is that between hot and cold. There are several suggestions of cold: being only partly covered by the bast matting, being bareheaded, the raw (or moist) distance, the numbness of the bound hands and the body. And several of heat: the warm oven, the burning candles, the fire of the last line. But I think that it would be difficult to assign the expected moral values to this opposition. The warm bread is 'good' but the arson or pyre or execution of the last line is 'bad.' The bracing cold of a sledge ride is much prized, but the numbness of bound hands and a frozen body is not. The poem does not even suggest an attitude to be taken toward the more basic opposition of legitimacy and violence.

The poem seems to me, then, for all its evident reference to questions of great moral and historical import, to be morally and historically mute. I think that it must stand as a masterpiece of the sort of tonal reference that I have attempted to suggest here. It is a structure of words and phrases which are, to a Russian reader, immensely evocative. But a structure of words, thus conceived, is not 'about' a ride through Moscow, or through a part of Moscow's history; nor is it the interior monologue of any identifiable historical personage – neither the murdered heir to the throne, nor the usurper, the False Dmitry, nor – least of all – Mandelstam himself.

And yet, it is a poem *by* Mandelstam, and there is one fact from his personal history and the history of the poem that strikes me as revealing and useful, especially in the context of the other poems of this triptych. The fact is that the poem was written to the woman with whom Mandelstam was briefly in love in 1916, the great Russian poetess Marina Tsvetaeva, whose memoir of that time we have discussed.

If the present discourse were being delivered as a talk to a mingled audience of Anglo-Saxons and Russians, I should expect to hear from the Russian component, or from some of them, certain satisfied sounds of recognition. And not just at the agreeably gossipy information that two of Russia's greatest poets were once linked in this way. It is the peculiar significance of her given name – Marina. I think that if one were to ask reasonably alert American schoolboys with a flair for history to supply the last names of women named 'Martha' and 'Betsy,' they would say 'Washington' and 'Ross.' The Russian opposite numbers, given 'Marina,' would probably say 'Mniszek.'

Marina Mniszek was the Polish princess who was courted and won by the usurper and who seconded him in his effort to defeat Boris. The very name of the woman to whom the poem was written summons up the entire history and atmosphere and locale of the Time of Troubles. The historical reference grows from her name, and the historical reference *is* the poem, or most of it. What of the muted and diffuse terror, the violence, the ambiguities of heat and cold? I am sure that at some distant remove these elements of the poem also depend upon the circumstances surrounding the dedication – but it is a remove forever, now, beyond our grasp.

I have noted as one of the arguments for reading Mandelstam extensively as well as intensively the fact that the poetic material of one poem is capable of rebirth, even after many years, in another. This poem, written to Tsvetaeva during the time of Mandelstam's attraction to her, evidently provides a context within which one ought to read a very different kind of poem, written during the Voronezh exile, No. 298, entitled 'Skripachka' (Woman Violinist).

> За Паганини длиннопалым
> Бегут цыганскою гурьбой—
> Кто с чохом чех, кто с польским балом,
> А кто с венгерской чемчурой.
>
> Девчонка, выскочка, гордячка,
> Чей звук широк, как Енисей,
> Утешь меня игрой своей—
> На голове твоей, полячка,
> Марины Мнишек холм кудрей,
> Смычок твой мнителен, скрипачка.
>
> Утешь меня Шопеном чалым,
> Серьезным Брамсом—нет, постой,—
> Парижем, мощно одичалым,
> Мучным и потным карнавалом
> Иль брагой Вены молодой—
>
> Вертлявой, в дирижерских фрачках,
> В дунайских фейерверках, скачках—
> Иль вальс, из гроба в колыбель
> Переливающий, как хмель...
>
> Играй же, на разрыв аорты,
> С кошачьей головой во рту,—
> Три чорта было,—ты четвертый:
> Последний, чудный чорт в цвету!

Behind long-fingered Paganini
they run in a Gypsy hullabaloo:
some Czechs with tics, some Poles with polkas,
and now Hungarians galore.

Jane-come-lately, stuck-up girl,
with a tone as wide as the Yenisey,
comfort me with the way you play...
Marina Mniszek's curly hillock
is piled on your head, you Polack girl,
and your fiddlestick is sickly, too.

Comfort me with a roan Chopin,
with weighty Brahms – no, wait a minute –
with the city of Paris, powerfully wild,
with floury, sweaty Mardi Gras,
with the bathtub beer of young Vienna,

that fidget in her conductor's tux,
in Danube fireworks, steeplechases,
or play a waltz that flows like a drunk
out of the coffin into the cradle...

But play to bust the heart's aorta,
with a mouth that could swallow a cat's whole head.
There've been three devils, you're the fourth,
you're in bloom, the last devil, prodigious!

The boisterous phonetic joviality and jangling of such poems as this are what prevent one from seeing the years of exile, illness and terror as unrelievedly bleak. I do not know who the violinist was or what role she played in addition to inspiring this poem, but it is the traces of Tsvetaeva that concern us now. Nadezhda Yakovlevna told me that the strange image of the cat's head in the mouth came from Tsvetaeva, who once used such an expression in commenting on the size of her own mouth. Perhaps Marina was one of the three devils, Nadezhda Yakovlevna suggested to me, and I think the conjecture would be fairly authoritative even if we did not have things like what Akhmatova calls her 'Don Juan list' of Mandelstam's various loves.

But even so slight a touch of Tsvetaeva is enough to send one back to the year 1916 and to discover that she has brought into this poem of 1935 other material: Marina Mniszek is there again, this time explicitly, and Tsvetaeva's association with the city of Moscow has also prompted an echo of the Muscovite 'Third Rome' formula. Once the hunt is on, one is tempted to hear other, fainter echoes, such as the words *kholm* 'hill' and *grob* 'coffin' (lexical souvenirs of the summer of 1916 in Aleksandrovo), but there the trail gives out.

No. 118   We shall gather again in Petersburg

В Петербурге мы сойдемся снова,
Словно солнце мы похоронили в нем,
И блаженное, бессмысленное слово
В первый раз произнесем.
В черном бархате советской ночи,
В бархате всемирной пустоты,
Всё поют блаженных жен родные очи,
Всё цветут бессмертные цветы.

Дикой кошкой горбится столица,
На мосту патруль стоит,

Только злой мотор во мгле промчится
И кукушкой прокричит.
Мне не надо пропуска ночного,
Часовых я не боюсь:
За блаженное, бессмысленное слово
Я в ночи советской помолюсь.

Слышу легкий театральный шорох
И девическое «ах»—
И бессмертных роз огромный ворох
У Киприды на руках.
У костра мы греемся от скуки,
Может быть века пройдут,
И блаженных жен родные руки
Легкий пепел соберут.

Где-то грядки красные партера,
Пышно взбиты шифоньерки лож;
Заводная кукла офицера;
Не для черных душ и низменных святош...
Что ж, гаси, пожалуй, наши свечи
В черном бархате всемирной пустоты,
Всё поют блаженных жен крутые плечи,
А ночного солнца не заметишь ты.

We shall gather again in Petersburg
As if we had buried the sun there
And for the first time we shall utter
The blessed meaningless word.
In the black velvet of Soviet night,
In the velvet of the universal void,
The dear eyes of blessed women still sing,
Immortal flowers still bloom.

The capital arches its back like a wild cat
A patrol stands on the bridge,
Only an angry motor will hurtle past in the murk
And scream like the bird in the clock.
I don't need a pass for the night,
I'm not afraid of the sentries:
For the blessed meaningless word
I shall pray in the Soviet night.

I hear a slight theatrical rustle
And a girl who murmurs 'Oh' –
And the immense bunch of immortal roses
In the arms of Aphrodite.
We warm ourselves from boredom at a fire.
Ages, perhaps, will pass
And the dear hands of the blessed women
Will gather the light ash.

228

> Somewhere there are the red flowerbeds of the stalls
> And the chiffoniers of the loges are richly stuffed;
> An officer like a mechanical manikin;
> Not for base souls and low hypocrites...
> So what if our candles are put out
> In the black velvet of the universal void,
> The sloping shoulders of the blessed women still sing
> But you will not notice the night sun.

This poem is dated '25 November 1920.' It appeared in the 1922 edition of *Tristia* but was omitted from the 1923 edition, possibly because it was reprinted that same year in a collection published in Berlin under the title *Petersburg in the Poems of Russian Poets*. As I have noted, Mandelstam published it in his last collection of 1928, but he put it among the poems of 1916, between numbers 85 and 86 – that is to say, where we are treating it now. He also slightly rewrote it, and the alterations are of interest. In lines five and sixteen he changed the words for 'Soviet night' to 'January night.' And he discarded lines 25–8 in favor of the following:

> Где-то хоры сладкие Орфея
> И родные темные зрачки,
> И на грядки кресел с галереи
> Падают афиши-голубки.

> Somewhere there are the sweet choirs of Orpheus
> And the dear dark eyes,
> And playbill-pigeons from the upper circle
> Fall onto the flowerbeds of stalls.

The word 'Soviet' has been removed from the context of a night that is equated with the 'universal void' and is obviously the source of some anguish on the part of the speaker; and in the latter changes the possibly offensive references to officers like mechanical dolls, base souls, and low hypocrites yield to some more neutral images. There can be little doubt that in 1928 Mandelstam was acting at least partly out of an instinct for self-preservation: the emendations are on the side of safety. So is the elimination of the date of composition and the displacement of the poem itself from those written during the Civil War to those written before the Revolution. That some 'camouflage' is involved in this, as the editors of the New York collection suggest, is hardly to be denied. In a private letter to me, Nadezhda Yakovlevna has also confirmed that concealment was one of the motives for displacing the poem.

I should like to argue, however, that in considering changes of this kind – 'from' one thing 'to' another – it is never enough to stop with the 'from.' After all, given that one wishes to replace the adjective *sovétskoi* with another trisyllabic word stressed on the second syllable, there is an immense list from which one might choose: in actual fact, Mandelstam wrote *ianvárskoi*. Why? Given that the mechanical officer is to be replaced by another image, why necessarily hit upon the choirs of Orpheus? Given that the poem is to be moved from its proper chronological place, the 'wrong' places to which it might be moved are extremely numerous: the fact is that it was put between the two other poems that we are now considering.

Finally, does any of this amount to much of a 'camouflage' after all? Censors are, to be sure, notoriously moronic, but could any literate reader fail to sense the comment on the 'new reality' that this poem – and not only this poem! – contains? It was not in Mandelstam's character to make concessions to the regime when those concessions would put his art rather than himself at risk.

On the other hand, it was very much in his character to rewrite poems long after they had been written, and even published, if by doing so he was able to bring the poem closer to his original conception of it. And the example of the 'Vos'mistishiia' and others makes clear that he was entirely willing to shift poems about, chronologically, for the sake of a more fully realized poetic statement. I wish therefore to argue that the changes I have spoken of might have been made for other reasons than those mentioned, or in addition to them.

As it chances, this famous poem is as easy to grasp on a first reading as any that Mandelstam ever wrote. It is far more explicit, for example, than the two poems that it was put between, and that is another reason to suppose that, had safety been the object, Mandelstam might have been better advised to omit it altogether. The pervasive menace of the previous poem had been established by the images from the ancient past of Muscovy. In this poem there is a similar motif of threat and surrounding horror, but the images are those of the contemporary moment in Petersburg (briefly going by the name of Petrograd when the poem was written, and already Leningrad when Mandelstam revised it in 1928). The only consolation that offers itself against the ravages of the present and the sure victory of Time over material things is, as everywhere in Mandelstam, Art. The art is of course the art of poetry, which is here called 'the blessed meaningless word.' So much, I think, is clear from even the most cursory reading. And it has evidently been enough to guarantee to the poem the devotion that so many readers, above all those in the city evoked by it, have felt for it. To read the poem on this primary level nothing else is needed, one might almost say, than a knowledge of Russian.

I think, however, that some readers will appreciate a discussion of the poem in the light of another of Mandelstam's writings.

It is a fact never to be sufficiently lamented that only fragments survive of the essay 'Pushkin and Scriabin,' of which the history itself is obscure. We depend, as for so many other things, upon Nadezhda Yakovlevna for our knowledge of its background.

Three poems of 'Tristia'

It appears that the article began as a talk delivered in Petersburg before some society or other – possibly the Religious and Philosophical Society. Kablukov, at any rate, who was a founder of that organization, had the manuscript in his possession. He died in 1921 while the Mandelstams were in the Caucasus, and his archive, together, presumably, with the manuscript, went to the Leningrad Public Library. Nadezhda Yakovlevna says that Mandelstam was dismayed at the loss (for such, evidently, it was) since he regarded the article as 'the chief thing that he had written.' Later in the 1920s Nadezhda Yakovlevna came across scattered fragments of a draft of it in a trunk belonging to Mandelstam's father, but by then the poet's attitude toward the article had, she says, rather altered. His reassessment belongs to an episode in his life which she herself calls 'the revaluation of values.' Perhaps he had changed his mind. Nadezhda Yakovlevna writes that he even satirized the whole business in the episode of *The Egyptian Stamp* where Parnok, the hero, is said to have been thrown out of some literary society for having read such a paper.[1] But none of this information reduces the importance of the essay for the background of the poem.

In order to argue that point, it will be necessary to look more closely at parts of the essay itself.

The Figure of Pushkin

The moment one does this, it becomes clear that elements of the central imagery depend upon the always seminal figure of Alexandr Pushkin. Pushkin is the *sun* who was *buried* on a *January night* in *Petersburg*. The italicized words indicate how much of the poem can be associated with Pushkin even on the basis of the fragmentary remains of the essay. In what is left, there is in fact very little about Pushkin. It was evidently a sort of memorial talk occasioned by the death of Alexandr Scriabin (25 April 1915), who occupies nearly all the remaining fragments. The comments about Pushkin are grouped near the beginning of the essay, which starts as follows (with puns on the Russian words for 'sun,' *solntse*, and 'heart,' *serdtse*.)

> Pushkin and Scriabin are two transformations of one sun, two transformations of one heart. Twice the death of an artist has gathered together the Russian people and lighted a sun above them. They [Pushkin and Scriabin] furnished an example of *soborny*[2] Russian death, they died a full death, as some live full lives. In dying, their personality expanded to the dimensions of a symbol of the entire nation, and the sun-heart of the dying man remained forever at the zenith of suffering and glory.

> I wish to speak of Scriabin's death as the supreme act of his creative activity. I think that the death of an artist should not be excluded from the chain of his creative achievements, but should be looked upon as the last, closing link. The death of Scriabin, seen from this altogether Christian

point of view, is astonishing. It is remarkable not only for the fabulous posthumous growth of the artist in the eyes of the masses, but also serves, so to speak, as the source of his creative work, its teleological cause. Remove the shroud of death from this creative life and it will follow freely from its cause – [from] death, around which it will take its place as around its sun, and absorb its light.

Pushkin was buried at night. He was buried secretly. The marble cathedral of St Isaac, that splendid sarcophagus, never did get the poet's radiant body. They put the sun into its coffin at night and the sledrunners scraped in the freezing January as they bore the poet's remains away for the funeral.

I mention this picture of Puskhin's funeral in order to summon up in your memory the image of the night sun, the image of the last Greek tragedy created by Euripides – the vision of the ill-fated Phaedra...

At a fateful moment of cleansing and storm we lifted up above us Scriabin, whose sun-heart burns over us, but – alas! – it is not the sun of redemption but the sun of guilt. Phaedra–Russia, making Scriabin her symbol at a time of world war....[the ending of this sentence is missing]

Time can go backwards: the entire course of recent history, which has, with terrible speed, turned away from Christianity to Buddhism and theosophy, testifies to this...

Unity does not exist! 'There are many worlds, all is arranged in spheres, one god reigns over another.' What is this: delirium or the end of Christianity?

Personality does not exist! Your 'I' is a transient condition, you have many souls and many lives. What is this: delirium or the end of Christianity?

Time does not exist! The Christian reckoning of time is in danger, the fragile calculation of the years of our era has been lost[3] and time is hurtling backwards with a rushing noise like a blocked torrent – and a new Orpheus flings his lyre into the boiling foam: art no longer exists...

One need read the essay no further than this, I think, to account for much of the central imagery of the poem, and especially for the major changes of the last redaction: the word for 'January' and the mention of Orpheus. Readers who have followed the discussion of Mandelstam's poems on Racine's *Phèdre* will note not only that the image of the black sun has changed its significance (now meaning Pushkin) but also that Phaedra herself has been identified, apparently, with Russia. But the essay is too fragmentary in that section to leave more than a hint of these matters.

The concealed references to Pushkin do not all derive from the essay. The punning equivalency established via the essay between *solntse* (sun) and *serdtse* (heart) means that the second line of Mandelstam's poem

> Slovno solntse my pokhoronili v nem
>
> As if we had buried the sun there

also derives from a line by Pushkin, *Eugene Onegin*, I: 50

> Gde serdtse ia pokhoronil
>
> where I buried my heart.

Three poems of 'Tristia'

As usually happens when Mandelstam refers in this way to an earlier line of poetry, the reference is not to that line alone but to its context. The context in this case is one of the most moving stanzas in Pushkin's novel-poem, which I quote here in Vladimir Nabokov's literal rendering:

> Will the hour of my freedom come?
> 'Tis time, 'tis time! To it I call;
> I roam above the sea,* I wait for the right weather,
> I beckon to the sails of ships.
> Under the cope of storms, with waves disputing,
> on the free crossway of the sea
> when shall I start on my free course?
> 'Tis time to leave the dull shore of an element
> inimical to me,
> and sigh, 'mid the meridian swell, beneath the
> sky of my Africa,
> for somber Russia, where
> I suffered, where I loved,
> where I buried my heart.

In his commentary Nabokov notes that 'here, as in other poems, Pushkin makes an allusion to his political plight in meteorological terms.' If Mandelstam's substitution of 'sun' for 'heart' makes the reference to Pushkin oblique, it can hardly be unimportant that it restores the meteorological imagery.

The line that ends the third stanza of Mandelstam's poem also derives from a poem written by Pushkin (1817) and entitled 'To Krivtsov' (Кривцову).

> Соберут их легкий пепел.

> [They] will gather their light ashes

That is the next to last line. I shall return to this same poem of Pushkin's at the end of this chapter on three poems of *Tristia*.

A Definition of Christian Art

It may be that in its complete form, Mandelstam's essay really justified the title 'Pushkin and Scriabin.' As we have it, however, it is hardly about Pushkin at all, and, though Scriabin is mentioned far more often, he seems to be little more than a pretext for the real subject: a definition of Christian art. Here is what strikes me as the heart of the essay:

> Christian art is always an activity based upon the great idea of redemption. In its manifestations it is an endlessly varied 'imitation of Christ,' an eternal return to the one creative act that marked the beginning of our historical era. Christian art is free. It is 'art for art's sake' in the fullest

* [Pushkin's note:] Written in Odessa.

233

sense of the word. No necessity of any kind, not even the highest, beclouds its luminous inner freedom, for its prototype, that which it imitates, is the very redemption of the world by Christ. So the foundation stone of Christian aesthetics is not sacrifice, not redemption in art, but the free and joyous imitation of Christ. Art cannot be sacrifice, since that has already been made; it cannot be redemption, since the world, including the artist, has already been redeemed. What is left? Joyous fellowship with God, the game, so to speak, of the Father with his children, the blind-man's-buff, the hide-and-seek of the spirit! The divine illusion of redemption which is Christian art is explained precisely by this game played with us by the Deity, who allows us to wander about the pathways of the mystery so that we might happen upon redemption on our own, as it were, by experiencing catharsis, redemption in art. Christian artists are like freedmen of the idea of redemption, and not its slaves or preachers. All of our two-thousand-year-old culture, thanks to the wonderful charitableness of Christianity, is the release of the world into freedom for play, for spiritual gaiety, for the free 'imitation of Christ.'

As regards art, Christianity adopted a completely free position, which no human religion either before or after it was ever able to do.

While it nourished art, surrendered its flesh to art, offered art the supremely real fact of redemption as an unshakeable metaphysical foundation, Christianity demanded nothing in return. Christian art is therefore not threatened by the danger of inner impoverishment. It is inexhaustible, endless, since, as it triumphs over time, it condenses grace into magnificent clouds and empties them out in life-giving rain. One cannot sufficiently emphasize the fact that European culture is beholden for its everlasting, unfading freshness to the charitableness of Christianity towards art.

The rest of the essay constitutes a similar doctrine concerning one art, the art of music. If I have understood it correctly – and given its fragmentary nature and my own slight capacity for its subject, I cannot be altogether sure that I have – what Mandelstam says is this. The Hellenes feared music and thought that it must at least always be accompanied by words, i.e. by some rational, 'meaningful' element. Christianity alone, for the reasons advanced above, could tolerate pure music. When Mandelstam calls Scriabin in this essay a *bezumstvuiushchii èllin* – a 'mad' or 'frenzied Hellene' – I think that the epithet is meant to convey that he is a 'pure' musician: a Hellene in music, but without the rational element. This is not to say that Scriabin is in every way an exemplar for Mandelstam of the Christian musician. For Mandelstam, the voice is the equivalent of 'personality,' and 'personality' is an essential of his version of Christianity. When, therefore, Scriabin deserted the voice for the 'siren' of pianism – and Mandelstam instances the 'mute' chorus of the *Prometheus* as a kind of pianism – he moved away from the ideal of Christian music.

If this seems uncomfortably nebulous, I beg the reader to remember that it is a résumé of the fragments of a draft of an essay concerning which the most reliable witness we have, the poet's widow, has testified that Mandelstam (1) thought it his 'credo' and (2) later had certain profound misgivings about it.

Approaching it, nevertheless, with all available caution, I cannot believe that Mandelstam would ever have changed anything more than a detail here and there in the essential argument, which I see in the declaration of the freedom and joyousness of genuine art. These qualities impart a third: invulnerability. And this brings us back to the poem from which we started, an infinitely more finished product of Mandelstam's pen, but one which we can now read with greater understanding after having read the remnants of his essay.

For the essential argument of the essay is the argument of the poem. The 'blessed' and 'meaningless' word for which the speaker of the poem 'prays' in the January night – a night now multitudinously alive with the spirit of Pushkin – is a poetry that knows no obligations to anything but itself. It is free. It, at least, is free, whatever the circumstance that binds the writer himself. Mandelstam prays for a poetry that will be the equivalent of Scriabin's music in its purity, freedom, and joyousness. And the purity of it will reside in its dissociation from 'meaning' in the ordinary sense.

It is clear that Mandelstam yearned, as did his contemporaries the Futurists, for a doctrine of the word that would establish its absolute value, a value to which its everyday task of 'standing for' something else made only a partial contribution. He argued for such a view in several places, most notably in the essays collected in 1928 under the title *About Poetry*.

Here is a central passage from 'The Word and Culture,' an essay first published in 1921:

> The main thing is: why identify the word with a thing, with the grass, with the object that it signifies? Is the thing master of the word? The word is Psyche. The living word does not signify a thing: it freely selects as its dwelling-place, so to speak, this or that objective significance, its concreteness, its dear body. And the word wanders about in the vicinity of its thing like a soul around its discarded but not forgotten body. [New York edition, II, 268.]

In the essay 'On the Nature of the Word,' first published in 1922, the same doctrine of the word occurs in the context of a polemic against the Symbolists. What is normally called Russian Symbolism is dubbed 'pseudo-Symbolism' by Mandelstam, for it was a Symbolism of things, the names of the things, the words themselves, being merely neutral pointers of some kind.

> They [i.e. the Symbolists] sealed all words, all images, having determined that they should be used exclusively for liturgical purposes. It turned out to be extremely awkward. One could neither go forward nor stand up nor

sit down. One could not have dinner on the table, since it was not simply a table. One could not light the fire, for that might mean something that one would later come to regret.

Man was no longer master of his own house. He had to live – one can't be sure in what – in a church or in a sacred grove of the Druids. Man's proprietary eye had nothing to rest upon, nowhere to be at ease. All the utensils had risen in rebellion. The broom asked for a day off, the pot no longer wanted to boil but demanded for itself an absolute significance (as if boiling were not an absolute significance). The master was driven from his own house and no longer dared to enter it. What is one to do with this attachment of the word to its meaning: surely this is not serfdom, is it? For the word, after all, is not a thing. Its signification is not in the slightest degree a translation of the word itself. As a matter of fact, it never happened that someone baptized the thing and gave it some name that had been dreamed up. The most convenient thing to do – and in the scientific sense, the most correct – would be to regard the word as an image, that is to say, as a verbal concept. By this means we rid ourselves of the question of form and content – the phonetics being the form and everything else the content. We eliminate also the question of what has primary significance, the word or its phonic nature. The verbal concept is a complicated complex of phenomena, a connection, a 'system.' The signification of the word can be regarded as a candle burning inside a paper lantern, and conversely, the sound concept, the so-called phoneme, can be placed within the signification, like that same candle in that same lantern. [II, 297–8.]

Structural linguists of the present day would hardly recognize Mandelstam's use of the term 'phoneme.' I do not know whether verbal philosophers and symbolic logicians would find his doctrine of word and meaning very edifying. But he was neither scientist nor philosopher: he was a poet. And the chief value of his essays, for the present undertaking, at least, is the light they cast upon the poems.

Mandelstam's doctrine of the word is not that of a philosopher but that of a lover. He adored words for their sounds, their shape, their meanings, their associations, their personality, their history and, no doubt, for the extraordinary power that they, like nothing else, gave him. He had the sort of mind that put things together into some sort of grand, overarching relationship, not the sort that takes things apart into their components. He was not an Acmeist because he subscribed to a doctrine of organicism: Acmeism was what it became in his conception because Mandelstam was born with a profound intuition of the interconnectedness of things. The word was his holy of holies. It could be analyzed into the sounds on human lips and the responses in human brains, but this had nothing to do with his conception of the wholeness of the word.

The wholeness was self-valuable and it was invulnerable. One cannot miss in all that he has to say about the word the same insistence upon freedom that forms the heart of the definition of Christian art. The word, the artist's instrument, is no more bound by necessity – 'not even the highest' – than the artist himself. By the time of these essays, written some six or seven years after the work on Pushkin and Scriabin and destined for a different audience, Mandelstam did not seek to establish his views upon any religious world view – science and philosophy seemed surer foundations – but it would be a great mistake to miss the identical theme. The word had been freed from any beggarly thralldom to its conventional association with a thing not, perhaps, by the fact of redemption, but it was not, for that, less free.

There is a good deal more to be said about this matter, but enough has probably been said to sustain the present argument, which is simply that the essays illuminate and reinforce the original conception of the poem, the changes that were made in it when Mandelstam last put his hand to it, and, as I propose to argue now, the positioning of the poem not elsewhere than just before 'Solominka.'

Solominka

The poem 'Solominka' ('The Straw') probably astonished more readers of Mandelstam than any other that he had written up to 1916. It is perhaps important to realize the extent to which, in *Tristia*, Mandelstam went beyond not only the accomplishments of *Stone* but also the capacities of his contemporaries, especially those of his former friends and associates who had joined the emigration. It is no doubt to be expected that Sergey Makovsky, a man very friendly to Mandelstam but belonging to an earlier generation, should have been unable to follow the former contributor to *Apollon* in his more advanced explorations. He saw Mandelstam's verbal audacity as a means of deluding the authorities. But it is surprising to note that Georgy Ivanov preferred *Stone* and had misgivings concerning the later work. (What *would* he have thought had he lived to see the ultimately 'later' Mandelstam?) In Russia as a junior member of the Acmeist group, Ivanov was a rather tedious and unoriginal poet; but in the emigration he became a poet of considerable power.

If we today are conscious of the effect produced by 'Solominka,' how much more conscious must Mandelstam have been in 1928, a dozen years after the poem was written? I think that one of the reasons why he put the poem 'We Shall Gather Again in Petersburg' where he did in the collection of 1928 was to 'introduce' the poem 'Solominka.' First, as it were, one prays for the 'blessed, meaningless word' and then...one demonstrates it. Twice in 'Solominka' we read: 'I have learned you, blessed words.'

СОЛОМИНКА

I.

Когда, соломинка, не спишь в огромной спальне
И ждешь, бессонная, чтоб, важен и высок
Спокойной тяжестью—что может быть печальней—
На веки чуткие спустился потолок,

Соломка звонкая, соломинка сухая,
Всю смерть ты выпила и сделалась нежней,
Сломалась милая соломка неживая,
Не Саломея, нет, соломинка скорей.

В часы бессонницы предметы тяжелее,
Как будто меньше их—такая тишина—
Мерцают в зеркале подушки, чуть белея,
И в круглом омуте кровать отражена.

Нет, не соломинка в торжественном атласе,
В огромной комнате над черною Невой,
Двенадцать месяцев поют о смертном часе,
Струится в воздухе лед бледно-голубой.

Декабрь торжественный струит свое дыханье,
Как будто в комнате тяжелая Нева.
Нет, не Соломинка,—Лигейя, умиранье--
Я научился вам, блаженные слова.

II.

Я научился вам, блаженные слова—
Ленор, Соломинка, Лигейя, Серафита.
В огромной комнате тяжелая Нева,
И голубая кровь струится из гранита.

Декабрь торжественный сияет над Невой.
Двенадцать месяцев поют о смертном часе.
Нет, не Соломинка в торжественном атласе
Вкушает медленный, томительный покой.

В моей крови живет декабрьская Лигейя,
Чья в саркофаге спит блаженная любовь,
А та соломинка, быть может Саломея,
Убита жалостью и не вернется вновь.

To speak of 'translating' *Solominka* is an impertinence. An extraordinarily high percentage of its meaning resides in the 'blessed, meaningless words' of the original Russian. The following is therefore proposed as nothing more than a sort of first-aid for those who want some help in working through what there is of prose sense in the poem. For many lines there might be equally correct alternative translations. 'Solominka' means 'a straw' in Russian. It is not always capitalized in the poem, but I shall

treat it throughout as the affectionate nickname for a woman, Solominka.
The word *solomka* is a diminutive of *soloma* 'straw.'

I.

When, Solominka, you can't sleep in the huge bedchamber
and wait sleeplessly for the ceiling, grand and lofty –
what could be sadder? – to descend with its tranquil weight
upon your sensitive eyelids,

ringing little straw, dry Solominka,
you have drunk up all of death and become tenderer;
the dear dead little straw has broken
not Salomeya, no, Solominka rather.

During hours of sleeplessness objects are heavier,
it's as though there were fewer of them, there's such quiet,
pillows are faintly seen in the mirror, scarcely showing white,
and the bed is reflected in the round tarn.

No, it is not Solominka in the solemn satin,
in the huge room above the black Neva,
the twelve months are singing about the hour of death,
pale blue ice streams in the air.

Solemn December streams its breathing,
it's as though the heavy Neva were in the room.
No, not Solominka – Ligeia, dying –
I have learned you, blessed words.

II.

I have learned you, blessed words –
Lenore, Solominka, Ligeia, Séraphita.
The heavy Neva is in the huge room
and light-blue blood streams out of the granite.

Solemn December gleams above the Neva.
The twelve months sing of the hour of death.
No, it is not Solominka in the solemn satin
partaking of the slow wearisome peace.

In my blood lives Decemberish Ligeia,
whose blessed blood sleeps in the sarcophagus,
but that one, Solominka, or perhaps Salomeya,
has been killed by pity and will not return again.

In these notes for English readers I have for the most part deliberately
neglected what is, of course, supremely important in the Russian – the
sound of the poem. In the case of 'Solominka,' however, one cannot
neglect it, for it is a poem that appeals first of all to the ear. The seductive
'acoustics' – a word that Mandelstam applied with some disdain to the
Symbolists in his essay 'On the Interlocutor' – have so entranced many

readers that they have never cared to penetrate beneath the level of the phonic surface. I think that it is a great mistake to suppose that the poem consists only of its sounds, but I readily admit that of Mandelstam's poems, this is among those that most cry out for some commentary on the sounds.

A phonemic transcription of the second stanza will reveal how enmeshed in phonic repetitions we immediately become. (Note that a phonemic transcription shows the meaningful sounds of the original. Most of the representations of Russian words in this book are in transliteration – i.e. they show the spelling of the original, not the sounds.)

> salómka zvónkaja salóm'inka suxája
> fs'u sm'ert' ti víp'ila i zd'élalas n'ižn'éj
> slamálas m'ílaja salómka n'iživaja
> n'i salam'éja n'ét salóminka skar'éj

There is a heavy alliteration on /s/ and its voiced counterpart /z/. The orchestration on /l/ and /m/ is very emphatic. The stressed vowels, marked with the acute accent ('), are dominated by /e/ and /o/. And all of these elements in the sound pattern derive from the two closely related words *Salomeya* and *Solominka*. The more one reads the poem, the more central seems the function of these two words – if only on the level of sound alone. They are heuristic, serving to discover other combinations. Thus, in the first hemistich of the second line

> i žd'oš *b'issónnaja*

one has already heard, however slightly, an echo of the first hemistich of the first line

> kagdá *salóm'inka.*

It is metrically identical, to begin with. The two italicized words occupy the second and third feet, just preceding the caesura of these iambic hexameter lines. The words are related by assonance: both consist of four syllables, the second being stressed, and of the sequence /s/ – /ó/ – /nasal consonant/ – /a/.

But I have begun with a word that is comparatively distantly related to the key word *solominka*. A more obvious fact is that *salomeya* and *solominka* have strewn their phonic progeny throughout the poem. Consider the syllables /óm/ and /ón/ in these expressions:

> v agrómnaj spál'n'i
> salómka zvónkaja
> b'issónn'ici
> v krúglam ómut'i
> v agrómnaj kómnat'i

And their influence is to be seen in the verb *slamálas* (in the third line of the stanza transcribed above).

If we turn now from this seemingly obsessive toying with certain phonic matter to the plainer sense of the poem, it is not surprising to find that it appears to involve two characters. The name of one is Salomeya – a perfectly standard if slightly uncommon Russian name, the equivalent of the French Salomé. The other is the eponymous Solominka. This word, meaning 'a straw,' is clearly a sort of transformation of Salomeya (in Russian pronunciation both begin with the syllable /sal/), and it looks rather as if it might be one of the familiar, diminutive forms of the name. In the poem as we have it, *solominka* is sometimes capitalized like a personal name and sometimes not. In the 1923 edition it is capitalized practically everywhere. But that it represents the name of a person cannot be doubted, for *solominka* is addressed as 'ty' (the familiar second person singular pronoun). What is more, *solominka* is clearly on a kind of equal footing with Salomeya since there is some question which is which, and that question of identity – Solominka or Salomeya? – forms a structural motif for this lyrical meditation. The physical ambience is a huge bedchamber in a house on the bank of the Neva in Petersburg. It is night in the month of December. The day is dead, the year dying, and a subject of the poem seems to be death and the transformation that death brings.

At the end of Part I a new name enters the poem in line 19 – Ligeia – and there is now another question of identity: not Solominka, or Salomeya, but Ligeia, a name with the same ending as Salomeya. In the last line of the first part, the speaker himself enters with a line that reads like the happy conclusion of an effort – the blessed words have been found. They are names, these blessed words, but whether of 'blessed women' we do not know. There is the new name that has just entered and others: Lenore, Solominka, Ligeia, Séraphita. The rest of this stanza and the greater part of the one following consist largely of repetitions, partial or exact, of earlier lines in the poem, and there is the same concern with the identity of Solominka–Salomeya. The final stanza contains in its first line references to blood, December, and Ligeia, but now in really new combinations.

В моей крови живет декабрьская Лигейя

And this is not merely the kind of incantatory reiteration to be found in the preceding lines of Part II.

The final stanza is thus truly final, and provides a conclusion. Though the identity of Solominka–Salomeya is left unclear to the end, what is clear is that it can hardly matter now, since she is dead and will return no more. Her place has been taken by the 'Decemberish Ligeia.'

This name, repeated three times, has attained a prominence in the poem that cannot be ignored. It signalled by its entrance the major structural break in the composition, and it has now provided a conclusion to the brief mental drama of the poem. It, and the other blessed words that appear to have given the speaker such relief, deserve further investigation.

Ligeia is one of the pale ladies of Edgar Allen Poe. She is the principal character in the weird tale of 1838 that bears her name. Married in a spiritual union to the narrator of the tale, she is an incarnation of the divinely unapproachable love-ideal: statuesque, ivory-skinned, possessed of miraculously luminous eyes, raven-haired, wise and incredibly learned. Her description recalls both Lilith and Sophia. The central element in her character is her 'gigantic volition,' and the theme of the tale, that death can be overcome by strength of will, is contained in the epigraph from Joseph Glanvill, which is also repeated three more times in the narrative:

> Man doth not yield him to the angels, nor unto
> death utterly, save only through the weakness
> of his feeble will.

Nevertheless, Ligeia falls ill and dies. In his grief the narrator begins to use opium, leaves the 'large, old, decaying city by the Rhine,' and goes to England, where he buys a ruined abbey and in order to forget his former wife takes a new one, the blond, blue-eyed Lady Rowena Trevanion of Tremaine. There follows an elaborate description, occupying two pages, of the chamber in the abbey to which he takes his bride. Situated in a high turret of the abbey, the room is huge in size and pentagonal in shape. 'The ceiling, of gloomy-looking oak, was excessively lofty, vaulted, and elaborately fretted with the wildest and most grotesque specimens of a semi-Gothic, semi-Druidical device.' In the angles of the chamber stand ancient sarcophagi with carved lids. The walls are hung with sumptuous draperies, the fabric and designs of which are found also on the bed and in the carpet. There is a kind of insanity that runs through all the furnishings of this fantastic apartment. Its most distinctive feature is the strange animation of it all: the wind sways the hangings and causes the arabesque designs upon them to assume terrifying shapes; the light thrown from the hanging lamp moves crazily over the 'Bedlam patterns of the carpets of tufted gold.' Rowena gradually becomes repellent to him as he obsessively compares her to Ligeia. Finally she, too, falls ill and, on drinking a goblet of wine into which some ghostly presence has let fall several drops of a ruby-colored fluid, dies. Her body, wrapped in a winding sheet, is laid on the bed, and the narrator, drugged by opium, keeps vigil beside it. Through a protracted and dreadful process of resurrection, the corpse is revived and the clothes fall away to reveal that the detested Rowena has become the ethereal Ligeia.

Mandelstam has of course made no mechanical transposition of the events of Poe's tale into his poem, but that he has altered and adapted the central elements seems beyond doubt.

There is, first of all, the prevailing mood, established in Poe's tale by the opium fog through which the narrator perceives the events which he relates and in the poem by the half-sleeping, half-waking state of insomnia. The setting in 'Ligeia,' so lavishly described and so centrally related to the other elements of the story that it becomes practically one of the characters, has clearly provided the tone and some of the actual details in Mandelstam's picture of the huge bedchamber where the ceiling threatens to sink from its great height down upon the sensitive eyelids. The general sense of movement in the room of Poe's story can be felt in the terms of Mandelstam's description: the ceiling moves, the reflection of the pillows in the mirror is conveyed by the verb *mercat'* 'to glimmer,' the blue ice streams in the air, as does the breathing of December. The latter features, and also the black Neva itself, which constantly threatens to fill the room, recall the ominous wind which forever stirs the heavy draperies in the room of Ligeia. The 'solemn satin' seems to have been prefigured in the shroud of the unfortunate Rowena, and the sarcophagus of line 30 – a word seldom if ever used elsewhere by Mandelstam except in the essay on Pushkin and Scriabin – almost certainly derives from Poe's tale.[4]

The central moment of Poe's tale involves the changed identity of the two female figures, the metamorphosis of one into the other, and the gradual revelation of this to the 'I' of the narrator, and this, as we have seen, is also the fundamental concern of 'Solominka.'

The suggestiveness of the line of 'blessed words' does not stop here. The name *Lenor* recalls an even better-known heroine of Poe – the dead lady of 'Lenore' and 'The Raven' – but it is the name *Sérafita* that sheds more light on the creative processes at work in this poem.

Séraphita is the title of one of the philosophical novels of Balzac, published in 1835. Practically devoid of any novelistic events whatsoever, *Séraphita* is devoted mainly to an exposition of the mystical philosophy of Swedenborg. The character from whose name the title is derived is related to this philosophy by birth – she is the daughter of a disciple of the master – and also by being a veritable incarnation of Swedenborgian doctrine. The great interest which Séraphita presents for an interpretation of 'Solominka' is to be seen in the fact of her disputed identity. To Minna, a young girl, she appears as a youth Séraphitus, but to Wilfred and to Pastor Becker she appears in female form as Séraphita. Ultimately, the character is both and neither, for its essence is ethereal and angelic, but as one of the blessed names, it makes its contribution to the unified effect of Mandelstam's poem.

The poem is about death, the death of a beautiful, loved woman. The names from Poe – Lenore and Ligeia – are of two of his famous dead ladies. The name Séraphita is that of a love-ideal, a creature who is finally transfigured and taken into heaven.

But the central character of Mandelstam's poem, Salomeya, is happily still living – and, as it chances, only a short ride on the London Underground from the spot where I am now writing. A famous Georgian beauty and once the toast of St Petersburg, Princess Salomeya Nikolaevna Andronikova was the object of more than one poet's attentions. She left Russia shortly after the Revolution and, now in her eighties, lives surrounded by a treasure of the paintings and books that belong to the last great flowering of her country's art. Her married name is Halpern. I am very grateful to her for the generous interest that she has taken in my studies of Mandelstam, and for the memories of him that she has so kindly shared with me. It appears that the picture of the enormous bedchamber looking out on the black Neva derives not only from literature but also from life.[5]

In concluding the discussion of these three poems, I should like to suggest – and admit that I can do no more than suggest, for there is no way to confirm it – that there might be another reason for Mandelstam's decision to place 118 between 85 and 86: I think that by doing so he made, as it were, a triptych of 'blessed women.'

That 85 was written out of his experience with Marina Tsvetaeva, and 86 out of that with Princess Andronikova, can scarcely be doubted. There is some evidence that 118 was, if not actually written to her, at least linked in his mind with an actress named Olga Nikolaevna Arbenina, with whom Mandelstam was in love in the last months of 1920. No. 118 is dated '25 November 1920.' Nos. 119 and 120, both dated 'December 1920' and No. 122, dated simply, '1920,' were certainly written to Arbenina, so the dates are very close indeed. Anna Akhmatova told me that 'everything connected with the theater in Petersburg had something to do with Arbenina' in Mandelstam's poetry, and this poem has much to do with the theater. Interestingly enough, it has to do specifically with the theme of Phaedra again. This time, however, the play would appear to be Euripides' *Hippolytus* (possibly in Annensky's translation) rather than Racine's *Phèdre*, for Aphrodite was not in the latter (cf. line 20). But there are the *candles* of the first poem on the *Phèdre*, and there is also the 'night sun' – i.e. the black sun of the second poem on the *Phèdre*. Finally, to complicate matters, or to tease the imagination, there is the fragmentary sentence about Phaedra in the essay. . .

Nor do I think that the full significance of the echo from Pushkin's poem can be clear until one looks at the context of the source:

> Смертный миг наш будет светел;
> И подруги шалунов
> Соберут их легкий пепел
> В урны праздные пиров.

Our dying moment will be bright;
And the pranksters' sweethearts
Will collect their light ashes
In urns left empty from the feast.

The first sentence bears a clear thematic relationship to the essay on Pushkin and Scriabin, where the death of the artist is seen as the supreme creative act of his life. And it strikes me that Mandelstam, in using the next-to-last line, could not have been entirely unmindful of the line that preceded it.[6]

THE POEMS TO OLGA ARBENINA

The linking of 118 to Olga Arbenina is a conjecture for which I have presented my arguments. But there is no need to conjecture about three of the poems of *Tristia*: 119, 120 and 122. Both Anna Akhmatova and Nadezhda Yakovlevna agree that Mandelstam wrote them to Arbenina. One of them at least (119) is a masterpiece; all are revealing in special and different ways of how the 'reality' that one can occasionally identify behind Mandelstam's poems became transformed in his making.

The reality, as usual, was dual: life and literature. In his extremely useful article on the classical themes in Mandelstam,[7] Victor Terras errs in his guess that 119 is written to the same woman – i.e. Marina Tsvetaeva – as Nos. 90 and 93, but he very helpfully identifies the literary source. It is the *Odyssey*, Book IV, lines 219–84. Menelaos tells in this passage of how Helen, led by some demonic power, came to the Trojan Horse at night, walked three times round it, and called the Greeks inside by their names, each in the voice of his own wife. Only Odysseus is sufficiently strong to resist, and to stop the mouths of the others. Reading the poem with this in mind, one can identify the remnants of Menelaos' narrative:

119

За то, что я руки твои не сумел удержать,
За то, что я предал соленые нежные губы,
Я должен рассвета в дремучем акрополе ждать.
Как я ненавижу пахучие древние срубы.

Ахейские мужи во тьме снаряжают коня,
Зубчатыми пилами в стены врезаются крепко,
Никак не уляжется крови сухая возня,
И нет для тебя ни названья, ни звука, ни слепка.

Как мог я подумать, что ты возвратишься, как смел!
Зачем преждевременно я от тебя оторвался!
Еще не рассеялся мрак и петух не пропел,
Еще в древесину горячий топор не врезался.

Прозрачной слезой на стенах проступила смола,
И чувствует город свои деревянные ребра,
Но хлынула к лестницам кровь и на приступ пошла,
И трижды приснился мужам соблазнительный образ.

Где милая Троя? где царский, где девичий дом?
Он будет разрушен, высокий Приамов скворешник.
И падают стрелы сухим деревянным дождем,
И стрелы другие растут на земле, как орешник.

Последней звезды безболезненно гаснет укол,
И серою ласточкой утро в окно постучится,
И медленный день, как в соломе проснувшийся вол
На стогнах шершавых от долгого сна шевелится.[8]

(Декабрь 1920.)

Because I was not able to restrain your hands,
because I betrayed your salty, tender lips,
I must wait for dawn in this dense acropolis.
How I despise these ancient reeking timbers.

Achaian men fit out the Horse in the dark,
cut deeply into the walls with toothed saws,
there's no way to calm the blood's dry commotion,
and there's no name for you, nor sound, nor plaster cast.

How could I have thought that you would come back, how dared I?
Why did I tear myself from you before it was time?
The darkness had not yet scattered, the cock had not crowed,
the hot axe had not yet cut into the wood.

The resin has oozed on the walls like limpid tears
and the city is feeling its wooden ribs,
but the blood has rushed to the ladders and begun the attack
and a seductive image come three times to the men in their dreams.

Where is dear Troy, where the royal house, where that of the
maidens?
It will be demolished, this lofty starling cage of Priam's.
And the arrows fall in a dry, wooden rain
as others grow from the earth like a grove of nut-trees.

The sting of the last star is guttering painlessly
and morning will knock on the window like a gray swallow,
and like an ox woken up in its straw deliberate day
stirs itself from long sleep on the harsh avenues.   (December 1920.)

I do not think it helpful to suggest a 'scenario' for such a dense and
intricate poem as this. There is no 'speaker,' no 'setting' – at least, no
single speaker or setting – for the statement of the poem is in the superimposition of several voices and scenes. I think the statement, however, is

single and coherent. In one degree or another, the poems to Arbenina are all unhappy – lamentations rather than erotic poems. This one is about the pain of separation. The first voice of the poem is that of one who waits alone for the dawn, the slow day that is stirring into its gray, animal life. This waiting, alone, separate from a loved woman and sensing guilt for the separation, is conveyed not by direct statement but by images from a literary parallel. The men in the Horse were waiting for the dawn, each alone in the silence and fear, and Helen's imitation of the loved women whom they have left behind in order to rescue that same Helen almost causes them to cry out, so great is their longing and anguish.

The episode from Homer occupies the interior stanzas and is framed by the first and last, where the first voice is heard. But the first voice also interrupts the scene from the *Odyssey* in order to speak directly to 'you,' the addressee of the poem. This maintains the essential imbalance and superimposition. The speaker speaks literally 'through,' as it were, the very images that he has summoned up as the 'objective correlative' of his state of mind. There is, after all, 'no sound, no plaster cast' for this emotion other than the oblique statement of Menelaos' story. The grammatical jumble of the fifth stanza, for instance, where the three utterances are all in different tenses and the voices seem at least three in number, does not bespeak a loss of control but rather its opposite, for the juxtaposition is essential to this montage of past and present, of Greek epic and gusty emotions on wet nights in Petrograd.

The other two poems to Arbenina are considerably more revealing of the circumstances surrounding their composition. No. 120 comes closest, in feeling, to a sort of emotional equilibrium: it is good humored and slightly teasing in a resigned sort of way. Of the three poems, No. 122 is the most conventional 'love poem' – a poem of unrequited love, about a love that is, on her part, at least, evidently a thing of the past.

120

Мне жалко, что теперь зима
И комаров не слышно в доме.
Но ты напомнила сама
О легкомысленной соломе.

Стрекозы вьются в синеве,
И ласточкой кружится мода;
Корзиночка на голове
Или напыщенная ода?

Советовать я не берусь,
И бесполезны отговорки,
Но взбитых сливок вечен вкус
И запах апельсинной корки.

Ты всё толкуешь наобум,
От этого ничуть не хуже,
Что делать, самый нежный ум
Весь помещается снаружи.

И ты пытаешься желток
Взбивать рассерженною ложкой.
Он побелел, он изнемог.
И все-таки еще немножко.

И, право, не твоя вина,
Зачем оценки и изнанки?
Ты так нарочно создана
Для комедийной перебранки.

В тебе всё дразнит, всё поет,
Как итальянская рулада.
И маленький вишневый рот
Сухого просит винограда.

Так не старайся быть умней,
В тебе всё прихоть, всё минута,
И тень от шапочки твоей—
Венецианская баута.   (Декабрь 1920.)

I'm sorry that it's winter now
and no mosquitoes can be heard in the house.
But you yourself reminded me
about the frivolous straw.

Dragonflies circle in the blue sky
and fashion twirls like a swallow:
will it be a basket on the head
or a bombastic ode?

I won't go giving advice
and it's no good making excuses,
but the taste of whipped cream lasts forever
and so does the smell of an orange skin.

You still make random explanations
but there's no harm in that.
What can you do? The tenderest mind
is all on the outside.

And you are trying to whip
the yolk of an egg with an angry spoon.
It's turned white, it's collapsed...
still, beat it a little more.

To tell the truth, it's not your fault.
Why weigh things and turn things inside out?
You were created as though on purpose
to squabble in comedies on the stage.

Three poems of 'Tristia'

You are all teasing and singing
like some Italian roulade.
And your small cherry mouth
asks for dry grapes.

So give up trying to be cleverer,
You're all caprice, all instantaneous.
Even the shadow of your hat
is like the chattering in Venice.

122

Я наравне с другими
Хочу тебе служить,
От ревности сухими
Губами ворожить.
Не утоляет слово
Мне пересохших уст,
И без тебя мне снова
Дремучий воздух пуст.

Я больше не ревную,
Но я тебя хочу,
И сам себя несу я
Как жертву палачу.
Тебя не назову я
Ни радость, ни любовь;
На дикую, чужую
Мне подменили кровь.

Еще одно мгновенье,
И я скажу тебе:
Не радость, а мученье
Я нахожу в тебе.
И, словно преступленье,
Меня к тебе влечет
Искусанный, в смятеньи,
Вишневый нежный рот.

Вернись ко мне скорее:
Мне страшно без тебя,
Я никогда сильнее
Не чувствовал тебя,
И всё, чего хочу я,
Я вижу наяву.
Я больше не ревную,
Но я тебя зову.   (1920.)

I want to serve you
equally with the others,
to mumble fortunes
with lips dry from jealousy.

249

The Word does not slake
my parched mouth,
and without you the dense air
is empty again for me.

I'm not jealous any longer
but I want you
and carry my own self
like a victim to the hangman.
I do not call you
either joy or love;
my blood has been exchanged
for another, savage blood.

One moment longer
and I shall say to you:
not joy but torment
I find in you.
And, as to a crime,
I'm drawn to you
by your bitten, tender,
confused cherry mouth.

Return to me quickly,
without you I'm afraid.
Never did I sense you
more strongly than now,
and all that I desire
I see in waking dreams.
I am no longer jealous,
but I am calling you.

Like the first poem to Arbenina, these are also linked to an earlier work
of poetic art, though this one is far less recognizable (certainly to non-
Russian readers) than a scene from the *Odyssey*. It is Nekrasov's poem
'P'ianitsa' (The Drunkard, 1845) – 44 lines of unstanzaed iambic trimeter.
This pathetic little sketch pictures the alcoholic trapped inside his
addiction, wishing but unable to reform, lashing himself with guilt over
the plight of his sick mother and his sisters and cringing with shame
over the poor figure that he cuts in public. The most relevant passage
is the following:

> Все, что во сне мерещится,
> Как будто бы назло,
> В глаза вот так и мечется
> Роскошно и светло!
> Все—повод к искушению,
> Все дразнит и язвит
> И руку к преступлению
> Нетвердую манит...

Three poems of 'Tristia'

> Everything seen in dreams
> [now] as though from spite,
> rushes to meet my eyes,
> luxurious and bright.
> Everything leads to temptation,
> everything teases and taunts,
> and entices to crime
> my unsteady hand...

Though No. 120 does contain an exact phrase from this (*vse draznit*), Nekrasov's poem has obviously contributed much more, including the meter, to 122. The third stanza contains not only the temptation to crime but also, in the adjective *iskusannyi* 'bitten,' a word evidently suggested by its near relative in Nekrasov's poem, *iskushenie* 'temptation.' And, in the last stanza, the idea of seeing what is desired not in dreams but waking obviously depends on the first four lines above. Other characteristics of the speaker of No. 122 link him to Nekrasov's drunkard: his lips are dry, the word does not slake his parched mouth; he carries himself like a victim to the hangman; and in the object of his passion he finds not joy but torment.

Whether 121 was written 'to' Arbenina or not, it clearly derives from the same general lexical and figurative drift as the others. The long syntactic unit that runs through the eight lines is never grammatically completed, and the poem strikes me as a work thrown off, as it were, in the process of composing the others – especially No. 119, written in the same meter (amphibrachic trimeter).

121

> Когда городская выходит на стогны луна,
> И медленно ей озаряется город дремучий,
> И ночь нарастает, унынья и меди полна,
> И грубому времени воск уступает певучий;
>
> И плачет кукушка на каменной башне своей,
> И бледная жница, сходящая в мир бездыханный,
> Тихонько шевелит огромные спицы теней,
> И желтой соломой бросает на пол деревянный...　　　(1920.)

When the municipal moon comes out onto the wide avenues
and slowly the dense city is illuminated by it
and night swells, full of bronze and melancholy,
and melodious wax yields to rude time

and the cuckoo weeps upon her stone tower
and the pale woman reaper, descending into the lifeless world,
slowly moves the huge spokes of the shadows
and bestrews the wooden floor with yellow straw...

This shares the words *soloma* 'straw' and *stogny* 'wide avenues' with No. 119 (as well as other, less conspicuous words), and in the collections of 1923 and 1928 Mandelstam placed the two poems side by side. Note also the verbal links between 119 and 120: *soloma* and *lastochka* 'swallow.' Both words summon up other recent poems: *soloma* inevitably recalls the poem to Princess Andronikova while *lastochka*, one of Mandelstam's most persistent classical images, brings to mind 112, 113 and 114, with their Greek version of the human soul (swallow) in its passage to the nether world.

13

Transparent sadness: the classical in 'Tristia'

The powder snow upon the wooden paving blocks
of Mandelstam's neoclassicism...

VLADIMIR NABOKOV, *The Gift*

It is about as common to find the word 'classical' in discussions of Mandelstam's poetry as it is to find the word 'birdlike' in descriptions of his person. To be sure, there are senses of 'classical' in which its application to his work is thoroughly justified, but there are so many unsuitable senses of this ill-defined term that one must handle it with the chariness now accorded that most deceptive of all critical labels, 'romantic.' In what follows I shall attempt not to define 'classicism' itself but to specify the ways in which, especially in *Tristia*, which I have called 'classical' and 'Greek,' Mandelstam employs his multitudinous reference to the ancient cultures of the Mediterranean world. A definition of his classicism, at least, ought to emerge.

In an exceedingly helpful and learned article, Professor Victor Terras has cleared much of the ground that must be cleared in a preliminary way.[1] In succinct readings of many poems, he demonstrates the extent to which Mandelstam drew on Greek and Roman myth in general and in particular on specific works of ancient authors. Like all ground clearing, the preliminary work begins in a negative way: to show the inapplicable senses of 'classical.' Noting the commonplace of calling Mandelstam's poetry by this term, Professor Terras writes:

> I find little substance in this notion – if it is to mean that Mandelstam's poetic style resembles that of Greek and Latin poetry in general, or of any individual poets of classical antiquity in particular. Only of some late and very sophisticated ancient poets (such as Ovid) can it be said that their verses are a 'quintessence of literature,' which is true of the Parnassians, and of Mandelstam. Yet Mandelstam goes even further than the Parnassians in eliminating from his poetry all that is 'non-poetry' (to use Croce's term). There is little rhetoric to be found in Mandelstam, but plenty of it in Horace, Ovid, and even Catullus. True, the early Mandelstam is the typical *doctus poeta*, who likes to shine with his erudition, but this is a trait he shares with many modern but not with all ancient poets. Mandelstam's tendency to reduce poetry to 'pure language' by eliminating the paralinguistic elements of abstract thought and logic, of subjective emotion, of personal involvement, and of actuality, this tendency reminds one of

Mallarmé or Valéry, and not of any ancient poet. Mandelstam's poems may be called polyphonic verbal compositions with a multidimensional (rhythmic, architectonic, euphonic, synaesthetic, emotional, and intellectual) expressive effect. Such an effect may be found, occasionally and I believe accidentally, in Pindar and the Aeolian poets, but is of course a consciously pursued goal in Mallarmé, Stefan George, or Mandelstam. It is quite untypical of the bulk of Greek and Latin poetry.[2]

And though there are poems, notably No. 62 and No. 65, in which Mandelstam seeks to convey a sense of Greek and Latin hexameters, his prosody in general hardly justifies the term 'classical.' 'His visions of classical antiquity,' concludes Terras, 'are not "Homeric", "Sapphic", or "Horatian", but Mandelstamian.'[3] To this statement one can only, as the Russians say, subscribe with both hands. It remains to define the exact ways in which classical reference contributes to what we think of as Mandelstamian, and specifically in *Stone* and *Tristia*. For the two books, the ways turn out to be very different.

When Aulus Gellius first applied the term 'classical' to literary matters in the second century it was laden with a combined socio-economic and finally a stylistic distinction traces of which can no doubt be detected in all the subsequent shades of meaning that the term has acquired. The opposition was that between *scriptor classicus* and *scriptor proletarius*. Both adjectives derived originally from the tax system, the first denoting the class of those whose property was taxed and the second that of writers too poor to be taxed. In time the distinction came to be that between a learned and cultivated style on the one hand and a popular, 'low' style on the other. If one may take this opposition as paradigmatic and apply it to the situation of a Russian poet eighteen centuries later, one can say that what is most characteristically Mandelstamian about his classical poems (let us drop the inverted commas) is the regularity with which he combines the two polarities. The epic, heroic world of Homer and the tragedies is practically never to be found without a leaven of the domestic, the low, the thoroughly Russian. Perhaps the best name for the lower end of the polarity is that nearly untranslatable Russian word *byt*, towards which Mayakovsky pointed just before he shot himself as a reason for his suicide, and which is normally rendered by 'everyday life.' His classicism is in a sense thoroughly unclassical, for the lofty, objective, and impersonal mode is always imbued with the naturalism and the homeliness of the New Testament. There is something Flemish about it. The mixture is prefigured in his very life, in the places where he lived and in the fate of the one classical author who presides over his most classical book. Much of Mandelstam's autobiography, *The Noise of Time*, grows out of the opposition felt between the life of a disadvantaged Jewish boy and that of the imperial Russian capital. Petersburg itself was celebrated in his vision of it not only as the classical city of its buildings and avenues but also as the 'Dutch' city of Peter, a city of handicrafts and commerce, belonging not to the imported architects alone but also to native carpenters. The Ovid whose presence is felt behind so much of Mandelstam's second collection of poems is not the author of the *Amores* and the *Metamorphoses*; he is the exile, a poet who, for Mandelstam as for Pushkin, was emblematic for that reason alone, for his symbolic linking of the classical world with the Slavic realm. The Crimea and the Caucasus, to which Mandelstam was so strongly attached, appealed to him under the double guise of classical and primitive Christian outpost in the Russian world.

No other definition of classicism can be made to fit Mandelstam's work. If, for example, one were to apply those canons of classicism that are nearest to him in time and native tradition – the classicism of the Russian eighteenth century, deriving from seventeenth-century France (Boileau) and ultimately from the prescriptions of Aristotle and Horace – one would succeed only in showing how essentially irrelevant they are. Take the rule of Cartesian clarity and logic. There is no need to repeat what Boris Bukhshtab has so convincingly shown, namely, that the trappings of logic, the transitional formulae, the formulae of deduction and proof, operate in his poetry rather as verbal gestures, as syntactic symbols that refer at large to the poetry of argument and reasoning but are completely at variance with the movement of thought in Mandelstam's own poems.[4] Other characteristics of Russian Classicism – the oratorical manner, the tendency to epigrammatic conclusions, the spirit of 'QED,' the cultivation of the ode – link Mandelstam, if they link him to any Russian poet of the eighteenth century, rather to Derzhavin than to anyone else. But Marina Tsvetaeva, who gave Mandelstam the soubriquet 'young Derzhavin,' was closer to the truth when she exclaimed, in a private letter, 'delo ne v klassitsime – v charakh!' (it isn't a question of classicism – but of sorcery).[5]

This preliminary definition of Mandelstam's classicism – the amalgam of Greco-Roman loftiness and distance with the familiar homeliness of Russian circumstance – will be seen to apply to practically every poem that refers to the ancient world of the Mediterranean. But it remains to be said that the classical in *Tristia* is very different from that in *Stone*. It evokes an entirely different world of feelings, and it draws upon a comparatively narrow segment of the world of Greek myth. To put it very plainly – and to ignore, for the moment, rare but important exceptions – one would retain practically all the classical reference in *Tristia* if one retained only that having to do with death and the underworld. The goddess of *Tristia* is Persephone, queen of the afterlife and wife to Hades, and Mandelstam's city, where she now presides and which, like Derzhavin, he calls Petropolis, might even more descriptively be called Necropolis. It is a place of burial. It is the place where Pushkin, who is referred to almost as frequently in *Tristia* as Persephone, though far less overtly, was secretly buried at night by a tyrannical government, an event to which Mandelstam repeatedly refers as the burial of the sun.[6] If a river is mentioned, it will be Lethe or the Styx; if a classical amulet, it will be lost or symbolically buried in the sand of a seashore; if spring, it will be that of Elysium, and bring forth asphodels, the flower of death.

That this is very far from the mood of the poems in *Stone* in which the classical world figures can be shown by a few examples. The poems are untouched by death. On the contrary, the first book celebrates the primal freshness of early myth (the birth of Aphrodite, goddess of love, beauty and fertility, who at the end of *Stone* and beginning of *Tristia* will invisibly preside over the tragedy of Phaedra and Hippolytus). There is a good deal of sunny, trivial fun: juxtaposing the strings of a lyre to those of a tennis racket and calling a silly American girl who is 'doing' Europe 'daughter of ocean' (she runs like a squirrel up the Acropolis).[7] The Ovid of *Tristia* is there in *Stone*, too, but the figure is that of a different writer, one who mingles Rome and the snow 'with love.'[8]

These statements must now be tested against the poems themselves. Here is the famous poem of 1914 (No. 62) in which Mandelstam conveys an impression of a long, lazy, satisfying day through images deriving from Homer. The meter is iambic hexameter with a caesura after the third foot.

62

Есть иволги в лесах, и гласных долгота
В тонических стихах единственная мера.
Но только раз в году бывает разлита
В природе длительность, как в метрике Гомера.

Как бы цезурою зияет этот день:
Уже с утра покой и трудные длинноты;
Волы на пастбище, и золотая лень
Из тростника извлечь богатство целой ноты.   (1914.)

There are orioles in the woods and in lines of tonic verse[9]
the single measurement is the length of vowels.
But only once a year does there occur in nature
the long-drawn lengthiness found in Homer's meter.

This day yawns as though it were caesural:
since daybreak it's been quiet, with troublesome longueurs;
the oxen are in the pasture, and golden lassitude
cannot draw from the reed the wealth of one whole note.

The other poem in *Stone* most directly inspired by Homer (No. 78) has the same languid, half-awake atmosphere. The speaker is afflicted with insomnia and evidently reads the catalogue of ships in *Iliad*, II: 494–759, as a kind of soporific, meanwhile musing upon the *casus belli* and finally, in the striking last line, subsiding under the dark sea of sleep.

78

Бессонница. Гомер. Тугие паруса.
Я список кораблей прочел до середины:
Сей длинный выводок, сей поезд журавлиный,
Что над Элладою когда-то поднялся.

Как журавлиный клин в чужие рубежи—
На головах царей божественная пена—
Куда плывете вы? Когда бы не Елена,
Что Троя вам одна, ахейские мужи?

И море, и Гомер—всё движется любовью.
Кого же слушать мне? И вот Гомер молчит,
И море черное, витийствуя, шумит
И с тяжким грохотом подходит к изголовью.   (1915.)

Insomnia. Homer. Taut sails.
I've read up to the middle of the catalogue of ships,
that long litter, that train of cranes,
that once set forth above Hellas.

Where are you sailing like a wedge of cranes
into alien zones, a godly foam
on your leaders' heads? Helen gone, Achaian men,
what would Troy alone be worth to you?

The sea and Homer both – all moves by force of love.
Whom should I listen to? Even Homer's silent now,
and now the dark sea roars rhetorically
its billowy thunder above my pillowed head.

As we have seen often enough before, Mandelstam frequently returns to the poetic material of an earlier poem and, as it were, reworks it in the spirit of a later manner, in response to the urgencies of some subsequent demand. The five years that separate 'The Admiralty' (No. 48, 1913) from 'Na strashnoi vysote' (At a terrible height; No. 101, 1918) also separate the classical impulse of *Stone* from that of *Tristia*. The two poems provide a bridge between the two books.

48. АДМИРАЛТЕЙСТВО

В столице северной томится пыльный тополь,
Запутался в листве прозрачный циферблат,
И в темной зелени фрегат или акрополь
Сияет издали, воде и небу брат.

Ладья воздушная и мачта-недотрога,
Служа линейкою преемникам Петра,
Он учит: красота не прихоть полубога,
А хищный глазомер простого столяра.

Нам четырех стихий приязненно господство;
Но создал пятую свободный человек.
Не отрицает ли пространства превосходство
Сей целомудренно построенный ковчег?

Сердито лепятся капризные медузы,
Как плуги брошены, ржавеют якоря—
И вот разорваны трех измерений узы
И открываются всемирные моря.   (1913.)

A dusty poplar languishes in the northern capital,
the translucent clockface has lost itself in the foliage,
and in the dark greenery a frigate or acropolis,
the brother of water and sky, gleams from far away.

An aerial ship and touch-me-not mast,
serving as a straightedge for the successors of Peter,
its lesson is that beauty is no demigod's caprice:
it is the simple carpenter's ferocious rule-of-eye.

The four elements in their sovereignty are well-disposed to us
but man, in his freedom, has created a fifth.
Does not the chaste construction of this ark
deny the dominance of space?

The whimsical medusas cling angrily,
anchors rust like discarded ploughs –
and, lo, the bonds of three dimensions are all sundered
and opened are the seas of all the world.

The poem is classical more by implication than by statement. The Admiralty – or strictly, the tower of the Admiralty building, which is the only visual subject of the poem – incarnates the original ideology of Petersburg and its dual, synthetic and paradoxical nature: the 'northern capital' that is touched by the 'medusas,' 'demigods,' and 'acropolis' of the Mediterranean world. Peter's will alone (he ordered that the tower and the arch beneath it convey the form of the Cyrillic, and Greek, initial of his name: П) ordained the irony that Russia's access to the sea routes of the world lie through the Baltic rather than the classical Pontine in the south, which was denied him. The poem is compact of the sciences and crafts (arithmetic, geometry, navigation, carpentry) upon which Peter's scheme depended: frigate, mast, ship, ruler, timepiece, plough, and anchor. But many of the words are also chosen with very concrete reference to actual details of the tower.[10] If it is figuratively a ship that conveys Peter's empire to hegemony not only over the traditional four elements and the three dimensions of space but even transcendently beyond them to a fifth element and a fourth dimension, the ship is also the actual three-masted ship atop the spire, the elements are the actual statues symbolizing them on the tower, the clockface is actually there (four times), and the 'acropolis' is an architecturally apt description of the colonnaded structure just beneath. The spire – or 'needle,' as Pushkin called it – does indeed serve as a point of reference (a rule) for the successors of Peter: it is the visual end-point for all three of the immense avenues that radiate from it – a fact that enables one, I think, to see in this exceedingly geometrical poem the other meaning of the word *lad'ia* – not only 'ship' but also 'rook' (the 'tower' of the chessboard).

By 1918 the soul of this poem had transmigrated, by Mandelstam's peculiar poetic metempsychosis, into a new body, that of No. 101. The contrast between its former and its new incarnation is in large part the contrast between *Stone* and *Tristia*. The second poem is darker in every way: its incantatory iterations yield little of the Acmeist visual, syntactic, or indeed intellectual clarity to be found in 'The Admiralty,' and far from being a celebration, it is a lament. The verbal correspondences hardly require comment.

101

На страшной высоте блуждающий огонь,
Но разве так звезда мерцает?
Прозрачная звезда, блуждающий огонь,
Твой брат, Петрополь, умирает.

На страшной высоте земные сны горят,
Зеленая звезда летает.
О, если ты звезда,—воды и неба брат,
Твой брат, Петрополь, умирает.

Чудовищный корабль на страшной высоте
Несется, крылья расправляет.
Зеленая звезда, в прекрасной нищете
Твой брат, Петрополь, умирает.

Прозрачная весна над черною Невой
Сломалась. Воск бессмертья тает.
О, если ты звезда—Петрополь, город твой,
Твой брат, Петрополь, умирает.

Preliminaries to a translation of No. 101

This poem has been translated more than once, but never, in my opinion, correctly. Before offering a literal version of it, I shall have to examine briefly its strange syntax and the contradictory texts that have come down to us. Because these difficulties are symptomatic of the difficulties that Mandelstam now increasingly builds into his poems, and also of the present state of our possibilities in studying his works, I retain this detailed analysis in the body of the text rather than relegating it to the notes. Non-specialists may wish to go at once to the translation, which follows shortly.

17-2

Here are the difficulties, and a proposal for resolving them.

It is clear from what can be understood that the poem is about a confusion of identity and that it represents this confusion in a deliberately ambiguous syntax. The punctuation and the use of apposition make the immediate constituents of the phrasal units unclear.

This inherent confusion is greatly increased by the fact that no two versions of the poem as published are exactly identical. And the divergences occur at precisely those points where they most confuse the statement of the poem. The editors of the New York edition unfortunately print a version that matches none of those preceding and fail, in their commentary, to acknowledge the existence of the relevant variants. Instead, they offer an exceptionally obtuse passage from Irina Odoevtseva, who chooses to put the poem into the context of the mad *gaiety* of Petersburg intellectuals in 1920–1.[11]

In the absence of an autograph, which might not be helpful even if we had it, one's interpretation of the syntax and thus of the meaning must depend upon how one sees the structural pattern, upon how this forces the interpretation of dubious points.

Here is my reading of the structure.

There are sixteen different nouns, but the essential shape of the poem is conveyed by only five of them: Height (*vysota*), Fire (*ogon'*), Star (*zvezda*), Brother (*brat*), and Petropolis (*Petropol'*). In the stanza these occupy the positions shown in the following diagram by their English initials:

1.	H	F
2.		S
3.	S	F/B/P
4.	B	P

The other nouns and noun phrases in the poem seem to be variants of these or in some way auxiliary. Three times, for instance, Height is the normal word for height or altitude (*vysota*), but in the last stanza the word for 'height' is replaced by a phrase expressive of 'height': *nad chernoiu Nevoi* 'above the dark Neva.' (The position within the line varies.) That would seem to be the most unarguable of the substitutions. About Fire the dubiety is very great, and it has the greatest number of variants: dreams (line 5), ship (9), and spring (13). Line 5 thus fulfils the pattern of line 1 by substituting for 'wandering fire' the phrase 'earthly *dreams* are *burning*.'

But it is about the identity of Star that the dubiety is greatest, and that image occurs in the two central lines, in the second of which (3, 7, 11, 15) the texts that we have blur the sense almost hopelessly. The position of Star is firmly fixed, however, in the first part of this troublesome third line. And in the first two stanzas a firm position seems to be fixed for Star in the second line also, thus making 'wings' and 'wax' substitutes for Star.

The movement of each stanza is thus from a first line that has a firm identity (established by the thrice repeated *na strashnoi vysote*) through the two central lines where, especially in the third, there is much fluidity, confusion, and change, to the last line, which is absolutely identical throughout. Note that line three is always direct address to the Star and note further the crucial regularity in the last three stanzas, namely, that the second component of line three always goes syntactically with the regular refrain of the last line. A failure to grasp this fact has caused most of the misunderstanding of editors and translators.

Finally, before proceeding to a translation, with interpolated commentary, here are the readings of lines 7 and 15 in Mandelstam's three collections of 1922, 1923, and 1928:

Line 7

1922   О, если ты звезда,—воды и неба брат,
1923   О, если ты, звезда, воды и неба брат,
1928   О, если ты, звезда, воде и небу брат,[12]

Line 15

1922   О, если ты звезда—Петрополь, город твой,
1923   О, если ты, звезда, Петрополь—город твой
1928   О, если ты, звезда, Петрополь—город твой,

On the basis of my reading, it is the version of *Tristia* (1922) that strikes me as best and most internally consistent. That is the one reproduced above, and here is the English sense of it:[13]

1 At a terrible height there is a wandering fire,
2 but does a star really twinkle like that? [Is the fire a star?]
3 [Direct address:] Transparent star, wandering fire, [yes, it is]
4 your brother, Petropolis, is dying.

5 At a terrible height earthly dreams are burning [it is the fire of dreams]
6 a green star is flying [not 'twinkling' as in later versions]
7 O, if you are a star, [then] the brother of water and sky,
8 your brother, Petropolis, is dying.
    [Here is the first confusion. The *Penguin Book of Russian Verse*, for instance, prints the version of *Tristia* but then ignores it in the translation: 'Oh, if you, O star, are the brother,' &c.][14]

9 A monstrous ship at a terrible height
10 is speeding [and] spreading its wings. [Star and Fire are united again, this time as a ship; *wings* justifies the *flying* of line 6]
11 Green star, in splendid poverty
12 [is] your brother, Petropolis, dying. [Petropolis is poor, not the star]

13 Transparent spring above the dark Neva [Star and Fire united again, as spring, which bears the epithet of Star]

14   has been broken. The wax of immortality melts. [Star = Fire = melting
     wax]

15   O, if you are a star, [then] Petropolis, your city,

16   your brother, Petropolis, is dying.

     [Examples of total confusion: 'Oh, if you, O star, are Petropolis...'
     (*Penguin Book of Russian Verse*); 'Oh star, if Petropolis is your city...'
     (*European Judaism*, Winter 1971–2)]

To return after this long excursus to the text which it has established,
we find the typical transformation that *Tristia* works upon the images of
Stone. The 'brother of water and sky,' Petropolis – it was the symbol
of Petropolis, the Admiralty tower, topped by its ship weathervane – is
now dying. It is the underworld of the second book, of which Persephone
is queen.

    Persephone makes her appearance early in the company of her city
and of certain other specially charged words to be seen in No. 48 and
101 (transparent, spring, northern, green, star, and medusa). The two
poems following, both dated 1916, clearly derive from a single verbal
and thematic impulse:

88

Мне холодно. Прозрачная весна
В зеленый пух Петрополь одевает,
Но, как медуза, невская волна
Мне отвращенье легкое внушает.
По набережной северной реки
Автомобилей мчатся светляки,
Летят стрекозы и жуки стальные,
Мерцают звезд булавки золотые,
Но никакие звезды не убьют
Морской волны тяжелый изумруд.   (1916.)

I'm cold. Transparent spring
clothes Petropolis in a green down,
but the Neva's wave, like a medusa,
fills me with a slight disgust.
Along the quay of the northern river
race fireflies of automobiles,
dragonflies and steel beetles fly,
the golden pins of stars glint
but no stars will kill
the sea waves' heavy emerald.

89

В Петрополе прозрачном мы умрем,
Где властвует над нами Прозерпина.
Мы в каждом вздохе смертный воздух пьем,
И каждый час нам смертная година.

Богиня моря, грозная Афина,
Сними могучий каменный шелом.
В Петрополе прозрачном мы умрем,
Здесь царствуешь не ты, а Прозерпина.   (1916.)

We shall die in transparent Petropolis
where Proserpine rules over us.
With every sigh we drink the lethal air
and every hour is the anniversary of our death.
Stern Athena, goddess of the sea,
take off your mighty helmet of stone.
We shall die in transparent Petropolis,
not you are empress here, but Proserpine.

Persephone is present in other poems. She is in No. 112 (discussed above in Chap. 6), one of the most explicit and detailed of the 'underworld' poems, where she is accompanied no less than three times by the word *prozrachnyi* 'transparent,' which joins with others to become one of the lexical signs of her presence. This word, plus *lastochka* 'swallow,' and the conspicuous amount of verbal overlap, suggest her presence in No. 113 as well, though she is not named there. Nor is she named in No. 114, but the poem begins

Чуть мерцает призрачная[15] сцена,
Хоры слабые теней

the *spectral* stage barely *glimmers*,
weak choruses of *shades*

and later contains other words which, like those italicized here, belong to her verbal regalia: *spring, green, Eurydice* (whom she allowed to depart from the underworld), and *swallow*. Persephone is named in No. 116, a strangely beautiful poem that combines the emotion of love with death in the horripilating images of kisses like dead bees and a necklace made of dead bees.

Возьми на радость из моих ладоней
Немного солнца и немного меда,
Как нам велели пчелы Персефоны.

Take for your pleasure out of my palms
a little sun and a little honey
as the bees of Persephone commanded us.

Before leaving the discussion of Persephone in these poems, it is worth asking why she should sometimes be called by her Latin rather than by her Greek name. The answer is suggestive also of the reason why she might be associated with the words for 'transparent' and 'spectral' and why, in addition to all the other reasons, the city should be called Petropolis in her presence. By this time, readers of this book will not

263

be surprised to learn that her genesis lies partly in the Russian consonants
and vowels of the words in question:

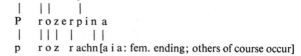

In this regard the poem resembles another of the classical poems of
Tristia, 'Kassandre' (To Cassandra, No. 95). As we know from her
memoir of Mandelstam, No. 95, like No. 97 and No. 98, was addressed
to Anna Akhmatova.[16] It is also one of the several poems in which the
upheaval of the Revolution is seen as the loss of all that part of the world
which Mandelstam identified, as Akhmatova and many others did, with
Alexandr Pushkin. No priority can now be determined, if it ever could,
but it is likely that one image was drawn into the poem on the basis of
its purely phonetic resemblance to the other: Kassandra – Aleksandra
(her other name in myth) – Aleksandra (the gen. sing. of Pushkin's first
name), as in line 19:

> зачем
> Сияло солнце Александра
> Сто лет тому назад, сияло всем?

> why
> did the sun of Alexander shine
> a hundred years ago, shine for everyone?

The one poem of *Tristia* that, though classical, is most untouched
by death is No. 92. Curiously enough, it resembles the poems of *Stone*
discussed above (No. 62 and No. 78) in two essential ways: the specific
classical reference is to Homer and the mood evoked is one of luxurious
idleness and tranquility. The long slow line is anapestic pentameter.

92

Золотистого меда струя из бутылки текла
Так тягуче и долго, что молвить хозяйка успела:
Здесь, в печальной Тавриде, куда нас судьба занесла,
Мы совсем не скучаем—и через плечо поглядела.

Всюду Бахуса службы, как будто на свете одни
Сторожа и собаки—идешь, никого не заметишь—
Как тяжелые бочки, спокойные катятся дни:
Далеко в шалаше голоса—не поймешь, не ответишь.

После чаю мы вышли в огромный коричневый сад,
Как ресницы на окнах опущены темные шторы,
Мимо белых колонн мы пошли посмотреть виноград,
Где воздушным стеклом обливаются сонные горы.

Я сказал: виноград как старинная битва живет,
Где курчавые всадники бьются в кудрявом порядке.
В каменистой Тавриде наука Эллады—и вот
Золотых десятин благородные, ржавые грядки.

Ну, а в комнате белой как прялка стоит тишина
Пахнет уксусом, краской и свежим вином из подвала.
Помнишь, в греческом доме: любимая всеми жена—
Не Елена—другая—как долго она вышивала?

Золотое руно, где же ты, золотое руно?
Всю дорогу шумели морские тяжелые волны,
И покинув корабль, натрудивший в морях полотно,
Одиссей возвратился, пространством и временем полный.

(1917.)

The stream of golden honey flowed from the bottle so long
and viscously that our hostess had time to say
'Here in sad Taurida where fate has carried us
we don't feel the least bit dull'...and she glanced over her shoulder.

The rites of Bacchus are everywhere, as though the world held
nothing more
than nightwatchmen and dogs, you won't see a soul as you walk
along –
the peaceful days roll by like heavy barrels:
far off, in the hut, there are voices, but you won't understand,
won't answer.

After tea we went out into the huge brown garden,
dark shutters like lashes were lowered on the windows,
past white columns we walked to look at the grapes,
where an air like glass pours over the sleepy hills.

I said: the grapes live a life like some long-ago battle
where curly-headed horsemen fight in leafy formations.
In rock-strewn Taurida Hellenic science lives, and here
are the noble, rusty beds of golden acres.

And in the white room silence stands like a spinning wheel,
it smells of vinegar, paint, and new wine from the cellar.
Do you remember, in the Greek house, the wife everyone loved –
not Helen, the other one – how long she would work at embroidering?

Golden Fleece, where are you, Golden Fleece?
All the journey long the heavy sea waves sounded,
and leaving his ship, its canvas worn out in the seas,
Odysseus returned, filled with space and time.

As in 'The Admiralty,' the classical furnishings of this poem written
in 1917 are more than merely literary. In the year of the Revolution
Mandelstam sought refuge at various places in the warm, safe, and

265

relatively well-fed south. This poem memorializes his sojourn in the Crimea at the house of the painter Sergey Sudeykin (cf. the smell of paint) and his wife Vera Arturovna, the hostess here, who was later married to Igor Stravinsky.[17] The 'science of Hellas' has brought to the rocky Crimean hills a varied cargo of Mediterranean lore: the cultivation of the grape, the white columns, the rites of Bacchus...and perhaps also Greek garrulity. For the poem consists of talk, wisps of conversation, most of it desultory and some of it inaudible. After the hostess has spoken and other distant, indistinct voices have been heard, the central consciousness takes over at the mid-point to make one remark from which the rest of the poem derives. It is his musing – whether exterior or interior is not clear – that seems to move from grapevines through a vignette, or perhaps a vase painting, of a battle scene and thence via the spinning wheel to the story of Penelope and the return of Odysseus.

The Bryusov who complained about the incorrectness of Mandelstam's mythology when he caused Persephone to accompany the souls of the dead into Hades, must have been outraged by the 'incorrectness' of this poem. Did Penelope (whose name itself seems to elude the speaker) 'spin' or 'embroider'? Like all Greek women, she was mistress of these skills, but the activity that identifies her was *weaving* at a *loom* a shroud for Laertes. And – unless one wishes to justify reference to the Golden Fleece by the presence in her household of the old hound Argos, who recognized the disguised Odysseus – she was very far from the events involving Jason, Medea, and the Argonauts.

As usual, it is the correctness of the imagistic progression that supersedes any other imaginable 'correctness.' In this poem, the movement is from the imagery of *liquid* to that of *textiles* (the traditional form of the textile being irrelevant), and in the last stanza the two are brought together: the canvas sails have been worn out in the water of the sea. The liquid imagery moves from *honey* (or *mead*; the Russian for both, *med*, is cognate with *mead*) to *Bacchus*, the god of wine, to *barrels* to *tea* to the glassy air *poured* about the sleepy hills to *grapes*, *wine* and *vinegar*. The imagery of textiles begins with the *spinning wheel* and moves by oblique ('incorrect') association to Penelope, to *embroidery* and the *Golden Fleece*. Finally, the synthesis of this dialectical movement of imagery is achieved with the waves and canvas, the liquid and the textile imagery brought together in the final resolution.

What stratagem of the poem brings Odysseus, that master of stratagems, into the scene of a painter's well-furnished house and garden in the Russian Crimea? There might have been something in the real-life situation, about which we can only conjecture, but about what is objectively there in the poem no surmise is needed: Odysseus returns here as he did in legend to vitalize, to lend directional force and form, to a domestic scene of tedious emptiness and expectation. One is reminded of the poem about the catalogue of ships. In that work as in this one, the Homeric element appears at the end with a kind of irresistible, obliterating power. 'Element' seems the right word: the dark sea in the poem of *Stone*, space and time in this one.

The best study of this poem, and one of the few truly excellent detailed studies of any poem by Mandelstam, is that by the Soviet scholar D. M. Segal.[18] It is a superlative exercise in 'slow reading,' as Segal calls it (citing M. O. Gershenzon as the source of that phrase), or, to give it the more traditional Western name, 'explication de texte.' His concern is to show how the specific denotation of individual words is altered by other words (and all other linguistic and prosodic features) in the context and how the poem moves among the general, necessarily abstract meanings that emerge. Thus, in his view, the overall movement of the poem is from what might be called 'solemn slowness of movement' through the 'nobility and bright cleanliness of the classical' to a resolution in the 'surmounting of difficulties.' To put it in this way is to confine his finely detailed argument, which ranges from the phonetics of single words to the large semantic suggestiveness of the abstract metrical pattern, within a very small nutshell. If I have any disagreement with him, it is perhaps implicit in my own analysis, namely, that the very breadth and abstractness of his focus prevents him seeing what I regard as the most fundamental, concrete and (to me) obvious structure of the poetic imagery: that from *liquid* to *textile*. For what it is worth, such attention to the concrete imagistic movement strikes me as a good deal more 'Mandelstamian'; see his own analysis of the Geryon passage in the XVIIth canto of the Inferno, which Mandelstam calls 'this truly miraculous demonstration of the transformability of poetic material, which leaves all the associative processes of modern European poetry simply nowhere.'[19] One of Segal's achievements, incidentally, is to expose clearly the enormous role played by classical imagery in a poem strangely neglected by Victor Terras, who practically dismisses it as 'not really classical' and concludes: 'The poet feels like Ulysses who has returned to his native Ithaca...'[20]

In two poems of 1918, among the most powerful and certainly the most famous that he ever wrote, Mandelstam takes leave of the past. The past is conceived as the upper world of light, air and freedom – the world of Pushkin; the future is the underworld that dominates *Tristia* throughout in its classical images. In the first poem the emblematic figures are Persephone and Pushkin. In the second the figure is the last of the trio, Ovid, whose fate colors all of Mandelstam's second book.

103. СУМЕРКИ СВОБОДЫ

Прославим, братья, сумерки свободы,—
Великий сумеречный год.

Mandelstam

В кипящие ночные воды
Опущен грузный лес тенет.
Восходишь ты в глухие годы,
О солнце, судия, народ.

Прославим роковое бремя,
Которое в слезах народный вождь берет.
Прославим власти сумрачное бремя,
Ее невыносимый гнет.
В ком сердце есть, тот должен слышать, время,
Как твой корабль ко дну идет.

Мы в легионы боевые
Связали ласточек—и вот
Не видно солнца; вся стихия
Щебечет, движется, живет;
Сквозь сети—сумерки густые—
Не видно солнца и земля плывет.

Ну что ж, попробуем: огромный, неуклюжий,
Скрипучий поворот руля.
Земля плывет. Мужайтесь, мужи.
Как плугом, океан деля,
Мы будем помнить и в летейской стуже,
Что десяти небес нам стоила земля.

(Москва, май 1918.)

THE TWILIGHT OF FREEDOM

Let us celebrate, brothers, the twilight of freedom –
this great twilight year.
Into the boiling waters of night
the forest of snares has been lowered.
The years are desolate in which you rise
O sun, judge, people.

Let us celebrate the fateful burden
taken by the people's leader in tears.
Let us celebrate the twilight burden of power,
its unendurable oppression.
Whoever, Time, has a heart must hear
your ship as it sinks to the bottom.

We have bonded the swallows together
into legions for battle – and now
the sun's invisible; all nature's element
twitters, stirs, is alive;
the sun can't be seen through the nets
of dense twilight, and the earth's afloat.

268

What then? Let us try: an immense
ungainly creaking turn of the helm.
The earth is afloat. Take courage, men.
Parting the ocean as though with a plough,
we shall remember even in Lethean cold
that the cost of this earth was ten heavens.

The figures of Persephone and Pushkin are as obscure in this crepuscular light as in any poem of the book, but they are there, she in the swallows conscripted for war and he in the vanished sun. That another sun – equated in the sixth line to a judge rising to make judgment – should have come into being in these 'desolate years' cannot weaken the association established in *Tristia* and elsewhere between the vanished sun and the spirit of Pushkin.

As might be imagined, Soviet commentators on Mandelstam must approach this poem with the greatest caution, and no one must be more cautious than those who are well-disposed toward his work. In the 1960s, when the rehabilitation of Mandelstam was making a certain stealthy progress, Nikolay Chukovsky, Ilya Ehrenburg, Vladimir Orlov, and Georgy Margvelashvili tended to cite this work (omitting, needless to say, the first two lines and other perfectly intractable bits of the poem) as evidence of Mandelstam's enthusiasm for Lenin, the Revolution, destruction of the exploiting classes, &c. For all one's sympathy with their good intentions, it is still refreshing, in a way, to have the good honest vulgarity of V. Nazarenko, who, in the course of a 1916 attack on Mandelstam in *Zvezda* (Star), wrote: 'In my opinion it is not only impossible to call this poem "a profound comprehension of the events" of 1918; on the contrary, the "comprehension" in it is profoundly reactionary, completely in accord with the howls of the bourgeois intellectuals of that day...'[21] Odd that the Philistine hack should do less of a disservice to Mandelstam than his friends.

Nazarenko is right, too, when he summons in support of his reading the whole context of *Tristia* and of Mandelstam's other work, for, as I have argued often enough by this time, it is only there that individual poems of Mandelstam yield their full meaning. It is by no means an accident that a poem of 1931 should be entitled 'Midnight in Moscow,' for not only does the first word of the title refer back to the 'Twilight' of this poem, but there are actual verbal resonances in the text as well:

Чур! Не просить, не жаловаться! Цыц!
Не хныкать!
　　　　Для того ли разночинцы
Рассохлые топтали сапоги, чтоб я теперь их предал?
Мы умрем, как пехотинцы,
Но не прославим ни хищи, ни поденщины, ни лжи!

(No. 260, 27–31.)

Beware! Don't ask for anything, no complaining! Sh!
No sniveling!
 Is that what the raznochintsy stamped
their cracked boots for – so I might now betray them?
We'll die like the infantry,
but we *won't celebrate* the plundering, the day-labor, the lying!

The Russian phrase translated in italics here is the negative of the first
word (twice repeated) in 'Twilight of Freedom': 'Let us celebrate...'
There is now no possible ambiguity. In the midnight of the 1930s things
were clearer than in the half-light of 1918.

It seems appropriate to conclude this discussion of Mandelstam's second
book of poetry with the poem 'Tristia,' from which Mikhail Kuzmin,
rightly in my opinion, drew the title of the whole collection.

104. TRISTIA

Я изучил науку расставанья
В простоволосых жалобах ночных.
Жуют волы, и длится ожиданье,
Последний час вигилий городских,
И чту обряд той петушиной ночи,
Когда, подняв дорожной скорби груз,
Глядели вдаль заплаканные очи,
И женский плач мешался с пеньем муз.

Кто может знать при слове—расставанье,
Какая нам разлука предстоит,
Что нам сулит петушье восклицанье,
Когда огонь в акрополе горит,
И на заре какой-то новой жизни,
Когда в сенях лениво вол жует,
Зачем петух, глашатай новой жизни,
На городской стене крылами бьет?

И я люблю обыкновенье пряжи:
Снует челнок, веретено жужжит,
Смотри, навстречу, словно пух лебяжий,
Уже босая Делия летит!
О, нашей жизни скудная основа,
Куда как беден радости язык!
Всё было встарь, всё повторится снова,
И сладок нам лишь узнаванья миг.

Да будет так: прозрачная фигурка
На чистом блюде глиняном лежит,
Как беличья распластанная шкурка,
Склонясь над воском, девушка глядит.
Не нам гадать о греческом Эребе,
Для женщин воск, что для мужчины медь.
Нам только в битвах выпадает жребий,
А им дано гадая умереть.

(1918.)

TRISTIA

I have studied the science of saying good-bye
in bareheaded laments at night.
Oxen chew, and the waiting stretches out,
it is the last hour of my keeping watch in the city,
and I respect the ritual of the cock-loud night,
when, lifting their load of sorrow for the journey,
eyes red from weeping have peered into the distance
and the crying of women mingled with the Muses' singing.

Who can know when he hears the word good-bye
what kind of separation lies before us,
what kind of promise the cock's exclaiming holds,
when a light burns in the acropolis,
when at the dawn of some new life
the ox chews lazily in his passage,
the reason why the cock, herald of new life,
beats his wings on the city wall?

And I love the habit of the woollen yarn:
back and forth the shuttle goes, the spindle hums,
and, flying like swansdown in our direction
look where barefoot Delia comes!
O, how threadbare is the language of joy,
the thin warping of our life!
Everything was before and will recur again,
our sweetness is all in the instant of recognition.

So be it then: the transparent little figure
lies on a clean terracotta dish
like the stretched pelt of a squirrel
and, bending over the wax, a girl inspects it.
Not for us conjectures about Greek Erebus,
wax is for women what bronze is for a man.
Only in battles do we learn our lot,
but they are granted death in the act of divination.

Victor Terras deals with this famous poem at some length in the article to which I have referred several times before. Here are some excerpts from his analysis:

> The title 'Tristia' (No. 104) suggests a connection with Ovid, a lifelong favorite of Mandelstam's who may have felt that his fate in Soviet Russia was that of Ovid in exile. The first stanza amply confirms this. There are several loud and clear echoes from Ovid, *Tristia*, I, 3: 'Cum subit illius tristissima noctis imago / Quae mihi supremum tempus in urbe fuit....'
> The second line, *v prostovolosykh zhalobakh nochnykh*, echoes Ovid's 'Illa etiam, ante Lares passis prostrata capillis' (I, 3$_{43}$). The vigil is that of Ovid's last, sleepless night in his beloved Rome. The weeping of women

(*zhenskii plach*) is clearly audible in Ovid's wonderfully musical composition: 'Miscuit haec lacrimis tristia dicta suis' (I, 3_{80}). But what does 'the night of the cock' mean? Mandelstam writes in one of his essays: 'In the stillness of night a lover pronounces one tender name instead of another, and suddenly realizes that this has happened once before: the words, and the hair, and the cock who has just crowed under the window, already crowed in Ovid's *Tristia*. And he is overcome by a deep joy of recognition....' [Terras' note at this point reads: 'To be exact, the cock crows in *Amores*, I, 4: 65, and not in *Tristia*. Cf. also the myth of Alectryon, told in the *Metamorphoses*.'] But no cock crows in Ovid's elegy. It is the morning star that announces the time of departure, not the cock. But then we know that in ancient Greece and Rome the cock was sacred to the Sun and to all the deities of light. He was sacred to Ares for being brave and pugnacious and vigilant. His crowing was an omen of victory. The cock was also sacred to Aesculapius, god of healing, to Nox Dea, and to the Lares for his vigilant custody of the home. Clearly, 'the night of the cock' cannot be the night of an old man departing for a sad exile. The first four lines of the second stanza still leave a shadow of doubt. The emphasis is still on parting, and on the fear of uncertainty. The man who sees the fire burning on the Acropolis could still be Ovid who, in his elegy, had written, 'Hanc ego suspiciens, et ab hac Capitolia cernens...' (I, 3_{29}). But then we hear, *i na zare kakoi-to novoi zhizni* [and at the dawn of some new life], and realize that this is no longer the aging Ovid departing for his melancholy exile, but a young man, perhaps an expedition of young men, warriors or adventurous colonists, seeking a new homestead. [...]

The third stanza begins with an image which is Greek to the core: the home and its keeper, the virtuous wife or daughter, were invariably associated with the spindle and the loom. But who is Delia? Just a light-footed young woman, the Delia of Tibullus, from whose elegy the image is taken? 'Tunc mihi, qualis eris, longos turbata capillos, / Obvia nudato, Delia, curre pede...' (Tibullus, *Elegies*, I, 3_{90-1}). Or the goddess Artemis, whose frequent epiclesis was Delia (e.g. Horace, *Odes*, IV, 33), flying from Delos across the sea to Athens?

The next four lines contain the conception underlying Mandelstam's philosophy, his aesthetics, and his poetic vision: philosophy, art, poetry, and life itself are acts of anticipation, of recognition, of rediscovery. Here it seems to be expressed in terms of Pythagorean metempsychosis.

The last stanza is again Greek to the very core: a waxen figurine, a young girl bent over it, seeking to divine the future. Waxen statuettes were common in Greek and Roman living rooms. We know, from numerous sources, that waxen images of Hecate, of Eros, and of other gods were used in magic and in divination.[22]

I have quoted this lengthy excerpt from Professor Terras' article not only for its intrinsic merit, and as a testimony of my gratitude and admiration for the classical erudition that it displays, but also to disagree slightly with some of the conclusions. It seems to me that Terras ignores one entire fund of allusion that has gone into the poem. As I have indicated, I thoroughly agree concerning the large debt that is owed to Ovid, but one cannot fail to take notice of the other figure who is almost equally there: Alexandr Pushkin. It is when one reads 'Tristia' in the context of the other poems near it that one comes to appreciate this.

It is a poem of parting. Everything that is about parting, the last vigil in the city, the weeping of women, etc., relates to Ovid's departure into exile. But it is equally a poem about what is to follow the separation, about the future, and above all about conjecturing what the future will bring. This refers to Pushkin.

It is very typical of Mandelstam that the mechanism of the reference should be oblique and that it should pass through another reference on the way. Line 27 is taken word-for-word from the second line of a poem by Anna Akhmatova written in 1911 and included in her first collection *Vecher* (Evening).[23] It will simplify matters to give a full literal translation of it:

> High in the sky one could see a small grey cloud
> like the stretched pelt of a squirrel.
> He said, 'It's no pity that your body
> will melt in March, frail Snow Maiden!'
>
> In my down muff my hands turned cold,
> I became afraid, somehow vaguely troubled.
> O, how could one return the hour, the fleeting weeks
> of his love, airy and momentary!
>
> I want neither bitterness nor revenge,
> let me die with the last white snowstorm.
> I divined about him on Twelfth Night eve,
> in January I was his friend.

In his memoirs Vladimir Pyast indicates that the line quoted by Mandelstam was already famous.[24] Viktor Shklovsky, writes Pyast, said somewhere that Akhmatova's 'stretched pelt of a squirrel' had become the banner of all Russian women poets, who were, at the beginning of the century, notoriously beholden to Mandelstam's great friend for so many of their poetic mannerisms. So the poet of *Tristia* could depend upon the line being very familiar to his first audience. As often happens when he quotes from another work, every detail of the context can play a role as relevant as – sometimes more relevant than – the actual words of the borrowing. It is therefore not to be overlooked that in Akhmatova's poem about parting, her eternal theme, the speaker *divines* the future on the eve of Twelfth Night. Even the *down* of the muff will have its relevance. But in this case the actual line itself is most relevant of all. The stretched squirrel skin appears in a simile of which the other member is the irregular shape of a cloud.

This provides a clue to correct the reading of Terras, who calls the means of divination in Mandelstam's poem 'Greek to the very core,' a mistake that arises from interpreting *figurka* as 'statuette.' On the contrary, the divination in question is 'Russian to the very core,' and Mandelstam's first readers would hardly have had to be more than normally literate to associate this passage with the most celebrated instance of divination in Russian literature, Pushkin's *Eugene Onegin*, v: 4–10. Tatyana's interest in divination is cited as proof of her thoroughly Russian nature, and the divination (a search for the identity of her future husband) takes place at the same traditional season (Twelfth Night fell on 6 January, O.S.) as it does in Akhmatova's lyric. The method was to melt a candle into a shallow dish of water, where the suddenly cooled wax would assume odd shapes like Rorschach blots or – what is more to the point – like a cloud or the stretched pelt of a squirrel. These were then to be interpreted. In *Onegin*, v: 8, we read (in Nabokov's translation):

> Tatyana with a curious gaze
> looks at the submerged wax:
> with its wondrously cast design,
> to her a wondrous something it proclaims.
> From a dish full of water
> rings come out in succession...

As I have mentioned, Akhmatova and Pushkin were together in an earlier poem of classical background (No. 95). It is not by accident, I think, that Akhmatova, who appeared there in the guise of Cassandra, the prophetess, should also enter this poem in connection with the theme of foretelling the future.

This wholesale reference to Pushkin via his greatest masterpiece makes it unnecessary, in my view, to go all the way to the *Elegies* of Tibullus or even more tenuously to Horace in order to find a source for Mandelstam's Delia in line 20: it is almost certainly Pushkin's Delia, who occurs several times in his early, exceedingly 'classical' poems, and twice in actual titles. Perhaps the epithet 'barefoot' comes from Tibullus, but does not the 'down' to which she is compared come from Akhmatova's poem?

What does this poem about parting and the uncertainty of the future have to say about the future? That comes in the famous lines that conclude the third stanza: what has been, will be. The science of leavetaking is a part of that science of Hellas which brought with it not only viticulture and white columns but also wisdom, and one of its axioms is that saying good-bye is an eternally recurrent pattern in man's life. Ovid's parting from his loved ones as he goes into exile is a paradigm of all partings. It may be laid over other partings, as it is in this poem, where as in the one preceding, Mandelstam speaks of leaving the old world for exile in the new, to check the accuracy of the emotional wrench. But the

The classical in 'Tristia'

Ovidian sadness is lightened for him, as it always was, by the calm courage, the stubborn joyousness of Pushkin. 'Pechal' moia svetla' (my sadness is luminous) wrote the greatest of Russian poets, and Mandelstam borrowed it. 'Tristia' is at the same time a lament and a celebration, not ironic, as in the 'Twilight of Freedom,' but genuine – and Pushkinian. The language of joy which is the warp of life's fabric may be scanty, but it is what conveys the instant of recognition, the everlasting renewal of art. The figure of Ovid is not replaced by 'adventurous colonists.' He is not, in a sense, replaced at all: he is combined with the spirit of Pushkin. Nothing could be more 'Acmeist' than the conclusion, where line 29 seems positively Gumilyovian in spirit.

I think it will depend upon the reader whether he responds most, in this equilibrium of sadness and joy, to the one or the other, but both are simultaneously there. One thing seems clear. If the Nazarenkos of the world were ever to read 'Tristia' at the deepest level of its meaning, they would surely find it as uncongenial as the celebration of the twilight of freedom, a much more explicit poem. The past to which adieu is bidden, and the future faced with resolute courage, are not such as to provide much solace for revolutionists, creators of a 'new reality,' or refashioners of nature. Only minds of a quite different cast will be gladdened by the doctrine of the twenty-third line, or of the poem.

14

Here writes Terror: Poems, 1921-1925

When B. sat down at the piano and made
A transparence in which we heard music, made music,
In which we heard transparent sounds, did he play
All sorts of notes? or did he play only one
In an ecstacy of its associates,
Variations in the tones of a single sound,
The last, or sounds so single they seemed one?

WALLACE STEVENS, 'Esthétique du mal'
Collected Poems, p. 316

At the end of 1925, Mandelstam's muse fell silent and was not to be heard from again until 1930. Only one poem in the New York edition (No. 199) is dated 1926, but the date, like the poem itself, is dubious, since the only known source for it is an article by Georgy Ivanov.[1] One of the poems to Olga Vaksel (No. 198) was dated 'January 1926' on a copy which I saw in Moscow, but that date, even if it should prove to be the correct one, is very early in the year.[2] In the last collection of his poetry that he himself was able to supervise, *Poems* (1928), he separated from *Stone* and *Tristia* the twenty poems that precede the silence, giving them no title other than the bare dates of their composition: '1921–1925.' These are practically all the poems he wrote in a period of five years, for he excluded from this last collection only two (195 and 197). Most of them were written in 1922 (eight) and 1923 (five).

The poems belong together, of course, on other grounds than chronology. In this chapter I should like to examine in somewhat greater detail a matter broached several times earlier – the question of 'drift.' 'Drift' is not an altogether comfortable word, but then neither are the other words – 'tonality,' 'dominant,' 'sound-image complex' – that come to mind. By drift, I shall mean a specifiable general tendency marking practically all the elements of a poem – the subject, theme, diction, sound, and images. It seems to me that practically all the poetry that came to Mandelstam in the five years before it ceased coming altogether for an equal period is marked by one drift. It is very difficult to specify a drift – and it is nearly impossible if one wishes to avoid impressionism completely, which I don't – but it is somewhat easier when the poems themselves are known. Here, then, are two poems that not only belong very closely together themselves but also exemplify the drift in a nearly palpable way. Like certain other poems of this period, they were first published together, in a different order, and under a common title. Nos. 131 and 132 appeared in 1922, in reverse order, under the title 'Senoval' (Hayloft). I think there are certain reasons for preferring that arrangement, but I shall give them as he finally placed them in 1928:

131

Я не знаю, с каких пор
Эта песенка началась—
Не по ней ли шуршит вор,
Комариный звенит князь?

Я хотел бы ни о чем
Еще раз поговорить,
Прошуршать спичкой, плечом
Растолкать ночь—разбудить.

Приподнять, как душный стог,
Воздух, что шапкой томит.
Перетяхнуть мешок,
В котором тмин зашит,

Чтобы розовой крови связь,
Этих сухоньких трав звон,
Уворованная нашлась
Через век, сеновал, сон.

I don't know how long ago
this little song began –
isn't it the tune the thief rustles to,
the one to which the mosquito prince whines?

Once again I'd like to talk
about nothing at all,
to scratch like a match, to give night
a shove with my shoulder and wake it.

To lift the air a little
like a choking hayrick, irksome as a cap.
To shake out the sack sewn up
with the caraway seeds,

so that the pink blood's link,
the ringing of these dry grasses,
will be found stolen away
after a century, a hayloft, a dream.

132

Я по лесенке приставной
Лез на всклокоченный сеновал—
Я дышал звезд млечных трухой,
Колтуном пространства дышал.

И подумал: зачем будить
Удлиненных звучаний рой,
В этой вечной склоке ловить
Эолийский чудесный строй?

Звезд в ковше Медведицы семь.
Добрых чувств на земле пять.
Набухает, звенит темь,
И растет и звенит опять.

Распряженный огромный воз
Поперек вселенной торчит,
Сеновала древний хаос
Защекочет, запорошит.

Не своей чешуей шуршим,
Против шерсти мира поем.
Лиру строим, словно спешим
Обрасти косматым руном.

Из гнезда упавших щеглов
Косари приносят назад,—
Из горящих вырвусь рядов
И вернусь в родной звукоряд,

Чтобы розовой крови связь
И травы сухорукий звон
Распростились: одна скрепясь,
А другая—в заумный сон.

I climbed into the tousled hayloft
on the ladder leaned against it –
I breathed the haydust of the milky stars,
the matted hair of space I breathed.

And I thought: why awaken
the swarm of lengthened lines of sound?
Why catch the miracle of Aeolian harmony
in this everlasting squabble?

There are seven stars in the Great Bear's dipper,
five good senses on the earth.
The darkness swells and rings
and grows and rings again.

The huge unharnessed load
sticks up athwart the universe,
and the old chaos of the hayloft
will start to tickle, to dust with powder.

They aren't our own, the scales we rustle;
singing, we brush the world's fur the wrong way.
We build a lyre as if we were hurrying
to be overgrown with shaggy fleece.

Mowers bring back the goldfinches
that have fallen from their nests.
I'll break loose from these burning lines
and return to my native passage of sound

so that the pink blood's link
and the one-armed ringing of the grass
will say their last good-bye: one nerving itself,
the other leaving for its dream beyond reason.

Ideally, a drift would be presented with visual aids, great poster-size reproductions of the twenty poems printed in various colors to highlight the salient evidence of the drift. Within the confines of a normal book one must do with excursive prose. I shall first examine these two poems, which are so closely bound together – even sharing whole lines in common – as to require no argument of their kinship, and then extend the inspection to other poems of the period.

To begin with, I should like to point to one of those literary allusions that Mandelstam so incessantly worked into the texture of his poems. It is what sustains the last stanza of 132, but I think it is also present behind most of the poem. Pushkin used the verb *skrepias'* only once and in this same form (the gerundive) that we find in 132, line 27. It means 'nerving oneself, overcoming fear.' It occurs at that point in *Eugene Onegin*, v:12:10, when Tatyana has a lurid and prophetic dream, filled with conventional monsters from some nasty corner of the Russian subconscious. She nerves herself because a bear has materialized out of the snow to help her across a rushing torrent to a cabin on the other side where she will spy on the monsters' feast, presided over by Onegin. The dream is not even surrealistic, let alone *zaumnyi* (the nonsense language affected by some of the Futurists), but the conjunction of a word used by Pushkin once in a familiar passage with the word *son* 'dream' is enough to make this almost certainly an allusion to that place in *Onegin*.

The allusion is a good deal richer than these two words suggest. The bear is shaggy. Pushkin calls him *vz"eroshennyi*, 'dishevelled, tousled' in v:12:7 and *kosmatyi*, 'shaggy' in v:13:3. Not only the bear is shaggy; the whole scene in the snowy forest is shaggy – a mélange of impressions – rushing water, trembling hands (and bridge), flocks of snow. Mandelstam describes the fleece with the word *kosmatyi* itself; and Pushkin's word for a 'flock' of snow (*klok*, v:13:9) is represented twice in Mandelstam by *vsklokochennyi* 'tousled' (132/2) and *skloka* 'squabble' (132/7).

Nevertheless, in spite of these and other, less evident, parallels, I think that this reference to Pushkin is what Nabokov somewhere calls 'the wayside murmur of [a] hidden theme.' It is diffuse and thematic, rather than specific. Mandelstam's theme, in part, is simply shagginess itself, 'the ancient chaos of a hayloft,' and consciously or unconsciously he conveys his theme, as is his wont, through partial reminiscence of an earlier literary instance of it.

'Shagginess' is one of the elements of the drift itself, though now that word has begun to look inappropriate for this larger application. 'Disorder' is perhaps the most abstract and least colorful name for it. Toward disorder, Mandelstam's poems reveal a perfectly ambivalent attitude. On the one hand, the disorder could be that of 'babbling,' 'shuffling of lips,' and this is a 'dear disorder' for it is the source of all poetry. This was a natural disorder, Herrick's 'tempestuous petticoat' – a sign of life itself. On the other hand, disorder could be violent, spiky, sharp, bewildering, hard to perceive – in a word, dangerous. The disorder, the shagginess, that characterizes the drift of 1921–1925 strikes me as lying at the dangerous end of this emotional scale. It is something from which, like the speaker of No. 132, one wishes to tear oneself away to return to what is native, to what is oneself.

As I have mentioned, in his critical writing at this time Mandelstam several times praised Pasternak and Khlebnikov for their masculine, purely Russian sound – above all for their consonantism: harsh, jagged, spiky sounds. He accompanied this by an equal dispraise for whatever fell under the heading of 'Russian Latin' – a phrase used of his own poetry, no doubt to his intense disgust, for he meant by it whatever was mellifluous, merely melopoeic, learned, divorced from the home-keeping genius of the Russian language.

All of Mandelstam's criticism is in one way or another revealing of his own practice. He was a poet first of all, and a critic second; his reading of other poets was among other things a method of measuring himself. Such criticism is excellent, because most committed and vulnerable, though one should add that the perception of its excellence depends heavily upon knowing the critic as well as his subject.

His articles therefore serve as an additional confirmation of the drift to which he himself was submitting at this period. The very phrases by which he praised the qualities of Khlebnikov and Pasternak are applicable to the poems he was then writing. He saw Pasternak's poetic genealogy, for instance, as stemming from the *shchelkan'e* 'clicking' and *tsokan'e* 'clatter' of that boisterous genius, Pushkin's contemporary, Nikolay Yazykov. 'There is always war in poetry,' he writes, and likens the distant influence of one poet on another to an exchange of fire between long-range artillery. All the word's belligerent virtue is in its root. Russian is a language of roots, short capsules of meaning, that grow at both ends by a series of regular accretions to form whole trees of words. 'Root-breeders, like generals, war against each other. Word roots fight in the dark, taking each other's food and earth saps away.'[3] This passage conveys, I am sure, what Mandelstam understood to have happened when he 'answered' Pushkin's *klok* with *vsklokochennyi* and *skloka*, and it illuminates similar procedures in many other poems.[4]

He quotes approvingly a line of Fet's

И горящею солью нетленных речей

And with the burning salt of immortal words

which contains two words (italicized here) that are vital to the drift itself – the first ('burning') in 132 and 137 and the other ('salt') scattered throughout these poems. And he introduces four almost painfully sibilant lines of Pasternak by a paragraph that would seem in English translation perfectly mysterious if one did not know that the Russian words for the 'sound made by a nightingale,' 'mating-call,' 'wood-grouse in its mating-place,' and 'bird's topknot' are there chiefly for their bristling, clattering, percussive sound: *tsokaiushchii*,[5] *tokovanie, glukhar' na toku*, and *khokholok*.

That this quality of sound is present in the poems once entitled 'Hayloft' can be easily seen by those who read Russian. For those who do not, here is a transliteration of lines 17–18 from 132:

> Ne svoei cheshuei *shur*shim,
> Protiv *sher*sti mira poem.

The particular word-images that form part of the drift are no doubt more immediately perceptible than the quality of sound. In No. 131 these words are: *krov'* 'blood,' *trava* 'grass,' *senoval* 'hayloft,' *spichka* 'match,' *sukhon'kii* 'dry,' *zvon* 'ringing,' *vozdukh* 'air,' and *noch'* 'night.' Some of the same occur in No. 132: *zvezda* 'star,' *krov', trava, senoval, sherst'* 'fur,' *runo* 'fleece,' *sukhorukii* 'one-armed,' *zvukoriad* 'passage of sound,' *zvon*, and *cheshuia* 'fish-scale.'

At this point I think that the word-images might best be presented in a simple graph. The words proceed down the left side roughly in descending order of frequency, and it should be clear that at the lower end the choice of a word-image as salient is rather personal. But it is not totally arbitrary: if *spichka* 'match' appears only twice, it is yet necessary to remember that the two occasions have so often struck commentators on Mandelstam's poetry that they have frequently quoted them. A word can be very conspicuous in its context (like Stevens's *funest*, Eliot's *maculate*) though used but once – more conspicuous, indeed, than words that are more frequent but less poetically alive. In its first occurrence (127: I spichka sernaia menia b sogret' mogla – 'Even a sulphur match could keep me warm') it carries one of the heaviest emotional loads in the poem; and in its second (131: Proshurshat' spichkoi... 'To scratch like a match...') it participates in the central tonality of this drift.

It should be equally clear that no single word or small cluster of words is sufficient to characterize a drift. Words such as *vozdukh* 'air' or *zvuk* 'sound' are among the most frequent in Mandelstam's poetic lexicon. What is more, when they occur at other periods they often occur, as I have shown several times, together. One may turn the pages of his collected works almost at random and find – as for example in No. 106 (1919) –

> I sumashedshikh skal koliuchie sobory
> Povisli v vozdukhe, gde sherst' i tishina.

281

	125	126	127	128	129	130	131	132	133	134
звезда	×	× ×	× ×					×	×	
star										
соль		× ×	× ×							
salt		—	—							
ночь	—	×	—				×		×	
night										
кровь					×		×	×		
blood										
песня	—						—			
song										
воздух	×						×			×
air										
век						×	×			
age										
звук	—				×			—		
sound										
время					×	×				
time										
губы				×	×					
lips										
яблоко			—							
apple										
трава			×				×	×		
grass			⊙				⊙	⊙		⊙
темнота							—	=		×
darkness										—
шерсть			×				×			
wool							⊙			
лес	×							~	×	
forest										
позвонок				⊙						
vertebra										
твердь	×	×							×	
sky										
(or earth)										
сухой						—	—	▬		
dry										
холодок					×	~				×
chill										—
чешуя								×	×	
scales										
спичка			×				×			
match										

1921   1922

282

135	136	137	138	139	140	141	142	143	144	
		× ×							×	звезда
										star
	×				×			×		соль
	−							−		salt
	×	×			×			×		ночь
					−					night
× ×			×		×					кровь
										blood
	× ×	×	=	−	−					песня
	−									song
	× ×	× ×	×						×	воздух
										air
× ×	×				× ×	× ×				век
										age
	× ×		−		×					звук
										sound
	×	×			×					время
										time
	×				×				×	губы
										lips
	×		× ×		× ×	× ×			−	яблоко
										apple
×	⊙				⊙			⊙		трава
					×					grass
	−	−			−				−	темнота
										darkness
	× ×									шерсть
										wool
	−									лес
	× ×	× ×								forest
=	×				⊙					позвонок
×	⊙									vertebra
⊙										
										твердь
										sky
										(or earth)
									−	сухой
										dry
							−			холодок
										chill
										чешуя
										scales
										спичка
										match

1923   1924   1925

And the spiny cathedrals of the crazy cliffs
Hung in the air, where the wool and silence are

that *koliuchii* 'spiny' has, as it were, 'hooked' both *vozdukh* 'air' and *sherst'* 'wool' into the line following. But this is a premonition of the drift, not yet the drift itself. The drift consists of a large complex: these word-images, these sounds, and this emotional tendency – the statement of this sequence of poems in the broadest sense, to which I shall come at the end of this section.

On the chart I have tried to show by different symbols features that are essential to what I mean by a drift.

× and × × indicate the single or multiple occurrence of the word as given on the chart or in one of its oblique forms.

– indicates, e.g. not the word 'salt' (*sol'*) but the derived adjectival form 'salty' (*solenyi*).

The two remaining symbols (⊙ and ∼) indicate features of the drift that will not strike the reader as so obvious and require some justification. By the symbol ⊙ I represent what might be called an image-variant. For example, what is signified by the word *trava* 'grass' is obviously very close in its sensory associations (tactile, visual, olfactory) to *soloma* 'straw,' *seno* 'hay' (in *senoval* 'hayloft'), *pshenitsa* 'wheat' and *murava* 'sward' – the latter partly identical in sound as well. These variants seem to me relevant, but subjective and difficult to keep within meaningful limits. Does *sherst'* 'fur' belong imagistically with *trava*? I should say no – no more than *voda* 'water' belongs with *krov'* 'blood.' But one wishes for some way to show that *kriazh* 'mountain ridge' belongs to a family of images, as Mandelstam himself makes clear, that includes *khrebet* 'backbone' and *pozvonok* 'vertebra' and, via the mediation of *khrebet*, its phonic shadow *khriashch* 'cartilage.' I shall discuss below the imagistic contribution made by these images to the totality of the drift.

I am dealing with the impressions left in the mind of one who reads these twenty poems. Impression is close to illusion, I realize. But, to paraphrase Svidrigailov, to say that something is an illusion is not to say that it does not exist. The illusion employed by the architect cannot be argued out of existence by 'disproving' its proportions, nor can the citation of words such as *plavat'* 'to swim,' *sfera* 'sphere,' etc., disprove the dominant impression of these poems, which is the opposite of whatever is fluent and oval.

The symbol ∼ is to be understood as follows. Mandelstam uses the actual word *kholodók* 'chill' only twice in these poems, but it is essential to an understanding of drift as a complex of sound *and* sense to realize that in No. 130 the word *kolobók* 'round loaf of bread' is in fact, so far as the drift is concerned, a *recurrence* of *kholodók*. There is not the slightest relationship in meaning between the two words, nor has either anything to do with the *khokholók* 'bird's topknot' from the essay on Pasternak, but they constitute for Mandelstam a kind of phonic 'root' on the grounds of their similar sound alone.

To take another example, and raise a problem, consider *pesnia* 'song' (and its stylistic variant *pesn'*). It occurs in 136 and 137. A closely related *pen'e* 'singing' is in 125, 137 and 138. The diminutive form *pesenka* is in 131, 138 and 140. The reference to song therefore occurs some eight times at least. Does it also occur in No. 132? Yes, it does: in a word that has nothing whatsoever to do with singing – *lesenka* 'ladder.' Why? Because in 132, a poem which is indubitably the twin of 131, the word *lesenka* occupies the same position, has the same diminutive meaning, except for the initial consonant is identical in sound, and is, in short, 'the same' as *pesenka*. There is, I mean to say, a series: *pen'e – pesnia – pesenka – lesenka*.

The idea of series, of one word-image being born out of another, is absolutely fundamental to the concept of drift and justifies more than anything else the choice of the term 'drift' to convey the essentially kinetic nature of this phenomenon. It is what Mandelstam himself repeatedly described as one of the most fundamental processes of poetry – most notably in the essay on Dante:

> As in all true poetry, Dante's thinking in images is accomplished with the help of a characteristic of poetic material which I propose to call its transformability or convertibility. It is only by convention that the development of an image can be called development. Indeed, imagine to yourself an airplane (forgetting the technical impossibility) which in full flight constructs and launches another machine. In just the same way, this second flying machine, completely absorbed in its own flight, still manages to assemble and launch a third. In order to make this suggestive and helpful comparison more precise, I will add that the assembly and launching of these technically unthinkable machines that are sent flying off in the midst of flight do not constitute a secondary or peripheral function of the plane that is in flight; they form a most essential attribute and part of the flight itself, and they contribute no less to its feasibility and safety than the proper functioning of the steering gear or the uninterrupted working of the engine.[6]

There is not necessarily any logical relationship between the terms of a series. If there were, its direction might be predictable and thus bereft of what is most basic to it: the surprise of perpetual discovery in unsuspected regions of the imagination. To the extent that one can recover the time sequence in which Mandelstam invented his poems, the most meaningful relationship among the terms is no doubt that of chronology. But I think it essential to keep in mind that the actual process by which one image is born from another lies beyond our reach in the central mystery of art. When we set it down in the linear fashion imposed by the conventions of writing, we are simply making a convenient notation. It is the very kinesis of the drift that makes one despair of ever exhibiting it in a very lucid manner. The drifts within the drift swirl in dizzying patterns.

To take an example involving this same series, it is obvious that *les* 'forest' is an important word-image in these poems. It contributes to the ideational node of primitive, vegetable world and also of density, baffling tangle. The railway station in Pavlovsk (No. 125) is a *stekliannyi les* 'glass forest' and later, in 133, a dragonfly's wing is an obvious development of this: *sliudianoi pereponchatyi les* 'a webbed mica forest.' And in 137 the air is a *prozrachnyi les* 'transparent forest.' *Les* is therefore *also* a contributor to *lesenka* 'ladder' in the series above and even to its exact homophone *lez* 'climbed' in the following line.

In precisely the same way, the situation in the *kholodok–kolobok* series is also more complex than might at first appear, for *kolobok* is the 'end product' of another phonic sequence: in the poem preceding it, one finds *kabluk* 'heel' and *kolobrodit* 'gads about' as clear antecedents. The syllable *kol* exists also, as it chances, as an independent word meaning – through no chance at all, in this context – 'stake,' the kind used for impaling. It is the nucleus of a parallel series in No. 128: *koleso* 'wheel' – *koliuchii* 'spiny, barbed' – *kliuch* 'spout' – *krucha* 'steep slope' – *ukliuchina* 'oarlock.'[7]

It is probable that no such series is so central to the drift as that in No. 136, *Nashedshii podkovu* (The Horseshoe Finder). Here is a portion of the series, put down in the order of its occurrence in the poem: *sherokhovatyi* 'rough' – *sherst'* 'fur' – *sharakhaiutsia* 'shy, vb.' – *shorokh* 'rustle' – *shar* 'sphere' – *sherst'* 'wool.'[8]

But that is only the most obvious group of words that participate in this particular complex of sound and meaning. Alerted by this group, one looks elsewhere in the sound pattern of the poem to find it bristling with nervous combinations of *sh*, *r*, and *kh*. I give these as they occur and dispense with translation, it being pointless to render such isolated words:

4	ver*kh*u*sh*ki	43	zapa*kh sh*ersti
11	*khr*upkii	48	*khr*ustal'
13	pover*kh*nost'	54	umer*sh*ikh
19	pute*sh*estvii...more*kh*oda	55	*khr*upkoe
22	*khr*ebet	65	*khr*apit
23	ver*kh*u*sh*kami	67	so*khr*aniaet
36	*khr*apiashchimi	81	so*khr*aniaiut

The cluster *sh–r–kh* proves to be one of the most seminal in the entire drift. If one follows its trail through the poems of 1921–1925 it will lead to discoveries, for such phonic kernels are as heuristic for the reader as they no doubt were for the poet. Here are other samples, taken from practically every poem that he wrote at this period:

125	*sh*ar	135	za*khr*ebetnik li*sh'*
126	stra*sh*nee		*khr*ebet
127	*sh*erst' i voro*sh*it'		*khr*iashch
	*sh*ar	136	(See above)
	*khr*upkii	137	pi*sh*et stra*kh*
	s petu*kh*om v gor*sh*ke		*sh*ershen'
128	no*sh*a *kh*rebtu		kor*sh*unitsa
	*sh*er*sh*avy*kh*		stria*kh*nut'
	*sh*irokaia		zly*kh* ovcharok *sh*uby
129	pro*kh*odit		dvuru*sh*nik
	*sh*evelen'e eti*kh* gub	138	popro*sh*aiki
	i ver*sh*ina		kro*kh*
130	*kh*oro*sh*a		goro*kh*
131	*sh*ur*sh*it		*sh*armankoi
	pro*sh*ur*sh*at'	140	skvore*sh*niam i zastre*kh*am
	peretria*kh*nut' me*sh*ok		ukryv*sh*is' ryb'im me*kh*om
132	*sh*ur*sh*im		*kh*rustit
	*sh*ersti		*khr*iashch
	iz goriashchi*kh* vyrvus'		pi*sh*ushchi*kh* ma*sh*in prostaia
133	*sh*estiruki*kh*	143	*khl*eba ezh⁹ briu*kh*atyi
	v che*sh*ue iskalechenny*kh*		po*khr*ustivaia
	kryl		

The poem from which we started on a search that has revealed an obsessive iteration of *sh–r–kh* is itself richest in that pattern. In other ways as well No. 136, 'The Horseshoe Finder,' strikes me as emblematic of the whole period. In one way it is, however, totally untypical of Mandelstam, who practically never wrote in irregularly metered lines of varying length, but the very atypicality, the 'disorder,' is part of its significance. For Mandelstam himself the poem was evidently a major statement: he included it in 1923 in both *Stone* and *Second Book* and republished it in 1928 in *Poems*. In what follows I give the version of these texts rather than that of the New York edition, where the divisions of the poem are unfortunately somewhat blurred. He meant it to have nine divisions, like the 'Slate Ode' (137) and '1 January 1924' (140), poems with which it has much in common.

НАШЕДШИЙ ПОДКОВУ

[1]   Глядим на лес и говорим:
Вот лес корабельный, мачтовый,
Розовые сосны
До самой верхушки свободные от махнатой ноши,
Им бы поскрипывать в бурю
Одинокими пиниями
В разъяренном безлесном воздухе;
Под соленою пятою ветра устоит отвес, пригнанный к пляшущей
палубе.

И мореплаватель,
В необузданной жажде пространства,
Влача через влажные рытвины хрупкий прибор геометра,
Сличит с притяженьем земного лона
Шероховатую поверхность морей.

[2]   А вдыхая запах
Смолистых слез, проступивших сквозь обшивку корабля,
Любуясь на доски
Заклепанные, слаженные в переборки
Не вифлеемским мирным плотником, а другим—
Отцом путешествий, другом морехода,—
Говорим:
И они стояли на земле,
Неудобной, как хребет осла,
Забывая верхушками о корнях,
На знаменитом горном кряже,
И шумели под пресным ливнем,
Безуспешно предлагая небу выменять на щепотку соли
Свой благородный груз.

[3]   С чего начать?
Все трещит и качается.
Воздух дрожит от сравнений,
Ни одно слово не лучше другого,
Земля гудит метафорой,
И легкие двуколки,
В броской упряжи густых от натуги птичьих стай,
Разрываются на части,
Соперничая с храпящими любимцами ристалищ.

[4]   Трижды блажен, кто введет в песнь имя;
Украшенная названьем песнь
Дольше живет среди других—
Она отмечена среди подруг повязкой на лбу,
Исцеляющей от беспамятства, слишком сильного одуряющего запаха—
Будь то близость мужчины,
Или запах шерсти сильного зверя,
Или просто дух чобра, растертого между ладоней.

[5]   Воздух бывает темным, как вода, и все живое в нем плавает как рыба,
Плавниками расталкивая сферу,
Плотную, упругую, чуть нагретую,—
Хрусталь, в котором движутся колеса и шарахаются лошади,
Влажный чернозем Нееры, каждую ночь распаханный заново
Вилами, трезубцами, мотыгами, плугами.
Воздух замешан так же густо, как земля,—
Из него нельзя выйти, в него трудно войти.

[6]   Шорох пробегает по деревьям зеленой лаптой;
Дети играют в бабки позвонками умерших животных.

Хрупкое летоисчисление нашей эры подходит и концу.
Спасибо за то, что было:
Я сам ошибся, я сбился, запутался в счете.
Эра звенела, как шар золотой,
Полая, литая, никем не поддерживаемая,
На всякое прикосновение отвечала «да» и «нет».
Так ребенок отвечает:
«Я дам тебе яблоко», или: «Я не дам тебе яблока».
И лицо его точный слепок с голоса, который произносит эти слова.

[7] Звук еще звенит, хотя причина звука исчезла.
Конь лежит в пыли и храпит в мыле,
Но крутой поворот его шеи
Еще сохраняет воспоминание о беге с разбросанными ногами—
Когда их было не четыре,
А по числу камней дороги,
Обновляемых в четыре смены
По числу отталкиваний от земли пышущего жаром иноходца.

[8] Так,
Нашедший подкову
Сдувает с нее пыль
И растирает ее шерстью, пока она не заблестит,
Тогда
Он вешает ее на пороге,
Чтобы она отдохнула,
И больше ей уж не придется высекать искры из кремня.
Человеческие губы,
                   которым больше нечего сказать,
Сохраняют форму последнего сказанного слова,
И в руке остается ощущение тяжести,
Хотя кувшин
          наполовину расплескался,
                              пока его несли домой.

[9] То, что я сейчас говорю, говорю не я,
А вырыто из земли, подобно зернам окаменелой пшеницы.
Одни
     на монетах изображают льва,
Другие—
       голову;
Разнообразные медные, золотые и бронзовые лепешки
С одинаковой почестью лежат в земле.
Век, пробуя их перегрызть, оттиснул на них свои зубы.
Время срезает меня, как монету,
И мне уж не хватает меня самого.

[1] We look at the forest and say
    here is a forest of ship timber, masts,
    the reddish pines
    are free of their shaggy burden clear to the top

they should creak in the storm
like lone pines
in the infuriate, unforested air
the plumbline will hold out, fastened to the dancing deck, under
                                        the wind's salt heel.
And the seafarer
in his unbridled thirst for space
dragging through the water furrows a geometer's fragile equipment
collates the ragged surface of the seas
with the tug of the earth's bosom.

[2] And breathing the smell
     of the resinous tears that ooze through the ship planking,
     admiring the boards
     riveted, arranged in bulkheads,
     (not by the peaceful carpenter of Bethlehem but by that other,
     the father of wanderings, friend of seafarers)
     we say:
     they also once stood on the earth,
     uncomfortable as the backbone of an ass,
     their tops forgetful of their roots,
     on a famous mountain ridge,
     and soughed under the freshwater deluge of rain
     fruitlessly offering heaven their noble burden
     in return for a pinch of salt.

[3] Where to begin?
     Everything cracks and shakes.
     The air trembles with similes.
     No one word is better than any other,
     the earth moans with metaphor
     and the light two-wheeled carriages
     in garish harness of birdflocks dense with effort
     fly to pieces
     competing with the snorting favorites of the racetrack.

[4] Thrice blest is he who puts a name into his song;
     a song adorned with a name
     lives longer than others,
     she is marked among her friends by the fillet on her brow
     that saves her from fainting, from any overstrong, stupefying scent,
     whether from a man's nearness
     or from the fur of a strong animal
     or simply the smell of savory rubbed between the palms.

[5] The air is sometimes dark as water and everything living swims in
                                        it like a fish,
     pushing with fins through the sphere,
     dense, resilient, hardly warm,
     crystal where wheels move and horses shy,

Neaera's moist black-earth, turned up anew every night
by pitchforks, tridents, mattocks and ploughs.
The air is mixed as thickly as the earth –
you can't get out of it, it's hard to get into it.

[6] Rustling races through the trees as through a mossy pasture;
children play jacks with the vertebrae of dead animals.
The fragile reckoning of the years of our age is nearing its end.
Thank you, for what there was:
I myself made mistakes, got lost, balled up the accounts.
The era rang like a golden globe –
hollow, unseamed, held by no one.
At every touch it answered 'yes' and 'no'
the way a child answers:
'I'll give you an apple,' or 'I won't give you an apple,'
its face an exact copy of the voice saying these words.

[7] The sound is still ringing, though the cause of the sound has gone.
The stallion lies in the dust, in a lather, and snorts,
but the sharp curve of his neck
recalls his racing with legs outstretched
when there weren't four of them
but as many as there are stones in the road,
travelled anew, four shifts at a time,
as often as a blazing hot pacer rebounds from the earth.

[8] And so,
the one who's found a horseshoe
blows the dust from it
rubs it with wool until it shines,
then
he hangs it over the door
to let it rest
where it won't ever have to strike sparks from the flint again.
Human lips,
            that have nothing more to say,
keep the shape of the last word uttered,
and the hand keeps feeling the weight
even though the jug
                splashed itself half empty
                            while being carried home.

[9] What I'm saying now isn't said by me,
it's dug up out of the ground like grains of petrified wheat.
Some
    depict a lion on their coins,
others
    a head;
Various lozenges of brass, gold and bronze

lie with equal honor in the earth.
Trying to bite through them, the age left the mark of its teeth.
Time wears me down like a coin
and there's not even enough of me left for me.

It is at the same time one of his least characteristic poems, in form, and one of his greatest masterpieces. It is not 'easy,' yet I find its statement so unambiguously present in the seemingly inevitable progression of images as to forestall commentary. But it might be worthwhile to observe how appropriate to this poem is the passage quoted from the essay on Dante.

The forest at the beginning is already a ship *in posse*, whipped by a salt wind. The plumbline (*otves*) and the geometer's apparatus are elements of order, the first recalling the equilibrium imposed upon the warring elements of 'Notre Dame' (No. 39), but the fury of 'mountainous atmospheres of sky and sea' is unabated. The ship image is superimposed upon that of the forest: the ship is wood that has been brought under control, mastered by a builder, but specifically pagan, not the Carpenter. Poseidon is the god not only of seafarers but also of horses, who enter the poem first in the degenerate guise of an ass (note also that the trees are twice made beasts of burden) but later become ennobled as steeds, racehorses. 'Where to begin?' the speaker asks after the poem is well begun. But the mannerism is sternly imposed by the tradition, for this is an ode (Mandelstam first subtitled it 'a Pindaric fragment'), and typically of the ode, it is concerned with itself, that is to say, with poetry. The world in which poetry must now exist is as turbulent as that of the forest and ship: Everything cracks and shakes.

A poem should have a name in it, and in the brief tranquillity of the fourth section there is a vision of a world where poetry is possible: a pastoral, classical world, celebrated in *Stone* and more often lamented in *Tristia*. But the point is that there is no name, it has been lost, and words have lost all meaning; there is a gray equality among them.

At line 55, about the midpoint of the poem, a thematic statement divides the work in two:

The fragile reckoning of the years of our age is nearing its end.

The epithet (*khrupkoe*) is the same as for that other instrument of measure, the geometer's apparatus. The speaker, from this point, speaks for himself alone (earlier, he had always spoken for 'us' – a public voice, suitable to the ode). But now there is hardly anyone else left. A leaden stillness settles over the images. The rhetoric that had stirred earth and air is reduced to infantile simplicities. The word 'fragment' of the subtitle was especially suitable not for the poem itself, one of the least fragmentary things that Mandelstam ever wrote, but for the dominant theme of the second part, where all the operative images are residua, remains, relics. The principal image of the poem, the horseshoe itself, is what is *left* of the stormy animal, now dead, whose former running is conveyed in an image that cries out to be painted by Chagall. The horseshoe was found and then displayed, and the mere happenstance of its discovery, plus the use to which it was put, suggest the archeological cast of all that follows. This is human life frozen in its last attitudes, as though surprised in Herculaneum. The speaker himself now speaks in a resurrected voice, turned to stone, and time, the element that erupted in this poem at line 55, finally flows like lava over everything, obliterating the very self of the speaker at the end.

The poem thus moves from the dynamic, stormy images of the first part to the absolute stasis and death of the second by a series of images that give birth to each other in a way that seems as inevitable as the onflowing of time. It is for this reason that I find it emblematic of the entire period. If the poems of 1921–1925 have the sound of agony, it is because they in fact came just before the death of Mandelstam's poetry. His fear of the imagery of stars derives no doubt from this time. He thought ever afterwards that they signalled a loss of contact with the earth – i.e. with human life and language – and thus meant, as they did on this occasion, the end of his gift.

I said that one of the themes of this drift was 'shagginess,' or 'disorder' to give it a more abstract name. To conclude this discussion, I should like to refine these terms somewhat. It seems to me that there are five qualities that predominate in the agony of 1921–1925: roughness, agitation, stridency, acuity, and disjunction. In what follows I list by no means all of the words that convey these general meanings but merely the most striking among them:

roughness:

    grubyi 'rough, coarse' 126
    shershavyi 'rough' 128
    kosmatyi 'shaggy' 132
    vsklokochennyi 'tousled' 132
    protiv shersti 'against the fur' 132
    mokhnatyi 'shaggy' 136
    sherokhovatyi 'rough' 136

agitation:

    drozhit 'trembles' 125, 136
    kishit 'teems' 125
    voroshit' 'to stir' 127
    sharit' 'to fumble' 127
    shchekochet 'tickles' 127, 129
    shevelen'e 'movement' 129
    trepeshchet 'tremble, flutter' 133, 135
    shevelilsia 'moved' 134

kolyshet 'rocks' 135
pliashushchii 'dancing' 136
vse treshchit i kachaetsia 'everything cracks and shakes' 136

stridency:

svistki 'whistles' 125
krik 'cry' 125
skripet' 'creak' 127
vereshchanie 'twittering' 127
skrip 'creak' 128
shelestit' 'rustle' 129
shurshat' 'rustle' 131, 132
proshurshat' 'rustle' 131
zvenit 'rings' 131, 132, 136, 139, 140
vizgi 'screeches' 137
shchelknut' 'click' 140
khrustit 'crunches' 140
pokhrustyvaia 'crunching' 143

acuity:

koliuchii 'prickly, spiny' 128, 144
ezh 'porcupine' 128, 143
tsarapalas' 'scratched' 137
tsarapina 'scratch' 137
zanoza 'splinter' 138, 139
ptichii kliuv 'bird beak' 137

disjunction:

This is less easy than the others to reduce to a list. I mean by the term to sum up all those references to jointed, articulated things that litter this drift. In the most literal sense, the time was out of joint. All the references to breaking, disruption, upheaval belong to this theme; but it seems to me that the references to articulated things also imply the opposite: they are fragile candidates for disarticulation. The insects – the dragonfly, ant, wasp, mosquito – are all endangered species here in the several poems where they occur, just as backbones seem to be there to come apart as the bones in a children's game of jacks. 'Razbit tvoi pozvonochnik' (Thy spine is broken) is a line addressed to the era itself, and one of the most famous in Mandelstam.

The word *koleno* refers to an articulation of the human skeleton, the knee. By extension, it refers to segmented things such as individual sections of bamboo, pipe, twisting rivers, passages of song (especially birdsong), and branches of a genealogical tree (e.g. the twelve *tribes* of Israel are called by this name in Russian). Mandelstam redoubles this image by calling the days whose passages must be soldered with a flute (poetry) 'knotted':

Uzlovatykh dnei kolena
Nuzhno fleitoiu sviazat'

The passages of knotted days
must be connected by a flute[10]

Those are lines 19–20 of the poem 'Vek' (The Age) (No. 135), with which I conclude this chapter, and the book:

Век мой, зверь мой, кто сумеет
Заглянуть в твои зрачки
И своею кровью склеит
Двух столетий позвонки?
Кровь-строительница хлещет
Горлом из земных вещей,
Захребетник лишь трепещет
На пороге новых дней.

Кровь-строительница хлещет
Горлом из земных вещей,
И горящей рыбой мещет
В берег теплый хрящ морей,
И с высокой сетки птичьей,
От лазурных влажных глыб,
Льется, льется без различья
На смертельный твой ушиб.

Чтобы вырвать век из плена,
Чтобы новый мир начать,
Узловатых дней колена
Нужно флейтою связать.
Это век волну колышет
Человеческой тоской,
И в траве гадюка дышит
Мерой века золотой.

И еще набухнут почки,
Брызнет зелени побег,
Но разбит твой позвоночник,
Мой прекрасный жалкий век.
И с бессмысленной улыбкой
Вспять глядишь, жесток и слаб,
Словно зверь, когда-то гибкий,
На следы своих же лап.   (1923.)

My age, my beast – who will be able
to look into your eyes
who will glue together with his blood
two centuries' vertebrae?
Blood the builder gushes
through the throat from earthly things,
the hanger-on is only trembling
on the sill of future days.

Mandelstam

Blood the builder gushes
through the throat from earthly things
and like a burning fish it throws
warm sea-cartilage on the shore
and out of the high bird-net,
from the damp blocks of azure,
pours, pours indifferently
onto your mortal wound.

To liberate the captive age,
to make a start at the new world
the passages of knotted days
must be connected by a flute.
That's the age that rocks the wave
with human melancholy
and in the grass the adder breathes
to the age's golden measure.

And the buds will go on swelling
and the sprint of green will burst,
but your backbone has been shattered,
my beautiful, pitiful age.
Cruel and weak, you'll look back
smiling senselessly
like an animal that used to be supple
on the tracks of your own paws.

Notes to the text

NOTES TO CHAPTER 1, pp. 1–8

1 Like many Russians, Natalya Shtempel is gifted with a memory that approaches total recall. I am much obliged to her for several long conversations in Moscow in the spring of 1966, when she caused certain episodes of Mandelstam's Voronezh exile to come alive for me with a vividness to be found elsewhere only in the pages of *Hope Against Hope*. She and her mother were for a time the only people in Voronezh to befriend the exiled (and therefore dangerous) Mandelstams. The beginning of their friendship was not auspicious: when she said that she admired his poetry, Mandelstam asked her to recite some of it, and she chose the slight *vers d'occasion* of 1916 about a lost amulet (No. 87). The irascible Mandelstam shouted, 'You've picked my worst poem!' and drove her away. Later on, his friendship with the beautiful lame girl flourished, and he addressed to her several of the last poems that he ever wrote (Nos. 389, 390, 391, 393 and 394), all written in May 1937. When Mandelstam had recited to her the most moving of these (394), he said, 'This is my best poem. When I die, see that it gets into Pushkinsky Dom.' Pushkinsky Dom is the Institute of Russian Literature in Leningrad, where very little of Mandelstam is preserved.
2 Vol. II, 182.
3 Nadezhda Mandelstam, *Hope Against Hope: A memoir*, translated from the Russian by Max Hayward; Introduction by Clarence Brown (New York: Atheneum, 1970). The Russian original (*Vospominaniia*, Memoirs) was published in New York by the Chekhov Publishing Corporation at the same time.
4 For a description of the works of Mandelstam published in the United States see the Bibliography.
5 Vladimir Nabokov, *The Gift* (New York, 1963), pp. 181f.
6 *The Prose of Osip Mandelstam: The Noise of Time, Theodosia, The Egyptian Stamp*, translated, with a critical essay, by Clarence Brown (Princeton, N.J.: Princeton University Press, 1965; second revised edition, 1967).

NOTES TO CHAPTER 2, pp. 9–31

1 *Prose*, p. 79.
2 Osip Mandelstam, 'Zapisnye knizhki. Zametki' (Notebooks and Notes), *VL*, 4 (1968), 184.

3 Translated in *Prose*, pp. 67–132.

4 Published annually in St Petersburg by A. S. Suvorin, this is an invaluable guide to the life of the imperial Russian capital. The Mandelstams' address in 1909 was No. 5 Kolomenskaya Street.

5 Yury Trubetskoy, *Mosty* (Bridges), 2 (1959), 415.

6 *Prose*, pp. 90f.

7 *Prose*, p. 90.

8 *Sobranie sochinenii* (Collected Works) (edited by Gleb Struve and Boris Filippov-Filistinsky, New York: Chekhov Publishing House, 1955), p. 5.

9 Georgy Ivanov, *NZh*, 43 (1955), 281.

10 Georgy Ivanov, *Peterburgskie zimy* (Petersburg Winters) (New York, 1952).

11 Sergey Makovsky, *Na Parnase 'Serebrianogo veka'* (On the Parnassus of the 'Silver Age') (Munich, 1962), p. 230.

12 Vladislav Khodasevich, *Literaturnye stat'i i vospominaniia* (Literary Articles and Recollections) (New York, 1954), pp. 151–8.

13 Irina Odoevtseva, *Na beregakh Nevy* (On the Banks of the Neva) (Washington: Victor Kamkin, 1967). The citations that follow are from the original journal publication.

14 *Prose*, p. 82.

15 *Prose*, p. 90. One of Mandelstam's relatives on his mother's side was the famous literary historian and bibliographer S. A. Vengerov.

16 *Prose*, p. 76.

17 *Prose*, p. 80.

18 *Prose*, p. 92.

19 *Prose*, p. 89.

20 *Prose*, pp. 81–2.

21 *Prose*, p. 79.

22 My translation of this appeared in the *Hudson Review* (April 1970) and in Michael Scammell (ed.), *Russia's Other Writers* (London, 1970).

23 See p. 35.

24 It is nearly pointless to be overly nice about some of the exact dates in Mandelstam's early life. The records might some day become available, but until they do one has to be content with informed conjecture. The Tenishev School had eight grades divided into two 'semesters' each. Viktor Zhirmunsky, a schoolfellow of Mandelstam's, told me that the poet had finished in 1907, when he was sixteen. Assuming that he entered the school in the first-year class, we arrive at 1899 as the year of his matriculation.

25 The latest version of this constantly evolving book is Vladimir Nabokov, *Speak, Memory: An autobiography revisited* (New York, 1966).

26 *Prose*, p. 100.

27 *Ibid.*

28 *Prose*, pp. 100–1.

29 *Prose*, p. 100.

30 *Prose*, p. 111.

31 B. P. Kozmin, *Pisateli sovremennoi epokhi* (Writers of the Modern Age) (Moscow, 1928), p. 178.

32 *Prose*, p. 109.

33 *Prose*, p. 112.

34 *Prose*, p. 116.

35 Years later Mandelstam was to depict the event as a kind of religious mystery-play. See p. 96.

36 *Prose*, p. 109.

37 *Prose*, p. 103.

38 *Prose*, pp. 105f.

39 Vladimir Vasilevich Gippius (1876–1941) was evidently the most important teacher in the Tenishev School for Mandelstam, and for others as well. See Mandelstam's letter to him, p. 35. He is the only teacher mentioned by Nabokov ('the spirited V. V. Gippius, one of the pillars of the school, a rather unusual red-haired man...', *Drugie berega* [Other Shores] (New York, 1954), p. 170. The mention occurs only in this Russian version of Nabokov's autobiography). Mandelstam devoted one of the longest character studies in *The Noise of Time* to his literary mentor, whose person embodies the poet's earliest conception of Russian literature just as Sergey Ivanych represented the revolution of 1905. Paradoxically, the love of literature was nurtured in his students by a man who hated literature, who saw in the length and breadth of its history an ample field for the spitefulness of his nature, whose own shaggy and unshaven presence was the embodiment of the feral and forever untamable element in the product of man's imagination. There is something bestial about the portrait of Gippius, though it is not unkind. Mandelstam depicts him as an unmanageable, slightly dangerous creature of alarmingly asocial habits who did not so much reside as hibernate in his lair-like rooms. That the picture is overdone cannot be denied (though in many respects it tallies with other recollections of Gippius, such as those in Bryusov's diaries), but a strictly human scale could hardly be preserved in figures who bear a so much larger than human significance. Gippius was the friend of Konevskoy and Dobrolyubov, those 'belligerent young monks of early Symbolism,' and he himself wrote verse under the pen-names of V. Bestuzhev and V. Neledinsky. He is the author of *Pushkin i khristianstvo* (Pushkin and Christianity) (Petersburg, 1915).

40 I am much indebted to the late Professor Zhirmunsky for alerting me to the existence of these school journals and for sharing with me his memories of Mandelstam. Y. M. Tager's memoir of Mandelstam in *NZh*, 81 (1965), 174, also contains a rare glimpse of Zhirmunsky as a schoolboy.

NOTES TO CHAPTER 3, pp. 32–52

1 Mikhail Karpovich, 'Moe znakomstvo s Mandel'shtamom,' *NZh*, 49 (1957), 258–61.

2 Since this was written the letter has appeared in Russian in *Vestnik*, 97 (1970) and in vol. II (1971).

3 These works of Mandelstam have never come to light.

4 The poems were first published in *Vestnik*, 97 (1970) and the letters in vol. II, 485–91, of the New York edition. The latter has enabled me to fill lacunae in my copies wherever foreign phrases and names in Roman script occurred, but I have often added information that was apparently unavailable to the editors of vol. II and made corrections where the reading of my versions seemed more accurate.

5 Akhmatova, II, 168–9.
6 The date as given in vol. II, 485, is wrong, in spite of the note on p. 679.
7 The book was Ivanov's *Po zvezdam* (By the Stars, 1909).
8 *Ostrov*: a poetry journal edited by Alexey Tolstoy and Nikolay Gumilyov. Only a few numbers appeared in 1909.
9 *Kormchie zvezdy* (Pilot Stars): Ivanov's first collection of poems (1901; second edition 1903).
10 The other two poems sent to Ivanov at this time were 'Ty ulybaesh'ia komu' (To whom are you smiling) and 'V prostorakh sumerechnoi zaly' (In the expanses of the twilit hall), both published in *Vestnik*, 97 (1970), 107–8, and in vol. II, 447.
11 Vladimir Pyast, *Gaudeamus*, nos. 4–5 (1911).
12 Vladimir Pyast, *Vstrechi* (Meetings) (1929), pp. 139–41.
13 The poems were 'V kholodnykh perelivakh lir' (In the cold playing of the lyres), 'Besshumnoe vereteno' (The silent spindle), 'Tvoia veselaia nezhnost'' (Your merry tenderness), 'Ne govorite mne o vechnosti' (Do not talk to me about eternity), and 'Ozareny lunoi nochev'ia' (Lit by the moon are the night lodgings). When these appeared in the above-mentioned issue of *Vestnik* the last stanza of the first poem was erroneously printed as a separate poem, an error repeated in vol. II, 449.
14 In vol. II, 445, these two versions are erroneously printed as if they were a single poem of six stanzas.
15 Sergey Makovsky, *Portrety sovremennikov* (Portraits of Contemporaries) (New York, 1955), pp. 377–98.
16 Akhmatova had alerted Mandelstam himself to such memoirs as early as February 1926. See his letter no. 15, vol. III, 209.
17 *Hope*, pp. 175–6.
18 *Hope*, p. 247.
19 Gleb Struve has exhaustively catalogued the Italian images in Mandelstam's poetry and shown how persistently they occur in the poems of every period. Especially valuable, for instance, is Struve's demonstration of how two lines in No. 69 – 'Prav narod, vruchivshii posokh / Mne, uvidevshemu Rim!' (The people are right to give the staff / to me, who have seen Rome!) – are actually meant to be understood as spoken by the philosopher Pyotr Chaadaev. A citation from Mandelstam's 1915 essay on Chaadaev is conclusive on this point. See Gleb Struve, 'Ital'ianskie obrazy i motivy v poezii Osipa Mandel'-shtama' (Italian images and motifs in the poetry of Osip Mandelstam) in *Studi in onore di Ettore Lo Gatto e Giovanni Maver* (Rome, 1962).
20 Vol. III, 197.
21 Steinberg told me that he had been 'cursed by God with a perfect memory,' and the contents of that memory are truly remarkable. He managed, for instance, to be acquainted with Suslova, the wife of Dostoevsky, married then to the philosopher V. Rozanov, who called her 'Mama.' Steinberg was a founder, along with Andrey Bely and R. V. Ivanov-Razumnik, of the Volnaya Filosofskaya Assotsiatsiya (Free Philosophical Association) and was closely acquainted with Blok, with whom he shared the peculiar experience of spending a night together on the same plank bed of a Cheka prison. Blok had been detained for his association with the Left SRs (see

The Memoirs of Ivanov-Razumnik, translated by P. S. Squire (London, 1965), pp. 24f.). Blok called him the 'Marburg philosopher,' quoting the sobriquet given to Steinberg by Andrey Bely in a poem entitled 'Moi drug' (My Friend, 1908). See Alexandr Blok, *Sobranie sochinenii* (Collected Works), VII (Moscow, 1963), 319 and n. 12, p. 506 A gentle man of exquisite courtesy, Steinberg answered my question about Blok's attitude toward Mandelstam with extreme reluctance, for the traces of anti-Semitism in that great poet's nature were still painful for him to contemplate.

22 Vol. II, 507.
23 Konstantin Mochulsky, *Vstrecha* (Meeting), 2 (1945), 30–1
24 The reference is to the famous phrase in the Futurist Manifesto of 1912 to the effect that Pushkin, Dostoevsky, Tolstoy, etc., etc., should be thrown overboard from the ship of modernity.
25 Mikhail Karpovich, *NZh*, 49 (1957), 261.
26 Georgy Adamovich, *VP*, II (1961), 95.
27 Yury Ofrosimov, *Novoe russkoe slovo* (New Russian Word), 13 December 1953. The Russian for 'Goldtooth' (Zlatozub) recalls both the name for St John Chrysostom (Zlatoust) and the famous character Skalozub from Griboedov's comedy *Gore ot uma* (Woe From Wit).
28 Rabinovich, *VP*, III (1963), 24–5. The other comic poems furnished by Rabinovich can be found in the New York edition as Nos. 416, 417, and 421.
29 Leonid Strakhovsky, *Craftsmen of the Word: Three Poets of Modern Russia* (Cambridge, Mass., 1949).
30 See D. Tschizewskij (ed.), *Russische literarische Parodien* (Wiesbaden, 1957), p. 66.
31 Viktor Shklovsky, *Sentimental'noe puteshestvie* (A Sentimental Journey) (Moscow–Berlin, 1923), p. 334. Renato Poggioli, *The Poets of Russia* (Cambridge, Mass., 1960), p. 309, wrongly attributes this to Shklovsky himself.
32 Vladislav Khodasevich, *Literary Articles*, p. 408.
33 Irina Odoevtseva, *NZh*, 71 (1963), 36.
34 Vsevolod Rozhdestvensky, *Zvezda* (Star), 12 (1958), 122. When Rozhdestvensky's memoirs appeared in book form as *Stranltsy zhizni* (Pages of Life) (Moscow, 1962), Mandelstam was finally identified by name on p. 129.
35 Em. Mindlin, *Neobyknovennye sobesedniki* (Unusual People to Talk To) (Moscow, 1968), pp. 77–95.
36 *Hope*, p. 306.
37 Vol. II, opp. p. 176.

NOTES TO CHAPTER 4, pp. 53–68

1 Vol. II, 233–40.
2 V. Kaverin, 'Kak ia ne stal poetom,' *Oktiabr* (October), 10 (1959), 131.
3 Vol. II, 414f.
4 Vol. II, 301–9; and see p. 151.
5 Blok, *Sobranie sochinenii*, v (Moscow, 1962), 756f.
6 *Ibid.* p. 427.
7 On Futurism, see Vladimir Markov, *The Longer Poems of Velimir Khlebnikov*

(1962) and *Russian Futurism: A history* (1968), both published by the University of California Press, Berkeley.

8 Akhmatova, II, 173f.

9 A facsimile edition of *Kamen'* was published by Ardis Publishers, Ann Arbor, Michigan, 1971.

10 Akhmatova, II, 167.

11 These and other facts on her life can be found in Gleb Struve's note on her in *NZh*, 81 (1965), 172–4.

12 Nikolay Gumilyov, *Sobranie sochinenii* (Collected Works), IV (Washington, 1968), 326–8.

13 Pasternak refers to several articles in which Mandelstam had praised his poetry. These were two entitled 'Literaturnaia Moskva' (Literary Moscow), published in *Rossiia* (Russia), nos. 2 and 3 (1922); 'Boris Pasternak' in *Russia*, 6 (1963); and 'Buria i natisk' (Storm and Stress) in *Russkoe iskusstvo* (Russian Art), 1 (1923). In the latter Mandelstam says of Pasternak's collection *Sestra moia zhizn'* (My Sister Life): 'Not since Batyushkov has such a new and mature harmony sounded in Russian poetry.' All of these have now been reprinted in vol. II. For my English translation of 'Storm and Stress,' see *Russian Literature Triquarterly*, no. 1 (1971).

14 Vol. III, 195.

15 Vol. II, 320–5. For a translation of this see p. 143.

16 For an excellent study of Tsvetaeva see Simon Karlinsky, *Marina Cvetaeva: Her life and art* (Berkeley, Calif., 1966).

17 Marc Slonim, *Oxford Slavonic Papers*, XI (1964), 112–36. Reprinted in the New York edition, vol. III, 306–44.

18 The poet Maximilian Voloshin, who with his mother (Pra), kept a famously hospitable villa in Koktebel. Karadag is a mountain in the Crimea.

19 See *Mosty* (Bridges), V (1960), 316.

20 This remark is omitted from the version printed in Akhmatova, II, 166.

21 Vol. II, 327f.

NOTES TO CHAPTER 5, pp. 69–84

1 Yelena Tager, *NZh*, 81 (1965), 184f.

2 See n. 31 to Chap. 2.

3 Artur Lourié, *VP*, III (1963), 169f.

4 Gumilyov, *Works*, II (Washington, 1964), 60–2. Irina Odoevtseva, who claims to have witnessed the very scene, adds other details in her memoir *Na beregakh Nevy* (On the Banks of the Neva), *NZh*, 72 (1963), 81f.

5 Sheila Fitzpatrick, *The Commissariat of Enlightenment: Soviet organization of education and the arts under Lunacharsky* (London, 1970).

6 *Hope*, p. 104.

7 See Mandelstam's letter to V. Ya. Khazina, his mother-in-law: vol. III, 199.

8 *Hope*, pp. 105f.

9 Felix Dzerzhinsky, in *Iz istorii Vserossiiskoi Chrezvychainoi Komissii* (From the History of the All-Russian Extraordinary Commission) *1917–1921*, ed. by G. Belov and others (Moscow, 1958), pp. 151–5.

10 Larisa Mikhaylovna Reysner (1897–1928), a great heroine of the Revolution,

was the wife of the Raskolnikov (Fyodor Fyodorovich, 1892–1939), Deputy People's Commissar of the Navy, mentioned by Dzerzhinsky. A woman with literary ambitions, she was devoted to Mandelstam's poetry, though not to intellectuals generally. Nadezhda Yakovlevna devotes a fascinating chapter to her, *Hope*, pp. 108–12.

11 See Gustav Hilger and Alfred G. Meyer, *The Incompatible Allies* (New York, 1951), pp. 2–6.

12 *Hope*, pp. 101f.

13 Igor Stravinsky and Robert Craft, *Retrospectives and Conclusions* (New York, 1969), p. 237. Yevtushenko 'topped' this story, in Craft's curious phrase, with an account of Mandelstam's death 'drowned by bread, literally choking on it; his dying request was for *Russian* bread.' Craft claims the italics; for Yevtushenko's sake, one might wish him to claim it all.

14 Yury Terapiano, *Vstrechi* (Meetings) (New York, 1953).

15 Vol. III, 197f.

16 My translation of the four chapters that constitute 'Feodosiia' may be found in *Prose*.

17 Mikhail Mabo, 'O Maximiliane Voloshine, Mandel'shtame i drugikh' (About Maximilian Voloshin, Mandelstam, and Others), *Novoe russkoe slovo* (New Russian Word), 14 January 1949. I should also like to record my indebtedness to Mr Mabo for an interview that I had with him in Freehold, New Jersey, shortly before his death in the spring of 1961.

18 Ilya Ehrenburg, *Liudi, gody, zhizn'* (People, Years, Life) (Moscow, 1961), pp. 495–6.

19 Vol. II, 195–200. Originally in *Ogonek* (12 August 1923). A variant, possibly an early draft of this article, appears in vol. III, 20–4, under the title *Vozvrashchenie* (Return).

20 Ehrenburg, *Liudi*, pp. 508f., gives a version of this story which he heard from Mandelstam. According to Ehrenburg, his release was secured by certain Georgian poets who happened to come to Batum and read in a newspaper that 'the double agent Osip Mandelstam had claimed to be a poet.'

21 Yashvili and Tabidze were close friends of Boris Pasternak, who has left a touching memoir of them in his *Avtobiograficheskii ocherk* (Autobiographical Sketch). See his *Proza* (Prose) *1915–1958* (Ann Arbor, 1961), pp. 48–52. Yashvili and Tabidze were inseparable companions who had grown up together and gone to school together (to the same Gymnasium attended by Mayakovsky). Their dates are identical: 1895–1937. The last year speaks eloquently of a fate to which neither Pasternak nor Ehrenburg could ever directly allude. Tabidze was arrested and vanished; Yashvili, when they came for him, shot himself dead with a rifle.

22 See *Russkaia kniga* (Russian Book), 1 (1921), 25.

23 Yadviga was Ehrenburg's daughter.

NOTES TO CHAPTER 6, pp. 85–98

1 Ehrenburg, *Liudi, gody, zhizn'* (People, Years, Life), p. 523.

2 The journal *Vestnik literary* (Messenger of Literature), 4–5 (1921), 22, listed Mandelstam along with 73 other writers and intellectuals entitled to the 'academic ration' of KUBU (Committee for Improving the Living Conditions of Scholars).

3 Olga Forsh, *Sumasshedshii korabl'* (The Insane Ship), p. 523 (Leningrad, 1931; reprinted, with an introduction by Boris Filippov, Washington, D.C., 1964).

4 Viktor Shklovsky, *Sentimental'noe puteshestvie* (A Sentimental Journey) (Moscow–Berlin, 1923), p. 335.

5 He confused *zhaba* 'toad' with *zhabo* 'jabot.' Nadezhda Pavlovich, 'Vospominaniia ob Aleksandre Bloke' (Memoirs of Alexandr Blok), in *Blokovskii sbornik. Trudy nauchnoi konferentsii, posviashchennoi izucheniiu zhizni i tvorchestva A. A. Bloka* (Blok Collection: Papers of the conference devoted to the study of A. A. Blok's life and work), Tartu, 1964, p. 493. Nadezhda Pavlovich has also described the same masked ball in a poem, two stanzas of which are devoted to Mandelstam. See her *Dumy i vosopominaniia* (Thoughts and Recollections) (Moscow, 1962), pp. 34f.

6 Blok, *Works*, VII, 371.

7 Pavlovich, *Memoirs*, p. 472.

8 Olga Arbenina later married Yury Yurkun, who perished in 1938. She herself was still alive as these words were being written.

9 See pp. 245ff.

10 Vladislav Khodasevich, *Nekropol'* (Necropolis) (Brussels, 1939), p. 128.

11 Adamovich, *VP*, II (1961), 93.

12 Akhmatova, II (1968), 176.

13 Vol. III, 255f.

14 Vol. III, 199. The letter was written in May or June of 1921.

15 *Hope*, p. 27.

16 Vol. I, 557.

17 In his article 'Batum' Mandelstam describes the workings of Tsentrosoiuz. See vol. III, 14.

18 Blok died in the same month as Gumilyov, on 7 August 1921.

19 Vol. III, 11–19.

20 Vol. III, 128–32.

21 Vol. III, 31–5.

22 In *Rossiia* (1 (1922), 28–9) the title was 'Alexandr Blok (7 August 1921–7 August 1922)' but when it was reprinted in altered form in the collection *O poezii* (On Poetry, 1928) the essay was entitled 'Barsuch'ia nora' (The Badger's Lair). See vol. II, 270–5.

23 Vol. III, 36–9.

24 Georgy Margvelashvili, *Literaturnaia Gruziia* (Literary Georgia), 1 (1967), 92.

25 Vol. II, 241–59. I also discuss this on pp. 153ff.

NOTES TO CHAPTER 7, pp. 99–120

1 Sergey Bobrov, *Pechat' i revoliutsiia* (Press and Revolution), 4 (1923), 259–62.
2 See Mandelstam's letter to his father, vol. III, 200, and also *Hope*, pp. 115ff.
3 Vol. III, 201.
4 Vol. II, 352–4.
5 Vol. II, 339–51. My English translation of this essay appeared in *Russian Literature Triquarterly*, 1 (1971), 154–62.
6 Akhmatova, II, 185.
7 Both were entitled 'Literaturnaia Moskva' (Literary Moscow), the second being subtitled 'Rozhdenie fabuly' (Birth of the Plot). They appeared, respectively, in the second and third issues of *Rossiia* (Russia) for 1922.
8 The first, subtitled 'I ikh sotni tysiach' (And their hundreds of thousands), appeared in *Ogonek*, no. 33 (11 November 1923); the second – 'Kto zhe oni takie?' (Who are They?) – in no. 34 (18 November 1923). See vol. II, 208–16.
9 Blok, *Works*, VI (Moscow–Leningrad, 1962), 168.
10 V. Kaverin, *Oktiabr* (October), 10 (1959), 131.
11 Nikolay Chukovsky, 'Vstrechi s Mandel'shtamom' (Meetings with Mandelstam), *Moskva* (Moscow), 8 (1964), 143–52.
12 Valery Bryusov, *Press and Revolution*, 6 (1923), 63–6.
13 *Hope*, p. 154.
14 Another reason for quoting the poem in full is to give some prominence to Mandelstam's final version of it, which differs from the version adopted by the editors of the New York edition. In an emendation dated '29/III–37' – and dating a poem or a change was for him always a significant act – he cancelled the last stanza and wrote the version given here.
15 *Hope*, p. 178.

CHAPTER 8, pp. 121–134

[*no notes*]

NOTES TO CHAPTER 9, pp. 135–158

1 Akhmatova, II, 185.
2 Sam Driver, 'Acmeism', *Slavic and East European Journal*, 2 (1968), 141–56; Howard William Chalsma, 'Russian Acmeism: Its history, doctrine and poetry', unpublished diss. (Univ. of Washington, 1967).
3 Gumilyov, *Works*, IV, 541.
4 Quoted from Robert H. Ross, *The Georgian Revolt, 1910–1922: Rise and fall of a poetic ideal* (Carbondale and Edwardsville, Ill., 1965), p. 248.
5 See *The Education of Henry Adams* (New York, 1931), p. 388.
6 Bely's account of the origin of the name in *Nachalo veka* (Beginning of the Century) (Moscow–Leningrad, 1933), p. 324, suggests that 'Adamism' was also his invention: 'Vyacheslav [Ivanov] once suggested with a wink that I make up a platform for Gumilyov: "You attack the Symbolists but you have no firm position of your own! So, Boris, make up a program for

Nikolay Stepanovich..." As a joke I proposed that Gumilyov create "Adamism" and proceeded in a parodying way to develop the platform that I had thought up. Vyacheslav joined in and added his own touches. Somehow the word *akme* "point" cropped up: "You Adams have got to be sharp." Gumilyov, keeping his composure, crossed his legs and said, "Splendid! You've made up a platform for me – against you. I'll show you what 'Acmeism' is!"'

Incidentally, it is curious to note the resemblance between the origin of this name for a rather fugitive Russian group and that for a literary movement of incomparably grander scale, Romanticism itself. In the second volume of his *History of Modern Criticism* (New Haven, Conn., 1955, p. 1) René Wellek writes that Achim von Arnim and Clemens Brentano took up the term in 1808 from a work by Jens Baggesen that was intended as a parody of them.

7 Gumilyov, *Works*, IV, 599.

8 Vol. II, 362–7.

9 As the editors of the New York edition point out in their commentary (vol. II, 582–3), this did not prevent critics from seeing Mandelstam as merely another Futurist theoretician.

10 Cf. *Razgovor o Dante* (Talking About Dante) (Moscow, 1967), p. 18: 'Every word is a bundle and the meaning sticks out of it in various directions, not striving toward any one official point.'

11 See also pp. 108–10.

12 Much later – in another book.

13 The word 'derivative' translates the Russian *proizvodnyi*, which is the reading of both the 1922 and the 1928 editions. In the New York edition *proizvol'nyi* 'arbitrary' is an error.

14 See Auden's essay 'The Poet and the City' in *The Dyer's Hand* (New York, 1968).

15 In an article on the poet Eduard Bagritsky, written after he had returned to Soviet Russia, the great literary historian D. S. Mirsky comments that only Narbut and Zenkevich actually fulfilled what he took to be the program of Acmeism, and they became Soviet poets. See *Literaturnaia ucheba* (Literary Education), 5 (1934), 34f.

NOTES TO CHAPTER 10, pp. 159–206

1 Some of the other meanings of *rakovina* are considerably dowdier – 'lavatory sink' for instance – and might have been disqualifying enough in 1913.

2 Max Vasmer does not associate the word *rakovina* 'shell' with *rak* 'crawfish' in his *Russisches etymologisches Wörterbuch* (Heidelberg, 1950–8), though Roman Jakobson, in his notes on Vasmer, does (*IJSLP*, 1–2 (1959), 267).

3 The meter of this poem has been much commented upon by Russian metrists, some of whom have ingeniously striven to accommodate it within the traditional schemes of their native prosody. American readers of my own generation might (or might not) wish to be reminded that this is the beat of a popular tune of the 1940s called 'Chattanooga Choo-Choo.'

4 Marina Tsvetaeva, *Ruski Arhiv* (Beograd), XXVI–XXVII (1934), 115.

5 The review of the 1913 edition appears in *Apollon*, 1–2 (1914), 122–30 and in Gumilyov, *Works*, IV, 326–8; that of the 1916 edition in *Apollon*, 1 (1916), 26–32, and in Gumilyov, *ibid.*, 363–6.

6 Vol. II, 306.

7 In a seminar on Acmeism which I conducted at Princeton Mr John Malmstad kindly drew my attention to the fact that this poem seems in some sense an answer to a poem by Bely, of whose poetry he has made an edition. It is the poem in *Urna* (The Urn) entitled 'Vstrecha' (The Meeting), the last of a four-part cycle addressed to Bryusov. I believe that Malmstad is right, regret my inability to pursue the full argument here, and urge interested readers to consider his valuable discovery.

8 See Chap. 2 above.

9 Vol. II, 150.

10 Since this has sometimes been translated as though the line meant 'bathed in peace' (e.g. *Penguin Book of Russian Verse*, p. 351; *Russian Literature Triquarterly*, 2 (1972), 189) it is worth noting that Mandelstam spelled the word мір 'world' before the reform of Russian orthography caused it to be written like its homophone мир 'peace.'

11 In 'The Admiralty' (No. 48) the primary significance of *lad'ia* is of course 'boat,' but since the word also means the tower-shaped chessman, the rook, whose power extends down long vistas on the board, it seems to me that this meaning cannot be left out of account.

12 The date given for No. 47 is that on the MS in Pushkinsky Dom, Leningrad. In the last published version (*Poems*, 1928), the last line is missing. But in the copy of that book belonging to N. E. Shtempel, the last line as given here was inserted by Mandelstam and dated '2/I/37. V[oronezh].'

13 A full understanding of the 'Ode to Beethoven' depends, I think, upon a reading of the fragments of Mandelstam's article 'Pushkin and Scriabin' (vol. II, 313–19), which must have been written at about the same time (Scriabin died in 1915) and has numerous verbal reminiscences of and a direct quotation from this poem. Reference should also be made to that text of the poem which has all the blank lines filled and appeared in the 1916 edition of *Stone*.

NOTES TO CHAPTER 11, pp. 207–218

1 This is the reading of *Stone* 1916 and 1923, though not, unfortunately, of the New York edition, where the variant goes unrecorded. Georgy Adamovich, *VP*, V (1967), 105, writes that he always heard the poem recited with *dushi* (rather than *dusha*) here and *zovushchii* 'calling' (rather than *zloveshchii* 'dire') in the line preceding. But there is no other evidence for the latter reading.

2 Mentioned by G. Ivask in his Introduction to vol. III of the New York edition. In the same volume the editors supply a lengthy discussion of the image of the black sun in literature.

NOTES TO CHAPTER 12, pp. 219–252

1 In the New York edition the episode occurs on pp. 48–9. In my English translation (*Prose*, 2nd edn, 1967), it is on p. 157.

2 An untranslatable Russian word for which 'collective,' 'conciliar,' 'pandemic' and so on, are pallid substitutes. It derives from the Slavophil philosopher A. S. Khomyakov (1804–60), who used it to indicate the principle of loving togetherness that bound the Orthodox Church and contrasted it to the authoritarianism of Catholicism and the individuality of Protestantism.

3 It is typical of Mandelstam that this phrase is practically repeated in the poem 'The Horseshoe Finder' (No. 136, line 55), written in 1923.

4 Vladimir Pyast did not fail to use the word 'sarcophagus,' either, in the second of the three poems that he wrote in 1912–13 on the theme of Poe's *Ligeia*. See his *L'vinaia past'* (Lion's Mouth) (Berlin–Petersburg–Moscow, 1922, p. 25).

5 The late Nikolay Chukovsky, who published an account of his encounters with Mandelstam in the journal *Moskva*, 8 (1965), 145, was quite wrong in asserting that the room described in the poem is the one occupied by the poet in the *Dom Uchenykh* (House of Scholars). If Mrs Halpern's testimony – and also, incidentally, that of Anna Akhmatova – were not enough, there would still be the matter of chronology. The poem is dated 1916; Mandelstam lived in the House of Scholars some three or four years after the Revolution.

6 I should add that when I suggested some of this to Nadezhda Yakovlevna in the abbreviated form of a letter, she replied that she regards No. 118 as having nothing at all to do with Arbenina. She says that it was written before Mandelstam's attraction to the actress. It still seems possible to me, however, that the poet, when he looked back at these poems from the standpoint of 1928, might easily have associated this poem with those so near to it in time.

7 Victor Terras, 'Classical Motives in the Poetry of Osip Mandelstam,' *SEEJ*, 3 (1966), 251–67. No. 119 is discussed on pp. 261f.

8 The New York edition unfortunately ignores two textual emendations in No. 119, though Mandelstam introduced them in *Second Book* and retained them in *Poems*. In line 4, for *plakuchie* read *pakhuchie*. In line 6, for *vgryzaiutsia* read *vrezaiutsia*. Note, incidentally, the conjunction of *pakhuchii* and *srub* in line 4 of No. 195 (*Akter i rabochii*, 'The Actor and the Worker').

NOTES TO CHAPTER 13, pp. 253–275

1 Terras, *SEEJ*, 3 (1966), 251–67. No one interested in the subject of this chapter can afford to ignore this article by Terras. Cf. especially his discussion of the following poems: 62, 70, 78, 79, 80, 92, 93, 104, 112, 113, 116, 119, and with the poem numbers of 1967 in brackets, 325 [356], 351 [383], 354 [387], 355 [385]. See also Struve, 'Ital'ianskie obrazy i motivy v poezii Osipa Mandel'shtama' (Italian images and motives in the poetry of Osip Mandelstam), pp. 601–14.

2 Terras, *SEEJ*, 3 (1966), 243.

3 *Ibid.*, p. 254.

4 Boris Bukhshtab's essay 'Poeziia Mandel'shtama' (The Poetry of Mandelstam) has not been published. My English translation of it appeared in *Russian Literature Triquarterly*, 1 (1971), 262–82.

5 From Tsvetaeva's letter dated 5–6 September 1923 to A. Bakhrakh: see *Mosty*, 6 (1961), 329.

6 See the discussion of Pushkin in connection with the analysis of No. 118 in Chap. 12.

7 Nos. 51 and 52.

8 No. 60. This poem contains, incidentally, one of the rare Ovidian allusions not cited by Terras. The last stanza reads

> Когда, с дряхлеющей любовью
> Мешая в песнях Рим и снег,
> Овидий пел арбу воловью
> В походе варварских телег.

> When with waning love
> in songs mingling Rome and the snow
> Ovid sang the ox-drawn cart
> in the barbaric wagon train.

and is based upon Ovid, *Tristia*, III, 10_{33-34}

> perque novos pontes, subter labentibus undis,
> ducunt Sarmatici barbara plaustra boves.

9 *Sic*. Specialists will regret 'tonic' where 'quantitative' is evidently meant.

10 See Omry Ronen, 'Mandelstam's *Kashchei*,' in *Studies Presented to Professor Roman Jakobson by his Students* (Cambridge, Mass., 1968), p. 252.

11 Vol. I, 443.

12 This is the only variant that exactly reproduces the phrase as it occurs in 'The Admiralty' (No. 48), that is, with 'water' and 'sky' in the dative case.

13 The Old Orthography of the 1922 edition has been modernized.

14 In his article 'Ship Metaphors in Mandelstam's Poetry,' in *To Honor Roman Jakobson. Essay on the Occasion of his Seventieth Birthday*, II (The Hague: Mouton, 1967), 1441, Nils Ake Nilsson does not translate the poem, but it is evident that he has read it in the same way: 'In *The Admiralty*, *vode i nebu brat* was used of a building; here it refers to a star.' It should be noted that the masculine *brat* 'brother' would be an awkward poetic image for the feminine *zvezda* 'star.'

15 Except for the first vowel and the stress, the Russian for 'spectral' is the same as that for 'transparent.'

16 Akhmatova, II, 174.

17 She was born Vera de Bosset in 1892. For a recent article about Mme Stravinsky see the *Saturday Review* for 26 February 1972.

18 D. M. Segal, 'Nabliudeniia nad semanticheskoi strukturoi poeticheskogo proizvedeniia' (Observations on the semantic structure of a poetic work), *International Journal of Slavic Linguistics and Poetics*, XI (1968), 159–71.

19 See Chap. 14, p. 285.

20 Terras, *SEEJ*, 3 (1966), 258.

21 *Zvezda* (Star), 9 (1961), 199.
22 Terras, *SEEJ*, 3 (1966), 259–60.
23 Akhmatova, I, 55. See Mandelstam, Vol. I, 444.
24 Pyast, *Vstrechi*, p. 156.

NOTES TO CHAPTER 14, pp. 276–296

1 See Vol. I, 484.
2 See p. 122.
3 Vol. II, 260.
4 One need hardly point out that what Mandelstam means by 'root' has no necessary relation to what linguists mean when using the term technically.
5 This verb has two meanings: (1) To pronounce 'ts' where the literary language has 'ch' – as in certain North Russian dialects; (2) to produce a clanging noise, as of metal striking stone.
6 *Razgovor o Dante* (Talking About Dante), vol. II, 382. The English translation by Robert Hughes and myself appeared in *Delos*, 6 (1971); this passage is on p. 81.
7 The classic exposition of the way Russian poets employ such consonantal sequences is that by the great Formalist critic and theoretician Osip Brik; see his essay 'Zvukovye povtory' (Sound Repetends), *Poetika* (Petrograd, 1919); reprinted in *Michigan Slavic Materials*, no. 5 (Ann Arbor, 1964).
8 *Sherst'* means the hair that grows on an animal's back and is therefore 'hair, fur, wool, coat,' etc., according to context.
9 The last consonant of *ezh* is pronounced unvoiced, as if spelt *sh*.
10 The words 'flute' and 'backbone' inevitably make this poem a relative in some degree of Vladimir Mayakovsky's poem 'Fleita pozvonochnik' (The Backbone Flute, 1915).

Bibliography

This selected bibliography lists the collected editions and the individual books of Mandelstam, and the works cited in the present volume. A full bibliography of works by and about Mandelstam will be found in vol. III of the 1964–1971 collection. Except where noted, I cite the texts of Mandelstam from vol. I, second edition, vol. II, second edition, and vol. III of that collection, referred to throughout in the preceding pages as the New York edition. For a discussion of Mandelstam's books of poems, see also the beginning of Chap. 10.

THE WORKS OF OSIP MANDELSTAM

COLLECTED WORKS

Sobranie sochinenii (Collected Works). Edited and introduced by Gleb Struve and Boris Filippov. New York: Chekhov Publishing House, 1955.

Sobranie sochinenii (Collected Works), 3 vols. Edited by Gleb Struve and Boris Filippov. New York: Inter-Language Literary Associates, 1964–1971.

   vol. I (Poetry). Introductions by Clarence Brown, Gleb Struve, and E. M. Rais, 1964. Second edition, revised and expanded, 1967.

   vol. II (Prose). Introduction by Boris Filippov. 1966. Second edition, revised and expanded, 1971.

   vol. III (Essays and Letters). Introductions by George Ivask, Nikita Struve, and Boris Filippov. 1969.

SEPARATE WORKS

POETRY

Kamen' (Stone). St Petersburg: Akme, 1913. Facsimile edition, Ann Arbor, Michigan: Ardis Publishers, 1971.

   Second edition, Petrograd: Giperborei, 1916.

   Third edition, with the subtitle 'First Book of Poems,' Moscow–Petrograd: GIZ (State Publishing House), 1923.

Tristia. Petersburg–Berlin, 1922. (The date on the cover is 1921.) Facsimile edition, Ann Arbor, Michigan: Ardis Publishers, 1972.

Vtoraia kniga (Second Book). Moscow–Petrograd: Krug, 1923.

Primus. Poems for children. Leningrad: Vremia, 1925.

Dva tramvaia (Two Streetcars). Poems for children. Leningrad: GIZ (State Publishing House), 1925.

311

Bibliography

Shary (Balloons). Poems for children. Leningrad: GIZ, 1926.
Kukhnia (The Kitchen). Poems for children. Leningrad: Raduga, 1926.
Stikhotvoreniia (Poems). Moscow–Leningrad: GIZ, 1928.

PROSE

Shum vremeni (The Noise of Time). Leningrad: Vremia, 1925.
Egipetskaia marka (The Egyptian Stamp). Leningrad: Priboi, 1928. (Includes the preceding. Translated by Clarence Brown under the title *The Prose of Osip Mandelstam*. Princeton, 1965; second edition, revised, 1967.)

CRITICISM

O prirode slova (On the Nature of the Word). Kharkov: Istoki, 1922.
O poezii (On Poetry). Essays. Leningrad: Academia, 1928. (Includes preceding.)
Razgovor o Dante (A Conversation About Dante). Afterword by L. E. Pinsky. Edited with commentary by A. A. Morozov. Moscow: Iskusstvo, 1967. (Translated by Clarence Brown and Robert Hughes under the title 'Talking about Dante.' *Books Abroad* (May 1965); revised translation, *Delos*, no. 6 (1971).)

WORKS CITED

Adamovich, Georgy, 'Moi vstrechi s Akhmatovoi,' *VP*, v (1967), 99–114.
  'Neskol'ko slov o Mandel'shtame', *VP*, II (1961), 87–101.
Adams, Henry, *The Education of Henry Adams*. New York, 1931.
Auden, W. H., *The Dyer's Hand*. New York, 1968.
Belov, G. *et al.* (eds.), *Iz istorii Vserossiiskoi Chrezvychainoi Komissii, 1917–1921*. Moscow, 1958.
Bely, Andrey, *Nachalo veka*. Moscow–Leningrad, 1933.
Blok, Alexandr, *Sobranie sochinenii*. Moscow, 1960–5.
Bobrov, Sergey (rev. of *Tristia*), *Pechat' i revoliutsiia*, 4 (1923), 259–62.
Brik, Osip, 'Zvukovye povtory,' *Poetika*. Petrograd, 1919.
Brown, Clarence, 'Into the Heart of Darkness: Mandelstam's Ode to Stalin,' *Slavic Review*, 4 (1967), 584–604.
  'Introductory Note to Mandelstam's *Fourth Prose*,' *Hudson Review*, 1 (1970), 49–52.
Bryusov, Valery, 'Sredi stikhov' (rev. of *Vtoraia kniga*), *Pechat' i revoliutsiia*, 6 (1923), 63–6.
Chalsma, Howard William, 'Russian Acmeism: Its history, doctrine and poetry.' Unpublished diss., University of Washington, 1967.
Chukovsky, Nikolay, 'Vstrechi s Mandel'shtamom,' *Moskva*, 8 (1964), 143–52.
de Coster, Charles, *La Légende de Thyl Ulenspiegel et de Lamme Goedzak* (Russian translation edited by Osip Mandelstam). Moscow–Leningrad, 1928.
Driver, Sam, 'Acmeism,' *SEEJ*, 2 (1968), 141–56.
Ehrenburg, Ilya, *Liudi, gody, zhizn*. Moscow, 1961.
Eykhenbaum, Boris, 'O Mandel'shtame' (notes for a talk given 14 March 1933), *Den' poezii*. Leningrad, 1967, pp. 167–8.
Fitzpatrick, Sheila, *The Commissariat of Enlightenment: Soviet organisation of education and the arts under Lunacharsky*. Cambridge, 1970.

Bibliography

Forsh, Olga, *Sumasshedshii korabl'.* Leningrad, 1931. Reprinted, with an introduction by Boris Filippov, Washington, 1964.

Glinka, Gleb, 'Po povodu,' *Novoe russkoe slovo,* 27 February 1966.

Gornfeld, A., 'Perevodcheskaia striapnia,' *Vecherniaia krasnaia gazeta,* no. 315 (1928).

Gumilyov, Nikolay, *Sobranie sochinenii.* Washington, 1962–8.

Hilger, Gustav, and Alfred G. Meyer, *The Incompatible Allies.* New York, 1951.

Ivanov, Georgy, 'Osip Mandel'shtam' (rev. of *Sobranie sochinenii,* 1955), *NZh,* 43 (1955), 273–84.

Peterburgskie zimy. New York, 1952.

Ivanov-Razumnik, R. V., *The Memoirs of Ivanov-Razumnik,* trans. by P. S. Squire. London, 1965.

Jakobson, Roman, 'Marginalia to Vasmer's Russian Etymological Dictionary (R–Ia),' *International Journal of Slavic Linguistics and Poetics,* 1–2 (1959), 266–78.

Karlinsky, Simon, *Marina Cvetaeva: Her life and art.* Berkeley, 1966.

Karpovich, Mikhail, 'Moe znakomstvo s Mandel'shtamom,' *NZh,* 49 (1957), 258–61.

Kaverin, V., 'Kak ia ne stal poetom,' *Oktiabr,* 10 (1959), 127–31.

Khodasevich, Vladislav, *Literaturnye stat'i i vospominaniia.* New York, 1954.

Nekropol'. Brussels, 1939.

Kozmin, B. P., *Pisateli sovremennoi epokhi.* Moscow, 1928.

Lure (Lourié), Artur, 'Detskii rai,' *VP,* III (1963), 161–72.

Mabo (Mabeau), Mikhail Vasilevich, 'O Maximiliane Voloshine, Mandel'shtame i drugikh,' *Novoe russkoe slovo,* 14 January 1949.

Makovsky, Sergey, *Na Parnase 'Serebrianogo Veka.'* Munich, 1962.

Portrety sovremennikov. New York, 1955.

Mandelstam, Nadezhda, *Hope Against Hope: A memoir.* New York, 1970. The Russian original, *Vospominaniia,* was published in New York by the Chekhov Publishing Corporation at the same time.

Mandelstam, Osip, 'Fourth Prose,' trans. by Clarence Brown, *Hudson Review,* 1 (1970), 53–66. Also in Michael Scammell (ed.), *Russia's Other Writers.* London, 1970.

'Journey to Armenia,' trans. by Clarence Brown, *Quarterly Review of Literature,* 3–4 (1973).

'Storm and Stress,' trans. by Clarence Brown, *Russian Literature Triquarterly* 1 (1971), 154–62.

'Zapisnye knizhki. Zametki,' *VL,* 4 (1968), 180–204.

Margvelashvili, Georgy, 'Ob Osipe Mandel'shtame,' *Literaturnaia Gruziia,* 1 (1967), 75–96.

Markov, Vladimir, *The Longer Poems of Velimir Khlebnikov.* Berkeley, 1962.

Russian Futurism: A history. Berkeley, 1968.

Mindlin, Em., *Neobyknovennye sobesedniki.* Moscow, 1968.

Mirsky, D. S., 'Ob Eduarde Bagritskom,' *Literaturnaia ucheba,* 5 (1934), 31–42.

Nabokov, Vladimir, *Drugie berega.* New York, 1954.

The Gift. New York, 1963.

Speak, Memory: An autobiography revisited. New York, 1966.

Nazarenko, V., 'Kstati o formal izme,' *Zvezda,* 9 (1961).

Bibliography

Nilsson, Nils Ake, 'Ship Metaphors in Mandelstam's Poetry,' in *To Honor Roman Jakobson*, vol. II. The Hague, 1967, pp. 1436–44.

Odoevtseva, Irina, *Na beregakh Nevy*. Washington, 1967.

Ofrosimov, Yury, 'O Gumilyove, Kuzmine, Mandel'shtame,' *Novoe russkoe slovo*, 13 December 1953.

Pasternak, Boris, *Sobranie sochinenii*, 3 vols. Ann Arbor, 1961.

Pavlovich, Nadezhda, *Dumy i vospominaniia*. Moscow, 1962.

'Vospominaniia ob Alexandre Bloke,' in *Blokovskii sbornik*. Tartu, 1964.

Pyast, Vladimir, *L'vinaia past'*. Berlin–Petersburg–Moscow, 1922.

'Po povodu sovremennoi poezii,' *Gaudeamus*, 4–5 (1911).

Vstrechi. Moscow, 1929.

Rabinovich, Grigory, (a note on Mandelstam), *VP*, III (1963), 24–5.

Ronen, Omry, 'Mandelstam's *Kashchei*,' in *Studies Presented to Professor Roman Jakobson by his Students*. Cambridge, Mass., 1968, pp. 252–64.

Ross, Robert H., *The Georgian Revolt, 1910–1922: Rise and fall of a poetic ideal*. Carbondale, Ill., 1965.

Rozhdental, S., 'Teni starogo Peterburga,' *Pravda*, 30 August 1933.

Rozhdestvensky, Vsevolod, 'Stranitsy zhizni,' *Zvezda*, 12 (1958), 116–35. Published as a book under the same title, Moscow, 1962.

Segal, D. M., 'Nabliudeniia nad semanticheskoi strukturoi poeticheskogo proizvedeniia,' *International Journal of Slavic Linguistics and Poetics*, XI (1968), 159–71.

Shklovsky, Viktor, *Sentimental'noe puteshestvie*. Moscow–Berlin, 1923.

Strakhovsky, Leonid, *Craftsmen of the Word: Three Poets of Modern Russia*. Cambridge, Mass., 1949.

Stravinsky, Igor, and Robert Craft, *Retrospectives and Conclusions*. New York, 1969.

Struve, Gleb, 'Ital'ianskie obrazy i motivy v poezii Osipa Mandel'shtama,' in *Studi in onore di Ettore Lo Gatto i Giovanni Maver*. Rome, 1962.

Tager, Yelena, 'Dve zapiski,' *VP*, IV (1965), 51–3.

'O Mandel'shtame,' *NZh*, 81 (1965), 172–99.

Terapiano, Yury, *Vstrechi*. New York, 1953.

Terras, Victor, 'Classical Motives in the Poetry of Osip Mandelstam,' *SEEJ*, 3 (1966), 251–67.

Trubetskoy, Yury, 'Iz zapisnykh knizhek,' *Mosty*, 2 (1959), 415–16.

Tschizewskij, D. (ed.), *Russische literarische Parodien*. Wiesbaden, 1957.

Tsvetaeva, Marina, 'Istoriia odnogo posviashcheniia,' *Oxford Slavonic Papers*, XI (1964), 112–36.

'Pesnici sa istorijom i pesnici bez istorije,' *Ruski arhiv* (Belgrade), XXVI–XXVII (1934), 104–42.

'Pis'ma Mariny Tsvetaevoi,' *Mosty*, 5 (1960), 299–318.

Vasmer, Max, *Russisches etymologisches Wörterbuch*. Heidelberg, 1950–8.

Ves' Peterburg na 1909 g. Adresnaia i spravochnaia kniga g. S.-Peterburga. Petersburg, 1909.

Wellek, René, *History of Modern Criticism*, vol. 2. New Haven, 1955.

Zaslavsky, David, (Letter to the editor), *Literaturnaia gazeta*, 20 May 1929.

'O skromnom plagiate i razviaznoi khalture,' *Literaturnaia gazeta*, 7 May 1929.

Index of names

Abercrombie, Lascelles, 136
Adalis (pseudonym of Adelina Yefimovna Efron), 105
Adamovich, Georgy, 11, 48, 56, 69, 91, 301, 304, 307
Adams, Henry, 138, 305
Akhmatova, Anna Andreevna, 4, 14–16, 36, 43, 45, 48, 49, 52, 55, 56, 68, 70, 71, 89–91, 97, 102, 104, 105, 121, 122, 124, 129, 130–2, 135, 136, 142, 155, 158, 185, 194, 196, 197, 209, 213, 227, 244, 245, 264, 273, 274, 300, 304, 305, 308–10
Alexander III, 10, 12
Amari, 58
Andreev (assassin of Count Mirbach, *q.v.*), 74
Andronikova, Princess Salomeya Nikolaevna (Mrs Halpern), 51, 244, 252, 308
Annenkov, Yury Petrovich (pseudonym of B. Temiryazev), 52
Annensky, Innokenty, 15, 42, 57, 89, 104, 153, 213, 244
Antokolsky, Pavel Grigorevich, 111
Arbenina, Olga Nikolaevna, 89, 244, 245, 247, 250, 251, 302, 304, 308
Arendt, Hannah, 3
Ariosto, 203
Aristotle, 255
Arnim, Achim von, 306
Ashkinazi, V. A., 52
Auden, W. H., 157, 177, 190, 306
Augustus, 196

Babel, Isaak Emmanuilovich, 76
Bach, Johann Sebastian, 142, 146, 194, 196, 200–4
Bagdatev, Sergey Yakovlevich, 93
Baggesen, Jens, 306
Bagritsky, Eduard (pseudonym of Eduard Georgievich Dzyubin), 306
Bakhrakh, Alexandr, 67, 309
Balmont, Konstantin Dmitrievich, 57, 153
Baltrushaitis, Yurgis, 92
Balzac, Honoré de, 243
Barats (a classmate in the Tenishev School), 24

Batyushkov, Konstantin Nikolaevich, 54, 178, 180, 181, 203, 302
Beethoven, Ludwig van, 196, 203, 307
Bely, Andrey (pseudonym of Boris Nikolaevich Bugaev), 38, 54, 85, 86, 105, 131, 139, 140, 153, 199, 300, 301, 305, 307
Berberova, Nina Nikolaevna, 91
Berdyaev, Nikolay Alexandrovich, 100
Bergson, Henri, 154, 197, 218
Berner, Nikolay, 111
Bestuzhev, V. (pseudonym of V. V. Gippius, *q.v.*), 299
Bezymensky, Alexandr Ilich, 92
Blagoy, Dmitry Dmitrievich, 100
Blake, William, 163
Blok, Alexandr Alexandrovich, 42, 54, 56, 57, 86, 88, 90, 93, 96, 100, 107, 139, 141, 174, 300, 301, 304, 305
Blokh (publisher of *Tristia*), 99
Blyumkin, Yakov Grigorevich, 71, 73, 74, 85, 92
Bobrov, Sergey Pavlovich, 99, 111, 305
Boileau, Nicolas, 255
Bomberg, David, 168
Borges, Jorge Luis, 207
Botticelli, Sandro, 166
Bottomley, Gordon, 136
Bozio, Angiolina, 123
Brahms, Johannes, 227
Brentano, Clemens, 306
Bridges, Robert, 137
Brik, Osip Maximovich, 100, 101, 310
Brooke, Rupert, 136
Bruni, Lev Alexandrovich, 51
Bruni, Nikolay Alexandrovich, 56
Bryusov, Valery Yakovlevich, 33, 35, 42, 54, 55, 57, 111, 112, 156, 167, 199, 266, 299, 305
Bukharin, Nikolay Ivanovich, 100, 102, 123–5, 131
Bukhshtab, Boris Yakovlevich, 255, 309
Bulgakov, Mikhail Afanasevich, 93
Bunting, Basil, 147
Burlyuk, David Davidovich, 48

Caesar, Julius, 196
Catullus, Gaius Valerius, 253
Chaadaev, Pyotr Yakovlevich, 153, 300
Chagall, Marc, 51, 88, 293

315

Chalsma, Howard William, 136, 305
Chaplin, Charlie, 197
Chebotarevskaya, A. N., 59
Chénier, André, 156
Chernyavsky (a member of the Guild of Poets), 56
Chicherin, Georgy Vasilevich, 72
Chigua, 82
Chopin, Frédéric, 227
Chukovsky, Korney Ivanovich, 52, 132
Chukovsky, Nikolay Korneevich, 107, 108, 269, 305, 308
Cicero, Marcus Tullius, 196
Coster, Charles de, 122–4
Craft, Robert, 75, 303
Crane, Hart, 7
Croce, Benedetto, 253
Crosby, Harry, 217

Daniel, Yuly Markovich, 99
Dante Alighieri, 46, 54, 96, 127, 151, 197, 202, 203, 217, 285, 292, 306, 310
Darwin, Charles, 11
Davies, W. H., 136
Dehmel, Richard, 38
del Re, Arundel, 137, 138
Denikin, Gen. Anton Ivanovich, 76
Derzhavin, Gavriil Romanovich, 221, 255
Diaghilev, Sergey Pavlovich, 73
Dickens, Charles, 8, 196, 200, 205, 206
Dimitry (Tsarevich), 222–4
Dimitry (Pretender), 225
Dobrolyubov, Alexandr Mikhaylovich, 299
Dos Passos, John, 76
Dostoevsky, Fyodor Mikhaylovich, 10, 17, 24, 97, 118, 223, 300, 301
Driver, Sam, 136, 305
Dubinskaya, Tatyana, 127, 128
Dzerzhinsky, Felix, 73, 74, 102, 302, 303

Eckermann, Johann Peter, 183
Efron, S. Ya., 64
Efros, Abram Markovich, 101
Ehrenburg, Ilya Grigorevich, 4, 25, 52, 74, 76, 77, 80, 83, 85, 269, 303, 304
Ehrenburg, Lyuba, 76, 77, 83, 84
Ehrenburg, Yadviga, 83, 303
Einstein, Albert, 97
Eliot, T. S., 7, 10, 163, 281
Etkind, Yefim Grigorevich, 90
Euclid, 38
Euripides, 42, 213, 232, 244
Eykhenbaum, Boris Mikhaylovich, 42, 105, 118, 129, 130

Fet, Afanasy Afanasevich, 280
Filippov, Boris, 4, 8, 298, 304
Filippov-Filistinsky, Boris, *see* Boris Filippov
Filofey (Philotheus), 223
Fitzpatrick, Sheila, 72, 302
Flaubert, Gustave, 196, 197
Flint, F. S., 136
Fondaminskaya, A. O., 34
Forsh, Olga Dmitrievna, 85, 86, 304
Freud, Sigmund, 97
Frost, Robert, 9, 137
Furmanov, Dmitry Andreevich, 131
Fyodor (son of Ivan IV), 223

Gandhi, Mohandas K., 108
Gapon, Georgy Apollonovich, 27, 96
Gautier, Théophile, 91, 137, 141, 185
Gavronskaya, L. S., 34
Gellius, Aulus, 254
George, Stefan, 254
Gershenzon, Mikhail Osipovich, 267
Gershuni, Grigory Alexandrovich, 34
Gippius, Vladimir Vasilevich, 21, 25, 29, 30, 32, 35, 56, 59, 299
Glanvill, Joseph, 242
Glinka, Gleb, 127
Goder, 30
Godunov, Boris, 210, 222–5
Goethe, Johann Wolfgang von, 19, 132, 183, 184, 187
Gogol, Nikolay Vasilevich, 24, 77, 131
Gorbunov, Nikolay Petrovich, 72
Goremykin, Ivan Logginovich, 59
Gorky, Maxim, 30, 85, 89, 101
Gorlin (editor at the State Publishing House), 122, 124
Gornfeld, Arkady Georgievich, 123, 124
Gorodetsky, Sergey Mitrofanovich, 14, 30, 55, 56, 92, 111, 136, 139, 141–3, 146, 149, 155, 157
Griboedov, Alexandr Sergeevich, 301
Gronfeyn, Yevgeniya Borisovna, 76
Gudzy, Nikolay K., 98
Gumilyov, Nikolay Stepanovich, 14, 17, 42, 49, 55–9, 71, 88, 90–3, 96, 111, 124, 136–43, 146, 148, 149, 151–3, 155, 157, 167, 178, 179, 184, 185, 199, 220, 300, 302, 304, 306, 307
Gusev, Sergey Ivanovich, 124

Hamsun, Knut, 35, 36
Hauptmann, Gerhart, 35
Hauser, Kaspar ('Gaspard Häuser'), 33, 34
Hayward, Max, 297
Hazlitt, William, 135
Hemingway, Ernest, 52
Herder, Johann Gottfried, 12
Herrick, Robert, 280

Hilger, Gustav, 303
Ho Chi Minh (Nguyen Ai Quoc), 108–10, 150
Hoffmann, E. T. A., 156
Homer, 47, 140, 156, 196, 247, 254, 256, 257, 264
Horace, 253, 255, 272, 274
Hughes, Robert, 310
Hugo, Victor, 21
Hulme, T. E., 137, 179
Huysmans, Georges Charles, 15, 54

Ibsen, Henrik, 35
Ionov (head of Land and Factory Publishing House), 124
Isaiah, 196, 201, 203
Ivan IV, 222
Ivanov, Georgy, 13–16, 18, 43, 56, 59, 60, 63–6, 73, 74, 91, 157, 158, 199, 237, 298, 310
Ivanov, Vyacheslav Ivanovich, 36–8, 40–2, 48, 54, 92, 139, 140, 146, 149, 155, 300, 305, 306
Ivanov-Razumnik (pseudonym of Razumnik Vasilevich Ivanov), 300, 301
Ivask, George, 307

Jacob, 91
Jakobson, Roman, 8, 71, 306
Joyce, James, 7, 76, 162
Justinian, 186, 196

Kablukov, Sergey Platonovich, 231
Kamenev, Lev Borisovich (pseudonym of L. B. Rozenfeld), 70, 73
Kameneva (wife of L. B. Kamenev), 73, 74
Kamensky, Vasily Vasilevich, 55
Kamkov, Boris Davidovich (pseudonym of B. D. Katz), 45
Kant, Immanuel, 46, 144
Kantakuzin, 30
Karlinsky, Simon, 302
Karpovich, Mikhail Mikhaylovich, 32, 34, 39, 47, 48, 54, 299, 301
Karyakin, V. N., 123, 124
Kastalsky, Alexandr Dmitrievich, 72
Kataev, Valentin Petrovich, 97
Kautsky, Karl, 25
Kaverin, Veniamin (pseudonym of Veniamin Alexandrovich Zilberg), 53, 107, 108, 301, 305
Kerensky, Alexandr Fyodorovich, 69
Kerner, J. A., 19
Khainsky, Alexandr Ivanovich, 45
Khardzhiev, Nikolay Ivanovich, 4, 8, 118, 129, 130
Khazin, Yevgeny Yakovlevich, 4
Khazina, V. Ya., 92, 132, 302

Khlebnikov, Velimir Vladimirovich, 50, 57, 129, 153, 154, 280, 301
Khodasevich, Vladislav Felitsianovich, 16, 50, 86, 90, 298, 301, 304
Khomyakov, Alexey Stepanovich, 308
Klyuev, Nikolay Alexeevich, 86, 90
Kolachevsky, 78
Komarovsky, Count Vasily Alexeevich, 15, 16, 57
Konevskoy, I. (pseudonym of Ivan Ivanovich Oreus), 299
Korsakov, Vanyusha, 24
Kozmin, B. P., 25, 90, 298
Kraevich, 25
Krivtsov, Nikolay Ivanovich, 233
Krupensky twins, 24
Kuzmin, Mikhail Alexeevich, 55, 56, 99, 151, 184, 219, 270
Kuzmin-Karavaev, Dmitry, 56, 141
Kuzmina-Karavaeva, Yelena, 56

Lakhuti, Abolgasem Akhmedzade, 133
Lamarck, Jean Baptiste Pierre Antoine de Monet de, 203, 204
Lask, Emil, 46
Legran, 93
Leibnitz, Gottfried Wilhelm von, 12
Lenin, Vladimir Ilich, 70, 110, 269
Lermontov, Mikhail Yurevich, 91
Leskov, Nikolay Semyonovich, 50, 97
Levberg, Maria, 69
Lewis, Wyndham, 162, 168
Lezhnev, Isay Grigorevich, 97, 101, 105
Livshits, Benedikt Konstantinovich, 52, 70, 184
Lobachevsky, Nikolay Ivanovich, 38
Lopatinsky, Boris Lvovich, 73, 92
Lourié, Artur Sergeevich, 70, 71, 200, 302
Lowell, Amy, 168
Lowell, Robert, 215
Lozinsky, Mikhail Leonidovich, 50, 53, 56, 86, 199
Lunacharsky, Anatoly Vasilevich, 69, 72, 73, 76
Lunts, Lev, 86
Luther, Martin, 194, 196, 203

Mabeau, see Mabo
Mabo, Mikhail Vasilevich, 79, 81, 303
Mabo-Azovsky, see Mabo
McKane, Richard, 166
Magritte, René, 188
Makkaveysky (a poet from Kiev), 77
Makovsky, Sergey Konstantinovich, 15, 42, 43, 237, 298, 300
Mallarmé, Stéphane, 89, 254
Malmstad, John, 307

Mandelstam, Alexandr Emilevich (Shura), 11, 68, 78, 79, 81, 83, 123, 125, 134
Mandelstam, Dr (eye specialist in Kiev), 11
Mandelstam, Emil Veniaminovich, 12, 13, 19, 20, 22, 92, 101, 121, 231, 305
Mandelstam, Flora Osipovna (*née* Verblovskaya), 13, 19, 22, 43, 44, 47, 68, 69
Mandelstam, Nadezhda Yakovlevna (*née* Khazina), 1, 2, 4, 8, 19, 43, 45, 46, 52, 58, 70–8, 80, 81, 83, 85, 88, 89, 92–4, 97, 98, 100–2, 111, 116, 121–4, 127, 128, 130–4, 160, 188, 219, 227, 229–31, 245, 297, 303, 308
Mandelstam, Yevgeny Emilevich, 11, 79, 100, 101
Mansfeld, Yu., 56
Maran, René, 109
Margolin, Yuly Borisovich, 51
Margvelashvili, Georgy, 97, 269, 304
Marinetti, Emilio Filippo Tommaso, 55, 137
Markov, Vladimir Fyodorovich, 14, 301
Marx, Karl, 25
Maupassant, Guy de, 89
Mayakovsky, Vladimir Vladimirovich, 25, 38, 70, 71, 100, 105, 106, 111, 254, 303, 310
Mazesa da Vinci, 78, 79
Merezhkovsky, Dmitry Sergeevich, 54
Metternich, Prince Klemens Wenzel Nepomuk Lothar von, 196
Meyer, Alfred G., 303
Mindlin, Emily Lvovich, 51, 78, 301
Minsky, N. (pseudonym of Nikolay Mikhaylovich Vilenkin), 35
Mirbach-Harff, Count Wilhelm von, 71, 73–5
Mirsky, Prince D. S. (Dmitry Petrovich Svyatopolk-Mirsky), 24, 306
Miturich, P. V., 51, 100
Mniszek, Marina, 225–7
Mochulsky, Konstantin Vasilevich, 47, 78, 301
Monro, Harold, 137
Montesquieu, Baron de, 109
Moore, Marianne, 167
Moravskaya, M., 56
Mozart, Wolfgang Amadeus, 37, 157

Nabokov, Vladimir Dmitrievich, 23
Nabokov, Vladimir Vladimirovich, 6, 23, 233, 274, 279, 297–9
Nadezhdin, 24
Nadson, Semyon Yakovlevich, 30
Nadya (nursemaid at Tsvetaeva's house), 60–3, 66

Napoleon, 21, 196
Narbut, Vladimir Ivanovich, 56, 102, 122, 124, 142, 155, 306
Nazarenko, V., 269, 275
Nekrasov, Nikolay Alexeevich, 54, 250, 251
Neledinsky, V. (pseudonym of V. V. Gippius), 299
Nerval, Gérard de, 217
Neumann, Fritz, 46
Nicholas I, 23
Nilsson, Nils Ake, 309
Novskaya, E., 111

Odoevtseva, Irina (pseudonym of Rada Gustavovna Geynike), 16–18, 48, 80, 260, 298, 301, 302
Ofrosimov, Yury Viktorovich, 48, 301
Orlov, Vladimir Nikolaevich, 269
Ossian, 204, 209–11
Ovid, 196, 203, 219, 253, 255, 256, 267, 271–5, 309
Ozerov, Vladislav Alexandrovich, 173, 196

Paganini, Nicolò, 226
Palkin, 15
Paperny, Z. S., 4
Pasternak, Boris Leonidovich, 57, 58, 90, 129, 131, 132, 280, 281, 284, 302, 303
Pavlovich, Nadezhda, 86, 88, 304
Peter the Great, 196, 255, 258, 259
Peter (Apostle), 203
Petnikov, Grigory Nikolaevich, 97
Petrarch (Francesco Petrarca), 54
Petrovykh, Maria, 131
Petrunkevich, Ivan Ilich, 24
Pindar, 254
Pletnyov, Dr, 129
Poe, Edgar Allen, 30, 173, 196, 200, 242, 243, 308
Poggioli, Renato, 8, 301
Potebnya, Alexandr Afanasevich, 105
Pra (nickname of Yelena Ottobaldovna Voloshina, mother of M. A. Voloshin, *q.v.*), 63, 302
Pound, Ezra, 7, 136–9, 147, 168, 176
Pronin, Boris, 69
Przesiecki, 24
Punin, Nikolay Nikolaevich, 121
Pushkin, Alexandr Sergeevich, 22, 25, 27, 28, 48, 51, 52, 57, 99, 107, 122, 163, 185, 194, 195, 204, 210, 222–4, 230–3, 235, 237, 243–5, 255, 264, 267, 269, 273–5, 279, 280, 301, 307, 309
Puslovsky, Count, 73, 74
Pyast, Vladimir Alexeevich, 38, 39, 200, 273, 300, 308, 310

Index

Rabelais, François, 141, 156, 185
Rabinovich, Grigory Semyonovich, 48, 301
Rachel (stage name of Élisa Félix), 196, 203, 209
Racine, Jean, 54, 156, 196, 204, 207–10, 213–19, 232, 244
Radlova, Anna, 105
Rakovsky, Kristian Georgievich, 97
Raskolnikov, Fyodor Fyodorovich, 73, 303
Read, Herbert, 135
Regatt, Anna (pseudonym of Yelena Tager, q.v.)
Reid, Captain Thomas Mayne, 160
Reysner, Larisa Mikhaylovna, 74, 302
Richard III, 223
Rodenbach, Georges Raymond Constantin, 36
Rodichev, Fyodor Izmaylovich, 24
Rodin, Auguste, 162, 188
Ronen, Omry, 309
Ross, Betsy, 225
Rousseau, Jean-Jacques, 12, 109
Rozanov, Vasily Vasilevich, 35, 153, 300
Rozental, S., 130
Rozhdestvensky, Vsevelod Alexandrovich, 51, 301
Rubinstein, Anton Grigorevich, 17, 18

Salieri, 157
Sarandinaki, Alexandr Alexandrovich, 78, 79, 81
Sargidzhan, Amir (pseudonym of Sergey Petrovich Borodin), 127–9, 131
Savinkov, Boris Viktorovich, 34, 69
Scammell, Michael, 298
Schiller, Johann Christoph Friedrich von, 12, 19
Schlegel, August Wilhelm von, 207
Scriabin, Alexandr, 230–5, 237, 243, 245, 307
Sedykh, Andrey, 78
Segal, D. M., 267, 309
Seneca, Lucius Annaeus, 213
Sergey Ivanych, 28, 299
Serov, Valentin Alexandrovich, 24
Setchkarev, Vsevolod, 8
Severyanin, Igor (pseudonym of Igor Vasilevich Lotaryov), 57
Shaginyan, Marietta, 86
Shakespeare, William, 19, 90, 135, 141, 156, 185
Shershenevich, Vadim Gabrielevich, 71
Shisov, Igor, 111
Shklovsky, Viktor Borisovich, 86, 105, 107, 273, 301, 304
Sholokhov, Mikhail Alexandrovich, 99
Shtempel, Natalya Yevgenevna, 1, 2, 161, 297, 307

Sh varts, Yevgeny Lvovich, 86
Si nani, Boris Borisovich, 24, 26, 27
Sinani, Boris Naumovich, 27
Sinani, Yelena Borisovna (Lena), 27
Sinani, Yevgeniya Borisovna (Zhenya), 27
Sinclair, Upton, 160
Sinyavsky, Andrey Donatevich, 26, 99
Słobodzinski, 24, 31
Slonim, Marc Lvovich, 60, 67, 302
Slonimsky, Mikhail Leonidovich, 86
Socrates, 196, 197, 203
Socrates (a servant), 65
Sologub, Fyodor Kuzmich (pseudonym of F. K. Teternikov), 36, 57, 59, 90
Solovyov, Vladimir Sergeevich, 144, 148
Spengler, Oswald, 97
Spinoza, Baruch, 12
Squire, P. S., 301
Stalin, 2, 11, 70, 125, 131, 132
Stavsky, Vasily P., 133
Steinberg, Dr Aaron Zakharevich, 11, 45, 46, 183, 300, 301
Stenich, Valentin Iosifovich (pseudonym of V. I. Smetanich), 76
Sterne, Laurence, 135
Stevens, Wallace, 7, 204, 281
Strakhovsky, Leonid, 49, 301
Strauss, Richard, 33, 34
Stravinsky, Igor, 74, 75, 266, 303
Struve, Gleb Petrovich, 4, 8, 13, 14, 298, 300, 302, 308
Sudeykin, Sergey Yurevich, 74, 75, 266
Sudeykina, Vera Arturovna (née de Bosset), 74, 75, 266, 309
Sumarokov, Alexandr Petrovich, 196
Surkov, Alexey Alexandrovich, 4
Suslova, Apollinariya Prokofevna, 300
Suvorin, Alexey Sergeevich, 298
Syrett, Kate, 136

Tabidze, Titsian, 83, 93, 303
Tager, Yelena Mikhaylovna, 57, 69, 70, 127, 130, 131, 299, 302
Tarkovsky, Arseny Alexandrovich, 51
Tchaikovsky, Pyotr Ilich, 17, 18
Terapiano, Yury, 76, 77, 80, 303
Terras, Victor, 245, 253, 254, 267, 271, 272, 274, 308–10
Tibullus, Albius, 272, 274
Tikhonov, Nikolay Semyonovich, 101, 125
Tolstoy, Alexey Nikolaevich, 90, 102, 127, 128, 131, 300
Tolstoy, Fyodor, 24, 26
Tolstoy, Lev Nikolaevich, 35, 97, 101, 140, 301
Tomashevsky, Boris Viktorovich, 38, 42

Index

Traherne, Thomas, 181
Trinkler, Prof., 97
Trotsky, Lev Davidovich (pseudonym of L. D. Bronstein), 72, 73
Trubetskoy, Yury Pavlovich, 11, 298
Tschizewskij, D., 301
Tsvetaeva, Alya, 60, 63
Tsvetaeva, Marina Ivanovna, 60–8, 89, 105, 174, 225–7, 244, 245, 255, 302, 306, 309
Tsygalsky, Colonel, 78–80
Tumpovskaya, Margarita, 69
Turgenev, Ivan Sergeevich, 45, 97, 155
Tyshler, Alexandr Grigorevich, 76
Tyutchev, Fyodor Ivanovich, 10, 144, 148, 190

Utkin, Iosif, 38

Vaksel, Olga, 121
Valéry, Paul, 254
Vasily III, 223
Vasmer, Max, 306
Vazha-Pshavela (pseudonym of Luka Pavlovich Razikashvili), 93
Vengerov, Semyon Afanasevich, 298
Verblovskaya, Flora Osipovna (*see* F. O. Mandelstam)
Verlaine, Paul, 33, 34, 36, 151, 183, 187, 196, 197, 203
Villon, François, 54, 55, 141, 151–3, 179, 184, 185, 187
Viollet-le-Duc, Eugène, 183, 193
Virenius, Dr, 24, 30, 52
Voevodsky, 23
Voloshin, Maximilian Alexandrovich, 63–5, 78, 80, 83, 302, 303

Wagner, Richard, 24
Washington, Martha, 225
Wellek, René, 306
Wilbur, Richard, 181
Wilde, Oscar, 34
Windelband, Wilhelm, 46
Winner, Thomas, 8
Wrangel, Gen. Pyotr Nikolaevich, 80, 88

Yakulov, Georgy, 70
Yashvili, Paolo, 83, 93, 303
Yazykov, Nikolay Mikhaylovich, 280
Yeats, William Butler, 7, 194, 195
Yeliseev, 85, 86
Yevtushenko, Yevgeny Alexandrovich, 75, 303
Yurkun, Yury, 304

Zaytsev, 121
Zamyatin, Yevgeny Ivanovich, 86
Zarubin, Leonid, 24
Zaslavsky, David Iosifovich, 124
Zelenetsky, Sergey, 111
Zenkevich, Mikhail Alexandrovich, 56, 142, 155, 157, 306
Zhdanov, Andrey Alexandrovich, 16, 129
Zhirmunsky, Viktor Maximovich, 8, 30, 46, 105, 138, 207, 298, 299
Zhukovsky, Vasily Andreevich, 57, 90
Zinovev, Grigory Yevseevich (pseudonym of G. Y. Radomylsky), 70
Zjuntan, 110
Zola, Émile, 196, 197
Zoshchenko, Mikhail Mikhaylovich, 86
Zubkov, 76